Cartesian Truth

D0075434

Cartesian Truth

THOMAS C. VINCI

DISCARDED

New York • *Oxford*

Oxford University Press

BOWLING GREEN STATE UNIVERSITY LIBRARY

1998

Oxford University Press

Oxford   New York

Athens   Auckland   Bangkok   Bogota   Bombay
Buenos Aires   Calcutta   Cape Town   Dar es Salaam
Delhi   Florence   Hong Kong   Istanbul   Karachi
Kuala Lumpur   Madras   Madrid   Melbourne
Mexico City   Nairobi   Paris   Singapore
Taipei   Tokyo   Toronto   Warsaw

and associated companies in
Berlin   Ibadan

Copyright © 1998 by Thomas C. Vinci

Published by Oxford University Press, Inc.
198 Madison Avenue, New York, New York 10016

Oxford is a registered trademark of Oxford University Press

All rights reserved. No part of this publication may be reproduced,
stored in a retrieval system, or transmitted, in any form or by any means,
electronic, mechanical, photocopying, recording, or otherwise,
without the prior permission of Oxford University Press.

Library of Congress Cataloging-in-Publication Data
Vinci, Thomas C., 1949–
Cartesian truth / Thomas C. Vinci.
p.   cm.
Includes bibliographical references and index.
ISBN 0-19-511329-2
1. Descartes, René, 1596–1650.   2. Metaphysics.
3. Science—Philosophy.   4. Sellars, Wilfrid.   I. Title.
B1875.V53   1997
194—dc21   96-48272

1 3 5 7 9 8 6 4 2

Printed in the United States of America
on acid-free paper

*To my wife, Carmen
and to my children, Christopher, Alexandra, and Rebecca*

Preface

My conception of what philosophy is and of how one should go about doing it owes much to the theory and practice of the late Wilfrid Sellars. Sellars regarded science and metaphysics as separate threads in a single web of philosophical inquiry. Since the most original and robust practitioners of philosophy, thus construed, must be masters of both science and metaphysics, it was natural for Sellars to begin his systematic thinking about philosophy by taking on the perspective of those practitioners best exemplifying that ideal. Sellars's philosophical heroes are Aristotle and Kant. Mine is Descartes.

It is not necessary to make the case that Descartes was both a metaphysician and a scientist of the first order. It is, however, necessary to make the case that he is, in Sellars's sense, a philosopher of the first order. To make this case it is necessary to show that one can extract from the Cartesian system neither an autonomous metaphysical "order of reasons" nor an autonomous theory of science. The point is not simply that Cartesian metaphysics is needed to save a scientific epistemology threatened by Cartesian skepticism about the senses but that the central doctrines of any one of these components—the metaphysical as well as the scientific—depend on threads of reasoning originating in the other. For example, some of the elements of the empirical psychology and some of the elements of the metaphysics and epistemology interlock in such an elegant and natural way that the overall result comes close to embodying the Sellarsian ideal.

But elegance and the embodiment of philosophical ideals are not the only reasons that Sellars had for studying figures in the history of philosophy. He also thought that he had something to learn from them about issues arising for, and within, contemporary philosophical disciplines. One such discipline is analytic epistemology.

In his recent book *The Fragmentation of Reason*,[1] Stephen Stich catalogs three major concerns of analytic epistemology—skepticism, the analysis of ordinary epistemic concepts, and the evaluation and reform of ordinary reasoning practices—all three of which he finds either pointless or somehow mismanaged. He does not have much to say about the first two but devotes the rest of the book to "deconstructing" the third. Unhappily for those of us in the business, responses of this sort are all too common, and I should like to locate my interest in Cartesian philosophy against the backdrop of a discussion of the merit of these complaints.

I regard modern analytic epistemology as a set of tools that philosophers have been trying to forge since the time of Descartes to solve some of the more intractable problems of fusing, to use familiar Sellarsian terminology, the manifest and scientific images. In general terms, the fusion problem is one of resolving tensions and inconsistencies that go right down to the bottom of those things to which we are most committed. As (I believe) Descartes saw it, these tensions arise because the world we experience through the senses is at odds with the world that is required by reason, yet we can bring ourselves to foresake neither.

Descartes's predicament is that of the engineer who knows that his or her best instrumentation is giving a collectively impossible picture of the state of the engine. To solve this predicament he or she must reflect in a deeper and more precise way than has been hitherto required about foundational concepts in the theory of instrumentation. This reflection must in the first instance be analytic. However, because in philosophy it is impossibility rather than necessity that mothers invention, this reflection must in the second instance be methodological and revisionary. This gives us two of Stich's three concerns. The third, skepticism, hovers nearby for Descartes as a consequence of the predicament and as a possible heuristic in aid of its resolution.

The preceding is of course an oversimplification of the origins of both Cartesianism and analytic epistemology but there is enough truth in it to say that without reference to these origins it is difficult to give a rationale for contemporary analytic epistemology in its parts as well as in the way it relates its parts to one another. Indeed, it may be that the reason that certain traditional components of this discipline, for example, research on the Gettier problem, have (as it seems to me) lost their vitality is that they have come to be pursued as ends in themselves rather than as means to help with the problem of reconciling the scientific and manifest images.

My own interest in the historical details of Descartes's philosophy stems in part from dissatisfaction with contemporary treatments of this problematic, including Sellars's own, in part from the conviction that the difference between philosophical systems that provide successful solutions to great problems and those that do not lie in matters of detail, and in part from the conviction that Descartes got many of the important details right.

Halifax, Nova Scotia   Thomas C. Vinci
1997

Acknowledgments

I cut my first philosophical teeth in a tutorial on Descartes and the British Empiricists given in 1968 by Francis Sparshott at Victoria College of the University of Toronto. I owe much to him and to my friend and fellow participant, Richard Fumerton, for initiating me into the heady stuff of rigorous philosophical discussion. Since then I have struggled with the issues that arose during the course of those discussions, one of the results of which is this book. I also owe a large debt of gratitude to Joseph Camp Jr., who was my supervisor, philosophical mentor, and friend during my days as a graduate student at the University of Pittsburgh and who (along with Wilfrid Sellars) taught me much of what I now know about philosophy.

The first major theme in the book took written shape eleven years ago in the form of a paper on the Cartesian notion of clear but not distinct ideas (developed here in chapter 7). I sent a copy of this paper to Professor Harry Frankfurt who, in his reply to an unsolicited paper from an author he had never heard of, said some very encouraging things—he liked the paper, and I should let him know when it was to be published. If you are reading this, Professor Frankfurt, the reply is that it, along with everything else I have ever published on Descartes, is being published now. Many others have given me encouragement during the long and, at times, difficult period of writing this book. Among those with expertise in Cartesian scholarship who deserve special mention are Jodi Graham, John Barresi, Calvin Normore, Tom Lennon, Gary Hatfield, Murray Miles, Ann MacKenzie, and Carlos Prado. I should also mention Jim Brown and Kathleen Okruhlik, and my colleagues Sue Campbell and especially David Braybrooke, whose advice (philosophical, literary, and personal) was an unfailing source of aid and comfort. In addition, I am also indebted to Steven Nadler, Stephen Menn, Dann Garber, Margaret Wilson, E. J.

Ashworth, Steven Maitzen, Duncan MacIntosh, and several anonymous referees for discussion of key issues and for written comments on portions of the manuscript. My greatest intellectual debts are to those whose ideas helped me turn the corner on some lines of thought that would otherwise have led to a dead end for this project. Let me especially mention Harry Frankfurt, Margaret Wilson, Gary Hatfield, Dan Garber, John Carriero, Hiram Caton, Maritial Gueroult, John Cottingham, Steven Menn, Stephen Gaukroger, Murray Miles, Norman J. Wells, Calvin Normore, Peter Markie, and Daisie Radner.

Although some of my colleagues in the philosophy department have occasionally expressed skepticism about the value of an intense philosophical study of figures in the history of philosophy, the commitment of all of them to rigorous thought in the best tradition of analytic philosophy has required me to maintain high standards of argument and clarity in my work on Descartes. I owe much to their influence. I also owe much to the participants in a Descartes seminar I led during the winter of 1996–97: David Cormier, Colin Kerr, Craig Mercer, and Nell Thurlow. Let me especially mention Adwoa Buahene and Anthony Skelton for their enthusiasm and demanding questions. The book is better for their efforts. I also thank members of the philosophy departments of the University of Western Ontario, the University of Toronto, York University, Queen's University, the University of Ottawa, and Acadia University for allowing me to read portions of this book to them. Many helpful discussions took place during those visits.

Chris Byrne, Steven Burns, and Michael Bishop provided advice on matters of translation. Sue McLeod did much of the painstaking work in the process of applying for permissions. Thanks to all. Appreciation is also due to the Research Development Fund (Arts) of Dalhousie University for financial help with travel and manuscript preparation costs as well as to Bob Fournier and the Office of Research Services for funds to help with permission fees. I also wish to thank Dalhousie University and the Dean of the Faculty of Arts and Social Sciences for granting me a six-month sabbatical leave in 1995–96 during which much of the final work was done on the manuscript.

I wish to thank my wife Carmen for her love, for her support, and for sharing with me the day-long smile that came on the occasion of the book's acceptance for publication by Oxford University Press. I also wish to express my gratitude to Cynthia Read, executive editor at the press, without whose decisiveness and faith in the book there would have been no smile. Thanks also to MaryBeth Branigan, my production editor, and a special thanks to Maura High, an outstanding copyeditor. Finally, to my mother, Ellen Suzette, and to my late father, Ernesto, who raised me to have faith in myself, let me say thank you.

Cambridge University Press and Professor John Cottingham kindly granted permission to quote numerous passages from Descartes's writings. This material is reproduced from René Descartes, *The Philosophical Writings of Descartes*, vols. 1 and 2, translated by John Cottingham, Robert Stoothoff, and Dugald Murdoch, copyright © 1985 and 1984, respectively, and vol. 3, translated by John Cottingham, Robert Stoothoff, Dugald Murdoch, and Anthony Kenny, copyright © 1991 by Cambridge University Press; reprinted with the permission of Cambridge University Press. Other passages from Descartes's writings are reproduced from *Meditations de prima philosophia / Meditations of First Philosophy* by René Descartes, translated by George Heffernan, copyright © 1992 by the University of Notre Dame Press. Reprinted by permission of the publisher; permission is gratefully acknowledged.

Other material reproduced in this book and gratefully acknowledged here are (where given, page numbers are those of the source) from:

Aristotle, *The Oxford Translation of Aristotle*, edited by W. D. Ross (Oxford: Oxford University Press, 1908–1952), by kind permission of Oxford University Press.

Robert Audi, *The Structure of Justification* (New York: Cambridge University Press, 1993). Copyright © Cambridge University Press 1993. Reprinted with the kind permission of Cambridge University Press. (Passages are from pp. 167–170; 362.)

Richard Foley, *Working Without a Net: A Study of Egocentric Epistemology.* Copyright © by Richard Foley. Used by permission of Oxford University Press, Inc. (Passages are from pp. 44, 121, 122, 123, 134.)

Maritial Gueroult, *Descartes' Philosophy Interpreted According to the Order of Reasons*, Vol. 2, translated by Roger Ariew (Minneapolis: University of Minnesota Press, 1985). Copyright © 1968 by Éditions Montaigne. Reprinted by permission of Georges Borchardt, Inc. for the author. (Passages are from pp. 62, 67.)

Maritial Gueroult, *Descartes Selon L'Order des Raisons II* (Paris: Aubier-Montaigne, 1968). Copyright © 1968 by Éditions Montaigne; reprinted with permission from Éditions Aubier. (Original passages occur on pp. 81, 87.)

Richard L. Gregory, *The Oxford Companion to the Mind* (Oxford, New York: Oxford University Press, 1987), by kind permission of Oxford University Press.

Eileen O'Neill, Mind-body interaction and metaphysical consistency: A defense of Descartes. *Journal of the History of Philosophy* 25 (1987): 239. The passage reproduced is a translation by A. Freddoso from Francisco Suarez, *Disputationes Metaphysicae, 4 (XXX, 1, 10)* (Hildeshiem: G. Olms, 1965). Permission to reproduce is kindly granted by the editors of *Journal of the History of Philosophy* and A. Freddoso.

Wilfrid Sellars, *Essays in Philosophy and Its History, Vol. II* (Dordrecht: D. Reidel, 1974). Copyright © 1974 by D. Reidel Publishing Company, Dordrecht, Holland, and copyright holders as specified on appropriate pages within. Reprinted with kind permission from Kluwer Academic Publisher. (Passages are from the preface, vii).

Portions of the preface are reproduced from my article "Why Is There Analytic Epistemology?" *Dialogue* 33 (1994). The passages are on pp. 518–19 and are reprinted with the kind permission of the editor of *Dialogue*.

Contents

Primary Works Used or Cited

C. Adam and P. Tannery (eds.). *Oeuvres de Descartes* (revised edition, Paris: Vrin/ C.N.R.S., 1964–76, 12 volumes.). Cited as AT.

F. Alquié (ed.). *Oeuvres philosophiques de Descartes* (Paris: Garnier, 1963–1973, 3 vols.). Cited as Alquié.

J. Cottingham, R. Stoothoff, D. Murdoch, and (vol. III only) A. Kenny (trans.). *The Philosophical Writings of Descartes, Volumes I, II, & III* (Cambridge: Cambridge University Press, 1984–1991). Cited as CSM I, CSM II or CSMK III respectively.

E. S. Haldane and G. T. R. Ross. *The Philosophical Works of Descartes, Volumes I & II* (London: Cambridge University Press, 1967). Cited as H&R.

T. S. Hall (trans.). *Descartes' Treatise on Man* (Cambridge, Mass.: Harvard University Press, 1972). Cited as Hall.

G. Heffernan. *Meditationes de prima philosophia/Meditations of First Philosophy* (Notre Dame: University of Notre Dame Press, 1990). Cited as Heffernan.

A. Kenny (trans.). *Descartes: Philosophical Letters* (Minneapolis: University of Minnesota Press, 1981). Cited as Letters.

P. J. Olscamp (trans.). *Discourse on Method, Optics, Geometry and Meteorology* (Indianapolis: Bobbs Merrill, 1965). Cited as Olscamp.

Cartesian Truth

For the juxtaposition of historical and systematic studies I make no apology. It has been suggested, with a friendly touch of malice, that if *Science and Metaphysics* consists, as its sub-title proclaims, of *Variations on Kantian Themes*, it would be no less accurate to sub-title my historical essays "variations on Sellarsian themes." But this is as it should be. Philosophy is a continuing dialogue with one's contemporaries, living and dead, and if one fails to see oneself in one's respondent and one's respondent in oneself, there is confrontation but no dialogue.

—Wilfrid Sellars from the preface to his
Essays in Philosophy and Its History

Introduction

In Meditation I Descartes lays the foundations for two distinct projects. One is what Bernard Williams has called "the project of pure inquiry."[1] In this Meditation Descartes begins to define a notion of absolute certainty, by showing that we cannot be absolutely certain of particular commonsense propositions like "I am seated by the fire." In Meditation II Descartes continues with the project by developing the idea of certainty, this time to more positive effect: he provides examples of propositions that are certain in the requisite sense and introduces a method for demonstrating certainty, one that he will characterize in Meditation III as a paradigm of his official method of clear and distinct ideas.

However, Descartes's *advertised* purpose in writing Meditation I is that of "providing the easiest route by which the mind may be led away from the senses."[2] This is a different goal from that of his project "of pure inquiry," where he does not present discrediting the senses as an essential objective. That these two objectives are distinct should be plain when we consider what would happen to them if the senses should be found to provide certainty in the requisite sense: the first project would not automatically fail, but the second would.

Why should Descartes want to discredit the senses? The answer that he offers is that he can provide a firm foundation for systematic knowledge (*scientia*) by freeing us from preconceived opinions based on the senses. Descartes suggests that there is a connection between the two projects: the sensory critique is a means to achieve the ends of the project of pure inquiry. But this answer increases our puzzlement rather than decreases it, for Descartes was himself a scientist who engaged in empirical research in the contemporary sense that relied heavily and essentially on observation. We know from the *Discourse*[3] that Descartes wished to include this research as part of systematic knowledge. For example, his work on rainbow effects required precise observation of the location of colors in a glass vessel formed when a ray of sunlight was passed through it.[4] Was this the sort of sensory-based opinion that Descartes wished to discredit? If so our question is still unanswered: Why should Descartes wish to discredit sensory-based opinion and, especially, why should he wish to do so as the first step in grounding systematic knowledge? If this was not the sort of observation he wished to discredit, what was?

My own answer to this question is that Descartes saw in commonsense observation reports a commonsense metaphysics about the ontological status of colors and other such sensible qualities according to which they are formally modes of external, extended objects. It was this metaphysics and its commonsense epistemic credentials that he wished to discredit.[5] The reason for his critique was that he sensed that failure to do so would fundamentally undermine his purely mechanistic conception of the physical order, a conception in which the world possesses only primary qualities. Commonsense metaphysics was Descartes's evil demon; the effort to exorcise it shaped the development not only of his epistemology but also of his empirical theory of perception and parts of his theory of representation. It is also the thread that connects the many and various critical things he has to say about the senses, allowing us to structure them into a sequence of critiques of increasingly fundamental significance.

I see five critiques in this series. The first arises within Descartes's psychological theory of the "material for error" afforded by the phenomenology of sense experience; the second is the dream argument of Meditation I; the third is the doctrine that sensory ideas are "materially false ideas," ideas that fail to carry out the central representational functions of intellectual ideas ("true ideas"); the fourth centers on the incomprehensibility of Scholastic explanations of the causal commerce between perceivers and what they are said to perceive; and the fifth shows that sensory awareness possesses an intrinsic "obscurity" that leaves the nature of its objects opaque to the understanding. This fifth critique is the final stage in Descartes's critical project against the senses; it also serves as an important element in what I see as the beginnings of a positive Cartesian sensory foundationalism.

As evidence from the *Meditations*[6] for the centrality of the project to defeat commonsense metaphysics, I offer the fact that in Meditation III Descartes says that the chief destructive effect of the First Meditation was to cast doubt on the following two propositions:

1. There is a world external to the senses.
2. It resembles our sensations.

For most readers of Meditation I, it will seem natural for Descartes to describe his purposes there as the casting of doubt on the first of these propositions but it will seem puzzling why he should describe himself as *additionally* casting doubt on the second. Where in Meditation I does Descartes raise the issue of resemblance or the principle that the world resembles our sensations? Where, indeed, does Descartes mention "sensations"? The answer to this puzzle is that Descartes is not directly interested in resemblance or hypotheses about the nature of sensations and their causes, but rather uses this idiom to describe the view that the same sensible qualities that form the content of immediate perceptual awareness also serve as the visible properties of objects in the material world (Meditation VI: AT VII, 82; CSM II, 56). This view arises in part from the way those objects appear to us and in part from errors we make on our own, the net effect of which is to create a conceptual image of the physical world as it manifests itself in sense experience. This is the image Sellars calls "the manifest image."[7]

According to Sellars, the manifest image is more than just a philosophically unstructured conception of our environment but contains an implicit Aristotelian (hylomorphic) metaphysics in which objects are taken to be combinations of matter[8] and form. The basic objects of this framework are composed of perceptible matter, for example, colored stuff, and perceptible spatial form. This perceptible matter is itself a combination of perceptible qualities and extended stuff: in Cartesian terminology, perceptible qualities are "modes" of extended matter. I shall call a framework having these characteristics "commonsense realism."

It may seem strange that Descartes should feel a threat from commonsense realism since from our perspective in the late twentieth century it is almost taken as axiomatic that commonsense metaphysics has little epistemic force and poses little threat to the materialist metaphysics apparently licensed by scientific method. And yet both scientific method and commonsense epistemology have a common source in the way in which the world presents itself to us in sense experience. It is because one object *seems* congruent in length with another that measurements can justifiably be made; it is because different objects *appear* in different places at the same time that we can reasonably differentiate between them; it is because one object *appears* in one place at one time and at a different place at a different time that we have grounds for believing in motion.

Without sense experience taking the form that it does, these operations and beliefs would not occur or possess rational warrant. However, colors appear located in space fused into the matter of objects, and this too counts as a form that sense experience takes, a form that explains and apparently justifies the commonsense metaphysics of the manifest image. If we now think that *this* evidence of the senses must be discounted while other evidence is retained, it is because we now think that science, as it is currently practiced, and the metaphysics it presupposes comprise the only conceptual framework of which we can have a clear and distinct vision. Though we believe this in part for systematic, ahistorical reasons, we also believe it because we now stand on an edifice that Descartes has built.

It is hard to discern from within our current conceptual scheme which elements are there because of the peculiarities of the perspective presented from this edifice and which elements would be there on any systematically adequate account. Perhaps Descartes's own practice establishes an ideal here—raze the current structure and build anew from the ground up—but it is an ideal we cannot expect to follow. What we can do, however, is see how Descartes himself proceeded in his project of inquiry, looking for crucial turns in the method that might help us understand our own systematic practices and prejudices.

Descartes's official explanation in Meditation I of the connection between the project of inquiry and the critique of the senses rests on two main premises. The first is that the senses provide us with beliefs that are subject to various kinds of doubt; the second is this:

> Reason now leads me to think that I should hold back my assent from opinions which are not completely certain and indubitable just as carefully as I do from those which are patently false. So, for the purpose of rejecting all my opinions, it will be enough if I find in each of them at least some reason for doubt. (AT VII, 18; CSM II, 12)

But why should reason lead Descartes to think this? Withholding belief from propositions known to be false is obviously rationally defensible, but withholding beliefs from propositions that are probably true though not one hundred percent certain—as Descartes thinks is the case with propositions derived from the senses (AT VII, 22; CSM II, 15)—is not obviously rationally defensible. We therefore are entitled to ask Descartes for some further defense of this doctrine or at least for some explanation of why he holds it. This he does not provide. But perhaps in the foregoing discussion of commonsense realism there is the basis for an explanation.

I have so far depicted commonsense realism as a doctrine attractive to philosophically untutored ordinary folk but not, of course, to Descartes himself. Suppose, however, that we allow that Descartes, too, is seduced by the attractions of this view and wonders whether its great power to influence his judgment may not, after all, be a sign of its truth. Yet Descartes also feels compelled to accept the alternative, incompatible view of mechanistic science, thinking that its great power to influence his judgment is also a sign of truth.

If this were Descartes's position he would be like the engineer I mentioned in my preface, whose only sources of knowledge yield an inconsistent picture of reality. One possibility for someone in this situation is to choose one source over the other—to choose reason over the senses or the senses over reason.

It may seem obvious that Descartes takes the first option right from the start of Meditation I. In the *Synopsis* he does, after all, characterize the method of doubt as "providing the easiest route by means of which the mind may be lead away from the senses." However, doubts about the senses can hardly be generated without some reliance on reasoning. For example, the doubts generated by considering mundane examples of perceptual mistakes, examples in which "the senses deceive us with respect to objects that are very small or in the distance" (AT VII, 18; CSM II, 12), rely on such logical facts as that the same object cannot be both round and square at the same time, and so on. Similar remarks apply to doubts generated by dreaming and evil demons. Moreover, knowledge of logical facts requires a source just as much as knowledge of empirical facts, and the lack of cotenability between the scientific and manifest images that, I am supposing, characterizes Descartes's set of belief inclinations undermines his confidence in the the former no less than in the latter.

It is of course well known that Descartes expressed doubts about the reliability of reason, as well as the senses, in a passage in Meditation I where he first introduces the device of the deceiving God (AT VII, 21; CSM II, 14). This device, if considered in isolation from other problems, seems capable of generating only the kind of remote, hyperbolic doubts in relation to which Descartes's stringent doctrine about belief-withholding seems so ill motivated. However, if considered in the context of a project of reconciling the manifest and scientific images, things look quite different; for, in showing that what we think we know on the basis of reason might in certain circumstances be mistaken, the device of the deceiving God shows that the deliverances of reason cannot be automatically excluded from the list of things that might have to be revised. Since Descartes thinks that the deliverances of the senses are certainly on this list, he must either abandon the project of reconciling the two images or look for a source of knowledge that cannot be contributing to the problem. In order to carry out this search in a systematic way, Descartes needs a doctrine of method as stringent as the one he prescribes at the beginning of Meditation I: "I should hold back my assent from opinions which are not completely certain and indubitable just as carefully as I do from those which are patently false" (AT VII, 18; CSM II, 12).

There is but one place where Descartes can turn for the requisite certainty, for however deeply infected with falsity and inconsistency his other beliefs may be, he knows at least that *he has those beliefs* and that *he exists*. This knowledge is self-knowledge and it provides the only foundation Descartes can trust in his project of rehabilitating his other sources of knowledge. Descartes goes about this task by identifying an inference from his thought to his existence that serves as a model for a more general inference from his clear and distinct ideas to the truth of certain propositions, and from the truth of certain propositions to the existence of things outside his ideas. The first inference is the cogito, the second is governed by the rule of truth and the third conforms to Descartes's general pattern of existential reasoning.

In chapter 1 I undertake to show how the general pattern of existential reasoning is based on the rule of truth and how the latter arises from the cogito. In subsequent chapters I show how the theory is put to work in establishing the existence of God—first in the guise of a causal argument in Meditation III and then in the guise of an ontological argument in Meditation V—and then in establishing the existence of the material world.

At the heart of the set of inferences comprising this theory lies the rule of truth, a principle or, rather, a set of principles that provide the main premises of Cartesian epistemology. My interpretation of these principles is initially based on a conservative reading of Cartesian texts, in which the scope of clear and distinct ideas is confined to ideas of the intellect. But there are tensions within some of the proofs, especially those concerned with the material world, which suggest the need for a less conservative interpretation according to which both ideas of the imagination and ideas of the senses are also seen by Descartes as falling within the scope of the rule of truth.

There has been much skepticism of late about whether there is a positive role for sense experience in Descartes's epistemological method.[9] Those who have found a role for it see it as confined to natural epistemology[10] or interpret it as an inductive inference from "sensation reports"[11]; none that I am familiar with has seen sense experience as playing a central role in the rule of truth. Yet there is a fairly strong case that Descartes does see sense experience in this light. Why should this case be so hard to discern? There are several reasons, but chief among them is the systematically negative view that Descartes takes of the senses and the imagination in the

Meditations. Here, however, I would urge some caution, for Descartes's account of the senses and the imagination serve two masters in the *Meditations*. One is the project of producing a set of epistemic tools that will in turn produce a worldview reconciling the senses and reason, the other is the project of Cartesian dualism. There is a tension between these two projects that arises at the very beginning of the epistemological project, in the account of self-knowledge in Meditation II. This tension gives rise to vacillation, perhaps even distortion, in the account that Descartes gives of his own doctrine of the metaphysics and epistemology of the senses. In order to gain a clear and distinct view of that doctrine it is, I think, necessary to understand the nature of that tension, something I undertake in chapter 1.

In attempting to resolve tensions among conflicting lines of theorizing within an existing philosophical system, a philosopher engaged in a project of reconstructing that system will have to make some choices not dictated by exegetical considerations alone about which of those lines of theorizing to include in the final reconstruction. Different philosophers will make different assessments, but my own is that it is Cartesian epistemology rather than Cartesian (dualistic) theory of mind that is of more abiding philosophical interest. Demonstrating this requires showing that Descartes's epistemology possesses more balance, more power, and more plausibility than contemporary Anglo-American philosophy has generally been able to see in it. This is what I aim to show in the following chapters and epilogue.

ONE

Self Knowledge and the Rule of Truth

1.1 Introduction

This is a lengthy chapter by the end of which I hope to have reconstructed—and to some extent defended—the foundation of Cartesian epistemology. The foundation is the rule of truth and the rock upon which it rests is Descartes's account of self-knowledge.

I have employed the foundational metaphor to indicate that Descartes maintains a form of foundationalism,[1] specifically, a form that is committed to the epistemic primacy of the immediate consciousness of nonpropositional entities. This form of foundationalism then confronts the problem of showing how it is possible to transform the awareness of nonpropositional items into knowledge of propositions. Contemporary critiques of foundationalism[2] have generally argued that it is impossible to show this.

I believe that Cartesian epistemology makes a philosophically defensible case that this transformation can be carried out. It is not easy to see this because at times Descartes seems simply to confuse propositional and nonpropositional forms of awareness. I will argue that although Descartes sometimes confuses the distinction, at other times he deliberately employs it in a theory of how items falling on the one side of the distinction can give rise to items falling on the other. At the heart of this theory is the rule of truth:

> So I now seem to be able to lay it down as a general rule that whatever I perceive very clearly and distinctly is true. (AT VII, 35; CSM II, 24)

But this rule itself seems to embody the same confusion: if "whatever I perceive very clearly and distinctly" is a nonpropositional item, then how can that item be

9

true; if it is a propositional item then what relation does it bear to the clear and distinct perception of *nonpropositional items*?

When the rule is first introduced at the beginning of Meditation III, Descartes gives us little by way of justifying it, little by way of explaining the puzzles surrounding it. He does, however, give us the cogito. The cogito crystallizes Descartes's account of self-knowledge, and I hope to show that Descartes uses this account as a paradigm for the rule of truth and that the rule serves as a kind of epistemologist's stone that transforms perception that is not knowledge into perception that is knowledge.

The main work on Descartes's account of self-knowledge begins in the next section. However, it will be helpful to say first some general things about Descartes's orientation to the family of concepts centering on knowledge, belief, and perception.

Cartesian philosophy of mind is generally credited with the view that individuals have special, first-person access to the contents of their minds (the special access doctrine). Oversimplifying somewhat for purposes of introduction, we can understand the special access doctrine as ascribing one or more of the following three properties: (1) My beliefs about my mental states are *infallible*: necessarily, if I believe that I am in a certain mental state then I am in that state; (2) my beliefs about my current mental states are *incorrigible*: necessarily, no one ever has overriding reason to think them false; and (3) my mental states are *self-presenting* to my beliefs: necessarily, if I am in a certain mental state then I know that I am in that state.[3]

One of the chief difficulties in deciding whether Descartes subscribes to the view expressed in (3) lies in translating the intended sense of knowledge and the intended scope of mental states into Cartesian terms. If knowledge is intended to be taken in the ordinary sense as implying belief then there are a number of passages in which Descartes says that we can make mistakes about our mental states, including mistakes about fundamental properties of these states. Consider, for example, a text from *Principles of Philosophy I, 46*[4]:

> [W]hen someone feels an intense pain, the perception he has of it is indeed very clear, but it is not always distinct. For people commonly confuse this perception with an obscure judgement they make concerning the nature of something which they think exists in the painful spot and which they suppose to resemble the sensation of pain; but it is in fact the perception alone which they perceive clearly. (AT VIIIA, 22; CSM I, 208)

In this passage Descartes countenances two kinds of mental state, perceptions and judgments. He maintains that we are in error about which is which: there is a perception of pain that we fail to recognize as such (we confuse it with judgment). Moreover, we falsely believe of this perception that it exists in a portion of the material world, namely, the "painful spot" in my foot.

The mistakes Descartes attributes to us in this passage are mistakes about where to locate things within Cartesian mental taxonomy. The principal division therein is that between *actions* and *passions*[5]: judgments fall in the former category[6] and perceptions in the latter. Descartes is thus allowing that we can be mistaken about important categorial aspects of our mental states even while we realize that we are in them.

Note also that the principal division within the overall Cartesian metaphysical taxonomy is that between mind and matter, and in allowing that we could think that a state of mind is really a state of matter, Descartes allows that we can even be confused and mistaken about the most fundamental metaphysical-categorial aspects of our mental states.

The reader may rest assured that I am not going to argue that Descartes rejects all forms of special access to mental states, but the foregoing example illustrates the need to interpret Descartes with much care on this issue. It is important to respect the distinction between judging and perceiving when it comes to analyzing other cognitive and epistemic concepts in the Cartesian system. Not doing so is the chief failing that Descartes attributes to common sense, embodied for example, in the confusion about pain mentioned above. It is of some importance, therefore, to take measures from the outset to ensure that it is not a chief failing of my own attempt to understand the basic concepts of Cartesian philosophy. Accordingly, I shall postpone further consideration of whether Descartes countenances special access in any of the three ways mentioned above until I have had an opportunity to further explore some of the underpinnings of the theory of ideas.

It is accepted as a truism among contemporary epistemologists that belief, knowledge, and certainty are "propositional attitudes." A propositional attitude is or implies an inclination to act in some way with respect to a proposition. For example, if I have a fear attitude toward the proposition that p, then I tend to avoid a situation in which it is true that p; if I have a doxastic (belief) attitude toward the proposition that p, then I tend to affirm that p is the case; if I have an epistemic (knowledge-like) attitude toward the proposition that p, then I not only tend to affirm that p is the case but I do so with certainty or with conclusive reasons as backing. I will assume without argument that ordinary English uses of "believe that," "know that," and "am certain that" are propositional attitudes in the sense just defined. We cannot assume without argument that this is the case with cognate concepts in the Cartesian system. (I will argue in section 1.3 of this chapter that this is *not* the case for one important conception of knowledge in the Cartesian system, *intuitive knowledge*.)

Speaking in Meditation IV of the freedom of the will Descartes says:

> [T]he will simply consists in our ability to do or not to do something (that is to affirm or deny, to pursue or avoid); or rather, it consists simply in the fact that when the intellect puts something forward for affirmation or denial or for pursuit or avoidance, our inclinations are such that we do not feel we are determined by any external force. (AT VII, 57; CSM II, 40)

That some of the "inclinations" mentioned here are directed toward propositions is indicated by the reference to affirmation and denial, a point reinforced by the fact that Descartes says that "falsity in the strict sense, or formal falsity, can occur only in judgments." (AT VII, 43; CSM II, 30): judgments are acts of affirmation or denial directed to the bearers of truth and falsity, namely, propositions. When Descartes speaks in Meditation I of his "habitual opinions," of his "habit of confidently assenting to these opinions" (AT VII, 22; CSM II, 15), he seems to have the doxastic inclinations of Meditation IV in mind. Since we may take beliefs and opinions to be much the same thing, we may take beliefs to be a species of judgment or, perhaps, a species of inclination to judgment. The Cartesian notion of belief thus accords well with the contemporary doctrine known as doxastic voluntarism.[7]

Beliefs in the Cartesian system also come in "weights" or degrees[8] that mirror strengths of inclination to affirm belief contents, and I shall assume that at least one version of the Cartesian concept of doubt and certainty—"psychological doubt" and "psychological certainty" as I shall call them[9]—can be defined within this apparatus as degrees of doxastic inclination. A high degree of inclination to affirm that p is a high degree of psychological certainty; a low degree of inclination to affirm that p is a high degree of psychological doubt.

In addition to a *psychological* notion of doubt and certainty, Descartes also appears to work with a concept, or family of concepts, of doubt and certainty—"epistemic doubt" and "epistemic certainty"[10]—that cluster around the idea that a proposition is certain if there are no *reasons* to doubt it.

> Reason now leads me to think that I should hold back my assent from opinions which are not completely certain and indubitable just as carefully as I do from those which are patently false. So, for the purpose of rejecting all of my opinions, it will be enough if I find in each of them at least *some reason* for doubt. (Meditation I: AT VII, 18; CSM II, 12; my emphasis)

Both notions of certainty seem to fit contemporary paradigms reasonably well—indeed, the former comprise the latter. However, it is more difficult to relate the Cartesian concept of knowledge to contemporary understanding of the concept of justified true belief. To demonstrate this, I first note that inclinations are a class of items that fall within the province of the will, not the intellect. The role of the intellect is to provide perceptions that *cause* the inclinations:

> I could not but judge that something which I understood so clearly was true; but this was not because I was compelled so to judge by any external force, but because a great light in the intellect was followed by a great inclination in the will. (Meditation IV: AT VII, 58–59; CSM II, 41)

Unfortunately, this doctrine creates some difficulty in seeing how the Cartesian notion of *knowledge* is to be handled. If we assume that knowledge entails psychological certainty (irresistible doxastic inclination) or at least belief, then we must see knowledge as falling at least partly on the side of the will. But Descartes denies this in the same article from *The Passions of the Soul* quoted at the outset:

> On the other hand, the various perceptions or modes of knowledge [*la connaissance*] present in us may be called its passions. (AT XI, 342; CSM I, 335; my emphasis)

Elsewhere,[11] however, Descartes employs a notion of knowledge—*scientia*—which does appear to entail psychological (and epistemic) certainty. Related to this is the question whether those forms of cognition that Descartes regards as intuitive can be regarded as a species of knowledge or should be assigned to some other form of awareness. In the same place (an important passage where intuitional modes of cognition are being discussed), Haldane and Ross have translated the term *cognitio* as "knowledge,"[12] but Cottingham et al. have rendered the term as "awareness," reserving "knowledge" for the translation of *scientia*.[13] What is important in this question is not which English word, "awareness" or "knowledge," best represents the logical properties of intuitive awareness—there are advantages and disadvantages to each—but what those properties are. Two properties interest me. The first has to do with the nature of the objects of these cognitions: are they propositional or are they non-propositional? The second concerns the nature of the epistemic properties of these cognitions.

1.2 Propositional Awareness and Nonpropositional Awareness

In the last passage but one quoted above (Meditation IV: AT VII, 58–59; CSM II, 41), Descartes is discussing an inclination to affirm a proposition based on clear and distinct perception. This inclination, located on the side of will in the Cartesian taxonomy, rests on two apparently distinct factors located in the intellect. The first factor is "understanding," which contributes the *propositional object* of the inclination; the second factor is the *cause of the inclination*. It is one thing to have a degree of understanding of the elements of a proposition sufficient to make it available for epistemic evaluation or affirmation; it is quite another to have sufficient evidence available to create an inclination to affirm that proposition.[14] Discussion of the two factors occurs within theories that are usually regarded as distinct—the first within theories of ideas and semantics; the second within a theory of knowledge. Yet Descartes seems to run the two factors together. This tendency is clearly evident in the passage quoted above from Meditation IV:

> I could not *but judge that something which I understood so clearly was true.* (AT VII, 58–59; CSM II, 41; my emphasis)

But the problem is not simply one of conflation. In *Objections and Replies*, Descartes declares: "By 'whatever we perceive' is meant any property, quality or attribute of which we have a real idea" (AT VII, 161; CSM II, 114), and in Meditation III Descartes identifies "true ideas" as those that are clear and distinct (AT VII, 43; CSM II, 30). In the latter passage examples cited of things clearly and distinctly perceived are "size, or extension in length, breadth and depth; shape; position . . . substance, duration and number." But none of these is a proposition. This would not be perplexing if Descartes had confined the role of clear and distinct ideas to the theory of understanding—we understand the nonpropositional concept of extension because we have a clear and distinct perception of the property of extension, a nonpropositional item—but he does not confine clear and distinct ideas to this role, employing them as well in the theory of doxastic inclinations. What is perplexing is how a clear and distinct perception of nonpropositional items can have sufficient structure to serve as a sufficient cause of an inclination to affirm a proposition.

This same problem appears in a somewhat different form in Descartes's commitment to what has come to be known as the rule of truth, introduced for the first time in Meditation III:

> In this first item of knowledge there is simply a clear and distinct perception of what I am asserting. . . . I now seem to be able to lay it down as a general rule that whatever I perceive very clearly and distinctly is true. (AT VII, 35; CSM II, 24)

If we read "whatever I perceive very clearly and distinctly" here to mean the same as "what we perceive" in the passage from the Second Replies, we find Descartes asserting that truth is a property of properties rather than of propositions. Yet Descartes clearly understands truth to be a property of judgments, a property of "what I am asserting,"[15] acts of the will directed toward propositional entities. Indeed, when we look to what "this first item of knowledge" is, we find that it is the *proposition* "*I am a thinking thing.*" Since this first item of knowledge seems to be what is clearly and distinctly perceived, we infer that Descartes does allow that clear and distinct perception can take propositional objects. But what is the connection between propositional and nonpropositional clear and distinct perception?

Frankfurt has argued that the propositional form is basic on the grounds that the property of clarity and distinctness is the same as the property of (epistemic) certainty and the latter is a property of propositions.[16] There are several difficulties with this proposal, of which I think two are fundamental. The first is that it may not respect the distinction between perception (in the domain of the intellect) and inclination (in the domain of the will):[17]clear and distinct perception is an act of the intellect exclusively, not the will; but certainty is an act of both faculties—an irresistible inclination of the will to affirm a proposition on the basis of clear and distinct perceptions of the intellect. Descartes would have been guilty of a profound confusion had he simply identified clarity and distinctness with certainty. The second difficulty in Frankfurt's proposal is that an identification of the two properties would fly in the face of Descartes's declaration that the clarity and distinctness of the proposition that I am a thinking thing is not by itself sufficient for certainty—what else is needed is the rule "whatever I perceive very clearly and distinctly is true."

Markie, too, rejects the identification of clarity and distinctness with certainty[18] but argues, chiefly on the grounds that clear and distinct perception seems to be regarded by Descartes as a form of *intuition*[19] and that Descartes often describes intuitions as taking propositional objects,[20] that Descartes is "a proposition theorist"[21] about clear and distinct ideas. Markie is right to characterize clear and distinct propositional knowledge as a form of intuitive knowledge but wrong to insist that all forms of intuition are of propositional objects.

Consider first Descartes's official characterization of intuition in Rule 4 of *Rules for the Direction of the Mind*:

> By intuition I do not mean the fluctuating testimony of the senses or the deceptive judgement of the imagination as it botches things together, but the conception of a clear and attentive mind, which is so easy and distinct that that there can be no room for doubt about what we are understanding. (AT X, 368; CSM I, 14)

Now consider his description in Rule 6 of the *objects* of intuition:

> we should note that there are very few pure and simple natures which we can intuit straight off and *per se* (independently of any others) either in our sensory experience or by means of a light innate within us. We should, as I have said, attend carefully to the simple natures which can be intuited in this way. (AT X, 383; CSM I, 22)

It is plain from this passage that the intuition is directed to things (natures). But Descartes also thinks that *truths* can be deduced from our intuitions of simple natures, a point he makes in the heading of Rule 6: "[W]e should attend to what is most simple in each series of things in which we have directly deduced some truths from others" (AT X, 381; CSM I, 21).

It is tempting to ignore those texts in which Descartes treats the objects of intuitions as things rather than truths (propositions) or to regard them as somehow infelicitous, since Descartes does not say very much about how the propositional formulations of intuitive perception might be related in a systematic way to the nonpropositional formulations. *Principles I*, 52, does, however, contain a suggestive remark: "[I]f we perceive the presence of some attribute, we can *infer* that there must also be present an existing thing or substance to which it may be attributed" (AT VIIIA, 25; CSM I, 210; my emphasis). Once we have a substance to which a property is attributed, we have a proposition. If we start from an assumption of a clear and distinct perception of a property and have grounds for asserting that the property is attributed to a substance, we have the means of inferring a proposition from the clear and distinct perception of a property. So, if this text can be relied upon, Descartes does provide a basis for linking nonpropositional clear and distinct perception to the assertion of propositions. And this is what we are looking for.

Unfortunately, Descartes does not offer an account here of how this principle is to be justified, nor how it may be connected to the official doctrine of intuition and deduction. However, if, primed with this suggestion, we now return to *Rules for the Direction of the Mind* I believe that a theoretical treatment of the link between nonpropositonal and propositional awareness can be extracted from central texts dealing with intuition and deduction.

In Rule 12 Descartes declares:

> [T]hese simple natures are all self-evident and never contain any falsity. This can be easily shown if we distinguish between the faculty by which our intellect intuits and knows things and the faculty by which it makes affirmative or negative judgements. (AT X, 420; CSM I, 45)

In this passage Descartes seems to leave open the possibility that intuitions of the simple natures comprise a form of propositional knowledge, one that has the special virtue of being guaranteed to be true. However, in a later passage Descartes seems to declare that intuitions of the simple natures are in themselves neither true nor false.

> By 'problems', moreover, we mean *everything in which there lies truth or falsity*. . . . As we have already said, there can be no falsity in the mere intuition of things, be they simple or conjoined. In that respect *they are not called 'problems'*; but they acquire that name as soon as we decide to make a definite judgement about them. (AT X, 432; CSM I, 53; my emphasis)

Although there is no explicit assertion that intuitions are not by themselves capable of truth, the clauses I have emphasized suggest that they are not, a suggestion reinforced by the final clause, in which the name "problems" (everything that is either truth or falsity) is associated with acts of judgment rather than with intuitions.

Van De Pitt has also maintained that intuitions of the simple natures are nonpropositional (not bearers of truth or falsity in themselves), arguing that what transforms nonpropositional intuitions into potential bearers of truth and falsity is that action of the mind Descartes calls deduction.[22] Van De Pitt's claim is supported by a list of texts in which Descartes associates deduction directly with a method of ascertaining truth—for example, "[D]eduction alone enables us to compose things so as to be certain of their truth"[23]—and indirectly with judgment through an association of judgment with the act of composing things.[24]

In treating deduction as a species of judgment, Van De Pitt treats deduction as an act of affirming a propositional content—an act of will. In Rule 3 Descartes does say that deduction is a process of inference for deriving with certainty the truth of things that are not self-evident to begin with (AT X, 369; CSM I, 15). This process comprises "a continuous and uninterrupted movement of thought in which each individual proposition (*propositio*)[25] is clearly intuited." However, Descartes does not say precisely that this movement of thought comprises a judgment. Indeed, the implication in this passage is that it does not, for deduction is there described as "another means of knowing in addition to intuition" and knowing is an act of the intellect not (as would be required for judgment) an act of the will. The chief difference between intuition and deduction seems to be that intuition is directed to a simple nature or to a single, necessary relation between two simple natures, whereas a deduction involves a *series* of intuitions requiring memory. This makes deduction a kind of "intuition on the move."[26] There is nothing here to support the view that deduction and intuition fall on opposite sides of what is, for Descartes, the very fundamental division between acts of the will and acts of the intellect.

My own interpretation will take an intermediate path between one in which deduction is treated as a species of judgment (Van De Pitt) and another in which deduction is treated as simply a series of intuitions with nonpropositional content. This interpretation sees intuitions as nonpropositional awarenesses of simple natures (properties or attributes) and deduction as a process that comes in two basic types: (1) as a process that produces (infers) a nonpropositional intuition of a second simple nature from the intuition of a necessary relation between a first simple nature and the second,[27] and (2) as a special variant of (1), in which a composite propositional entity is inferred from an intuited consequence between two rather special kinds of simple nature. Once this special kind of deduction has occurred, the mind then has available the kind of content that it needs in order to be in a position to make a judgment of truth or falsity.

The special deduction occurs in the case where we "compose" the objects of intuition ourselves. I suggest that the object in question is best designated by a sentence of the form: "There is something that bears a certain relation to an intuited simple nature." Among objects of intuition, it is these entities for which I shall reserve the term "proposition," and it is propositions that are the sole objects of judgment. However, among propositions of this form there are two variants, one proper and produced in the manner just described, the other improper and produced in several other ways. What distinguishes these two kinds of proposition is the nature of the relation between the simple nature and its subject. Descartes's case for this is developed systematically in the sixth and seventh paragraphs of Rule 12 (AT X, 422–425; CSM 1, 46–48).

In the sixth paragraph Descartes introduces a class of natures he calls "composite." These are divided into two classes by an epistemic criterion: class 1 comprises those whose characteristics we know by experience, and class 2 those whose characteristics we know because we have put them together. Knowledge by experience in this context seems to include anything that reaches our intellect from external sources or from inner reflection. Intuition is included under this class (as coming from inner reflection). Descartes devotes the rest of the sixth paragraph to a discussion of ways in which we can go wrong. For example, we go wrong when we judge that "the imagination faithfully represents the objects of the senses, or that the senses take on the true shape of things, or, in short, that external things always are just as they appear to be." Descartes asserts that erroneous judgments arise only when "we believe that an object of our understanding contains something of which the mind has no immediate perceptual experience: and this cognition is to be found only among those we put together ourselves."

For my purposes the chief interest of these passages is what they tell us about the nature of judgment, not what they tell us about how judgments come to be liable to error. A judgment is directed toward something that conveys the idea that something other than the object of an intuition, namely, an object in the world external to our senses, bears a certain relation, namely, resemblance, similarity of appearance, or transmission in an unaltered form to the object of intuition. Something that conveys an idea of this form is a proposition in the sense introduced above; it is also a class 2 composite entity—something we put together ourselves.

Descartes does not, however, restrict class 2 composite entities only to those that are unreliable, for in the next (seventh) paragraph Descartes introduces a taxonomy of causes for the creation of this class of entity that includes deduction, a process that "remains as the sole means of compounding things in a way that enables us to be certain of their truth."[28] The phrase "compounding things" is a bit misleading here since it suggests a process of conjoining things rather that drawing necessary conclusions from things, but in its proper employment deduction always does the former by means of doing the latter:

> [I]t is within our power to avoid this error, *viz.* by never conjoining things unless we intuit that the conjunction of the one with the other is wholly necessary, as we do for example when we deduce that nothing which lacks extension can have a shape on the grounds that there is a necessary connection between shape and extension and so on. (AT X, 425; CSM I, 48)

Among the things that would replace the words "and so on" is the deduction of the proposition that there is a subject in which a given simple nature inheres.[29] All chains of deduction can be followed until they terminate in a cognition of this form, an intuitively based proposition suitable for affirmation or denial.

This analysis has found that compositeness comprises two classes of cognitions having the logical form of existentially generalized propositions:

1. Those that assert of a certain simple nature n that there is something x conceptually (but not actually) distinct from n such that n is contained in x.
2. Those that assert of a certain simple nature n that there is something x actually distinct from n such that x bears a resemblance relation to n.

These two classes of cognitions are not in themselves judgments but provide objects with a logical structure suitable for judgments. What else is needed is an action of the will affirming or denying them. When the will affirms propositions of class 1 it is guaranteed to assert the truth; when it affirms propositions of class 2 it is not guaranteed to assert the truth.[30] This is so because the latter class of propositions contain elements that go beyond those elements presented immediately in intuitive consciousness. The only cognitions that are candidates for truth or falsity in the Cartesian system are propositions of class 1 or class 2 or propositions that can be generated from them by means of generalization or other logical operations.

The doctrine that judgments based on intuitions are directed to class 1 propositions inferred from intuited simple natures is a doctrine that Descartes never abandoned, even after he abandoned the project of *Rules for the Direction of the Mind* itself. It is, for example, reflected in article 52 of the *Principles of Philosophy* in the words quoted earlier: "[I]f we perceive the presence of some attribute, we can infer that there must also be present an existing thing or substance to which it may be attributed" (AT VIIIA, 25; CSM I, 210). I shall call the principle embodied in this passage the *deductive judgment principle*.

The Deductive Judgment Principle

If we perceive the presence of some attribute, we can infer that there must also be present an existing thing or substance to which it may be attributed.

I will argue later that this same principle is[31] reflected in the formulation that Descartes gives of the rule of truth in Meditation III: "So I now seem to be able to lay it down as a general rule that whatever I perceive very clearly and distinctly is true" (AT VII, 35; CSM II, 24).

The deductive judgment principle should be distinguished from a principle that states that if we assume the presence of an actualized property P then there is a *subject* in which P is exemplified. This is a principle that Descartes also endorses in many passages, including the following from Rule 14:

> Let us now proceed to the sentence, 'Body possesses extension'. Here we understand the term 'extension' to denote something other than 'body'; yet we do not form two distinct ideas in our imagination, one of extension, the other of body, but just the single idea of extended body. . . . This is a peculiarity of those entities which exist only in something else, and which can never be conceived apart from a subject. (AT X, 444; CSM I, 60)

There is, nevertheless, a distinction of some sort between a substance and the attributes that inhere in it, the drawing of which "is entirely the work of the pure intellect: it alone has the ability to distinguish between abstract entities of this sort" (AT X, 444; CSM I, 60).

In this passage Descartes does not specifically identify the "subject" of the properties as a substance, but in his definition of the notion of substance in the Second Replies, he does so (this passage is from AT VII, 161; CSM II, 114; it is quoted in section 1.7, below).[32] Accordingly, I shall call this principle the *substance/attribute principle*.

The Substance/Attribute Principle

If a property *P* is actualized, then there exists an actual substance *s* such that *s* exemplifies *P*

The deductive judgment principle is an epistemic principle, since it allows us to move from an immediate awareness of an object that is not by itself a subject of judgment to an object that is a subject for judgment. The substance/attribute principle, on the other hand, is not an epistemic principle, since it does not specify a cognitive state in its antecedent. It is, rather, a metaphysical principle that specifies a necessary relation between one state of affairs and another.

I ended section 1.1 with the question whether we should allow that intuitional cognition should be treated as a form of "knowledge" or as a more general form of "awareness." We have found that intuition can be properly described in both ways: when intuition takes a propositional object, it can fairly be called *knowledge*; when it takes a nonpropositional object, it seems best to regard it as a form of *awareness*. Moreover, since there is strong evidence that Descartes regards clear and distinct perception as a kind of intuitional awareness, we expect to find Descartes treating the former correspondingly: when clear and distinct perception takes a propositional object, it is treated as knowledge; when it takes a nonpropositional object, it is not.

1.3 Intuitive Knowledge and Certain Knowledge

There is an important text from the Second Replies that has suggested to some commentators that even intuitive propositional cognition is not really worthy of the name "knowledge." Since it is an important text upon which I shall draw subsequently, I quote it in full:

> Now awareness[33] of first principles is not normally called [*scientia*][34] by dialectitians. And when we [notice][35] that we are thinking things, this is a primary notion which is not derived by means of any syllogism. When someone says "I am thinking, therefore I am or exist", he does not deduce existence from thought by means of a syllogism, but recognizes it as something self-evident by a simple intuition of the mind. This is clear from the fact that if he were deducing it by means of a syllogism, he would had to have had previous knowledge of the major premise 'Everything which thinks is, or exists'; yet in fact he learns it from experiencing in his own case that it is impossible that he should think without existing. It is the nature of the mind to construct general propositions on the basis of our knowledge [*la connaissance/cognitione*] of particular ones. (AT VII, 140–141; CSM II, 100; my interpolation; changes from Cottingham's translation are indicated by square brackets.)

Descartes is here contrasting awareness of first principles with what dialecticians call *scientia*, a concept usually translated as "knowledge." However, the contrast need not be taken as a contrast between a form of awareness that is not knowledge and one that is, for Descartes goes on to say that our perception of first principles is due to (propositional) intuition, and intuition in the Cartesian system yields something much stronger than just belief or perceptual awareness—it yields something possessing a foundational role in the development of the system of knowledge Descartes called *scientia*. Not only is intuitive cognition epistemically stronger than belief, it is drawn from a fundamentally different category in the Cartesian taxonomy of ideas. Beliefs are inclinations to affirm contents presented by ideas to the will. Intuitions are ideas that both present contents for affirmation and also cause inclinations to affirm. Intuitions thus cause beliefs; they are not a species of belief. So Descartes's conception of intuitive cognition shares some properties with our concept of knowledge and exhibits some contrasts with several other concepts with which our concept of knowledge also exhibits contrasts. Does such a role confer on intuition an epistemic character that merits the name "knowledge"? Clearly there is some element of arbitrariness in any decision on this matter, but I assume that it does.

However, the text of the immediately following paragraph appears to pose a problem for this assumption because Descartes there goes on to explain the difference between intuitive awareness and *true knowledge* in such a way as to suggest that intuition is not a form of knowledge. This suggestion is embodied in Cottingham's translation of the Latin term *cognitio* as "awareness" and *scientia* as "knowledge":

> The fact that an atheist can be "clearly aware that the three angles of a triangle are equal to two right angles" is something I do not dispute. But I maintain that this awareness of this is not true knowledge, since no act of awareness that can be rendered doubtful seems fit to be called knowledge. (AT VII, 141; CSM II, 101)

Cottingham explains the difference between the mathematician's intuitive awareness and *scientia* as the difference between "an isolated act of awareness" and "systematic, properly grounded knowledge" (CSM II, 101, n.1). But Descartes would regard the "ungrounded" and "isolated" nature of intuitive awareness as unsuiting it for the role of knowledge only if he has a fundamentally coherentist account of knowledge. Presumably Cottingham is suggesting that this is just how we should understand Cartesian epistemology.

There is, however, another way to understand Descartes's doctrine that does not have this rather drastic effect on our traditional understanding of Cartesian epistemology as paradigmatically foundational.[36] Consider the version of this passage, translated from the French:

> Now, that an atheist is able to know [*connaître*] clearly that the three angles of a triangle are equal to two right angles, I do not deny; I only maintain that the way he knows it is not as true and certain knowledge, for no knowledge which can be made doubtful should be called by that name. Since we are supposing that our subject is an atheist, he cannot be certain that he will not be mistaken in those things that seem to be most evident to him, as we have shown above. (My translation; AT IX, 11; Alquié II, 565)

What is brought out in this text more clearly than in the Latin is that the difference between intuition and *scientia* is the difference between *knowledge* and *certain knowledge*. I suggest that the difference amounts to this: certain knowledge is second-order knowledge; it is being certain that I have first-order, intuitive knowledge. There is, thus, no need to see in this text a denial that intuitive awareness is a form of knowledge for Descartes, and thus no compelling evidence that Descartes is (simply) a coherentist.

As support for this suggestion consider what has been "shown above." What has been shown (in Meditation III) is that Descartes must admit that "some God could perhaps have given to me such a nature that I were to be deceived even about those things which would seem most manifest" (AT VII, 36; Heffernan, 121). It is not clear from this passage by itself that what is "most manifest" is the object of intuition, but this is suggested by the previous sentence:

> When I considered something very simple and easy about things arithmetical or geometrical such as that two and three added together were five, or similar things, did I not then intuit [*intuerbar*] at least these things perspicuously enough that I might affirm that they are true. (AT VII, 36; Heffernan, 121)

What exactly is it that God's power makes possible? Is it (1) that if I have an intuition that two plus three is five, I may be mistaken that two plus three is five? But this is not quite what Descartes says, for, interpreting what is "most manifest" as what is intuitively cognized, he speaks of things that *seem* intuitively cognized, not of things which *are* intuitively cognized. Then is what makes God's power possible (2) that if I think that I have an intuition that two plus three is five, I may be mistaken about that opinion, namely, *that I have an intuition that two plus three is five?* Although it is difficult to extract a decisive argument from this text, I can find no indication in this portion of Meditation III that Descartes clearly affirms that it is actual rather than merely apparent intuited propositions that God can make false.[37] In all of the cases we have considered (including the text from the Fourth Replies quoted earlier) where he speaks of the power of God to deceive us concerning intuitional subject matter it is apparent intuitions that are at issue:

> [I]t is easy for him [God] to effect that I would err even in the things that I *think* I most evidently intuit with the eyes of the mind. Yet so often as I turn to those things which I *think* that I very clearly perceive . . . (AT VII, 36; Heffernan 121; my emphasis)

This counts in favor of (2). Furthermore, I note a text in the Fifth Replies (to Gassendi) where Descartes assigns great importance to the question of determining whether we have a clear and distinct perception, more even than the matter of the rule of truth itself:

> You say at the end of this section that what we should be working on is not so much a rule to establish the truth as a method for determining whether or not we are deceived when we think we perceive something clearly. This I do not dispute; but I maintain that I carefully provided such a method in the appropriate place, where I first eliminated all preconceived opinions and afterwards listed all my principle ideas, distinguishing those which were clear from those which were obscure or confused. (AT VII, 361–362; CSM II, 250)

There are, however, a number of apparently contrary texts. These are the texts in which Descartes asserts that God's benevolence is required to validate the rule of truth itself. For example, in Meditation V Descartes says:

> Now, however, I have perceived that God exists, and at the same time I have understood that everything depends on him, and that he is no deceiver; and I have drawn

the conclusion that everything which I clearly and distinctly perceive is of necessity true. (AT VII, 70; CSM II, 48)

In the Synopsis of the *Meditations* Descartes says, "In the Fourth Meditation it is proved that everything that we clearly and distinctly perceive is true" (AT VII 15; CSM II, 11). The relevant text in Meditation IV is this:

[E]very clear and distinct perception is undoubtedly something, and hence cannot come from nothing, but must necessarily have God for its author. Its author, I say, is God who is supremely perfect, and who cannot be a deceiver on pain of contradiction; hence the perception is undoubtedly true. (AT VII, 62; CSM II, 43)

Descartes says that clear and distinct perception is "something," but what is the something? It is, I believe, two things: intuitive awareness plus an additional component intimately connected with the irresistible inclination to affirm the propositional knowledge arising from the intuitive awareness. I will develop this case in detail in the section 1.4, but if the case is successful then a second case can be made, that God's nondeceiving property is needed more for the inclination component of clear and distinct perception than for the intuitive component.[38] The case for this is as follows. For persons practicing Cartesian method, one main subjective indication that they have correctly identified a case of intuitive awareness among the clutter of other sorts of mental state is the existence of an irresistible inclination to affirm the contents of that case of awareness.[39] Since irresistible inclination and intuitive awareness are not the same thing, nor does the existence of one seem to logically entail the existence of the other, Descartes needs a demonstration that irresistible inclination is a reliable indicator of intuitive awareness. Since the only device available to Descartes to provide this demonstration is a draft on God's benevolence,[40] validating the *use* of the rule of truth depends on God's existence, but not in a way showing that it is logically possible that actual *intuitions* give rise to false propositions.

Perhaps Descartes has something along these lines in mind in a text from *Principles I, 30*:

[T]he light of nature or faculty of knowledge which God gave us can never encompass any object which is not true insofar as it is indeed encompassed by this faculty, that is, insofar as it is clearly and distinctly perceived. For God would deserve to be called a deceiver if the faculty which he gave us was so distorted that it mistook the false for the true <even when we were properly *using* it>. (AT VIIIA, 16; CSM I, 203; my emphasis)[41]

To *use* the faculty of clear and distinct ideas properly requires that we properly identify intuitional awarenesses by the subjective indicators available to us, namely, irresistible doxastic inclinations, and Descartes may be saying here that we need to rely on God to validate this use.

There is, however, a text from a letter to Gibieuf where Descartes introduces God's nature as a nondeceiver in a way that seems to focus exclusively on the veridicality of ideas themselves—not on our inclinations to affirm ideas—and on the rule of truth itself—not on the employment of the rule:

I do not . . . deny that that there can be in the soul or the body many properties of which I can have no ideas; I deny only that there are any which are inconsistent with the ideas of them that I do have . . . for otherwise God would be a deceiver and we would have no rule to make us certain of the truth. (AT III, 478; CSM III, 203)

In this passage Descartes says that God would be a deceiver if ideas (intuitive awarenesses) did not give a true picture of their objects. Notice, however, that this is different from saying that knowledge of the rule of truth depends on knowledge of God's existence: it simply asserts that the conjunction of the two propositions, (1) we have a *faculty of knowledge that is not veridical* and (2) *there is a nondeceiving God*, is inconsistent. Asserting this (that these propositions are jointly inconsistent) does not entail that God exists; hence knowledge of God is not needed prior to knowledge of the rule of truth in contexts such as these. Why should Descartes be interested in making this logical point? Perhaps because it would serve as a *reductio* of the supposition that the rule of truth is false: if there were a being sufficiently powerful to make the supposition true then there would be a deceiving God, but there can be no such being; hence the supposition is false.[42]

In Meditation III, on the other hand, when Descartes says that if I do not know that there is a nondeceiving God "it seems that I can never be quite certain about anything else" (AT VII, 36; CSM II, 25), he does commit to knowing the existence of God before other things can be known for certain. But, as we have seen, that passage occurs in a context where the doubts that need to be removed by God's nondeceiving nature are doubts about whether apparent intuitions are actual intuitions, not doubts about whether actual intuitions could be false, namely, doubts about the rule of truth. This interpretation draws additional strength from the fact that it excludes the rule of truth itself from the Cartesian circle. Without this exclusion it is very difficult to see how Cartesian epistemology as a whole can be defended from the charge that it is subject to a vicious circularity.[43]

In any case, and to return to the main line of argument, if it is accepted that Descartes is not maintaining that actual intuitions might have false propositional content, then there is no warrant for denying the term "knowledge" to the actual intuitive awareness of such propositions. The epistemic position of the atheist mathematician appears, then, to be that she in fact possesses intuitive knowledge of basic geometrical propositions, believes that she possesses such knowledge, but lacks the means to remove the last vestiges of doubt that reside in the possibility that God is a deceiver regarding her belief that she possesses such knowledge. In contrast, a theist can be certain that he has intuitive knowledge, a state which Descartes characterizes as "true and certain knowledge" *(science)*.[44] The distinction between *true and certain knowledge* and *intuition* is a distinction not between a cognition that is knowledge and one that is not, but a distinction between knowledge that is both first-order (intuitive) knowledge and second-order (reflective) knowledge and one that is only first-order (intuitive) knowledge.

1.4 The Method of Clear and Distinct Ideas

The picture of Cartesian (first-order) method that has emerged from my discussion so far is of a first level of intuitive awareness of nonpropositional items, an inference from first-level intuition to intuition of propositional items, and then the presentation of the latter to the will as a content worthy of affirmation. If the mind is to make an inference from first-level intuitive awareness, the mind must, of course, *notice* that it has the first-level content of intuitive awareness in a form that makes it amenable for its acts. Clear and distinct perception thus requires not only that we *have* intuitive awareness but that we have somehow *attended to* this awareness as such. The importance of the notion of attending in the concept of clear and distinct perception is made clear in the official definition of clear and distinct perception in *Principles* I, 45:

> A perception which can serve as the basis for a certain and indubitable judgement needs to be not merely clear but also distinct. I call a perception 'clear' when it is present and accessible to *the attentive mind* — just as we say that we see something clearly when it is present to the eye's gaze and stimulates it with a sufficient degree of strength and accessibility. I call a perception 'distinct' if, as well as being clear, it is so sharply separated from all other perceptions that it contains within itself only what is clear. (AT VIIIA, 24; CSM I, 207; my emphasis)

It may seem strange that Descartes should think that intuitions need to be made "accessible to the attentive mind." Are they not automatically disclosed to the attentive mind? Is it not the defining feature of Cartesian ideas that they be self-disclosing? Consider what he says about *thoughts* in the Second Replies:

> *Thought.* I use this term to include everying that is within us in such a way that we are immediately aware of it. Thus all the operations of the will, the intellect, the imagination and the senses are thoughts. I say "immediately" so as to exclude the consequences of thoughts, a voluntary movement, for example, originates in a thought but is not itself a thought. (AT VII, 160; CSM II, 113)

In the French text the first sentence reads as follows:

> Par le nom de *pensée*, je comprends tout ce qui est tellement en nous, que nous en sommes immédiatement connaissants. (AT IX, 124; Alquié II, 586)

In a note appended to the term *connaissants* (a form of the verb *connaître*, to know) Alquié observes that it would be better to say "conscients" (conscious/aware), since the Latin reads "ut ejus immediate conscii simus,"[45] concluding that, for Descartes, thought and awareness are synonymous. This suggestion has received considerable criticism from commentators[46] on the grounds that the grammatical structure of the definitions of thought and idea makes it clear that thought and idea are the *objects* of consciousness rather than constituted by consciousness. This by itself is not decisive against the synonymy thesis, however, since Descartes may intend *both* that thought and consciousness are synonyms and that thought is the object of consciousness.

It is clear that the second-order character of the Second Replies definition is not just an accident, for it appears in the definition of thought in *Principles* I, 9 (AT VIIIA, 7; CSM I, 195), and in the following passage from the Fourth Replies:

> As to the fact that there can be nothing in the mind, in so far as it is a thinking thing, of which it is not aware, this seems to me to be self evident. For there is nothing that we can understand to be in the mind, regarded in this way, that is not a thought or

dependent on a thought . . . and we cannot have any thought of which we are not aware at the very moment when it is in us. (AT VII, 246; CSM II, 171)

It is possible, therefore, that Descartes is committed to the existence of a univocal kind of awareness that is constitutive of the relation that first-order thoughts bear to their immediate objects and to the existence of a necessary principle asserting that if I have first-order awareness then I am aware (in the same sense) that I have it. I shall call the doctrine attributed to Descartes by this suggestion, the *iteration doctrine*.

The first contributor to the Sixth Set of Objections seems to have thought that Descartes subscribed to this doctrine and worried about the potential that such a doctrine might have for generating infinite iterations of awarenesses required for even first-level cognition to occur.[47] This is the difficulty which Descartes seeks to answer in his reply:

> It is true that no one can be certain that he is thinking or that he exists unless he knows what thought is and what existence is. But this does not require reflective knowledge, or the kind of knowledge that is acquired by means of demonstrations; still less does it require knowledge of reflective knowledge, i.e. knowing that we know, and knowing that we know that we know, and so on *ad infinitum*. This kind of knowledge cannot possibly be obtained about anything. (AT VII, 422; CSM II, 285)

Descartes seems to be making two main points here: (1) Knowledge that I think or that I exist does not require reflective knowledge (*scientia reflexa/une science réfléchie*): and (2) reflective knowledge does not require reflective knowledge of reflective knowledge and so on. I am here concerned only with the second point, which I take to embody a rejection of any generalized, logical requirement that first-level knowledge obtains only if second-level knowledge obtains. Writing on a similar topic in the Seventh Replies, Descartes makes an even stronger claim:

> The initial thought by means of which we become aware of something does not differ from the second thought by means of which we become aware that we were aware of it, any more than this second thought differs from the third thought by means of which we become aware that we were aware that we were aware. (AT VII, 559; CSM II, 382)

The thrust of this passage is clearly against any commitment on Descartes's part to a general principle of iteration and, thus, against any commitment to the iteration doctrine itself.

Another interpretation is due to McRae. He has proposed that second-level awareness is simply the paying attention to first-level awareness:

> That act of thought by which we know that we believe . . . is the act of *attending* to our belief, so that we clearly and distinctly perceive what it is, although prior to any such attention we are conscious of our belief or have an implicit knowledge of it.[48]

As the passage from the definition of clear ideas in *Principles* I, 45, indicates, Descartes clearly does think that our ideas attain their highest status only when we are somehow noticing them and that noticing them and being aware of them are closely related concepts. There are, however, passages indicating that these concepts are not simply identical. A central one occurs in the Sixth Replies:

> This inner awareness [*connaissance intérieur*]⁴⁹ of one's thought and existence is so innate in all men that, although we may pretend that we do not have it if we are overwhelmed by preconceived opinions and pay more attention to words than to their meanings, we cannot in fact fail to have it. Thus, when anyone notices [*aperçoit*] that he is thinking. . . . (AT VII, 422; CSM II, 285)

In this passage Descartes denies that inner awareness is the subject of automatic attention (being "noticed") for we "cannot fail" to have the former, the latter occurs sporadically. Both the use of the French term *connaissance*, used in the French text of the passage from the Second Replies quoted earlier in this section (AT VII 140–141; CSM II, 100–101)⁵⁰ to denote intuitive knowledge, and the contrast drawn between inner awareness and reflective knowledge *(scientia)* (a contrast also drawn in a passage from the Second Replies just prior to the one quoted) make it fairly clear that inner awareness is a form of intuition. This passage thus serves to reinforce the moral from *Principles* I, 45, that intuition (perception) does not make itself automatically accessible to mind. In that passage Descartes suggests that what does make intuition accessible is a kind of clearer vision made possible, as it were, by turning up the wattage in the light of the mind. But the passage from the Second Replies suggests otherwise: it suggests that accessibility requires removing obstacles in the form of prejudices and other mistaken beliefs. (I will take this theme up again later in this section.) In any case, this passage shows decisively that immediate awareness of one's thoughts and paying attention to one's thoughts are not simply synonymous.

A final suggestion that I shall consider comes from Radner. Her idea is that there are two different conceptions of consciousness at work in the Cartesian theory of mind, one constitutive of *thought* (C1 consciousness) the other constitutive of *immediate consciousness* (C2 consciousness):

> My consciousness is of the C1 variety if and only if the following two relations hold between it and its object x:
>
> > (i) It is possible that I am conscious of x and x does not exist.
> > (ii) It is possible that x exists and I am not conscious of it. . . .
>
> My consciousness is of the C2 variety if and only if the following conditions hold:
>
> > (iii) Necessarily, if I am conscious of x, then x exists.
> > (iv) Necessarily, if x exists, then I am conscious of x.⁵¹

Radner is quite right to maintain that there are examples of C2 consciousness in the Cartesian theory of mind, and, moreover, that immediate awareness is such an example. I think that Radner is not, however, right to maintain that there are legitimate examples of C1 consciousness in Cartesian theory. Her case that there are such examples rests on the assumption that Cartesian thoughts are forms of perception that take intentional objects. This is a very natural assumption to make, since Descartes often speaks of thoughts that are about things that do not exist, for example, thoughts about fictional objects. Nevertheless, thoughts that are apparently about ordinary physical objects, whether real or unreal, have a complex structure that shows that they are not forms of perception with intentional objects.

Making this case depends on arguments I make in detail only in chapter 5. Here I offer the argument in summary form. In *The Passions of the Soul* Descartes divides thoughts into two broad categories, *actions of the will* and *perceptions*. In Meditation III Descartes divides ideas (equivalent there to perceptions) into those that are clear and distinct and those that are not. Clear and distinct ideas are intuitive awarenesses, and they satisfy the conditions for C_2 consciousness, not C_1 consciousness. Ideas that are not clear and distinct are "materially false" — they are not in fact about any objects, intentional or otherwise. Descartes maintains that ideas of colors, sounds, and so on (secondary qualities) fall entirely into the category of materially false ideas. What we would call ordinary perceptual or cognitive consciousness is a hybrid entity composed partly of intuitive awarenesses of geometrical properties and partly of materially false ideas of the senses combined in the overall form of *an act of judgment* "referring" these ideas to properties of the material world. But acts of judgment fall on the action side of thoughts and are not candidates for consciousness — although they are candidates for objects of consciousness — of either the C_1 or the C_2 variety. Materially false ideas *are* ideas but they have no objects and thus have no intentional objects so they are not a candidate for C_2 consciousness. The only remaining class of ideas, intuitive awarenesses, are, by common agreement, examples of C_2 consciousness, not C_1 consciousness. In short, the Cartesian theory of mind countenances no entity that is both a perception and satisfies the conditions for C_1 consciousness.

We have now come full circle back to the intepretation due to Alquié that Cartesian perceptions (thoughts on the side of passions) are states of consciousness. It will be recalled that I initially rejected that idea because it seemed to entail the iteration doctrine, a doctrine that Descartes rejects. This doctrine is objectionable to Descartes because it pointlessly and automatically iterates awarenesses — first-order awareness requires second-order awareness, second-order awareness requires third-order awareness, and so on. But in postulating that all the operations of the intellect, the senses, and the imagination are objects of immediate awareness, Descartes might not be pointlessly iterating the same notion of consciousness. Although, as we shall see in chapter 5, the faculty of sense, and even that of the imagination, has its own proper form of intuitive awareness, only the intellect is the proper locus of epistemic activity:

> But [nature] does not appear to teach us to draw any conclusions from these sensory perceptions about things located outside us without waiting until the intellect has examined the matter. For knowledge of the truth about such things seems to belong to the mind alone, not to the combination of mind and body. (Meditation VI: AT VII 82–83; CSM II, 57)

It is therefore crucial that sensory and imaginative awareness be linked to the intellect by means of a postulate asserting the necessary connection between these forms of awareness. A form of awareness proper to the intellect would be needed for this connection and *la connaissance intérieur* appears to be the best candidate for this office. My suggestion, then, amounts to the claim that the transparency doctrine articulated in the Second Replies is a postulate whose main function is to link sensory and imaginative forms of awareness to those of the faculty of intellect. This doctrine could be expressed in two versions:

The Transparency Postulate (Version 1)

Necessarily, if A is the property that a person x possesses when x has an intuitive awareness of something proper to either the senses or the imagination or the intellect then x *also has an intellectual awareness of* A.

The Transparency Postulate (Version 2)

Necessarily, if A is the property that a person x possesses when x has an intuitive awareness of something proper to either the senses or the imagination[52] then A *is a form of intellectual awareness*.

Version 1 postulates that first-order awarenesses of the imagination or the senses are the objects of second-order (reflective) intellectual awarenesses. In the case of first-order awarenesses of the intellect, Descartes's view that iterations of the same sort of awareness should collapse into first-order awareness[53] could be invoked here. There is a text from *the Conversation with Burman* which suggests that Descartes endorses version 1:

> It is correct that to be aware is both to think and to reflect on one's thought. But it is false that this reflection cannot occur while the previous thought is still there. This is because . . . the soul is capable of thinking of more than one thing at the same time. (AT V, 149; CSM III, 335)

But even in this passage Descartes seems to vacillate about whether thinking *automatically* requires reflective awareness, for he adds in the next sentence of this passage: "[The soul] has the *power* to reflect on its thoughts *as often as it likes*, and to be aware of its thoughts in this way" (my emphasis).

A more conservative interpretation is due to Gueroult. In explaining this point, Gueroult says that when an act of second-order awareness A* takes a first-order awareness A as its apparent object, A* is not distinct from A but rather produces a "better vision"[54] of A. Perhaps Gueroult's metaphor simply means that that the original act of awareness is now accessible to (is perceived by) the intellect for epistemic operations. I shall leave it open which formulation best expresses Descartes's underlying intentions, although when I need to rely on the transparency doctrine in the course of subsequent discussion I shall generally rely on the first formulation.

It should also be recalled that Descartes does not take intellectual awareness itself to be self-disclosing. What I take this to mean is that intellectual awareness (a form of awareness directed to properties not propositions) is not automatically *known* for what it is. This is the main burden of the passage quoted earlier from the Sixth Replies:

> This inner awareness [*connaissance intérieur*] of one's thought and existence is so innate in all men that, although we may pretend that we do not have it if we are overwhelmed by preconceived opinions and pay more attention to words than to their meanings, we cannot in fact fail to have it. (AT VII, 422; CSM II, 285)

It appears from this that coming to notice intellectual intuition requires overcoming the obstacles of preconceived opinion, and for that purpose a doctrine of method is needed.[55] "Coming to notice" the existence of intellectual intuition is an epistemic notion amounting to propositional knowledge, knowledge that I am aware of my thought and existence. We thus seem to need a postulate that not only links sensory and imaginative awareness with intellectual awareness but also one that postulates the conditions under which nonpropositional intellectual awareness can be known as such. This is not a version of the transparency postulate but is, rather, the central postulate of the method of clear and distinct ideas.

The Central Postulate of the Method of Clear and Distinct Ideas

If A* is a state of intellectual awareness possessed by a person x then, upon proper application of Cartesian method, x can come to know that he or she is in A* and that A* is a state of intellectual awareness.

To come to know that a certain idea amounts to an intuitive awareness requires *identifying* the idea among the clutter of opinions, beliefs, and other apparent contents of mind. Only once this process of identification has occurred can an idea be said to be clear and distinct. There seem to be three main methods and criteria by means of which Descartes accomplishes this identification. In summary form they are as follows.

1. In Descartes's main taxonomy of thoughts there are but two dichotomous kinds: actions and perceptions . All genuine perceptions are forms of intuitive awareness. To show that a given thought is an intuitive awareness it thus suffices to show that no component of that thought can be attributed to the will. Since Descartes thinks that it is introspectively obvious whether any action of the will has occurred as part of a composite thought, this can be used as a criterion for identifying intuitive awarenesses. (I call this the *passivity criterion for clear and distinct ideas.* Supporting details for this interpretation are given in chapter 5.)

2. Descartes seems to think that when two states of mind are perceptually indistinguishable, for example, the state of dreaming that I am sitting by the fire and the state of seeing that I am sitting by the fire, the explanation is that each state comprises an intuitive awareness of the *same* objects or object types. This explanation provides a component of a method of identifying the objects of intuitive awareness. This method is an application of the method of doubt. I call the explanatory principle, the *principle of perceptual indiscernibility* and the method as a whole can operate in coordination with criterion 3, following. (The supporting details of this interpretation are provided in section 1.8.)

3. We have seen that in Meditation IV Descartes supposes that there is an irresistible inclination to affirm the proposition associated with a clear and distinct idea. Since an irresistible inclination to affirm a proposition is uniquely associated with a clear and distinct idea and its presence is introspectively obvious, Descartes can use the presence of an irresistible impulse as a sign that the idea to which it is di-

rected is clear and distinct. However, the existence of an irresistible inclination to affirm a proposition emerges only after practicing Cartesian method and does not, thus, by itself constitute that method. Rather, it serves as a psychological indication that the termination of that method has been reached. I call this the *criterion of psychological certainty for clear and distinct ideas*, and it should be used in coordination with criterion 2.

If the thrust of my argument in this section has been correct, we need to add to the two components previously identified in the Cartesian method of clear and distinct ideas — nonpropositional intuitional awareness and inference to propositional intuitive knowledge — a third component, a method for making the first step accessible to the mind for cognitive action. This step is afforded by the central postulate of the method of clear and distinct ideas.

As just mentioned, the method of clear and distinct ideas has three components:

1. Nonpropositional intuitive awareness of properties,
2. A means of identifying the first component,
3. A means of inferring from the first component to a proposition suitable for judgment.

The inference in question in (3) is governed by the deductive-judgement principle:

> If we perceive the presence of some attribute, we can infer that there must also be present an existing thing or substance to which it may be attributed.

There is, however, what appears to be a rather large difficulty for this principle, since it seems to imply that there are no properties that are not exemplified. This is an extremely strong claim that makes existential proofs far too easy and surely, at least without some further qualification, cannot be what Descartes means.[56]

To begin to make sense of Descartes's intentions here, it is useful to observe that the inference from an intuited property to exemplification in an existing substance does make sense in one very special instance: reasoning from an intuition of my *thought* to the proposition that there is an existing substance exemplifying that property. This is the *cogito*.

Descartes treats the cogito as holding a very special place in the development of his doctrine of method. Before Descartes begins Meditation II, he is adrift on a sea of hyperbolic doubt; by the time he is finished Descartes is about to proclaim the rule of truth and implicitly, the whole of the three-step method of clear and distinct ideas. The means by which Descartes accomplishes this impressive task is the existence of a paradigm of that method in the case of first-person knowledge (the cogito).

I shall argue, however, that there are *two* accounts of first-person knowledge in Descartes's writings or, rather, two phases of a single argument. The first phase occurs in Meditation II and is the most explicit; the second phase is present in the Replies and a few other places where Descartes emphasizes the intuitive nature of self-knowledge. The paradigm for the rule of truth present in Descartes's account of reasoning to self knowledge occurs in the second phase, the phase not explicitly present in Meditation II.

Making this case overall will require an analysis of the texts regarding self-knowledge in Meditation II as well as those texts relevant to the second phase. Moreover, there is important material in the account of the first phase that bears crucially on a subsequent case that I make regarding Descartes's theory of sense perception and the imagination. For both of these reasons, I will now undertake a fairly detailed examination of the account of self-knowledge in Meditation II.

1.5 The First Phase of Descartes's Account of Self-Knowledge: *Meditation II*

One of the most dramatic moments in the *Meditations*, perhaps in all of Western philosophy, is the moment when Descartes asserts in evident triumph:

> [L]et him deceive me as much as he can, he will never bring it about that I am nothing as long as I think that I am something. . . . *I am, I exist* is necessarily true whenever it is put forward by me or conceived in my mind. (AT VII 25; CSM II, 17)

But the cogito is more than existential triumph in the teeth of doubt: it is a paradigm of reasoning that will help Descartes to structure the way in which he will carry out his program. There is, however, some controversy about the nature of that paradigm.

Frankfurt[57] has given an account of this paradigm that depends on an analogy between it and the notion of clear but not distinct perception present in the passage from *Principles* I, 46, quoted near the beginning of this chapter. Frankfurt identifies clear (and clear and distinct) perception, with certainty arrived at through arguments showing that no reason for doubt exists — the paradigmatic version of which is the cogito. Frankfurt also notes that our situation when we have completed the argument of the cogito is

> similar to that of a man suffering pain who perceives clearly that he has a pain, but who is not sure whether this is tantamount to perceiving clearly that some part of his body is affected. In both cases we are certain that something exists but lack a clear understanding of just what the nature of that something is.[58]

There is surely some basis in Meditation II for seeing the cogito in this way. After presenting his dramatic conclusion Descartes says that he does "not yet have a sufficient understanding of what this 'I' is, that now necessarily exists," adding that he wishes to avoid error "in this item of knowledge that I maintain is the most certain and evident of all"(AT VII, 25; CSM II, 17). The item of knowledge is that he exists. Descartes then spends more than a page wondering about the nature of this being whose existence has now ceased to be a source of wonder. Eventually Descartes finds that he is essentially a "thing which thinks" ("thought; this alone is inseparable from me") but still finds it necessary to ask again "But what kind of thing?" and to answer, "As I have just said — a thinking thing."

But what *is* a thinking thing? What is thinking? What is Descartes's method of answering these questions?

Gueroult answers these questions by claiming that there are "three truths" that immediately emerge from the cogito: (1) "I exist as a thinking thing"; (2) "My nature is no other than pure thought and pure intelligence, exclusive of all corporeal element"; and (3) "[B]ody is less easy to know than soul, since soul is known before it in the order of reasons."[59]

There is, of course, much more to Meditation II than the cogito argument itself and its immediate product, (1). The question arises whether this additional content contains material essential to determining the second and third "truths." Gueroult thinks not, arguing that the remainder of Meditation II is used essentially to "persuade" readers of the three truths in the teeth of various obstacles created by the senses and the imagination.[60] Carriero, on the other hand, has argued that the rest of Meditation II is vital to Descartes's project of specifying the nature of oneself once one's existence has been established.[61] The core of the disagreement between these two views lies in the question whether Meditation II embodies the scholastic precept that "it is better to know the *quod* [what exists] before seeking the *quid* [the nature of what exists],"[62] as Carriero and Frankfurt maintain, or the reverse, as Gueroult would have it. Gueroult is, of course, aware of the passages in Meditation II that are suggestive of the *quod*-to-*quid* interpretation but, if I understand him, believes that this suggestion is misleading since the fact that I exist (the *quod*) is itself derived from the knowledge of my nature as a thinking thing (the *quid*). But this is not quite how the argument of Meditation II goes.

My interpretation of how it does go assigns three stages to the argument. I call these the *paradigm argument*, the *res cogitans argument*, and the *sufficient condition argument* respectively.

The Paradigm Argument

In paragraph 3 of the CSM II text (CSM II, 16–17) Descartes establishes that he exists because denying that he exists would be self-defeating in some sense. This is the paradigm argument. Although there are a variety of ways in which the notion of self-defeat at issue here has been taken,[63] two seem to be most natural. The first is that to deny that I exist runs against the assumption that my existence is entailed by all of the skeptical possibilities that Descartes has been discussing in the previous Meditation, including those in which he is actually deceived as well as those in which he simply doubts but is not deceived.[64] The second is that the formulation ("performance") of a skeptical hypothesis by Descartes, including the possibility that he does not exist, presupposes that he does exist.[65] The former of these possible readings is suggested by the sentence:

> But there is a deceiver of supreme power and cunning who is deliberately and constantly deceiving me. In that case I too undoubtedly exist.

The latter is suggested by the sentence:

> I must finally conclude that this proposition, *I am, I exist*, is necessarily true whenever it is put forward by me or conceived in my mind. (AT VII, 25; CSM II, 17)

This is the official end of what I am calling the paradigm argument, but it is clear from a letter to Clovius that Descartes expects more of the cogito than this conclusion:

I am obliged to you for drawing my attention to the passage of St. Augustine relevant to my own *I am thinking, therefore I exist.* I went today to the library of [Leiden] to read it, and I do indeed find that he does use it prove the certainty of our existence. He goes on to show that there is a certain likeness of the Trinity in us, in that we exist, we know that we exist, and we love the existence and the knowledge that we have. I on the other hand use this argument to show that this *I* which is thinking is an *immaterial substance* with no bodily element. These are two very different things. In itself it is such a simple and natural thing to infer that one exists from the fact that one is doubting that it could have occurred to any writer. (AT III, 247–248; CSM III, 159)

The argument from the existence of this I that thinks to the conclusion that *I am an immaterial substance* begins in the paragraph immediately following the one in which the paradigm argument is given, paragraph 4. There Descartes begins the quest for knowledge of his nature as a *res cogitans*.

The Res Cogitans *Argument*

Here, as at the beginning of Meditation I,[66] Descartes initiates discussion with a statement of his preconceived opinions on the subject at hand, (here the subject is his nature as a "man") and then states what his method will be:

I will then subtract anything capable of being weakened, even minimally, by the arguments now introduced, so that what is left at the end may be exactly and only what is certain and unshakeable. (AT VII, 25; CSM II, 17)

The starting point for this process of subtraction is what he formerly thought himself to be, namely, "a man." "But what is a man?" Descartes asks next. In the next two paragraphs, (5) and (6), Descartes discusses various answers to the question, concluding:

At last I have discovered it—thought; this alone is inseparable from me. I am, I exist—that is certain. But for how long? For as long as I am thinking. (AT VII, 27; CSM II, 18)

What Descartes claims to have discovered is at least that thinking is a necessary condition for his existence as a person. (I shall take this as the official conclusion of the *res cogitans* argument.) Notice that the fact that thinking is one necessary condition of his existing does not preclude the possibility that there are other necessary conditions, including conditions entailing the existence of body. Indeed, the view taken by Descartes's interlocutor in paragraph 5 seems to be that persons are essentially bodies with a set of physicalistically irreducible intellectual properties. This position can be represented by the following, apparently consistent, set of statements:

1. If I am thinking then I exist.
2. Thinking is a necessary condition of my existence.
3. Having a body is a necessary condition of my existence.
4. Thinking is a noncorporeal property of me.

Despite some contrary indications in the text, I do not take Descartes to have claimed to have shown,[67] by the end of this phase of the argument, that the position characterized by these four statements is untenable. What he has shown is simply that statement 2 is true.

But Descartes has bigger fish to fry in Meditation II: he seeks to establish a key premise in his argument for the real separation of the mind and the body.[68] In the Fourth Replies (AT VII, 219; CSM II, 154ff.) Descartes declares that his objective in Meditation II is to show that mind is a "complete thing," by which he means "a substance endowed with the forms or attributes which enable me to recognize that it is a substance" (AT VII, 221–222; CSM II, 156). Strictly speaking, a substance is "a thing which exists in a way as to depend on no other thing for its existence" (*Principles* I, 51: AT VIIIA, 24; CSM I, 210) but since only God satisfies this definition, Descartes allows in the French text the concept *substance* to be used in a derivative sense for things whose existence is independent of everything other than God. Showing that the mind is a substance in this sense is not accomplished by the *res cogitans* argument. Accomplishing this is the role of another argument that I call the sufficient condition argument.

The Sufficient Condition Argument

Descartes was forced to clarify the structure of his case for mind-body dualism as a result of a difficulty Arnauld detected in the case he believed Descartes was making in Meditation II for mind-body dualism:

> [S]o far as I can see the only result that follows from [the reasoning in Meditation II around AT VII 28, CSM II, 19] is that I can obtain some knowledge of myself without knowledge of the body. But it is not yet transparently clear to me that this knowledge is complete and adequate, so as to enable me to be certain that I am not mistaken in excluding body from my essence. (AT VII, 210; CSM II, 141; my interpolation)

To this objection Descartes responds that he is not claiming to have complete and adequate knowledge of himself or of the nature of mind and body but only such knowledge *as is required for him to know* that the mind is a complete thing, knowledge that Descartes claims to have demonstrated in Meditation II. But such knowledge comprises a set of *sufficient conditions* for the mind being a substance known as such in virtue of its properties.

It is not easy to see what Descartes's case might be. In paragraph 7, Descartes seems to be making much the same point as Arnauld: it would be fallacious to argue from "I am aware of myself" and "I am not aware that I have a body" to "I am aware that I am not essentially a body":

> What else am I? I will use my imagination <to see if I am not something more>. I am not that structure of limbs which is called a human body . . . or whatever I depict in my imagination; for these are things which I have supposed to be nothing. Let this supposition stand; for all that I am still something. And *yet may it not perhaps be the case that these very things which I am supposing to be nothing, because they are unknown to me, are in reality identical with the 'I' of which I am aware?* (AT VII, 27; CSM II, 18; my emphasis)

His response is simply to say that he intends not to "argue the point" but to observe that

> it is quite certain that *knowledge* of it ["this I"] does not depend on things of whose existence I am as yet unaware; so it cannot depend on any of the things which I invent

in my imagination. . . . [I]magining is simply contemplating the shape or image of a corporeal thing. (AT VII, 27–28; CSM II, 19; my emphasis)

The principle on which this observation relies is that the current knowledge of "this I" cannot in general depend on premises that are not currently known. Since it is currently in question, hence currently unknown, whether the objects that the imagination ostensibly presents to the mind (physical objects) are real, Descartes concludes in light of the principle that he cannot depend on the imagination for sources of knowledge about the nature of the self. This is a reasonable enough claim, one quite distinct from the objectionable claim that Arnauld attributes to him.

So Descartes asks for the fourth time "But what then am I?" and answers:

A thing that thinks. What is that? A thing that doubts, understands, affirms, denies, is willing, is unwilling, and also imagines and has sensory perceptions. (AT VII, 28; CSM II, 19)

It does not seem that Descartes is simply asking whether he is essentially a thinking thing—a question that has been asked and answered previously (in paragraph 5). What else might he be wondering about? Perhaps Descartes believes that merely possessing the property of being a substance with thoughts essentially is not *sufficient* for that substance to be a "complete" mental substance in Descartes's special sense. After all, could there not be a substance of kind *K* possessing both mental and material properties essentially[69] such that when the physical properties are removed, the subject of the remaining properties lacks the metaphysical integrity needed for substancehood *of any kind*? This is in principle different from the question whether those properties will continue to be actualized once bodily properties are removed, since someone might hold that properties can be actualized without existing in a substance. This is not, however, Descartes's doctrine—he maintains that an affirmative answer to the latter question depends on an affirmative answer to the former.[70]

In order to meet these difficulties I suggest that Descartes is at this point in Meditation II embarked on a new phase of argument, one designed to determine a set of conditions that are sufficient for complete mental substancehood. This is the sufficient condition argument.

The argument has five main stages:

1. Descartes carries forward the "preconceived opinion" that he is a person (a "man"). Let us suppose he also takes persons, whatever other metaphysical category (categories) they may fall into, to be substances. This is premise 1.
2. Descartes identifies a certain set of cognitive powers that are logically sufficient for personhood. This is premise 2. In the presence of premise 1, premise 2 establishes a set of properties sufficient for its possessor to be a substance. It is important that the argument move from the properties of the mind to its substantiality since, as Descartes reminds us in the Fourth Replies,

[W]e do not have immediate knowledge of substances, as I have noted elsewhere. We know them only by perceiving certain forms or attributes which must inhere in something if they are to exist; and we call the thing in which they inhere a 'substance.' (AT VII, 222; CSM II, 156)

3. Descartes shows that these powers, or a reasonable selection from them, are purely intellectual powers, that is, powers that do not depend, either in the way in which they are deployed or in their objects, on things that are essentially material.
4. Descartes deduces from premises 2 and 3 that there is a set of purely intellectual properties that jointly are sufficient for its possessor to be a substance.
5. If there is a set of properties sufficient to identify myself as a substance and if that set is composed of purely intellectual properties, then, by the definition of *complete intellectual substance*, I am complete intellectual substance.

This is the conclusion of the sufficient condition argument. There is evidence of something like stages 2 and 3 in paragraphs 8 to 9. In paragraph 8 (AT VII 28; CSM II, 19) Descartes provides a list of things that he (as a thinking thing) can do. He "doubts, understands, affirms, denies, is willing, is unwilling and also imagines and has sensory perceptions." This is stage (2). Some of the capacities on this list can be simply assumed by Descartes not to depend on body because they are assumed not to depend on body in that portion of the set of preconceived opinions which has not been "subtracted away" by the method of doubt. This portion contains the power of "self-movement," the power of "sensation" and the power of "thought" (AT VII, 26; CSM II, 17).[71] Significantly, it does not contain the power of *imagination*.

It would seem that the easiest way for Descartes to deal with the fact that the imagination cannot be assumed to be independent of the body is simply to omit the imagination from the list of properties jointly sufficient for personhood. In fact, this is just what he does in Meditation VI:

> I find in myself faculties for certain special modes of thinking, namely imagination and sensory perception. Now I can clearly and distinctly understand myself as a whole without these faculties. (AT VII, 78; CSM II, 54)

But he does not drop sense experience and the imagination from the list in Meditation II. Why not? The answer must be that in Meditation II he is working from our ordinary conception of a person, and this conception does not obviously survive the removal of sense experience or imagination. So Descartes is operating under a considerable pressure in Meditation II to retain sense experience and the imagination within his sufficient conception of himself, yet he is also under considerable pressure to exclude those powers because of their danger to his ultimate program of dualism. The danger comes from the possibility that the imagination (and also, perhaps, sense experience) depends essentially on the existence of body. One way in which we might expect Descartes to resolve the tension that these contrary pressures create is simply to deny that the imagination does depend essentially on the body. Although Descartes is never entirely clear on this in his philosophical writings[72], I think that he does not take this step.

Consider, for example, this text from the *Conversation with Burman*:

> When external objects act on my senses, they print on them an idea, or rather a figure of themselves; and when the mind attends to these images on the gland in this way, it is said to perceive. . . . The difference between perception and imagination is thus really just this, that in perception the images are imprinted by external objects which are actually present, whilst in imagination the images are imprinted by the mind without any external objects. (AT V, 162; CSM III, 344–345)

The gland mentioned in this passage is the pineal gland, a corporeal object, and Descartes's doctrine appears to be that attending to corporeal images is definitionally constitutive of both imagining and perceiving. Since attending to corporeal images entails the existence of corporeal objects, it would seem that Descartes's official position is that both imagination and perception entail the existence of corporeal objects.

In a passage from Meditation II quoted earlier in this section, Descartes also asserts that imagining is a matter of "contemplating the shape or image of a corporeal thing" (AT VII, 28; CSM II, 19). Although Descartes does not argue there that imagination entails the existence of corporeal images (hence of corporeal things), a case can be made that he has provided such an argument in the sequel to the dream argument of Meditation I:

> Suppose then that I am dreaming. . . . Perhaps, indeed, I do not even have . . . a body at all. Nonetheless, it must surely be admitted that the visions which come in sleep are like paintings. . . . For even when painters try to create sirens and satyrs . . . at least the colours used in the composition must be real. By similar reasoning, although these general kinds of things—eyes, head, hands and so on—could be imaginary, it must at least be admitted that certain other even simpler and universal things are real. These are as it were the real colours from which we form all the images of things, whether true or false, that occur in our thought. . . . This class appears to include corporeal nature in general, and its extension . . . and so on. (AT VII, 19–20; CSM II, 13–14)

Although interpreting Descartes's intentions in this passage is not a straightforward matter,[73] on the most straightforward interpretation he is saying that just as the power of the painter to produce images depends on the actual existence of the paint from which the images are constructed so the power of imagination to produce images depends on the actual existence (exemplification) of the corporeal properties comprising the images. Although Descartes does not make it clear here just where these actual corporeal properties are exemplified, we have already seen that his view is that the imagination contemplates corporeal images in the brain.[74] (Descartes is not, of course, saying that when we use imagination in the ordinary way to conceive of unicorns and other imaginary objects, we are conceiving only of parts of the brain but rather that our ability to conceive of ordinary imaginary objects depends logically on parts of the brain.) It is only subsequent to this passage that the ultimate reason for doubting the existence of all corporeal things is put forward:

> [F]irmly rooted in my mind is the long-standing opinion that there is an omnipotent God who made me the kind of creature that I am. How do I know that he has not brought it about that there is no earth, no sky, no extended thing, no shape, no size, no place, while at the same time ensuring that all of these things appear to me to exist just as they do now? (AT VII, 21; CSM II, 14)

In light of this background it is worth looking more closely at the reasons Descartes advances for ignoring the imagination in his quest for self-knowledge. The central text is this:

> Once this point has been grasped [that the existence of corporeal objects is in question], to say 'I will use my imagination to get to know more distinctly what I am' would seem to be as silly as saying 'I am now awake, and see some truth; but since

my vision is not yet clear enough, I will deliberately fall asleep so that my dreams may provide a truer and clearer representation'. I thus realize that *none of the things that the imagination enables me to grasp is at all relevant to the knowledge of myself which I possess.* (AT VII, 28; CSM II, 19; my emphasis)

Descartes appears to be making this point in order to demonstrate that it would be futile to appeal to the imagination as a source of reliable self-knowledge, since the existence of corporeal objects, including the brain, remains in the shadow of the hyperbolic doubt of Meditation I. It is important to note that the force of this point rests on the assumption that the existence of the imagination *depends necessarily* in some way on the existence of actual corporeal structures. If Descartes were not committed to a necessary dependence, why would he make the point that doubts about the existence of these structures generate doubts about the utility of the imagination to reveal at least *some things* about ourselves? The force of this point can hardly depend on the representational aspect of imagination, since the objects of the representations of the imagination typically don't exist anyway—that is why we call them "imaginary objects." No one, least of all Descartes's commonsense interlocutors, would think that they are essentially, for example, of a vegetative nature because they can imagine themselves to be pumpkins. But what else could Descartes have in mind? Perhaps it is to discredit the view that we can learn something about ourselves from *the elements out of which the imagination constructs its representations*, not from the intentional objects of those representations. What might this something be? The only relevant answer seems to be that it is the proposition that *we (considered here as persons) are essentially connected to our bodies.* This proposition is inconsistent with his ultimate objective of showing that persons are complete intellectual substances.

To prevent this answer occurring at this stage of the argument Descartes must remove from this stage of the argument the imagination as a source of possible knowledge. This he does, if I have him right, by arguing that *the very existence* of imagination is cast in doubt by the fact that the existence of corporeal structures in the brain, upon which its operations necessarily depend, are themselves cast in doubt.[75] (In the case of the intellect it is precisely because Descartes assumes its independence of body that doubts about the existence of body do not undermine the utility of the intellect as a source of self-knowledge.)

So Descartes does not take the step of denying that the imagination depends on the body to resolve the tension arising within stage 3 of the sufficient condition argument. I suggest that his strategy is, rather, to propose a *special sense of imagination and sense experience,* an attenuated sense in which imagination and sense experience do not depend on the body, and then to propose that the inclusion of this kind of imagination and sense experience (rather than the full-blooded sense) is sufficient for his purposes in this stage of the argument. The "attenuated" kind of imagination and sense experience that I have in mind here is the kind of *awareness of* imagination and sense experience mentioned in the Fifth Replies (to Gassendi):

When, for example, we are asleep and are aware that we are dreaming, we need imagination in order to dream, but *to be aware that we are dreaming we need only the intellect.* (AT VII, 358–359; CSM II, 248; my emphasis)

In saying that we need only the intellect in order to be aware that we are dreaming, Descartes seems to be denying that awareness of dreaming possesses an essential property of dreaming itself, namely, dependence on the brain. In a text just preceding this, Descartes seems to say that the imagination itself does depend on the brain:

> I also distinctly showed on many occasions that the mind can operate independently of the brain; for the brain cannot in any way be employed in pure understanding but only in imagining or perceiving by the senses. (AT VII, 359; CSM II, 248)

If Descartes's position is as it seems in these texts, then he sees a difference between first-order acts of the imagination (and sense experience?), which depend on the brain, and reflective awarenesses of first-order acts of the imagination, which do not.[76]

Evidence that Descartes is also employing a special sense of sense experience comes in the last few sentences of paragraph 9 where Descartes explains that sense experience "in this restricted sense of the term is simply thinking" (AT VII, 29; CSM II, 28). I take the "restricted sense" of sense experience mentioned here to be the kind of second-order cognition of first-order operations of the senses and of the imagination mentioned in the Reply to Gassendi. It is, therefore, only sensing and imagining in this rather attenuated, second-order sense that Descartes can rightfully take to be independent of the body and, thus, only sensing and imagining in this sense that can rightfully appear on the list of cognitive powers sufficient for a purely intellectual entity to count as a person.

I think that it is an open question whether a list of cognitive powers that contains only attenuated imagination and sense experience would be sufficient for Descartes's purposes in this stage of the argument, namely, to convince someone operating with a commonsense conception of personhood that an entity possessing only the powers on the list would be a genuine person. What would it be like to be able only to think about sensing or dreaming or imagining without actually being able to sense, dream, or imagine? Doubts about the coherence of this possibility infect the coherence of Descartes's conception of an intellectual, complete substance and with it the soundness of his case for dualism (completed later in Meditation VI). On the other hand, the inclusion of first-order sensing, dreaming, and imagination on the list would very much constitute for Descartes a trip from the frying pan into the fire. I would venture the suggestion that recognition of this fact accounts for much of Descartes's vacillation about the status of the imagination and for at least some of his attempts to discredit its epistemic significance in the *Meditations*. With this observation I conclude my discussion of the first phase of Descartes's account of self-knowledge.

The second phase of the account depends on the intuitive awareness that Descartes thinks we have of our thought and existence.

1.6 The Intuitive Phase of Descartes's Account of Self-Knowledge

Recall that in the *res cogitans* argument Descartes maintains that he is a real thing with the essential property of thought. The kind of real thing in question is a "substance," a "complete being" that can exist independently of all things other than God. Claiming that a thing that has only intellectual properties is a complete being is a strong claim, stronger than would be warranted by an immediate inference simply from the knowledge that I am a thinking thing, stronger than would be warranted by the argument laid out in the second stage. This is the case since the "thing" in question could lack the integrity needed for substancehood—it could, for example, be an entity metaphysically dependent on a body. I have maintained above that Descartes argues against this possibility in a third stage of argument[77] by showing (1) that there is a set of purely intellectual properties logically sufficient for personhood. But (1) by itself will not lead to the desired conclusion; what is needed in addition is (2), the premise that persons are substances.

We have yet to see where Descartes makes the case for (2). He does not make it in Meditation II. For in Meditation II premise (2) is simply *assumed* as part of Descartes's original conception of himself as a person ("man") that stands at the head of the dialectic that Descartes develops in subsequent paragraphs. Within the constraints of the method of subtraction operating at that point in Meditation II, carrying forward an assumption drawn from the original conception of himself is allowed until the assumption is refuted or cast into doubt by Cartesian reasoning. Since Descartes never casts the substantiality of persons into doubt by subsequent reasoning, the method allows him to continue to carry that assumption on the books at the beginning of the sufficient condition argument.

But if not in Meditation II, where *does* Descartes make the case for premise (2)? My answer begins with the suggestion that there are two methods operating in that class of texts comprising Descartes's account of self-knowledge. One method, the method of subtraction, begins with a set of ordinary beliefs and subtracts those subject to doubt. The other method begins with intuitive knowledge and proceeds to deduce consequences from this knowledge.

From the point of view of the intuitive method, premise (2) is simply an unproved statement in need of rigorous demonstration. The most straightforward prospect for proving (2) within this method rests on the possibility that each person has immediate knowledge of herself as a substance. Unfortunately, there are several passages in which Descartes denies that we are immediately aware of substances, for example,

> But as for corporeal substance and mind (or created thinking substances), these can be understood to fall under this common concept [*substance*]: things that need only the concurrence of God in order to exist. However, we cannot initially become aware of a substance merely through its being an existing thing, since this alone does not of itself have any effect on us. We can, however, easily come to know a substance by one of its attributes, in virtue of the common notion that nothingness possesses no attributes, that is to say, no properties or qualities. Thus, if we perceive the presence of some attribute, we can infer that there must also be present an existing thing or substance to which it may be attributed. (*Principles* I, 52: AT VIIIA, 24–25; CSM I, 210)

What is needed in order to secure a demonstration of our own substantiality by this method is both the existence of the right kind of inference leading to the attribution of substancehood and the existence of a kind of immediate knowledge of something that, together with this kind of inference, implies that we are are a substance but that does not itself amount to immediate knowledge of ourselves as a substance. Within the class of methods contemporary logicians would character-ize as deductive, Descartes distinguishes between those that rely on immediate inferences (the *analytic method*) and those that rely on syllogistic arguments (the *synthetic method*).[78] Although the analytic method is the one Descartes preferred[79] (and is the officially designated method of the *Meditations*), for the sake of logical perspicuity and expository clarity I will initially present the reasoning in a synthetic manner that exhibits dependence on the substance/attribute principle. What we need to find is the immediate knowledge meeting these conditions. I suggest that we begin to look for the latter in a passage from the Sixth Replies:

> It is true that no one can be certain that he is thinking or that he exists unless he knows what thought is and what existence is. But this does not require reflective knowledge. . . . It is quite sufficient that we should know it by that internal aware-ness which always precedes reflective knowledge. (AT VII, 422; CSM II, 285)

The prereflective awareness that I am a thinking thing is not intuition of thought in the abstract but intuition of actual thinking. Consistent with what he says else-where, Descartes does not say here that we have prereflective awareness that we are a substance; what he says is that we have prereflective awareness that we exist. The difference is that substantiality is a *metaphysical* category, whereas existence (actu-ality) is an *ontological* category. Someone who was reluctant to think that the metaphysical category of an entity could be the object of immediate awareness might nevertheless think that in at least certain special cases, ontological status could be known in this way. I believe that this is exactly Descartes's position. The passage from the Sixth Replies indicates that the special cases are *the actuality of our thought* and *the actuality of ourselves*.

The parallel structure of this formulation may suggest that, according to Descartes, the actuality of our thoughts and the actuality of ourselves are known independently of one another. However, I think that Descartes's view is we have awareness of our actual existence *through* the awareness we have of our actualized thoughts. There are a number of passages in which Descartes asserts precisely this, most notably the following from the Second Replies:

> And when we become aware that we are thinking things, this is a primary notion which is not derived by any syllogism. When someone says 'I am thinking, therefore I am, or I exist', he does not deduce existence from thought by means of a syllogism, but recognizes it as something self-evident by a simple intuition of the mind. This is clear from the fact that if he were deducing it by means of a syllogism, he would have to have had previous knowledge of the major premiss 'Everything which thinks is, or exists'; yet in fact he learns it from experiencing in his own case that it is im-possible that he should think without existing. It is in the nature of our mind to con-struct general propositions on the basis of our knowledge of particular ones. (AT VII, 140–141; CSM II, 100)

Recall that an immediate awareness of one thing through the immediate aware-ness of another is the kind of awareness that licences an immediate inference from the first thing to the second thing.[80] When Descartes says, "I am thinking, *therefore* I am or exist," the word "therefore" indicates that he is drawing an immediate inference from thought to existence. This in turn indicates the presence of an awareness of my existence through an awareness of my thinking. However, in order to avoid transgressing the doctrine that we do not have immediate awareness of substances, including ourselves, we need to be a bit careful in the way we characterize Descartes's position here. I suggest that we say that the immediate object of our intuition is actualized thoughts and that in the actualized thoughts we perceive, not our existing selves simpliciter, but a further property that ties these thoughts to our existing selves by way of first-person attribution.[81] This latter need not be construed as an immediate awareness of ourselves as a substance but as an immediate awareness of a second-order property. This property then becomes part of a two-level property *actualized thinking belonging to me*, which can serve as a component in an inference to the proposition that we are actualized, thinking substances. The major premises of this argument are premise A, the substance/attribute principle,

If a property *P* is actualized, then there exists an actual substance *s* such that *s* exemplifies *P*.

and premise B, a principle that intuition is an extensional relation. We can derive the conclusion that I am an existing substance by means of an argument that I shall call the *intuitive cogito*. It can be formally represented as follows:

The Intuitive Cogito

1. If we immediately perceive the two-level property *actualized thinking belonging to me*, then there is the two-level property *actualized thinking belonging to me*. (B)
2. We immediately perceive the two-level property *actualized thinking belonging to me*. [assumption]
3. There is the two-level property *actualized thinking belonging to me*. (1, 2, logic)
4. There exists an actual substance *s* such that *s* exemplifies the two-level property *thinking belonging to me*. (A, 3, logic)
5. I am an existing substance. (4, logical implication)

This reasoning gives us the result we were seeking and does so within the constraints provided by Cartesian metaphysics and the doctrine of intuitive method.

It is worth mentioning that Descartes sees the philosophically interesting use of the cogito to lie not in the inference to his own existence — that "could have occurred to any writer" — but in the inference to his existence as "an immaterial substance."[82] One advantage of my interpretation is that it shows how Descartes might have thought that the cogito (i.e., the *intuitive cogito*) helped in that task. Another is that this interpretation employs both inference and intuition and thus accounts for the importance that Descartes assigns to both intuition and inference in the various texts concerned with the cogito.

There is, however, a notorious difficulty with reconciling everything that Descartes has to say about these two elements of the cogito that comes to light when we compare the passage quoted earlier in this section from the Second Replies (AT VII, 140–141; CSM II, 100) with a passage from *Principles* I, 10:

I have often noticed that philosophers make the mistake of employing logical definitions in an attempt to explain what was already very simple and self-evident; the
result is that they only make matters more obscure. And when I said that the proposition *I am thinking, therefore I exist* is the first and most certain of all to occur to
anyone who philosophizes in an orderly way, I did not in saying that deny that one
must first know what thought, existence and certainty are, and *that it is impossible
that that which thinks should not exist*, and so forth. But because these are very simple
notions, and ones which on their own provide us with no knowledge of anything
that exists, I did not think that they needed to be listed. (AT VIIIA, 8; CSM I, 195–6;
my emphasis.)

The emphasized clause "that it is impossible that that which thinks should not
exist" is a general principle. The fact that Descartes says here that a general principle must be known before the intuitive deduction of my existence from my thought
suggests that the cogito is an enthymeme for a syllogism with the emphasized clause
as the major premise. But this is just what Descartes has denied in the passage from
the Second Replies. The existence of a tension between these passages was known
to Descartes's contemporaries and was noted by one of them, Burman, in a conversation he had with Descartes. Descartes replied that

the major premiss comes first, namely because implicitly it is presupposed and prior.
But it does not follow that I am always expressly and explicitly aware of its priority,
or that I know it before my inference. This is because I am attending only to what I
experience in myself—for example 'I am thinking therefore I exist'. I do not pay
attention in the same way to the general notion 'whatever thinks exists'. As I explained
before, we do not separate out these general propositions from the particular instances; rather it is in the particular instances that we think of them. (AT V, 147;
CSM IIIK, 333)

In these passages Descartes is focusing on the nature of the inference from his
thought to his existence simpliciter rather than on the inference from his thought
as his own to the existence of himself as a thinking substance. Neverthless there is
a general lesson to be derived from the reply, namely, that although a general
premise—in the case of interest to us, the general premise is the substance/attribute
principle—is presupposed in the proof of the proposition that we are a substance,
we derive the general principle by means of immediate intuitive inference.[83]

1.7 The Rule of Truth and the Intuitive Cogito

At the beginning of Meditation III Descartes summarizes the main result of the
previous meditation and indicates what conclusion can be drawn from it:

I am certain that I am a thinking thing. Do I not therefore also know what is required for my being certain about anything? In this first item of knowledge there is
simply a clear and distinct perception of what I am asserting; this would not be enough
to make me certain of the truth of the matter if it could ever turn out that something
which I perceived with such clarity and distinctness was false. So I now seem to be

able to lay it down as a general rule that whatever I perceive very clearly and distinctly is true. (AT VII, 35; CSM II, 24)

Descartes says a number of things in this very condensed passage. First, he says that there is a connection between clear and distinct ideas and truth. This is the rule of truth. Second, he says that there is a connection between what is needed for certainty in general and the special certainty that obtains in the case of the proposition that I am a thinking thing. Third, he says that there is a connection between the rule of truth and the notion of certainty.

The first time in the *Meditations* that the rule of truth is explicitly *employed* in a proof is in Meditation V: "But if the mere fact that I can produce from my thought the idea of something entails that everything which I clearly and distinctly perceive is true, is this not the basis of another argument to prove the existence of God?" (AT VII, 65; CSM II, 45) This passage taken by itself suggests that the conclusion of the rule of truth is an existence claim derived from a clear and distinct conception of certain properties. But a closer look at the ontological argument will show that it is a special case and that the rule of truth in general does not give rise to existence claims without the help of additional premises, a point that Descartes makes explicitly to Mersenne in a letter of March 1642:

> Thus, you quote as an axiom of mine: whatever we clearly conceive is or exists. That is not at all what I think, but only that whatever we perceive clearly is true, and so it exists, if we perceive that it cannot not exist; or that it can exist, if we perceive that its existence is possible. For although the objective being of an idea must have a real cause, it is not always necessary that this cause should contain it formally, but only eminently. (AT III, 542; *Letters*, 132)

In the last sentence of this passage Descartes mentions three notions we have not previously encountered: *objective being, formal containment*, and *eminent containment*. Descartes offers a formal definition of each of these notions in the Second Replies, just after his definitions of "thought" and "idea" (AT VII, 161; CSM II 113–114). We will have a chance to study these notions in more detail later[84] but for present purposes it will suffice to say that the *objective reality* of an idea is its content, and its content is a property or attribute. When a property P in the content of an idea is *contained formally* in a substance x, we can say that x is (in the predicative sense) actually P. (For example, if triangularity is formally contained in x then x is triangular.) This in turn supports an inference to the existence of the P-thing. When a property P is *contained eminently* in a substance we cannot say that x is actually P, hence cannot infer that the P-thing exists. (This is so, paradoxically, even though there is an existing substance that eminently contains P! But more of this later.)[85] Moreover, Descartes asserts in this passage that not all of the properties associated with the content of clear and distinct ideas are necessarily formally contained in a substance — that is the force of denying the axiom "whatever we clearly conceive is or exists."

It appears from this passage that the truth of a clear and distinct idea is equivalent to the containment of the content of the idea either formally or eminently in its cause. The existence of the thing associated with this content obtains when and only when the form of containment is formal not eminent. Now Descartes does not say very much about the nature of the cause of the objective reality of an idea in this passage, but if we take the objective reality of an idea to be what we perceive by means of the idea, then a passage in the Second Replies tells us that the cause of what we perceive by means of a (true) idea is a substance in which what we perceive is contained ("exists"):

> *Substance.* This term applies to every thing in which whatever we perceive immediately resides, as in a subject, or to every thing by means of which whatever we perceive exists. By 'whatever we perceive' is meant any property, quality or attribute of which we have a real idea. The only idea we have of substance itself, in the strict sense, is that it is the thing in which whatever we perceive (or whatever has objective being in one of our ideas) exists, either formally or eminently. For we know by the natural light that a real attribute cannot belong to nothing. (AT VII, 161; CSM II, 114)

If we interpret the passage from the letter to Mersenne in light of this definition, we find Descartes endorsing the following principle. I shall call it the rule of truth (preliminary version):

The Rule of Truth (Preliminary Version)

If I have a clear and distinct idea of properties $P_1 \ldots P_n$ (the objective reality of the idea) then there exists a substance containing $P_1 \ldots P_n$ either eminently or formally.

This principle operates upon a clear and distinct idea (an intuitive awareness) of a set of properties and warrants an inference to a proposition about the containment of properties in a substance. The truth of the idea consists in this containment. This account does not, however, amount to a *general definition* of truth, for it only explains truth in the special case where it is attributed to the clear and distinct perception of nonpropositional entities (properties). It does not, for example, attempt to define truth for the propositions expressed in the consequent of the rule of truth: *There exists a substance containing* $P_1 \ldots P_n$ *either eminently or formally.* For Descartes, what makes this entity true is something for which no informative answer is possible.[86]

To reach the conclusion that an object *actually exists*, the further premise that the substance does not contain $P_1 \ldots P_n$ eminently is also needed. I shall call this the *elimination premise*. For technical reasons I will postpone giving a formal representation of the full inference from clear and distinct ideas to the actual existence of an object, but for now it suffices to say any general proof of an existence claim occurring within Descartes's method of clear and distinct ideas will involve the rule of truth and a suitable elimination premise.

As noted at the beginning of this section, there is a close connection in Descartes's thinking between the rule of truth (in its initial formulation in Meditation III) and the intuitive cogito. Part of what is special about the latter is its reliance on a special kind of intuitive awareness in which the second-order property of *actualization* of a first-order property (our thinking) is part of its content. It is possible, however, by means of the rule of truth to arrive at the same conclusion as the intuitive cogito without reliance on this special kind of intuition. The rule of truth does not presuppose that the objects of clear and distinct perception are actualized properties but derives an equivalent result by a disjunctive syllogism operating on the premise that there is a substance that contains my thoughts either formally or eminently and a premise that eliminates the possibility that my thoughts are in me in some way other than formally. A proof of the latter premise might very well take the form of showing that a denial of it would be self-defeating, the very sort of proof that Descartes offers in the paradigm argument of Meditation II. What this reveals, I suggest, is that the premises of the intuitive cogito are equivalent to the rule of truth and an elimination premise provided by the paradigm argument.

Although in the special case of my own thought and existence I do not need the paradigm argument or the rule of truth to establish that I possess those properties—the intuitive cogito accomplishes those tasks independently—Descartes seems to say that in the *general* case I need both the rule of truth and an argument for the elimination premise modeled on the paradigm argument. That, I take it, is one of the points of the passage quoted at the outset of this section. But Descartes also suggests in that passage that the rule of truth is somehow derived from the intuitive knowledge ("clear and distinct perception") I have of my existence as a thinking thing. The latter is the intuitive cogito, and I now want to make a suggestion about how Descartes might have derived the rule of truth from it.

In its general form, the intuitive cogito is an argument from a premise asserting that someone is aware of the presence of a property (and one other metaphysical premise—the substance/attribute principle) to a conclusion asserting the existence of a substance possessing those properties. The deductive judgment principle is also of this general form:

> If we perceive the presence of some attribute, we can infer that there must also be present an existing thing or substance to which it may be attributed.

The differences are, first, that the intuitive cogito is an inference explicitly employing a general premise (the substance/attribute principle) and, second, that the attribute perceived in the intuitive cogito is a special two-level property entailing its own actualization. This makes the argument of the intuitive cogito a special case of the inference sanctioned by the deductive judgment principle.

There is, thus, a logical priority to the latter over the former. However, in the passage quoted at the outset of this discussion[87] Descartes appears to assign epistemic priority in the reverse order, suggesting that we derive the general principle (the deductive judgment principle) from the instance (the intuitive cogito). This is not a trivial derivation since the instance takes the strong starting point of the perception of *actualized* properties and infers the actual existence of a substance to which those properties may be attributed, whereas the deductive judgment principle takes the much weaker starting point of the perception of the presence of properties *in general* (actualized or not) as the object and licenses an inference to the same thing.

To assess the significance of this difference it is necessary to distinguish between a conservative and a nonconservative interpretation of the notion of property attribution in the consequent of the deductive judgment principle. If we suppose that this notion is equivalent to *formal* property containment, then the deductive judgment principle is a very strong principle, since it licenses an inference from a very weak premise to a strong conclusion. Indeed, it is too strong to plausibly attribute to Descartes, for it entails that there are no ideas of objects that do not exist, something which seems patently false. (This is the nonconservative interpretation.) However, if we take the deductive judgment principle as asserting that if we perceive the presence of certain properties then there is a substance to which these properties must be attributed *in one way or another*, we arrive at a more conservative version of the principle that we might plausibly attribute to Descartes.

This version is still inadequate, however, because it does not make explicit provision for a distinction between ideas of objects that do exist and those of objects that do not. This is something that Descartes clearly needs to accommodate and that he does accommodate in the rule of truth. He does so by introducing into the rule of truth an explicit disjunction between formal and eminent modes of containment.

Consequently, I suggest that we see the derivation of the rule of truth from the intuitive cogito not as an attempt on Descartes's part to provide a strict deduction[88] of the former from the latter but, rather, as a case in which he saw the inference of the intuitive cogito as a striking, concrete example of how one gets in a deductively rigorous way from intuitions of nonpropositional contents to the intuitions of propositions about the actual existence of something that posseses (in way or another) that content. With this example in hand, I then suggest that Descartes may (or at least could reasonably) have moved to the rule of truth in two intermediate stages: first to the (conservative version of the) deductive judgment principle by a kind of abductive generalization[89], then to the rule of truth by a refinement of its predecessor, in which a vague notion of property attribution is replaced by a disjunction between two more specific notions.[90]

There is, however, a difficulty with the present proposal that I would now like to consider. A central text for the introduction of the rule of truth is the second paragraph of Meditation III (quoted at the beginning of this section) and in that text Descartes does not say that the truth of a clear and distinct idea entails the existence of a subject possessing the objective reality of the idea. On the contrary, Descartes seems to assign the task of connecting the objective reality of ideas to underlying substances solely to a causal principle introduced later in Meditation III (AT VII, 41; CSM II, 28–29). In another central text, the letter to Mersenne of March 1642 (quoted just after the paragraph mentioned), although still connecting the objective reality of an idea to an underlying subject by means of a causal principle, this connection is there absorbed into the rule of truth.

There are a number of reasons for preferring the account of the letter to that of Meditation III as expressing Descartes's underlying view. In the first place, the letter is written to correct a misunderstanding and seems to embody a more careful setting out of Descartes's view than the short and rather slogan-like formulation of Meditation III. In the second place, the account in the letter fits well with the general need to provide a propositional object for judgments and with the line of thought in the *Rules* leading to the formulation of the deductive judgment principle.[91] A third reason is this: unless we interpret the rule of truth of Meditation III as asserting that there is a substance possessing the properties to which clear and distinct ideas are directed, the rule is disanalogous to the intuitive cogito in a way that would fatally undermine the derivation of the former from the latter. Since I take this derivation to be a most important link in the order of reasons leading from self-knowledge to knowledge of the wider world, it would be a considerable disadvantage for any interpretation if it were not able to show how the derivation might have gone, and a correspondingly great advantage for any interpretation that could show how it might have gone. This is an advantage that the present interpretation possesses. (It should be recalled in connection with this point that although the rule of truth implies the existence of a substance formally or eminently containing a given property P, this is not equivalent to asserting that a P-thing exists.)[92]

1.8 Identifying Intuitional Awareness

The method of clear and distinct ideas relies on the rule of truth as the chief principle for reasoning from our ideas to the existence of things outside our ideas. But the method of clear and distinct ideas also relies on a method for the identification of intuitions and their objects. Without such a means, the rule of truth could not be systematically applied. As Descartes has noted in agreement with Gassendi[93] providing this method is more important and more difficult than proving the rule of truth itself.

To date in this chapter I have provided considerable discussion of the intuitive cogito and of its role in the derivation of the rule of truth at the outset of Meditation III. For all the importance of intuition in all of this, it is worth noting that none of the key texts on intuition—and I have discussed most of them in the chapter to date—have come from Meditation II. Yet this is the place where we would most expect to see a discussion of intuition, if Descartes is to respect his own doctrine that the order of presentation should match the order of reasons.

Perhaps we can begin to see an emergence of it in the following passage from Meditation II, in which Descartes concludes the discussion of the piece of wax:

> [T]he perception I have of it [the piece of wax] is a case not of vision or touch or imagination . . . but of purely mental scrutiny. (AT VII, 31; CSM II, 21)

I shall assume that by the term "mental scrutiny" Descartes means to designate intuitive awareness.

A reader who has been taken up in the intellectualist arguments of Meditation II will naturally think that Descartes is thinking of perception in this passage as a kind of *understanding*: perceiving the wax means understanding the nature of wax, something that depends on the intellect grasping essences. But Descartes seems to intend more than this, for he makes a point of saying, "I am speaking of this particular piece of wax; the point is even clearer with regard to wax in general" (AT VII, 31: CSM II, 21). He goes on to discuss what happens in cases where we would ordinarily have said—would have said prior to reading Meditation II—that "we see the wax itself." What really happens in such cases, Descartes maintains, is that "we judge it *to be there* from [our perception of] its colour or shape" (my interpolation; my emphasis). This is the first appearance in the *Meditations* of Descartes's general form of existential inference, and it conforms to the pattern of reasoning in the deductive judgment principle, namely, as an inference from the perception of properties to the existence of something possessing those properties.[94]

Descartes seems to make a similar point in his discussion of "men in the street in hats and coats" in the passage immediately following the discussion of the piece of wax (AT VIII, 32; CSM II, 21). He pointedly denies there that ordinary objects like the men in the street in hats and coats are the proper objects of (ordinary) perception: we *think* that such objects are what we see, but what we actually see is only their clothing and we "judge that they are men" (AT VII 32, CSM II 21). Of course, clothing is itself a collection of physical objects, not a collection of qualities. However, a few sentences later Descartes speaks of "taking the clothes off as it were," that is, taking off the "outward forms" of material objects, in order to contemplate their real nature intellectually.[95] The "outward forms" appear to involve both secondary qualities and primary qualities ("We [mistakenly] say that we see the wax itself, if it is there before us, not that we judge it to be there *from its colour or shape*" (AT VII, 32; CSM II, 21; my interpolation; my emphasis). I infer from this that seeing, in the basic sense, depends on an intuition of properties, not objects. The seeing of objects, if it occurs at all, must be defined in terms of the intuition of their properties.[96]

We may also see in these passages the implicit operation of a *method* for identifying among those states we might believe to involve an immediate awareness (intuition) of something, those that actually do involve such an awareness and, among the kinds of things we might think are the objects of intuition, those that actually are such objects. This is a method that is analogous to the method of subtraction that Descartes employs earlier in Meditation II to reach the conclusion that he is essentially a *res cogitans*. What indicates the implicit presence of this method in these passages is the fact that Descartes undertakes to identify the real object types of visual perception by following a line of retreat from, first, taking the object types of ordinary perception to be men wearing hats and coats, next, by subtracting the men arriving at the conclusion that the object types are just the hats and coats (in a shape as if they were worn by men), finally, by subtracting the hats and coats arriving at the conclusion that the objects are just "appearances" of hats and coats, namely, qualities of shape and color. This line of retreat provides a method for identifying what is essential to the contents of perception by eliminating from the complex of ideas comprising ordinary perception those objects whose absence is compatible with having experiences with the same qualitative phenomenology. Thus, in the perceptual experience of men in the streets in hats and coats, the men are inessential to its intrinsic characteristics because the same qualitative characteristics could be present even if the hats and coats are worn by automatic machines. Similarly, the hats and coats are dispensable, since the same qualitative characteristics could be present in a dream. What is left after this process has been completed is what is essential to the experience.

In order for Descartes to employ this procedure as a general method to identify intuitions and the nature of their objects, he needs to show that what is introspectively indistinguishable between different tokens of a consciousness type entails the existence of intuitional awareness of the same properties. I take it that Descartes simply *postulates* the latter as the explanation for the former. We can use this explanation as the basis for a criterion of intuitional awareness that I shall call the *postulate of phenomenological indiscernibility*:

The Postulate of Phenomenological Indiscernibility

If s and s' are phenomenologically indiscernible perceptions then there is an intuitive awareness of object x, $I(x)$, and there is an intuitive awareness of object x', $I(x')$ such that s contains $I(x)$ essentially; s' contains $I(x')$ essentially; and $x = x'$.

We have been allowing ourselves to characterize the form of "mental scrutiny" directed towards properties, both sensory-given and intellectual, as intuitional awareness without any very direct evidence that this is how Descartes himself would characterize this form of mental scrutiny. Indeed, Descartes does not ever speak specifically of "intuitional awareness" in connection with the Meditation II discussion of the cogito and related matters. He does, however, speak this way often in connection with discussion of the cogito elsewhere in his writings, chiefly in the Replies. We have already seen two such passages, one quoted in section 1.6 from the Second Replies (AT VII, 140–141; CSM II, 100), one quoted in section 1.4 from the Sixth (AT VII, 422; CSM II, 285). Consider a passage that occurs immediately subsequent to the latter:

This inner awareness of one's thought and existence is so innate in all men that, although we may pretend that we do not have it if we are overwhelmed by preconceived opinions and pay more attention to words than to their meanings, we cannot in fact fail to have it. Thus when anyone notices that he is thinking . . .

The main issue of interest to us when I first considered this passage was the difference between inner awareness (a form of intuitional awareness) and the noticing of same. Descartes here says that the noticing of intuitional awareness occurs when we are not "overwhelmed by preconceived opinions." The method for establishing that all acts of perceptual consciousness contain elements of intuitional awareness of properties other than those true of ourselves will also reveal that these elements themselves imply an intuitional awareness of our own thought and existence. I suggest, therefore, that we see in the concluding stages of the Meditation II the introduction of a general method for identifying all intuitional awarenesses, including those of our own thought and existence.

1.9 Foundationalism and Privileged Access Revisited

I began this chapter with a preliminary account of where Cartesian philosophy of mind and epistemology has generally been located within the standard categories of analytic philosophy. The philosophy of mind has been treated as falling within the class of theories countenancing privileged access to mental contents, and the epistemology has been classified as foundationalist. To explore the merit of these classifications it will be helpful to have specific version in front of us. We can take that which Robert Audi offers as representative.[97]

Audi offers the following characterization of Cartesian foundationalism as the standard view, one which he "assumes" to be correct:

> (i) [O]nly beliefs (or other cognitions) that, owing to, say, their basis in the clarity and distinctness of their propositional contents, achieve epistemic certainty are admissable for the foundational level — call this *axiomatism* about foundations; (ii) only deductive inferences can transmit justification to superstructure elements — call this *deductivism about transmission*; and (iii) if one has these strong foundations, one can (or even does) know that one has the relevant kind of certainty (whatever that is) — call this *second-order foundationalism*.[98]

If we reformulate the foundations clause, clause (i), in terms of the rule of truth, then, with one further qualification, I take Audi's characterization to be generally correct. The qualification concerns the description in clause (iii) of the second-order knowledge as foundational. It is not clear that the method for identifying intuitional awareness described in the last section is foundational in the same sense as the method for coming to know first-order propositions. The latter relies on the rule of truth, but the former does not. I shall argue in the epilogue that, on its most compelling reading, the second-order method is, nevertheless, foundational in some sense — a psychologically realistic, defeasible foundationalsm closer in spirit to Audi's own preferred brand of foundationalism[99] than to axiomatism.

On Audi's characterization, privileged access concerns "one's sincere avowals of current mental states" and comes in four possible variants:[100]

1. *incorrigibility*: no one ever has overriding reason to think them false.
2. *infallibility*: necessarily, if the subject (S) makes such a report then it is true.
3. *indubitability*: necessarily, if S makes such a report, then no one ever has good grounds for doubting it.
4. *self-presentation*: necessarily, if [a mental state M] is present then S directly knows that it is.

There are at least three obstacles to directly considering which (if any) of these properties applies to Cartesian philosophy of mind.

The first is that beliefs for Descartes are tendencies to affirm propositional contents, not avowals. Avowals employ descriptions or natural kind terms to pick out linguistically the mental states in question (e.g., "I am in pain"; "I am experiencing a red after-image"), whereas Cartesian beliefs allow for nonlinguistic ways of identifying contents for which affirmation is to be given. However, if we allow some latitude in the form which these avowals take (for example, allowing the avowals to be expressed in *de re* formulations or allowing the inclusion of demonstrative elements), and if we assume that avowals are linguistic expressions for doxastic acts, then we can translate Audi's categories into Cartesian categories.

The second obstacle is that Audi takes it for granted that if a given form of privileged access applies to a content, the content is necessarily a mental state. Since the status of privileged access will be derivable, if at all, from Cartesian accounts of intuition and the rule of truth, determining whether this status applies only to claims about mental states depends on whether Cartesian intuitions are only about mental states. This is a metaphysical question that we are not yet in a position to answer definitively. However, when, in later chapters, I take this question up, we will find a somewhat ambiguous situation in the Cartesian philosophy of mind but one that tends in the direction of allowing both for a form of intuition directed to properties of our minds and also for a form of what I call "concrete intuition." Concrete intuitions are intuitions directed at corporeal images (properties) instantiated in the brain. If this is so, then privileged access is not only of mental states. Even if in the end it seems advisable not to include concrete intuitions in Cartesian philosophy of mind, their absence may be a contingent matter.

Third, there is also the question of whether, given that there is a mental state M that does fall within the scope of one of the categories of privileged access, does *the fact that M* is a mental state (or possesses some other metaphysical category) automatically do so as well? For example, even if pain is mental rather than a physical state (as Descartes agrees it is), and even if the avowal that I am in pain is, say, incorrigible, does that mean that the claim that the pain is a mental state is itself incorrigible? It is unclear how Audi would answer this question, but I shall argue that the answer is negative.

With these qualifications in place, let me say the following about the privileged status of Cartesian judgments. Cartesian judgments come in two basic forms: proper judgments about intuited subject matter, improper judgments about nonintuited subject matter. A proper judgment J is an act of affirmation (1) that presupposes the immediate presence to consciousness of a property P and the inferred presence of a proposition Q to the effect that there is an existing substance that possesses (in one way or another) P, and (2) that is directed to Q. If, by employing Cartesian method, we have identified (not necessarily linguistically) the property and drawn the inference mentioned in the presupposition, then the judgment J is infallible and incorrigible but not indubitable. (The case that proper judgments are not indubitable depends on material developed in the epilogue.) Notice that these ascriptions of privileged status are conditional on the presupposition that the intuited subject matter is known by other means. The other means is the method of clear and distinct ideas, a method that probably does not not yield infallible or incorrigible results. (The case for this also rests on material developed in the epilogue.) Finally, the properties presented are not *self-presenting* in the sense defined by Audi, since they are not known directly but are known in virtue of the application of a method.

Appendix A : Defending Descartes against the Charge of Circularity

In section 1.4 I argued that there are three kinds of subjective indicators that persons applying Cartesian method can use to distinguish genuine intuitive awareness from other forms of perception.[101] The second, already introduced, is irresistible inclination, and it needs God's benevolence because of the contingent nature of the connection between inclination and intuition. The third seems to be used in concert with irresistible inclination and cannot be validated without it.

The first, however, seems to stand apart from the other two. It is the criterion of passivity.

Innate ideas, in the sense at issue here, are defined as those that do not arise by a process containing acts of the will.[102] Moreover, as Descartes thinks, whether a person has willed something is simply self-evident to that person. Consequently no criterion of innateness is needed, hence no validation (theological or otherwise) of a criterion of innateness is needed. I note that when it comes to establishing the key premise in the Meditation III proof regarding the status of the idea of God as an intuitive awareness of a real entity (a clear and distinct idea of God) (AT VII, 46; CSM II, 41), it is the *innateness* of our idea of God that justifies this premise,[103] not an irresistible inclination to affirm the idea. Once God's existence is in place in Meditation III, a criterion of irresistible inclinations can be introduced, validated noncircularily, and henceforth made available for general work in other applications of Cartesian method.

In further support of this suggestion I note that the notion of irresistible inclination and its connection with clear and distinct ideas is introduced by Descartes in Meditation IV (AT VII, 58–59; CSM II, 41), and it is only after this that Descartes establishes the theological validation of clear and distinct perception at AT VII 62 (CSM II, 43). Although Descartes does not say that it is the matter of determining whether I have a clear and distinct idea rather than that of vindicating the rule of truth that in general requires reference to God, it may be relevant to recall that Descartes endorses Gassendi's claim that the former rather than the latter is of the most importance. (See the passage quoted in section 1.3 from the Fifth Replies: AT VII, 361–362; CSM II, 250.)

T W O

Truth, Existence, and Ideas

2.1 Introduction

In the previous chapter I put forward the proposal that within his method of clear and distinct ideas Descartes reasons to the existence of actual things outside our ideas in two stages. The first, the rule of truth, takes us from an intuitive awareness of the presence of certain attributes to the existence of a substance in which the attibutes are contained either actually (formally) or in some other way (eminently). The second stage, the elimination premise, shows that the form of containment cannot be other than formal.

However, because of some technical difficulties I did not attempt to give a formal representation of this pattern of reasoning that I shall call the *general pattern of existential reasoning*. One of the technical difficulties concerns an ambiguity in the subject of a crucial clause in the account of the relationship between truth and existence in the letter to Mersenne quoted in chapter 1: "[W]hatever we perceive is true, and so it exists, if we perceive that it cannot not exist" (AT III, 520; *Letters*, 132) In some texts the subject appears to be a property or attribute[1] in others it would appear to be an object.[2] Another technical difficulty concerns a multiplicity of terminology that Descartes uses to express the notion of existence and cognate notions such as actuality. Settling these difficulties will clear the way for a formal account of the general pattern of existential reasoning. Perhaps the best place to begin this task is with a discussion of the ontological argument of Meditation V, since it is in this argument that Descartes first makes express use of the rule of truth in deriving an important existential claim, and it is in this argument that both of the difficulties mentioned are most strikingly evident.

2.2 Descartes's Concepts of Truth and Existence

In Descartes's hands the ontological argument is an argument from the true and immutable nature of God to his existence.

> There are many ways in which I understand that this idea [the idea of God] is not something fictitious which is dependent on my thought, but is an image of a true and immutable nature. First of all, there is the fact that, apart from God, there is nothing else of which I am capable of thinking such that existence belongs to its essence. (AT VII, 68; CSM II, 47)

The argument that he employs is, of course, the infamous ontological argument, an argument that rests on the premise that the nature of God implies his existence.

> I am not free to think of God without existence (that is, a supremely perfect being without a supreme perfection). (AT VII, 67; CSM II, 46)

Thus Descartes proves the existence of God for the second time in the *Meditations*.

Perhaps the simplest, preliminary representation we can give to this cryptic formulation of the argument can be made as follows:

A Standard, Simplified Formulation of the
Ontological Argument

1. God has all perfections.
2. Existence is a perfection.
Therefore,
3. God has existence.

Objections to the argument thus formulated[3] seem to fall roughly into two categories: those that object that existence is not a property, hence not a perfection property, and those that object that the argument presupposes its conclusion.

The first objection, originally due to Kant,[4] is that existence is not a property that can be listed alongside other properties describing the nature of an object. If I describe the contents of my wallet as containing one hundred gold coins, I might enlarge my description of those contents by specifying what is inscribed on the coins, what they weigh, and so on, but adding the property of existence does not seem to enlarge the description in the same way. What then *is* existence? Since Russell's time one standard answer has been that "existence is a quantifier," an operator on open sentences like "*x* is F." For those not afraid of Platonism or other forms of realism about properties, an analogous answer takes the form of asserting of properties that *there is something that exemplifies them*. In either form, existence is not simply another first-order predicate.

The second objection, that God's existence is presupposed by the first premise of the argument, made by Caterus in the First Set of Objections (AT VII, 99; CSM II, 72), rests on the fact that the logical form of premise 1 is that of a property predicated of a subject and on the assumption that the truth of this premise cannot be known unless it is first established that the subject exists.

To assess the merits of this objection we need to consider Descartes's detailed discussion of the ontological argument in the First Replies. There Descartes presents a formulation of the argument that clearly exhibits its reliance on the rule of truth:

> That which we clearly and distinctly understand to belong to the true and immutable nature, or essence, or form of something can be truly asserted of that thing. But once we have made a sufficiently careful investigation of what God is, we clearly and distinctly understand that existence belongs to his true and immutable nature. Hence we can now truly assert of God that he does exist. (AT VII, 116; CSM II, 83)

Does this formulation beg the question in favor of God's existence? Not necessarily, for Descartes could maintain that the true predication of properties clearly and distinctly perceived simply does not entail the existence of the subject. Since Descartes has written this portion of the First Replies in part to dispel the charge of begging the question, we are invited to see in this passage a kind of Meinongianism in Cartesian ontology.[5] The ontological argument then appears to make the case that the actual existence of a Meinongian subject can be inferred from the nature of that subject only in the special case where actual existence or, as he claims in a later formulation (AT VII, 119; CSM II, 85), necessary existence, is contained in the nature of the subject. This, at least, is the picture we get of the ontological argument from reading Meditation V and the relevant passages of the First Replies.

Nevertheless, I believe that this is the wrong picture because it is inconsistent with Descartes's general claim, made in the definition of *substance* in the Second Replies and elsewhere, that the objects of "true ideas," namely, clear and distinct ideas, *are properties not substances*:

> *Substance.* This term applies to every thing in which whatever we perceive immediately resides, as in a subject, or to everything by means of which whatever we perceive exists. By 'whatever we perceive' is meant any property, quality or attribute of which we have a real idea. The only idea we have of substance itself, in the strict sense, is that it is the thing in which whatever we perceive (or whatever has objective being in one of our ideas) exists, either formally or eminently. For we know by the natural light that a real attribute cannot belong to nothing. (AT VII, 161; CSM II, 114)

Since God is a substance, Meinongian or otherwise, not a property, God is not an object of a "true idea." This creates considerable difficulty for interpreting those texts where Descartes speaks as if God himself were an object of our ideas. A more general version of this difficulty also appears in a passage from a letter to Mersenne we saw in chapter 1:

> [Y]ou quote as an axiom of mine: whatever we clearly conceive is or exists. That is not at all what I think, but only that whatever we perceive clearly is true, and so it exists, if we perceive that it cannot not exist; or that it can exist, if we perceive that its existence is possible. For although the objective being of an idea must have a real cause, it is not always necessary that this cause should contain it formally, but only eminently. (AT III, 542; *Letters*, 132)

It is evident from the reference in this passage to beings that "cannot not exist" that Descartes has God in mind here and God is a substance. But he also speaks of "whatever we perceive," and according to the doctrine from the definition of substance, that object is a property not a substance. This is the same difficulty we have just described; but this passage does more than simply repeat it, it suggests a solution. To be in a position to understand the solution we need to carry out some analytical work on Descartes's several notions of being or existence. There seem to be at least three. The first is a *monadic predicate of substances*, which occurs in the conclusions of the official proofs of the existence of God and the material world, for example, "God exists." The second is the concept of a *relation between properties and substances*, as in this sentence from the definition of substance: "[S]ubstance ... is ... the thing *in which whatever we perceive ... exists*, either formally or eminently."[6] Third, we have the concept of the *existential quantifier* as in the following sentence from *Principles* I, 52: "[I]f we perceive the presence of some attribute we can infer that *there must also be present an existing thing* or substance to which it may be attributed" (AT VIIIA, 25; CSM I, 210; my emphasis).

If we now return to the passage from the letter to Mersenne we find that Descartes seems to derive the notion of the actuality of a being (the monadic concept of existence) from the notion of the formal containment of something in something else (the relational notion of existence) and the notion of the mere possibility of a being from the notion of the eminent containment of something in something else. The first "something" is described as "the objective being of an idea" in this passage, an item identified as a property in the passage from the definition of substance, the second "something" is described as what contains the first, namely, a substance. We therefore seem to have the result that the concept of the actuality (monadic existence) of a subject is reducible to the concept of the formal containment of properties in a substance and the concept of the possibility of a subject is reducible to the concept of the eminent containment of properties in a substance. This is the second notion of existence. The third notion, the quantificational, shows up in a logical expansion of the concept of properties being contained in *a substance*.

If I have understood Descartes correctly here this means that Descartes takes the second and third notions of existence as basic, the first as derivative. I postulate that this doctrine takes the form of a reductive definition of statements ascribing the monadic existence predicate to Meinongian objects to statements asserting that there exists a substance bearing the formal containment relation to a set of properties associated with the Meinongian object. There is, however, some difficulty in determining just what kind of reductive definition to adopt. There is also the problem of determining which sets of properties are associated with which Meinongian objects. Regarding the latter problem, I propose that the specific properties to be ascribed in the case of a proposition of the form "*t* is F", where "*t*" is a constant term or definite description, is a function of the individual concept or 'sense' of *t*. I shall call this the Fregian approach. Thus, the proposition "God exists" is to be reduced to the proposition "Properties determined by the individual sense of the word 'God' are formally contained in a substance."[7]

In seeking a reductive definition of one thing in terms of another we have several choices. We can employ a *contextual elimination* of one proposition by another. In this case the first proposition apparently commits us to one kind of object, the second apparently commits us to another kind of object, and we treat the second proposition as equivalent to, but more ontologically fundamental than, the first. A famous example of this is Russell's contextual elimination of apparently singular propositions in favor of existentially quantified propositions.[8] This procedure provides a very tempting model on which to understand the Cartesian account.

Statements such as "So from what has been said it must be concluded that God necessarily exists" (AT VII, 45; CSM II, 31) or "The existence of God can be known merely by considering his nature" (Second Replies: AT VII, 166; CSM II, 117) are the characteristic ways in which Descartes states the results of his proof procedures, and he clearly regards such statements as formally true.[9] But Descartes also sees the notion of the formal containment of a property in a substance as equivalent to the actual existence of the object possessing the property and sees the former as ontologically fundamental. This is the moral to be drawn from the letter to Mersenne read in light of the definition of substance in the Second Replies.[10]

I propose to implement the contextual elimination of sentences in which an existence property is apparently ascribed to a possible object by means of a definition of the (formal) truth predicate ascribed to sentences of the form "t exists," where "t" takes an individual sense as its meaning.

Definition of the Existence Predicate

<t exists>[11] is (formally) true iff there is a substance s such that the properties, $P_1 \ldots P_n$, determined by the sense of t are formally contained in s.

The definition is a biconditional, combining two conditionals. The conditional from left to right effects the "reduction" of a proposition expressing a monadic existential predication of a subject that might be a merely possible subject (a *possibile*) to a proposition expressing a containment relation between substances and properties none of which are *possibilia*. I shall call this the *reduction principle*.

The Reduction Principle

If <t exists> is formally true then there is a substance s such that the properties, $P_1 \ldots P_n$, determined by the sense of t are formally contained in s.

The conditional from right to left is the conditional that governs the final stage of Descartes's ontological reasoning—the move from formal property containment to the formal truth of an existence statement. I shall call this inference the *truth move* and the conditional statement warranting it the *truth conditional*."

The Truth Conditional

If there is a substance s such that the properties, $P_1 \ldots P_n$, determined by the sense of t are formally contained in s then <t exists> is (formally) true.

It needs to be observed that on the truth definition approach what is being defined is not the proposition "God exists" but the proposition "That God exists is formally true." However, for convenience I will use the two formulations interchangeably, on the understanding that the latter is canonical.

The reducibility doctrine has an immediate corollary for the ontological argument: the formal truth of the judgment that God necessarily exists must be derived from a premise asserting that God's essential properties x are necessarily formally contained in a cause. How are we to determine if this premise is true?

Consider again the passage from the letter to Mersenne just quoted. We have seen that in this passage that Descartes associates formal containment with actual existence and eminent containment with possible existence. Necessary existence thus implies the necessary absence of the eminent mode of containment of a property. Descartes does not seem to allow for an introspective test to distinguish between those clear and distinct ideas that are directed to properties formally contained in a substance and those that are directed to properties eminently contained in a substance; he requires that an additional premise be supplied from nonintrospectable resources to determine which of the alternatives obtains. In the case where Descartes wishes to prove the necessary formal containment of the essential properties of an object, he must find premises allowing the *necessary elimination of the possibility that these properties are contained eminently.*

On the face of it Descartes's official explanation of the ontological argument does not employ an elimination premise—we move directly from our concept of God to his necessary existence:

> So we shall come to understand that necessary existence is contained in the idea of a supremely powerful being, not by any fiction of the intellect, but because it belongs to the true and immutable nature of such a being that it exists. (AT VII, 119; CSM II, 85)

The difficulty with this answer is that it seems to leave open the possibility that the property of necessary existence is itself contained eminently rather than formally in a being, a circumstance which, if it obtained, would be insufficient to warrant the assertion of God's existence via the truth move. However, when a property P is eminently contained in a substance s, it will transpire[12] that P is contained in a "higher form" than would be the case if P were contained formally in s. Hence, since necessary existence is a property lying at the head of the hierarchy of forms of being, it is impossible that necessary existence should be contained within its substance eminently. In effect, this is an elimination premise and we shall see that it functions here in much the same way as it functions in the causal argument.[13]

This makes for a much more complex structure in Cartesian ontological inference than we might at first glean from official formulations of the rule of truth or its application in the case of the ontological argument. Moreover, without attributing this structure to the ontological argument, we will be unable to show how it derives its conclusion from the canonical version of the rule of truth and the assumption that we have a clear and distinct idea of God's essential properties. Since the ontological argument is essentially an application of the rule of truth we are compelled to assign to the argument a canonical form more complex than any of the forms in which Descartes expressly presents the argument in the central texts. This is certainly a difficulty for my interpretation but one that is overridden by the need to reconcile the specific ontological inference at issue in the proof of God's existence with the central principles of Descartes's theory of general existential reasoning.

2.3 Descartes's General Theory of Existential Reasoning

This theory describes the inferences that need to be made from the assumption of a clear and distinct idea to the assertion of the formal truth of a judgment and from thence to the assertion of the existence of certain objects outside our ideas. For example, suppose we wish to establish the contingent existence of an object x. We assume a clear and distinct idea of a set of properties essential to x. From this we infer by means of the rule of truth (preliminary version) (RTP) introduced in the last chapter that there is a substance containing these properties formally or eminently. We then appeal to an elimination premise (established on other grounds) to yield the preliminary conclusion that there is a substance in which the properties are not eminently contained; hence they are formally contained. Elimination premises come in two modal forms: a necessary elimination premise (NEP) and a general elimination premise (EP). Applying the truth conditional (TC) yields the final conclusion that a statement of the form <x exists> is formally true. This sequence of inferences comprises the general pattern of existential reasoning, and the theoretical account of its component premises and concepts comprises Descartes's general theory of existential reasoning. A preliminary formulation of this pattern can be given as follows:

The General Pattern of Existential Reasoning
(First Version)

1. Assume that t is a constant term or definite description for an object and that there is a set of properties $P_1 \ldots P_n$ comprising the individual sense of t.

Then we reason as follows:

2. I have a clear and distinct idea of properties $P_1 \ldots P_n$ comprising the individual sense of t. (Assumption)
3. There is a substance s such that $P_1 \ldots P_n$ are contained formally or eminently in s. (RTP, 2)
4. $P_1 \ldots P_n$ are not contained eminently in s. (EP)
5. $P_1 \ldots P_n$ are contained formally in s. (3, 4)
6. A sentence, <t exists>, is true. (TC, 1, 5)

This theory also comes in a version with a necessary conclusion:

The General Pattern of Necessary Existential Reasoning
(First Version)

1. Assume that t is a constant term or definite description for an object and that there is a set of properties $P_1 \ldots P_n$ comprising the individual sense of t.

Then we reason as follows:

2. I have a clear and distinct idea of properties $P_1 \ldots P_n$ comprising the individual concept of t. (Assumption)
3. There is a substance s such that $P_1 \ldots P_n$ are contained formally or eminently in s. (RTP, 2)
4. Necessarily, $P_1 \ldots P_n$ is not contained eminently in s. (NEP)
5. Necessarily, $P_1 \ldots P_n$ is contained formally in s. (3, 4)
6. The sentence <t necessarily exists> is true. (TC, 1, 5)

I have contended that Descartes's main method of arguing for the actual existence of something is an eliminative argument demonstrating that the objects of our true ideas are not contained eminently in the substance containing it (its "grounding substance," as I shall call it). This method seems to be employed in this passage taken from the proof of the external world in Meditation VI:

> [S]ince God is not a deceiver, it is quite clear that he does not transmit the ideas [of sensible objects] to me either directly from himself, or indirectly, via some creature which contains the objective reality of the ideas not formally *but only eminently.* . . . I do not see how God could be understood to be anything but a deceiver if the ideas were transmitted from *a source other than corporeal things.* It follows that corporeal things exist. (AT VII, 79; CSM II, 55; my interpolation; my emphasis)

This passage is cast in a causal idiom but if we translate it into the ontological idiom of property containment, we find the clear implication that our belief in the truth of the proposition that the material world exists is a direct consequence of our being able to eliminate the possibility that the property of being a corporeal thing is contained eminently rather than formally in the ground of that property. This is an instance of steps 3 through 6 of the general form of existential reasoning described above.

We now have in place most of the elements of Descartes's general theory of existential reasoning. I have yet to consider Descartes's general theory of ideas, something required if I am to show in the next chapter that what look like instances of purely causal reasoning in Descartes's proofs of the existence of God and of the external world are in fact instances of a general pattern of existential reasoning derived from the rule of truth. Central to the theory of ideas is the notion of the *objective reality of ideas*, and I devote the reminder of this chapter to an interpretation of this notion and consideration of issues in Cartesian general ontology arising therefrom.

2.4 The Objective Reality of Ideas: The Basic Picture

I begin with Descartes's official definition of the concept of objective reality:

> The *objective reality of an idea.* By this I mean the being of the thing which is represented by an idea, in so far as this exists in the idea. In the same way we can talk of 'objective perfection', 'objective intricacy' and so on. For whatever we perceive as being in the objects of our ideas exists objectively in the ideas themselves. (AT VII, 161; CSM II, 113–114)

In attempting to sort out Descartes's notion of objective reality, an interpreter encounters a number of obstacles, not the least of which is an apparent departure in Descartes's use of "objective reality" from its standard Scholastic use.

In its standard use *objective reality* is something had by things, not ideas, a property that simply signifies the fact that the thing is considered as an object of someone's thought. This at least is how Caterus understands the standard usage of the term "objective being in the intellect": "According to what I was taught", he writes, "this is simply the determination of an act of the intellect by means of an object. And this is merely an extraneous label which adds nothing to the thing itself" (AT VII 92; CSM II, 66–67). On the other hand, the term "objective existence" was standardly used to connote the object had by a thought.[14] Given these conventional usages it makes sense to speak of the *objective reality of an object* and of the *objective existence of a thought*; it does not make sense to speak of the objective reality of a thought. Unfortunately, it is precisely this latter usage that Descartes most frequently employs.

In his Reply to Descartes's Meditation III discussion of material falsity, Arnauld uses the term "objective existence" in its standard sense when he says that an idea is "called positive not in virtue of the existence it has as a mode of thinking (for in that sense all ideas would be positive) but in virtue of the *objective existence* which it contains and which it represents to the mind" (AT VII, 207; CSM II, 145). Given Descartes's self-proclaimed indifference to correct technical philosophical usage (AT VIII, 235; CSM 164), it is certainly possible that Descartes is simply using the terms "objective existence" and "objective reality" interchangeably to mean the object of our thought. Certainly this suggestion fits many texts. It does not, however, fit them all, including his official definition in the Second Replies.

The first half of the first sentence characterizes objective reality as an ontological property of a *thing*, thus — it is gratifying to report — employing the terminology in its conventional way:

> The objective reality of an idea. By this I mean *the being of the thing which is represented by the idea*.

When Descartes wishes to speak of what was conventionally called the *objective existence* of an idea in the third sentence he simply speaks of "the objects of our ideas." Of course Descartes also characterizes the objective reality of a thing as the mode of being it has "insofar as it exists in the idea" in the second half of the first sentence, a puzzling qualification that we take up below. But, this qualification aside, these two ways of speaking appear to be two ways of describing the same state of affairs — *an object's being represented by an idea*.

There is, however, another element to the account that appears in the first half of the third sentence:

> For whatever we perceive as being in the objects of our ideas exists objectively in the ideas themselves.

It seems that Descartes is speaking here of a manner or form or content of the perceiving of objects. There are, then, apparently three elements contained in the account of objectively reality:

1. the notion of the objects of ideas
2. the notion of the way in which the objects of ideas exist in those ideas (*objective being in the intellect*)
3. the notion of the way in which the objects of ideas are perceived (the form or content of the perception)

The First Element: The Objects of our Ideas

In the definition of substance (in the same set of definitions from which we have taken the definition of objective reality), Descartes tells us that the object of "real ideas" are properties:

> By 'whatever we perceive' is meant any property or quality or attribute of which we have a real idea. The only idea we have of a substance itself, in the strict sense, is that it is the thing in which whatever we perceive (or whatever has objective being in one of our ideas) exists, either formally or eminently. (AT VII, 161; CSM II, 114)

The Second Element: Objective Being in the Intellect (The Way in which the Objects of our Ideas Exist in our Ideas)

This notion is one which puzzled even Descartes's scholastic contemporaries. Caterus, as we have seen, took the notion to be "the determination of an act of the intellect by an object." But Descartes explains in his reply that this is not how the notion is to be understood:

> 'Objective being in the intellect' will not here mean 'the determination of an act of the intellect by means of an object', but will signify the object's being in the intellect in the way in which its objects normally are there. By this I mean that the idea of the sun is the sun itself existing in the intellect—not of course formally existing, as it does in the heavens, but objectively existing, i.e. in the way in which objects normally are in the intellect. (AT VII, 102; CSM II, 75)

There are a number of things that are puzzling about this passage. The first is the identification of the idea of the sun with the object of the idea of the sun. This puzzle can be disposed of by appealing to an ambiguity in Descartes's use of the term "idea":

> 'Idea' can be taken materially, as an operation of the intellect, in which case it cannot be said to be more perfect than me. Alternatively, it can be taken objectively, as the thing represented by that operation; and this thing, even if it is not regarded as existing outside the intellect, can, still, in virtue of its essence, be more perfect than myself. (AT VII, 8; CSM II, 7)

It is in the objective sense of idea that the idea of the sun *is* the sun. Of course the sun "as it is in the heavens" is not in the intellect. But what other sun is there? Are there perhaps two suns, one sun-in-the-intellect, one sun-in-the-heavens? Descartes's answer to this, I think, is that there are not two suns but only one that exists in two ways: in the heavens and in the intellect. What Descartes needed to explain to

Caterus is the second way of being, not the first, but Descartes's answer is very unhelpful: the sun exists in the intellect "in the way in which objects normally" are there.

But how *are* objects normally in the intellect? Descartes's answer to this is fairly simple and is already implicit in the doctrine that the immediate objects of our ideas are properties, not substances (see the definition of substance, above): *Objects are normally in the intellect in virtue of their properties being the objects of ideas of the intellect.*[15] For example, the sun exists objectively in the intellect because the properties of the sun are the objects of our ideas.

Some confirmation for this view comes in a passage from Meditation I in which Descartes explains that the power of our ideas to represent objects depends on simple and universal things. "These are as it were the real colours from which we form all the images of things, whether true or false, that occur in our thought" (AT VII, 20; CSM II, 14). Examples of such simple and universal things are "corporeal nature in general, and its extension; the shape of extended things" (AT VII, 20; CSM II, 14). Our representations of ordinary actually or possibly existing substances like the sun are composed of sets of ideas of properties. That is how ordinary *objects* "normally exist in the intellect." But how do their *properties* exist in the intellect? We begin our search for an answer with a consideration of Descartes's general theory of the ontological status of immutable essences.

2.5 The Ontological Status of Immutable Essences

The clearest and most direct statement Descartes makes on the ontological status of immutable essences comes in a passage from Meditation V:

> [T]he most important consideration at this point is that I find within me countless ideas of things which even though they may not exist anywhere outside me still cannot be called nothing; for although in a sense they can be thought of at will, they are not my invention but have their own true and immutable natures. When, for example, I imagine a triangle, even if perhaps no such figure exists, or has ever existed, anywhere outside my thought, there is still a determinate nature, or essence, or form of the triangle which is immutable and eternal, and not invented by me or dependent on my mind. This is clear from the fact that various properties can be demonstrated of the triangle . . . it follows that they cannot have been invented by me. (AT VII, 64; CSM II, 44–45)

The first thing to note about this passage is that true and immutable essences are *what (intellectual) ideas represent*, namely, the "objects of ideas," not the ideas themselves taken in the "material sense", that is, as mental events. We may broadly distinguish between three interpretations of the ontological status of these objects: (1) that the objects of (intellectual) ideas are abstract entities, understood in a straightforward Platonic sense as possessing mind-independent reality; (2) that the objects of (intellectual) ideas are abstract entities, understood as possessing *some kind* of mind-independent reality, but not in a straightforward sense; and (3) that the objects of (intellectual) ideas are straightforwardly mind-dependent.[16]

Let me first present some arguments against attributing to Descartes the doctrine that immutable essences are properties of ideas and that ideas are properties of minds. I shall call this the mode of idea doctrine, a version of interpretation (3). (For a contemporary version of this doctrine we might consider the class of theories of intentionality known as "adverbial theories," according to which the locution "*x* is thinking of *y*" is to be paraphrased as "*x* is thinking in an *of-y* manner," where "of-y" is understood as a modifier of the verb "is thinking" and thinking is regarded as a monadic property not of minds but of persons. The most notable contemporary exponent of this view is Wilfrid Sellars.[17] (Chappell appears to maintain that this view was Descartes's position.)[18]

The first argument is one we have alluded to above: it would be hard to see how Descartes could escape inconsistency if he subscribed to the view that immutable essences are independent of minds in some important sense while also maintaining that immutable essences are modes of ideas, that ideas are modes of mind, and that modes are dependent on the things of which they are modes.

The second argument is the one that Descartes himself gives to justify the claim that the essence of a triangle is not "invented or dependent on my mind":

> This is clear from the fact that various properties can be demonstrated of the triangle. . . . [I]t follows that they cannot have been invented by me. (AT VII 64; CSM II, 45)

We must, however, exercise caution in resting too much on this argument: while it establishes that immutable essences are not "invented by me," it does not establish that they are not modally dependent on my ideas or on my mind, since modal dependence on mind and invention by the mind are different kinds of mind dependence, a point to which Descartes himself seems to give recognition in the phrase "not invented by me or dependent on my mind" in the full passage quoted above.

With respect to the third argument against the mode of idea reading, there are, of course, many passages in which Descartes discusses innate ideas. But those in which he emphasizes the independence of the objects of innate ideas from mind are few and far between: most discussions of innate ideas occur in contexts where Descartes's main point is to insist that innate ideas have always been present in the mind, perhaps even from birth.[19] There is, of course, a notable exception to this tendency in a passage from *Comments on a Certain Broadsheet*, a late work in which Descartes clearly states that he never intended his doctrine of innate ideas to be understood in this way, indicating that innate ideas are innate only in the sense that we have the *capacity* to generate these ideas—they "came solely from the power of thinking within me"—much in the way we might say that certain people have a tendency to develop gout (AT VIIIB, 358–359; CSM I, 303–304).

The dispositional account does not by itself imply that we have the power to create the *objects* of innate ideas in addition to the ideas themselves but it does have this consequence when taken in conjunction with option 3. On that reading, the objects of ideas are ontologically dependent on the ideas themselves: creating the ideas creates their objects. I see no way of reconciling this result with the doctrine from Meditation V that the objects of innate ideas are discovered, not invented. Whatever Descartes may have meant when he described immutable essences as "not nothing," in saying that they are not "invented" he means that we do not create them by the power of our thought alone. We can reconcile the doctrine of the *Broadsheet* passage with that of Meditation V only if we say that the mind has an innate power to access through cognitive activity a realm of abstract entities with some measure of mind-independent reality.

It seems to me, therefore, that the case against the mode-of-idea interpretation (a version of the interpretation that essences are straightforwardly mind dependent) and for a "quasi-Platonic"[20] interpretation of the objects of innate ideas (the intermediate interpretation) is overwhelming *if* we accept Descartes at his word in the *Broadsheet*. Should we do so?

Certainly some commentators have argued that those passages apparently expressing the occurrent-idea conception of innate ideas can be satisfactorily explained in terms of the dispositional conception,[21] others, however, have argued that the occurrent-idea conception is fundamental and ineliminable.[22] I shall not attempt to settle this controversy here. I simply note that if the occurrent interpretation of innate ideas is accepted as fundamental, it is essentially neutral on the question of the ontological status of the objects of those ideas. I therefore conclude that our initial judgment in favour of the intermediate interpretation is either reinforced by a consideration of the disposition/occurrent controversy about innateness or substantially unaffected by it.

There are at least a few other textual indications that Descartes regarded the objects of innate ideas as not simply reducible to aspects of ideas. For example, there is the set of passages where Descartes differentiates between those ideas having "real things" as their objects and those that do not. The notion of a "real thing" is applied to the objects of innate ideas, for example, God ("something real": AT VII, 46; CSM II, 31–31), or mathematical qualities (AT VII, 43; CSM II, 29–30), and seems to ascribe to them an ontological status somewhat independent of ideas.

Perhaps it can be argued that these texts taken by themselves are not entirely decisive against the view that immutable essences have mind-dependent existence. However, when these texts are taken together with those in which Descartes characterizes the objects of sense perception as "sensations,"[23] namely, modes of thinking, then it seems inescapable to me that the contrast between objects of clear and distinct perception and sense perception is that the objects of the latter have (second-order) modal dependence on minds, the objects of the former do not.[24] In view of this, had Descartes believed that immutable essences are modally dependent (in either the first or second order) on minds he would, quite simply, have said so. This he did not do.

Descartes does, however, insist that immutable essences are in the mind—even if not in the mind as modes of ideas. This is puzzling enough, but in the same passage from Meditation V where Descartes insists that immutable essences are in the mind (do not exist "outside the mind"), he also insists that they are not "dependent" on the mind. The juxtaposition of saying that immutable essences are not dependent on mind with the claim that they exist in the mind creates a tension in the Cartesian theory of ideas. How can something be in the mind in some sense and yet not be dependent on the mind in some sense?

One possible answer comes from Berkeley:

[I]t may perhaps be objected that, if extension and figure exist only in the mind, it follows that the mind is extended and figured; since extension is a mode or attribute which (to speak with the Schools) is predicated of the subject in which it exists. I answer, those qualities are in the mind only as they are perceived by it, that is, not by way of *mode* or *attribute* but only by way of *idea*; and it no more follows that the the soul or mind is extended because extension exists in it alone, than it does that it is red or blue.[25]

Berkeley's point is that in saying that objects of ideas are "in the mind" we do not need to be saying the objects of ideas are features of a monadic mental substance but, that mind is a substance whose essential property, perception, involves a *cognitive relation* to a special class of objects (qualities), which are themselves not properties of mind. In this view the objects of perception count as *being in the mind* because the existence of the cognitive relation is essential to the existence of the objects, they count as *being not dependent on the mind* because they are not properties of the mind.

So far we have considered two possible readings of the Cartesian notion of an immutable essence being in the mind : the *mode-of-idea version* and Berkeley's theory—the *relational version*, as I shall call it. I have earlier presented several arguments against attributing the former to Descartes, I shall now present some against attributing the latter.

First, Descartes says in Meditation V that he has ideas of countless things "which *may not* exist anywhere outside thought" (AT VII, 64; CSM II 44; my emphasis). If Descartes took the notion of *being in the mind* (not being "outside me") to be definitionally equivalent to the notion of *being the object of an idea*, he would not have said "may not"; he would have said "could not." Second, in the First Replies, he says to Caterus that "if the question is about what the idea of the sun is," his answer is "that it is the thing which is thought of, in so far as it has objective being in the intellect" (AT VII, 102; CSM II, 75). Here Descartes seems to be explaining the notion of an idea[26] in terms of the notion of a way of being in the intellect, the reverse of what would be required if immutable essences were relationally dependent on minds.

So the question remains. How can something be in the mind in some sense for Descartes and yet not be dependent on the mind in some sense? I have to say that I do not know whether Descartes has a clear answer to this question, but an answer along the following lines is at least potentially available to him. Suppose that we see a distinction between the Cartesian notion of *modal dependence* and the Cartesian notion of *property containment*. The notion of modal dependence can be explained as follows:

If an entity *x* is modally dependent on one of the two basic Cartesian finite substances—matter or mind—then *x* is a property of that substance and cannot be a property of the other.

This part of the doctrine is suggested by a passage in *Principles* I, 61:

[M]ode[s] cannot be understood apart from the substance in which they . . . inhere. For example, if a stone is in motion and is square-shaped, I can understand the square shape without the motion and, conversely, the motion without the square shape;

but I can understand neither the motion nor the shape apart from the substance of the stone. (*Principles* I, 61; AT VIIIA, 29; CSM I, 214)

For another example, if we assume[27] that color is a *mode* of mind then color not only is a property of mind (possibly a second-order property of mind) it *must* be a property of mind—it cannot be a mode of matter. All properties are entities that are ontologically dependent on the substances in which they inhere, but some can inhere in only one of the two basic substance types. Properties that behave in this way are modes, and modes consequently exhibit a special kind of dependence on the substance type in which they inhere that goes beyond the fact that they are properties.

On the other hand, Descartes's notion of property *containment* seems to work differently. If *x* is a property *contained* (in Descartes's technical sense) in one of the two basic kinds of substance, then it can—and often will—be contained in the other. For example, although the property of shape can be contained in a mind in a nonformal way (eminently), it can also be contained in matter formally. Since immutable essences and only immutable essences bear the containment relation to the substances they characterize, immutable essences and only immutable essences can be in one of the basic kinds of substance (be contained in a substance) while not being necessarily *only* in that kind of substance. It is in this sense that immutable essences can be in thought and yet not be dependent on thought.

As indirect support for the proposal I note an article of *Principles* I in which Descartes speaks of a class of entities that are neither modes of matter nor modes of mind. The article is number 48 and the entities are the eternal truths: "All the objects of our perception we regard either as things, or affections of things, or as eternal truths which have no existence outside thought" (AT VIII, 22; CSM I, 208). Eternal truths are characterized two articles later as "these common notions." In the formal portion of the Second Replies Descartes offers a list of common notions, for example "It is impossible that *nothing*, a non-existing thing, should be the cause of the existence of anything, or of any actual perfection in anything" (AT VII, 165; CSM II, 116). Now, the eternal truths are principles that *apply* to both kinds of substance: a mode of mind no less than a mode of matter is subject to the causal law just mentioned. The notion of application employed in this last observation is or implies an inherence of properties that crosses the boundary between the two basic kinds of substance. Eternal truths are also said to be the objects of clear and distinct perception and to "have no existence outside thought." This is analogous to what Descartes says about immutable essences in Meditation V:

[T]he most important consideration at this point is that I find within me countless ideas of things which even though they may not exist anywhere outside me still cannot be called nothing; for although in a sense they can be thought of at will, they are not my invention but have their own true and immutable natures. (AT VII 64; CSM II, 44)

Although eternal truths are not essences—the former are general propositions, the latter are not—Descartes sees a close connection between them.[28] For example, in the *Conversation with Burman*, speaking of the genesis of the truth, "[W]hatever thinks, exists," he says: "As I have explained before, we do not separate out these general propositions from the particular instances; rather it is in the particular instances that we think of them" (AT V, 147; CSM III, 333). The connection between eternal truths and immutable essences in Descartes's account is somewhat speculative. What is less speculative is the fact that immutable essences are accorded a special, if ambiguous, status in Meditation V and eternal truths are accorded an analogous status in *Principles* I, 48. Associated with that special status for the eternal truths is the property of cross-categorial application. This provides some support for my proposal that the special status of immutable essences is also associated with the possibility of cross-categorial application.

My conclusion is that, for Descartes, immutable essences are in the mind but not dependent on the mind because, although they are contained in the mind, they are not modally dependent on minds.[29] This proposal has significance for the problem left over at the end of the previous section: in what sense are immutable essences *in the intellect*? (This is the second element of the three comprising Descartes's theory of the objective reality of ideas.) The answer is that they are contained, in this special technical sense, in the intellect. However, there are, as we know from previous discussion, two modes of containment, *formal* and *eminent*. Since immutable geometrical essences—the kind of properties at issue in our ideas of external substances—are not formally contained in the mind, they must be *eminently* contained therein. Ultimately, this is how immutable essences are in the intellect.

To introduce a discussion of the third element—the form of our perception of objects—and also to deepen our understanding of the second, I now propose to take a closer look at the Cartesian notion of eminent containment.

2.6 Descartes's Notion of Eminent Containment: An Epistemic Interpretation

In the previous chapter I said that a property P is formally contained in a substance s just in case s is P, and a property P is eminently contained if it is contained in some other way not implying that s is P.[30] These characterizations have served us well enough, but we now need to sharpen our understanding of them. To do so we need to look to the definitions of these notions in the Second Replies (AT VII, 161: CSM II, 114):

> Whatever exists in the objects of our ideas in a way which exactly corresponds to our perception of it is said to exist *formally* in those objects.

> Something is said to exist *eminently* in an object when, although it does not exactly correspond to our perception of it, its greatness is such that it can fill the role of that which does so correspond.

Both of these notions are defined in terms of the fidelity of a property as it actually is to the way in which it is perceived, together with some other terms involved in the definition of eminent containment. Considering the former set of terms first, I note that if there is a property P that we perceive, then the rule of truth tells us that it must be exemplified in something, either eminently or formally. This manner of describing the situation suggests that Descartes countenances two kinds of exemplification. However, the official definitions suggest a different understanding, implying that there is only one kind of exemplication but two kinds of perception: (1) there is the case in which a property is perceived as it is and is exemplified in its ground, and (2) there is the case in which a property is not perceived as it is exemplified in its ground. In case 1 Descartes speaks of the property being formally contained in its ground; in case 2 he speaks of eminent containment; but in both cases there exists a property actually exemplified in a substance. Since this account describes one of the central differences between formal and eminent containment in epistemic terms, my account can be categorized as an *epistemic interpretation of the notion of eminent containment*. Nonepistemic interpretations are more common, two of which I consider in the next chapter.[31]

It is not surprising that Descartes should allow that sometimes we perceive things as being other than they really are, but it is surprising that Descartes allows that we can clearly and distinctly perceive properties to be other than they are. Yet this is just what is allowed by the inclusion of the disjunction *either formal or eminent* in the rule of truth. However, even in the case where a clear and distinct perception is of the presence of a property that does not correspond to reality, there is enough "greatness" in the property to ensure that "it can fill the role of that which does so correspond." In a curious sense it is the fact that eminently contained properties are "great" ontologically that makes it possible for our perception of them to be deficient epistemically.

To help fix our understanding of this difficult notion, it would have been helpful if, along with the definition, Descartes had provided us with an example of how we misperceive an eminently contained property. Unfortunately, he does not do this.[32] He does, however, say a number of things in other places that collectively suggest an example.

In the *Conversation with Burman* Descartes speaks of mathematical objects as if they were *possibilia*, namely, possible objects ontologically independent of existing substances :

> [A]ll the demonstrations of mathematicians deal with true entities and objects, and the complete and entire object of mathematics and everything it deals with is a true and real entity. This object has a true and real nature, just as much as the object of physics itself. The only difference is that physics considers its object not just as a true and real entity, but also as something actually and specifically existing. Mathematics, on the other hand, considers its object as merely possible, i.e. as something which does not actually exist in space but is capable of so doing. (AT V, 160; CSM III, 343)

On the other hand, in the letter to Mersenne that I have been relying upon so heavily in my discussion of the rule of truth, Descartes associates the distinction between actual and possible existence with the distinction between the formal and eminent containment of properties in an actually existing substance (cause):

> [Y]ou quote as an axiom of mine: whatever we clearly conceive is or exists. That is not at all what I think, but only that whatever we perceive clearly is true, and so it exists, if we perceive that it cannot not exist; or that it can exist, if we perceive that its existence is possible. For although the objective being of an idea must have a real

cause, it is not always necessary that this cause should contain it formally, but only eminently. (AT III, 542; *Letters*, 132)

When I quoted this passage earlier, I noted that Descartes seems to be maintaining that the reason something has merely possible existence is that its cause contains the objective being of the thing eminently rather than formally. Since then I have argued for three additional points: (1) that the objective being of a thing consists in its properties being objectively in the intellect—in the case of an ordinary physical substance the properties in question are geometrical properties; (2) that the way in which geometrical properties are objectively contained in the intellect is eminently; and (3) that properties eminently contained in something are somehow misperceived. But how? We now have the makings of an answer to that question: geometrical essences are perceived as *mathematical possibilia ontologically independent of actually existing substances* although their actual status is of *properties ontologically dependent (by means of the relation of eminent containment) on an actual substance (the mind)*.

If I have Descartes right here, then his doctrine of mathematical thought is somewhat analogous to that maintained by Aristotle in *De Anima*:

> [T]he mind when it is thinking the objects of Mathematics thinks as separate, elements which do not exist separate. In every case the mind which is actively thinking is the objects which it thinks. (*De Anima* III, 7: 431b 15.)

In the foregoing I have been simply *assuming* that I have Descartes right in order to provide a concrete illustration of the way in which a set of properties eminently contained in myself might be misperceived as something independent of myself. Of course it is possible to use this same passage for the contrary purpose of claiming that Descartes was committed to the existence of *possibilia* and that it was through this device that Descartes proposed to explicate the concept of nonactualized possibility. If this alternative reading proves to be closer to Descartes' intentions[33] than the one I have proposed, it undermines a central contention of my interpretation of Cartesian epistemology: that the rule of truth is a logical guarantee of the existence of an actual substance containing any property which is the object of a clear and distinct perception. If, that is, what the rule of truth guarantees is only that there is a possible object containing such a property, then Descartes is still left with the task of deciding which possible objects are actual and which are not. But this requires that Descartes provide an additional principle to accomplish this, that he justify this principle to the same standards as the rule of truth and that he deploy it in a way that does not run foul of circularity. I do not find any such principle in Descartes's writings and, if one were detected, I do not see how it could be justified and deployed independently of the rule of truth.[34] (On the version of the rule of truth that I assign to Descartes no additional criterion of the actuality of the subject containing the content properties of the clear and distinct perception is needed, although some means for showing that this content is formally rather than eminently contained in that subject is still required.)[35] So there is much at stake here both for my reading of Cartesian epistemology and for the power and cogency of the epistemology itself. It would, therefore, be useful to find some further argument from other central aspects of Cartesian doctrine to show that Descartes cannot be committed to the existence of merely possible objects.

There is, I believe, such an argument based on the doctrine of the free creation by God of the eternal truths.[36] Eternal truths are necessary truths, truths that cannot possibly be false. Suppose we interpret the notion of possibility here in terms of an assumed commitment on Descartes's behalf to the existence of *possibilia* (merely possible objects that are not in the actual world). The supposition is that God creates the eternal truths by means of creating a suitable set of *possibilia* to which the truths apply.[37] Call this "the *possibilia* supposition." We can also allow for the sake of argument that the awareness of these entities (by us or by God) does not by itself compromise their nonactual status.

The argument against the *possibilia* supposition proceeds by way of dilemma. If there are *possibilia* in the Cartesian system then either they exist causally independently of God's creative power or they do not. *First horn*: If they exist independently of God's creative power, then God does not freely create necessary truths, contrary to assumption. *Second horn*: If they do not exist causally independently of God's creative power, that is if they are causally dependent on God's power, then they are in the actual world, contrary to assumption. *Conclusion*: there are no *possibilia* in the Cartesian system.

The second horn of the dilemma rests on the principle that causal relations are not "transworld relations": if *a* is actual and *a* causes *b*, then *b* must be actual. It is possible to deny that this principle is sound, maintaining that causality is a transworld relation, but that seems to me to be a high price to pay to defend the proposition that Descartes countenances merely possible objects. Since there is an alternative interpretation (the one I have just proposed) of how Descartes proposes to explicate the notion of nonactualized possibility that has at least some independent textual evidence, the alternative interpretation is the one that should be adopted.

This interpretation explains the notion of unactualized possibility in epistemic rather than ontological terms and requires a distinction between the properties that we clearly and distinctly perceive and the way in which we clearly and distinctly perceive them. We can describe the latter as the *content* of our clear and distinct ideas. In this interpretation, the greatness of an eminently contained geometrical property consists in its ability to be perceived as if it were a clearly and distinctly perceived property formally contained in something. To perform this function, eminently contained ideas must possess a structure *analogous to* but *greater than* that of the corresponding formally contained idea.

Descartes does not say precisely how the analogy between the role of eminently contained ideas and the role of formally contained ideas is to be understood, but we can find a need for such an an analogy to explain the correspondence between the demonstrations of pure mathematics and those of physics mentioned in the passage quoted earlier in this chapter from the *Conversation with Burman*. If the results of pure mathematical demonstrations are to hold formally of actual matter as well as of mathematical abstracta there will have to be some way for Descartes to secure the correspondence.[38] Postulating a structural analogy between mathematical properties eminetly contained in mind and their formal counterparts in matter would be one way for Descartes to accomplish this.

In order to explicate the epistemic dimension of the notion of eminent containment, I have taken recourse to the way in which the objects of our ideas are perceived, namely, to the notion of the content or form of our ideas of objects. This also amounts to the third and final element in the analysis of Descartes's notion of the objective reality of ideas. I now consider that element in more detail.

2.7 The Third Element of Objective Reality: The Form or Content of Perceptions of Objects

There are a number of places in which Descartes discusses the form of ideas and it is in these texts that we can find some additional evidence for the present interpretation. Consider, for example, Descartes's official definitions of *thought* and *idea* in the Second Replies. It will be recalled from the previous chapter that Descartes there defines "thought" as "all the operations of the will, the intellect, the imagination, and the senses" (AT VII, 160; CSM II, 113). He also explicitly distinguishes "thought" from "idea" explaining the latter in terms of the notion of "form":

> *Idea.* I understand this term to mean the form of any given thought, immediate perception of which makes me aware of the thought. Hence, whenever I express something in words, and understand what I am saying, this very fact makes it certain that there is within me an idea of what is signified by the words in question. Thus it is not only the images depicted in the imagination which I call 'ideas'. Indeed, in so far as these images are in the corporeal imagination, that is, are depicted in some part of the brain, I do not call them 'ideas' at all; I call them 'ideas' only in so far as they give form to [*informant*] the mind itself, when it is directed toward that part of the brain. (AT VII, 160–161; CSM II, 113)

The reference to "form" here has seemed baffling to many commentators. Though we might expect to find a Scholastic doctrine of "forms" here, Kenny says, no such doctrine is in fact present: ideas are "non-material representations of things."[39] The doctrine is a "terminological thicket" according to Jolly: "Ideas are called forms because it is of the essence of a thought that it is a mode of mind or, as Descartes sometimes says, an operation of the understanding."[40] Finally we note Costa's explanation: "All that we are justified to conclude is that the 'form' of my thought is that which makes it a thinking about Vienna rather than some other thought; it is simply that which all thoughts *of that type* have in common."[41]

None of these explanations seem to me to make especially good sense of the passage in question. An important part of the reason for this is that there are two contexts in the passage where the notion of form occurs and they each suggest a different interpretation. The first context is the discussion of the transparency property of thoughts in general; the second is the discussion of the effects of the mind's contemplation of corporeal images. The generality of the first context seems to count against the restrictive function assigned to forms in both Kenny's and Costa's accounts, but Jolly's explanation is so general that it has Descartes saying not much more than that operations of the will, the understanding, the senses, and the imagination are collected under the rubric of operations of the mind. Of course they are, but in the second context Descartes seems to make a point of saying that the mind itself is given "form" by the corporeal image, a use of "form" that seems more Aristotelian (viz., hylomorphic) than Scholastic.

The Aristotelian conception is also implied in a letter written to Mesland in 1644:

> I regard the difference between the soul and its ideas as the same as that between a piece of wax and the various shapes it can take. Just as it is not an activity but a passivity in the wax, to take various shapes, so, it seems to me, it is a passivity in the soul to receive one or other idea and only its volitions are activities. It receives its ideas partly from objects in contact with the senses, partly from impressions in the brain, and partly from precedent dispositions in the soul and motions of the will. (AT IV, 110; *Letters*, 148)

If ideas are Aristotelian forms, what is the Cartesian "material cause" in the case of the soul? The answer comes from the first definition—ideas are forms of *thoughts*. Thoughts are "operations," acts of the various mental faculties, the generic form of which is *immediate awareness*. In the case of clear and distinct mathematical thoughts, they are immediate awarenesses of mathematical essences eminently contained in the mind. But the essences do not individuate the *contents* of the thoughts, since the essences can be perceived in a form that does not correspond to the way they really are.[42] That is why Descartes makes ideas as forms of thoughts the content of our awareness rather than the objects of said thoughts: "*Idea*. I understand this term to mean the form of any given thought immediate perception of which makes me aware of the [object of the] thought" (my interpolation). It is forms of thoughts in this sense that comprise Descartes's notion of the objective reality of ideas.

It seems, therefore, that when we put things together in this way we are led to the conclusion that ideas as forms are not the objects of acts of immediate awareness, nor the acts themselves, but properties of the acts. Ideas as forms of thought are like adverbial properties modifying perceptual relations between observers and objects. This relation is most perspicuously characterized as a *three*-place relation between a person, an object and the *way* the object looks to the person. In the case of Cartesian clear and distinct perception we also need three parameters to individuate such acts: the person, the object, and the form of the perception of the object. This will require a modification in the logical form that I have initially attributed to ascriptions of clear and distinct perception. To effect this modification I will introduce the technical notion of the *form of a perception*:

The Form of a Perception

If f is the property of *its appearing as if property* $\emptyset$ (or a *possibile* possessing $\emptyset$) *is present to me* and f is true of a perception x, then f is the form of x. (I shall say that $\emptyset$ is the "content property" of f.)

The Objective Reality of an Idea

If x is a perception (idea in the material sense), f is the form of x and $\varnothing$ is the content-property of F then $\varnothing$ *is the objective reality of x.*

I will express clear and distinct perceptions in the following canonical way:

The Canonical Formulation of Clear
and Distinct Perception

x has a clear and distinct perception [idea] of a set of content properties [with objective reality] $\varnothing_1 \ldots \varnothing_n$ determining the sense of t, where t is a singular term for an individual object. (The words in brackets are alternative formulations]

To reflect these formulations in Descartes' theory of eminent containment and formal containment, I propose the following definitions:

Eminent Containment (EC)

For any actual substance s and content property $\varnothing$, if I have a clear and
    distinct perception of $\varnothing$ then $\varnothing$ *is eminently contained in s* iff
1. There is a property P such that P is nonidentical with $\varnothing$
2. s exemplifies P
3. P appears as if it were $\varnothing$ or a *possibile* formally containing $\varnothing$
4. P is epistemically analogous to $\varnothing$
5. P is metaphysically greater than $\varnothing$.

Formal Containment (FC)

For any actual substance s and content-property $\varnothing$ if I have a clear and
    distinct perception of $\varnothing$ then $\varnothing$ *is formally contained in s* iff
1. There is a property P such that P is identical with $\varnothing$
2. s exemplifies P
3. P appears as it is.

Next, I incorporate these ideas in a revised version of Descartes's general rule of truth:

The Rule of Truth *(Final Version)* *(RTF)*

If I have a clear and distinct idea i of a set of content properties $\varnothing_1 \ldots \varnothing_n$ determining the sense of a singular term t for an individual object, then there is a substance s and there is a set of real properties $P_1 \ldots P_n$ corresponding to the set of content properties $\varnothing_1 \ldots \varnothing_n$ such that $\varnothing_1 \ldots \varnothing_n$ are contained formally or eminently in s and $P_1 \ldots P_n$ are the objects of i.

Then I use RTF to revise the definition of the existence predicate:

The Definition of the Existence Predicate
(Final Version) (DEF)

<t exists> is (formally) true iff there is a substance s and there is a set of real properties $P_1 \ldots P_n$ such that $P_1 \ldots P_n$ are identical with the corresponding content properties $\emptyset_1 \ldots \emptyset_n$ comprising the sense of the term t and s exemplifies $P_1 \ldots P_n$.

Finally, I use RTF as the chief principle underlying a revised general pattern of existential reasoning:

The General Pattern of Existential Reasoning (Final Version)

1. Assume that t is a constant term or definite description and that there is a set of content properties $\emptyset_1 \ldots \emptyset_n$ determining the sense of t.
2. Assume that I have a clear and distinct idea of $\emptyset_1 \ldots \emptyset_n$.

Then we can reason as follows:

3. There is a substance s such that $\emptyset_1 \ldots \emptyset_n$ are contained formally or eminently in s. (RTF, 1, 2)
[4. If the content properties $\emptyset_1 \ldots \emptyset_n$ are contained eminently in s then they are not identical with the corresponding real properties. (EC, 2)]
5. If the content properties $\emptyset_1 \ldots \emptyset_n$ are contained formally in s there is a set of real properties $P_1 \ldots P_n$ such that $P_1 \ldots P_n$ are identical with the corresponding content properties and s exemplifies $P_1 \ldots P_n$. (FC, 2)
6. $\emptyset_1 \ldots \emptyset_n$ are not contained eminently in s. (elimination premise: EP)
7. $\emptyset_1 \ldots \emptyset_n$ are contained formally in s. (3, 6)
8. There is a set of real properties $P_1 \ldots P_n$ such that $P_1 \ldots P_n$ are identical with the corresponding content properties and s exemplifies $P_1 \ldots P_n$. (5, 7)
9. A sentence, <t exists>, is formally true. (DEF, 8)

This pattern also comes in a necessity version:

The General Pattern of Necessary Existential
Reasoning (Final Version)

1. Assume that t is a constant term or definite description and that there is a set of content properties $\emptyset_1 \ldots \emptyset_n$ determining the sense of t.
2. Assume that I have a clear and distinct idea of $\emptyset_1 \ldots \emptyset_n$.

Then we can reason as follows:

3. There is a substance s such that $\emptyset_1 \ldots \emptyset_n$ are contained formally or eminently in s. (RTF, 1, 2)
[4. If the content properties $\emptyset_1 \ldots \emptyset_n$ are contained eminently in s then they are not identical with the corresponding real properties. (EC, 2)]
5. If the content properties $\emptyset_1 \ldots \emptyset_n$ are contained formally in s there is a set of real properties $P_1 \ldots P_n$ such that $P_1 \ldots P_n$ are identical with the corresponding content properties and s exemplifies $P_1 \ldots P_n$. (FC, 2)

6. Necessarily, $\emptyset_1 \ldots \emptyset_n$ are not contained eminently in s. (EP)
7. Necessarily, $\emptyset_1 \ldots \emptyset_n$ are contained formally in s. (3, 6)
8. There is a set of real properties $P_1 \ldots P_n$ such that $P_1 \ldots P_n$ are necessarily identical with the corresponding content properties and s exemplifies $P_1 \ldots P_n$. (5, 7)
9. A sentence, <t necessarily exists> is formally true. (DEF, 8).

I noted earlier in this chapter that Descartes countenances an ambiguity in the word "idea":

'Idea' can be taken materially, as an operation of the intellect. . . . Alternatively, it can be taken objectively, as the thing represented by that operation; and this thing, even if it is not regarded as existing outside the intellect, can be more perfect than myself. (AT VII, 8; CSM II, 7)

However, if I have Descartes right on the notion of idea as form, then it seems that we must recognize not two but three different official Cartesian uses of idea terminology:[43] to refer to the objects of acts of awareness, to refer to the acts of awareness, and to refer to the "forms" of the acts of awareness.

Why should Descartes tolerate such multiple ambiguity in one of his central theoretical terms? The reason has in part to do with the transitional nature of Descartes's conception of ideas in the course of his philosophical development. In the *Rules for the Direction of the Mind* "ideas" refer only to ideas in the corporeal imagination (AT X 414–417; CSM I, 41–41); in the *Treatise on Light* "ideas" refers to *ideas we have in our mind* (AT XI 3; CSM I, 81) although in the *Treatise on Man* (AT XI, 176–177; Hall, 86), written in the same period, Descartes retains the corporeal usage; by the time of the *Meditations* Descartes expressly disavows the corporeal usage. However, in coming to have a new doctrine of mental ideas, Descartes transferred many of the features of the old (corporeal) conception to the new. That, I shall argue, is the ultimate source of his Meditation III analogy of ideas to images. One part of that analogy on the side of corporeal images lies in the property of representing an (external object) to mind, the other part lies in the property of serving as the immediate object of the "cognitive power":[44] both properties show up on the side of mental ideas in the ambiguous usage of the word "idea" in the passage from the Preface to the *Meditations*.

The distinction between ideas-as-forms and ideas-as-acts also appears in a distinction drawn in the Fourth Replies between ideas in the *formal* sense and ideas in the *material* sense:

When M. Arnauld says 'if cold is merely an absence, there cannot be an idea of cold which represents it as a positive thing', it is clear that he is dealing solely with an idea in the *formal* sense. Since ideas are forms of a kind, and are not composed of any matter, when we think of them as representing something, we are taking them not *materially* but *formally*. If, however, we were considering them not as representing this or that but simply as operations of the intellect, then it could be said that we were taking them materially, but in that case they would have no reference to the truth or falsity of their objects. (AT VII, 232; CSM II, 162)

This passage has seemed puzzling to interpreters for at least two reasons.[45] The first has to do with the reference to ideas as "forms of a kind," the second has to do with a comparison between the notion of formality as it figures here (*ideas taken in the formal sense*) and the notion of formality as it figures in Descartes's standard distinction between the *formal reality* of ideas and their objective reality.

The reference to ideas "as forms of a kind" should be taken not as a reference to Scholastic forms—sensible or intelligible species—but to the hylomorphic forms we have just been discussing. There is, however, a puzzle that still remains. The context in which this passage is presented is one in which Descartes is discussing the "material falsity" of a certain class of awarenesses. This property seems to amount to the absence of a "real thing" as the object of the awareness. The difference between an act of awareness that represents something and one that does not is that in the former case, the act has a real thing for an object and in the latter it does not.[46] Why does Descartes insist that only acts with real objects have "forms"? Why not say that acts without objects—acts taken materially—also have a form?

Descartes's answer, suggested by the second use of "form" in the definition of *idea* quoted above, would seem to be that ideas-as-forms are forms not of the relation of awareness *abstracted from its object* but of the state of affairs that obtains when the relation of awareness is *satisfied by its object*.[47] The point seems to be that the form of awareness, though not identical with the object of the awareness, is nevertheless dependent on that object for its character. That is why Descartes describes the form as *given* to the mind by the corporeal image in the Second Replies' definition.

This result is of some importance to resolving the second ground of puzzlement this passage provides, namely, that concerning the relation between the notion of *an idea taken in the formal sense* and the notion of the *formal reality of an idea*. This is puzzling because Descartes contrasts the formal reality of an idea with the objective reality of an idea and yet seems to identify the objective reality of an idea with an idea taken in the formal sense. Descartes thus sees a contrast between *ideas taken in the formal sense* and *the formal reality of ideas*, a bit of terminological imperspicuity that would be tolerable were it not for the opacity of the contrast itself.

We can shed light on this contrast if we make one crucial interpretive hypothesis: that the notion of *idea taken in the formal sense* is to be explained in terms of the hylomorphic notion of the *form* of an act of awareness. This notion then stands in clear contrast to the notion of the existence of an idea considered simply as a event in the natural order, namely, to the notion of the *formal reality of an idea*. Because Descartes identifies ideas taken in the formal sense with the objective reality of ideas, this text provides some additional support for my contention that the notion of the objective reality of an idea is the notion of a *form* of the relation of awareness between the intellect and an object. Because forms are functions of relations embodied by their objects, the objective reality of an idea must be seen as dependent on the object of the idea-as-act, but is not identical with that object.

Without seeing cognition as a three-place relation among a subject, an object, and a mode of awareness, the various dichotomies that Descartes draws between ideas will indeed seem perniciously confusing. I take as one of the chief virtues of my account that it avoids attributing an inexplicable degree of expository and conceptual confusion to Descartes on matters of central doctrinal importance.[48]

Can this treatment of ideas as forms be reconciled with those many passages where Descartes treats ideas as if they were images of things? I take this question up in the next section.

2.8 Ideas as Images: Presentation versus Representation

There is no doubt that Descartes says many things about representation in many different places, not all of which seem to point in the same direction. Still, some passages are more central than others, chief among which must surely be the discussion in Meditation III where Descartes likens an idea to an image (*imagio*).

One school of thought sees this analogy as a picturesque way of saying that ideas represent objects and sees no significant mileage to be derived from any further exploitation of the analogy to pictures. Students of Scholastic thought are apt to see much of the import of the image metaphor deployed in Meditation III in terms of standard Scholastic uses of the notion of an image. Calvin Normore[49] has given us an ingenious and illuminating reconstruction of Descartes's theory of representation that relies upon this usage. He locates Descartes's conception of images in the tradition of Suarez, who sees them as having two defining characteristics: (1) ideas refer to items or represent them in virtue of an extrinsic causal relation to the (actual) causes, (2) they are "similar" to them. This is the "Janus-faced" aspect of ideas that allows Descartes to have both the epistemological benefits of an "internalist" theory of meaning and the semantic benefits of an "externalist" theory. Of course Descartes rejects the straightforward interpretation of the resemblance theory, giving to both the causal and the internal features of images his own twist. Normore takes God's images of the things he will create as exemplars and goes on to show how a good deal of Descartes's views about objective reality might be explained by this interpretation.

Another interpretation sees Descartes's account of the representation of corporeal bodies as also depending heavily on images, but on the corporeal images formed in the brain rather than on images of interest to the Scholastic tradition.[50] Such interpretations argue that Descartes holds to a traditional representational theory of ideas and that in making the analogy between ideas and images Descartes is giving expression to this theory. By a *traditional representational theory of ideas* I mean a theory that construes intentionality as a symbolic relationship of natural sign or resemblance.

A chief source of the naturalistic interpretation of Descartes lies in writings such as the *Optics*, where Descartes presents his empirical account of perception as well as in those writings (to be considered in a subsequent chapter) where Descartes develops his theory of the objects of the passions.

There are striking parallels both in content and in (rough) order of discussion between a segment of the *Optics* running from about AT VI 112–147 (CSM, 165–175) (in Discourses 4–6) and a segment of Meditation III running from AT VII, 37–40 (CSM, 27–29), a parallelism that we can exploit to gain some insight into Descartes's intentions with the image analogy of Meditation III.

First we get a discussion of images and resemblance at AT VI, 112–114 (CSM I, 165–166) in *Optics* IV, and at AT VII, 37–38 (CSM II, 25–27) in Meditation III; then in *Optics* VI we get a discussion on the general theme of judgment at AT VI, 138 (CSM I, 169) to the end of Discourse VI,[51] and at AT VII, 37 (CSM II, 26) in Meditation III; finally we get a discussion of the difference between sensory ideas and intellectual ideas introduced by the "two suns" discussion at AT VI, 144–145 (CSM I, 173–174) in *Optics* VI, and at AT VII 39 (CSM II, 27) in Meditation III.

Even more significant than similarity of order and content is the fact that in important respects each passage takes in the other's theoretical laundry.

For example, though Descartes relies upon a notion of judgment in the empirical theory of the *Optics*, a theory telling us how a certain class of judgments is determined, he does not tell us there what judgment is. This he tells us in the Meditation passage: when I judge ("affirm or deny") "there is always a particular thing which I take as the object of my thought" plus "something more." My thought of a particular thing is "as it were an image." This is an analogy but not one spelled out in the *Meditations*. This he does in the *Optics*, explaining what an "image" in the brain is by drawing an analogy to an engraving. As I read that analogy, engravings of objects are images, though they need not, indeed generally will not, resemble what they are images of. I take it, therefore, that when Descartes denies in the Meditation III passages that images resemble their objects, he is not thereby withdrawing the analogy to engravings. Of course ideas and engravings are not categorially similar—ideas are modes of mind and engravings are modes of matter—but, for the analogy to have point, they must share some characteristics. The question is, *which ones?*

When Descartes speaks of engravings he is interested in conditions under which engravings "better represent objects," adding that brain images should be thought of "in the same way" (AT VI, 113; CSM I, 166–167). It is clear that Descartes is here thinking of corporeal images in the sense of the traditional theory of representation, that is, as effects carrying information about their causes in a form decipherable by the mind.

In light of the existence of the parallelism between the text of the *Optics* and the *Meditations*, the existence of this passage in the *Optics* might suggest that Descartes was thinking of the representational property when he likened ideas to images in the *Meditations*. In fact, in the French edition Descartes explicitly speaks of representation in connection with the image analogy a few paragraphs after introducing the analogy: "But considering them [ideas] as images [*comme des images*] some of which represent [*répresentent*] one thing, some another" (AT IX, 31; Alquié II, 437, my translation).

There is, however, also evidence from the *Optics* pointing in the other direction, suggesting, that is, that Descartes is not thinking of images primarily in their role as traditional representations.

Ordinary images have the characteristic that they are "of" things in what appear to be at least two senses: they make a content "cognitively accessible" [52] (or, I shall sometimes find it more convenient to say, they "present a content") to the mind and they carry information about the things which cause, or could cause, their production by some standard means. Both of these features of images are present in Descartes's discussion of corporeal images. We have seen that he conceives of images as effects when he speaks of the conditions under which engravings "better represent objects"; he also conceives of images as *causes* when he speaks of corporeal images "as what occasions the soul to have sensory perceptions" (AT VI, 114; CSM I, 166) and other related passages.

We should note, however, that the latter feature is the one most frequently discussed and is apparently of central interest to Descartes, as indicated by his summary observation:

[T]he problem is to know simply how they [corporeal images] can enable the soul to have sensory perceptions of all the various qualities of the objects to which they correspond—not to know how they can resemble these objects. (AT VI, 114; CSM I, 166)

Consequently, when Descartes speaks of an analogy between images and ideas in the Third Meditation he is thinking of images from the perspective he takes on corporeal images in the *Optics*, a perspective in which the role of images as causes (presenters of contents) rather than as effects (representers of objects) is in focus. This is not to say that Descartes denies that sensory ideas naturally signify objects; it is to deny that when Descartes attributes to ideas the property of being like images he is attributing to them this property. But what property is he attributing? My answer is that in virtue of their nature as forms of thoughts, ideas *present* the objects of those thoughts to the mind for cognitive action.

It is true that in the Third Meditation Descartes introduces the idea of resemblance soon after introducing his analogy of ideas to images, but, *pace* Bolton,[53] he does not do so in order to discuss common misconceptions regarding the nature of representation. In fact, the first time that the notion of representation explicitly appears in this part of Meditation III is in the guise of objective reality at AT VIII, 40 (CSM II, 27) just after Descartes has finished with his investigation of resemblance. As he makes clear there, Descartes takes himself to be now engaged in "another investigation." Where he does talk about resemblance the point of interest is in our (naive) reliance on the resemblance principle as either a conjecture causing us to form naive, commonsense beliefs or as a principle we might use to justify those beliefs. It is, thus, the role of ideas as causes rather than as effects that is in focus in the Third Meditation just as it is in the corresponding passage in the *Optics*.

I therefore find myself in disagreement with those, like Normore,[54] who see in the image analogy a primary significance on the side of images as effects rather than as causes (presenters of contents) and conclude that Descartes's characterization of ideas by means of the the metaphor of images is not inconsistent with the formal-epistemic interpretation. An image, for Descartes, is an entity which "presents" rather than "represents" a content to the mind. I will often employ the term "(re)presentation" to retain the connection with traditional Cartesian terminology but to remind the reader of the nontraditional sense that that terminology carries for Descartes.

THREE

Causes, Existence, and Ideas

3.1 Introduction

This chapter continues the project launched in the last. In chapter 2 I set out to provide an interpretation of Descartes's theory of existential reasoning—Descartes's theory of what justifies an inference from our ideas to things outside our ideas—moving from Cartesian epistemology into the heart of Cartesian theories of ideas and metaphysics. I am now ready to take up discussion of the epistemological part of the enterprise once again.

In the Second Replies Descartes declares that a principle ascribing certain properties to the causes of the objective reality of our ideas provides the central premise in all reasoning to the existence of things "whether they are perceived by the senses or not."[1] The central task of the first two sections of this chapter is to establish the relationship between the main premises figuring in Descartes's general theory of existential reasoning (including, of course, the rule of truth) and Descartes's causal principles. My conclusion will be that the rule of truth is fundamental and provides the content for the version of the causal principle that Descartes employs in the two central existence demonstrations of his metaphysics—that of the existence of God and that of the existence of the material world. I call this the *fundamentality thesis*.

The fundamentality thesis is a thesis about relations of logical priority and logical equivalence between propositions, not a thesis about whether Descartes recognized or exploited these relations. However, I also believe that Descartes did recognize these relations, perhaps somewhat confusedly at first, more clearly later on. I see evidence of this within the Meditation III proof of the existence of God and, more decisively, in the evolution of Descartes's argument for the existence of the external world from Meditation VI to *Principles* II, I. I deal with these applications in later sections of this chapter.

It is, therefore, of considerable importance that we get clear at the outset about the nature and variety of Descartes's causal principles. In the main, following Radner,[2] my interpretation sees Cartesian causal principles coming in three forms of increasing strength: the at-least-as-much principle, the preexistence principle, and the communication principle.

The first principle appears in Meditation III:

> Now it is manifest by the natural light that there must be at least as much <reality> in the efficient and total cause as in the effect of that cause. (AT VII, 40; CSM II, 28)

Just before giving this principle Descartes introduces a hierarchy in levels of reality: at the highest level is infinite substance, then there is finite substance; finally there are modes of substances. The effect of combining the at-least-as-much principle with the three-level hierarchy yields a rather weak causal theory — sufficient, as we will see later, for playing a role in the proof of God's existence in Meditation III, but not sufficient, as we are about to see, for the purpose of giving a general theory of cause and effect.

The third principle appears in the sentences following the one just quoted:

> For where, I ask, could the effect get its reality from, if not from the cause? And how could the cause give it to the effect unless it possessed it? (AT VII, 40; CSM II, 28)

Radner supposes that the "giving" [*dare*] is a form of communication or "transference" of properties from cause to effect. She takes these sentences to demonstrate that the communication principle is the basic principle from which the at-least-as-much principle is derived. The remaining principle appears in the Second Replies:

> The fact that 'there is nothing in the effect which was not previously present in the cause, either in a similar or higher form' is a primary notion which is as clear as any we have. (AT VII, 135: CSM II, 97)

Like the communication principle, the preexistence principle requires that the same properties be present in the cause as in the effect although the reference to "communication" is absent.

Although some commentators have defended the minimal (at-least-as-much) principle as the only one of the three to be clearly endorsed by Descartes,[3] it seems plain that more than this minimal principle will be needed if Descartes is to explain how qualitatively different effects can occur from causes lying *within* one any of the three levels of reality. Consider this example provided by Descartes in the First Replies:

> Thus if someone possesses in his intellect the idea of a machine of a highly intricate design, it is perfectly fair to ask what is the cause of this idea. . . . For in order for the idea of the machine to contain such and such objective intricacy, it must derive it from some cause. . . . But notice that all the intricacy which is to be found merely objectively in the idea must be necessarily found, either formally or eminently, in its cause. (AT VII, 104; CSM II, 75–76)

The logical form of the last sentence is that of a universal quantification over details of intricacy such that the same details present objectively in the idea are present formally or eminently in the cause. It appears, therefore, that Descartes is giving expression here to a causal principle at least as strong as the preexistence version. Moreover, nothing like the at-least-as-much principle can account for qualitatively different effects, such as having an idea of this particular machine versus an idea of that particular machine—something Descartes clearly must provide for—when the causes of each lie within the same level of reality. However either of the other two principles—which I shall call collectively the *qualitative principles*—will account for same-level, differential effects. I shall therefore take it that Descartes accepts a causal principle at least as strong as the preexistence principle.

But if the case for seeing a Cartesian commitment to qualitative causal principles is this straightforward, why have commentators been reluctant to accept it? There seem to be two notable reasons. (1) The qualitative principles imply that there must be a likeness between cause and effect, something that has long been taken to cause trouble for Descartes's thesis of the real distinction between mind and body.[4] An especially puzzling version of this problem concerns the application of the qualitative principles to the cause of the objective reality of ideas. (2) The qualification in the last sentence of the quotation, that the cause must contain the effect formally *or eminently*, is regarded by some commentators as allowing that a different property may be present in the cause than in the effect, something apparently not allowed by either of the qualitative principles.[5] I will argue in section 3.2 that the resolution of the first difficulty can be afforded by showing that the qualitative causal principles for the objective reality of our ideas can be derived from the rule of truth. This is the fundamentality thesis, to which I now turn. I take up the second difficulty in Appendix A.

3.2 Descartes's Causal Principles and the Rule of Truth

The Fundamentality Thesis

Descartes does not himself establish a connection between the rule of truth and the qualitative causal principle concerned with the objective reality of ideas but I believe that one nevertheless exists. The connection takes the form of an equivalence between the qualitative version of the causal principle applied to the objective reality of ideas and the rule of truth, final version (RTF), which I reproduce here for convenience.

(RTF) If I have a clear and distinct idea i of a set of content properties ϕ_1 ... ϕ_n determining the sense of a singular term t for an individual object, then there is a substance s and there is a set of real properties $P_1 \ldots P_n$ corresponding to the set of content properties $\phi_1 \ldots \phi_n$ such that $\phi_1 \ldots \phi_n$ are contained formally or eminently in s and $P_1 \ldots P_n$ are the objects of i.

My argument for the equivalence is influenced by the thesis that inference and explanation can be symmetrical.[6] This is not to say that every inference serves as an explanation nor that every explanation serves as an inference[7] but it is to say that in some cases they do. For example, if we begin with the knowledge that someone has carried out action A then we can *explain* why he or she does so by citing a law-like principle P connecting action A with cognitive state S. If, on the other hand, we begin with knowledge of the cognitive state S then we can use the same principle P to *infer* what action will occur. When P is used in an inferential role it serves as a rule of truth, when used in an explanatory role it serves as a causal principle. It would not, of course, be surprising that a causal principle can be used both to explain why something (which is known to have occurred) did occur and to infer that something (which is not known to have occurred) will occur. It would, however, be surprising if a rule of truth formulated in purely ontological terms should turn out to be a causal principle as well. Yet I believe that this is the case. In its original form the rule of truth is a principle of inference, reformulated as one of the qualitative causal principles (the communication principle or the preexistence principle) it serves as a principle in Descartes's explanation of the objective reality of ideas.

This account depends on the acceptability of the thesis that the communication principle (or the preexistence principle) is the basic form of the causal principle that Descartes employs in Meditation III[8] and that the weaker, quantitative version is derived from the stronger. At the end of the previous section, we encountered the objection to this interpretation that it saddles Descartes with an inconsistency between his commitment to the real distinction between mind and body and his commitment to applying the causal principle, construed in its strong form, to the objective reality of ideas. There are two responses that I propose to this objection. (1) This objection can be met on exegetical grounds by showing that specific employments of the various causal principles in specific texts do not commit Descartes to any consequences inconsistent with his brand of dualism. (2) This objection can be set aside on systematic grounds by showing that the strong form of the causal principle applied to the objective reality of ideas is equivalent to the rule of truth, for then we will have shown that this principle is compatible with every other legitimate Cartesian doctrine, including that of the real distinction between the mind and the body, since each of the latter is derived by means of the rule of truth. I shall attempt both responses, beginning with the second.

The second response consists in showing that there is a natural reformulation of the rule of truth that renders it equivalent to the communication principle. This task assumes the success of the formal-epistemic interpretation of the Cartesian notion of objective reality defended in section 2.7. On that interpretation the objective reality of an idea is the form of an act of cognizing a property (the latter is a real thing [a *res*] formally or eminently contained in a substance), and the form exhibits a certain characteristic content that can be used to infer the existence of the property. The conditional statement expressing this inference then affords the basis for an explanation: a clear and distinct idea has the content it does because there is a set of properties corresponding to the content properties formally or eminently contained in an actual substance and the idea takes the set of properties as its object.

An analogy with attributions of visual appearances may help. Various theories about the logical form of appearance attributions have been proposed, but suppose, for the sake of the analogy, that we that we attribute appearances by employing sentences of the form *x appears y to z*. Moreover, suppose that we treat *y* as the content of the appearance. In this case the content has the logical status of being a second-order property of the relation of appearing holding between *x* and *z*. For this reason the content counts as a kind of form in the Cartesian sense. One explanation for the appearance having content *y* is that the object of the attribution *x* actually is *y*. Suppose that we interpret this in the following way: if an apple looks red to me then the content of the appearance is *redness*, and one reason that the *appearance* possesses this form is that the *object* of the appearance, the apple, possess the first-order version of the same property, *redness*. In this case we can say that things appear as they do because the reality of the content simply reflects ("transmits") the reality of the object. This, I suggest, corresponds to the case in Cartesian theory where the content property of an idea is formally contained in the substance that grounds that property and where the reality of the content property is causally explained as a reflection ("transmission") of the reality of the object property.

Alternatively, the content of an appearance may not reflect the same reality as the object of the appearance, although it will reflect some, presumably structural, aspects of the reality of the object. This corresponds to the case in Cartesian theory where the content property of a perception is eminently contained in its grounding substance. Although there is not, in these cases, a clear transmission of the reality of the object property to the content property, there is a reflection of some structural aspect of the object in the content sufficient, I think, to sustain a causal explanation of the content of the idea by means of its object.

The rule of truth is not officially employed as part of a causal explanation of content properties by object properties but it does provide the material for such an explanation. All that is needed for the explanatory formulation to emerge is that we extract some of the implications of the notions of formal and eminent containment from the rule of truth and rearrange some of its elements. Let me propose the following. (I shall call this principle the *general qualitative causal principle*.)

The General Qualitative Causal Principle (GQCP)

My having a clear and distinct idea *i* of content properties $\emptyset_1 \ldots \emptyset_n$ comprising the individual sense of (a singular term) *t* is causally explained by there being a substance *s* and there being a set of real properties $P_1 \ldots P_n$ corresponding to $\emptyset_1 \ldots \emptyset_n$ such that $\emptyset_1 \ldots \emptyset_n$ are contained formally or eminently in *s* and $P_1 \ldots P_n$ are the objects of *i*.

Rearranged in this way the rule of truth is a general formulation of the qualitative causal principle for the objective reality of ideas. To qualify as such, a principle must minimally satisfy two conditions: (1) it must explain why an idea has one specific content property rather than another, and (2) in doing so it must quantify over the same variable in both the clause ascribing content properties to an idea and the clause ascribing a cause to the content properties of the idea. The GQCP meets both of these conditions. The conditions can be strengthened by adding a third: (3) the content property and the property causally responsible for the content property must be the same entity. In the case where the mode of containment is formal rather than eminent we can infer from the GQCP and the formal containment principle that this strengthened condition is met. This yields a form of the preexistence principle. Adding a fourth condition, (4) the cause property must communicate its form to the effect property, yields the communication principle, which is the principle in its strongest form. It is, therefore, possible to propose that the rule of truth, suitably restructured, provides the content of the strongest and most fundamental of Descartes's causal principles relating to the objective reality of our ideas.

Saying that the rule of truth meets the requirements of a qualitative causal explanation of the content of our ideas (the fundamentality thesis) is not the same as saying that Descartes explicitly recognized the thesis. Nevertheless, I claim that he is *committed* to this thesis because, once the objective reality of ideas is treated as a form of acts of thinking, there does not seem to be any way for Descartes to explain types of *forms* of thoughts except by reference to types of *objects* of thought consistent with his view that the thoughts themselves "considered simply <as> modes of thought" have "no recognizable inequality among them: they all appear to come from within me in the same fashion" (AT VII, 40; CSM II, 27–28).

A Corollary

The interpretation of the previous section has a corollary for the persistent worry that Descartes's commitment to the strongest of the causal principles, the communication principle, requires the transmission of material forms into the mind itself. This is a worry because it violates Descartes's doctrine of the real and absolute distinction between the mind and the body. However, on the present interpretation the "communication" occurs *within* the mental realm alone between the objects of our ideas and the form in which they are perceived.

But if this account can explain the *form* of our ideas, it clearly does not explain their *occurrence*. For that we need to consider a second application of the causal principle, this time to ideas taken in the material sense.

When Descartes applies the causal principle to ideas in the material sense, he is explaining why the idea occurred to a particular person at a particular time with its particular formal properties. Such causes are *external* to the ideas they produce. However, in the case of applying the causal principle to explain the particular objective reality of an idea it is the GQCP that governs, and the GQCP is a qualitative principle in which the cause of the objective reality of an idea is the object of the idea. The cause in this case is *internal* to the idea. There is, thus, an important distinction within the class of causal explanations of ideas between *external causes of the occurrence of ideas* and *internal causes of the objective reality of ideas.*

Internal causes, in this sense, are governed by the communication principle. Notice, however, that in the text from Meditation III where Descartes discusses applying the causal principle to ideas in the material sense he seems to deny that any communication of reality is taking place:

> But it is also true that the *idea* of heat, or of a stone, cannot exist in me unless it is put there by some cause which contains as least as much reality as I conceive to be in the heat or in the stone. For *although this cause does not transfer any of its actual*

or formal reality to my idea, it should not on that account be supposed to be any the less real. (AT VII, 41; CSM II, 28; emphasis in last sentence is mine)

Here, the most that we can say is that the *degree* of reality of the cause is at least as great as that of the effect. If we now compare this passage with the following:

For where, I ask, could the effect get its reality from, if not from the cause? *And how could the cause give it to the effect unless it possessed it.* . . . And this is transparently true not only in the case of effects which possess <what the philosophers call> actual or formal reality, but also in the case of ideas, where one is considering only <what they call> objective reality. (AT VII, 40–41; CSM II, 28; my emphasis)

It does appear that here Descartes is countenancing some kind of communication of the reality of cause to effect. Notice, however, that this occurs in only two cases: (1) the general case of physical cause and physical effect and (2) the special case of the cause of the objective reality of our ideas. Missing from this set of cases is that of the material cause of the ideas taken simply as mental occurrences. For these latter cases only a quantitative causal principle seems to be countenanced by Descartes. In that special case Descartes treats causality as occurring in its weakest form, a form that does not require the communication of anything. This helps to remove any remaining source of worry that the present interpretation of Descartes's theory of the causes of our ideas violates Descartes's doctrine of the real distinction between the mind and the body.

I now turn to a test of the fundamentality thesis. The test consists of seeing whether the attribution of this thesis to Descartes can shed light on some of the obscurities of the main causal argument for the existence of God in Meditation III.

3.3 The Fundamentality Thesis and the Main Causal Argument for the Existence of God in Meditation III

The Argument

Of several causal arguments for the existence of God in the *Meditations* III the main one traces a circuitous route, beginning in the paragraph where Descartes takes up a new method of investigating "whether some of the things of which I possess ideas exist outside me" (AT VII 40; CSM II, 27) coming to a temporary halt with the words "So from what has been said it must be concluded that God necessarily exists" (AT VII, 45: CSM II, 31), continuing into a second phase concluded by the sentence "And finally, I perceive that the objective being of an idea cannot be produced merely by potential being, which strictly speaking is nothing, but only by actual or formal being" (AT VII, 47; CSM II, 32). There is more that follows, but our attention will be focused on the fifteen paragraphs comprising the main argument.

The first three paragraphs introduce three essential elements of the proof. In the first paragraph Descartes asserts the *hierarchy principle*: that ideas of finite substances "contain within themselves more objective reality than the ideas which represent modes or accidents" and that the idea of God ("eternal, infinite, <immu-

table>, omniscient, omnipotent and the creator of all things that exist apart from him") has more objective reality than the idea of finite substances (AT VII, 40; CSM II, 28). In the second paragraph Descartes introduces several variants of his causal principle including this one: "[I]n order for a given idea to contain such and such objective reality, it must surely derive it from some cause which contains at least as much formal reality as there is objective reality in the idea" (AT VII, 41; CSM II, 28). This is a quantitative version of the causal principle applied to objective realities.

Taken in conjunction with the hierarchy principle, this principle would permit Descartes to conclude that God exists. The argument goes as follows. The objective reality of our idea of God has the content of a being at the highest level of reality (the hierarchy principle), hence there is a being existing at this or a higher level (the minimal at-least-as-much causal principle), but there is no level higher than the highest level, so a being identical with God exists. I shall call this the *levels argument*. There is however, an important reason for thinking that Descartes does not employ the levels argument as the primary causal proof for the existence of God: all of its premises are in place by the end of paragraph 2 and yet there are seven more paragraphs of reasoning before Descartes actually asserts the existence of God. This must come as a considerable puzzle if we see the levels argument as comprising the main causal argument that Descartes offers for God's existence. The solution that I propose to this puzzle is that the main causal argument for God's existence is not the levels argument, relying as it does on a quantitative version of the causal principle, but is, rather, an argument which I shall call the *archetype argument*,[9] an argument relying on the communication principle, the strongest and most fundamental of the causal principles.

The archetype argument gets its clearest statement in paragraph 3:

> And although the reality which I am considering in my ideas is merely objective reality, I must not on that account suppose that the same reality need not exist formally in the causes of my ideas, but that it is enough for it to be present in them objectively. . . . And although one idea may perhaps originate from another, there cannot be an infinite regress here; eventually one must reach a primary idea, the cause of which will be like an archetype which contains formally <and in fact> all the reality <or perfection> which is present only objectively <or representatively> in the idea. (AT VII, 42; CSM II, 29)

The archetype argument also depends on a version of the causal principle for objective realities but the reason for taking the principle to be *qualitative rather than quantitative* is that the function of the expression "the same reality" seems to be anaphoric,[10] thus suggesting that specific content properties are to be reflected in specific causes. The conclusion of the argument is that there must be a class of "primary ideas," the content of which is reflected formally in its cause. I note that the main causal premise as formulated in paragraph 3 differs from the GQCP in that the disjunction between eminent and formal containment is missing. However, when Descartes formulates the causal principle in *Principles* I, 17, he says:

> All the intricacy which is contained in the idea merely objectively—as in a picture—must be contained in its cause, whatever kind of cause it turns out to be; and it must be contained not merely representatively, but in actual reality, *either formally or*

eminently, at least in the case of the first and principle cause. (AT VIIIA, 11; CSM I, 198–199, my emphasis)

In this passage Descartes includes reference to the possibility of eminent containment. Moreover, the reference to "first and principle cause" suggests that he is concerned here with causes of primary ideas, as with the archetype argument of Meditation III. I will take it, therefore, that the formulation of the causal principle in the *Principles* is the most perspicuous and represents the formulation that Descartes intends to be operative in the archetype argument.

Descartes does not move directly from the statement of the causal premise of the archetype argument to its ultimate theological conclusion but engages in an investigation of various candidates of things "other than myself" whose formal existence might be proved by the archetype argument.

This is as we should expect. Descartes employs two methods in Meditation III, one of which investigates whether ideas taken in abstraction from their representational properties necessarily "resemble" their causes, the other of which investigates "whether some of the things of which I possess ideas exist outside me," a general way of stating the central question of Cartesian epistemology. The first investigation was carried out from AT VII 38–40 (CSM II, 26–27) and a generally negative answer resulted. Considerations of symmetry and completeness suggest that Descartes will eventually provide some kind of general answer to the question posed for the second method of investigation. This investigation will need to rely on qualitative principles and the only passages in Meditation III in which such principles seem to be employed in a relevant manner are those comprising the archetype argument.

There seem to be four main possibilities investigated. (1) In paragraphs 5 to 6, Descartes considers various kinds of ideas which he possesses to determine if "they could be put together from the ideas I have of myself, of corporeal things and of God," concluding that they could (AT VII, 43; CSM II, 29). In paragraphs 7 to 9, Descartes considers the other possibilities. (2) He considers whether sensory ideas, "ideas of light, colours, sounds" might have originated from within myself, concluding that they could (AT VII, 44; CSM II, 30). (3) Regarding clear and distinct ideas of corporeal things he asserts that "I could have borrowed some of these from my idea of myself, namely substance, duration, number and anything else of this kind" (AT VII 44; CSM II 30). (4) It is only in paragraph 10 that Descartes finally turns to an application of (what we may presume to be still) the archetype argument to the idea of God.

If my conjecture is right we should find in arguments 1 to 4 above an attempt to eliminate the possibility that either the formal or the eminent containment of the relevant content property occurs in ourselves. At least this is what we expect from his statement of the objectives of the archetype argument in paragraph 4:

> But what is my conclusion to be? If the objective reality of any of my ideas turns out to be so great that I am sure the same reality does not reside in me, either formally or eminently, and hence that I myself cannot be its cause, it will necessarily follow that I am not alone in the world, but that some other thing which is the cause of this idea also exists. But if no such idea is to be found in me, I shall have no argument to

convince me of the existence of anything apart from myself. For despite a most careful and comprehensive survey, this is the only argument I have so far been able to find. (AT VII, 42; CSM II, 29)

We find an application of this method in argument 3 where Descartes considers the possibility that geometrical content properties are contained within himself eminently[11] but finds that he cannot eliminate this possibility. In arguments 1 and 2 Descartes does not use the concept of the eminent containment of properties and speaks only of the possibility that certain ideas "originate in myself." He also finds that this possibility cannot be eliminated. In argument 4 Descartes gives his proof for God's existence:

By the word 'God' I understand a substance that is infinite, <eternal, immutable>, independent, supremely intelligent, supremely powerful, and which created both myself and everything else (if anything else there be) that exists. All these attributes are such that [*are so great and so eminent that*] the more carefully I concentrate on them, the less possible it seems that they [*the idea I have of them*] could have originated from me alone. So from what has been said it must be concluded that God necessarily exists. (AT VII, 45; CSM II, 31; the bracketed phrases are my interpolations from the French text: AT IX, 36; Alquié II, 445)

This proof seems to achieve the objective of the archetype argument, showing that there must be *something* existing apart from myself, but it also concludes more than this: it concludes that the something has the properties of God. To justify this stronger conclusion Descartes must show that the cause of the idea of God contains the properties of God—which I shall call collectively *infinite-beinghood*—formally rather than eminently. For it is only with the formal containment of properties that we can infer the existence of the thing containing those properties.[12] To achieve its purpose of proving the existence of something outside of our minds with a nature at least partly specifiable in terms of the content of our ideas, the archetype argument must, therefore, employ a minor, elimination premise in addition to the major, causal premise. The argument as a whole may be formally represented as follows:

The Archetype Causal Proof for the Existence of God

1. I have a clear and distinct idea of a set of content properties $\phi_1 \ldots \phi_n$ determining the sense of the term "God." The set of content properties will henceforth be called *infinite-beinghood*. (Assumption)
2. My having a clear and distinct idea i of the set of content properties *infinite-beinghood* is causally explained by there being a substance s and there being a set of real properties $P_1 \ldots P_n$ corresponding to *infinite-beinghood* such that *infinite-beinghood* is contained formally or eminently in s and $P_1 \ldots P_n$ are the objects of i. (GQCP)
3. There is a substance s and there is a set of real properties $P_1 \ldots P_n$ corresponding to *infinite-beinghood* such that *infinite-beinghood* is contained formally or eminently in s. (GQCP, 1)
4. *Infinite-beinghood* is not contained eminently in s. (EP)

5. *Infinite-beinghood* is contained formally in s. (3, 4)
6. There is a set of real properties $P_1 \ldots P_n$ such that $P_1 \ldots P_n$ are identical with the corresponding properties in *infinite-beinghood* and s exemplifies $P_1 \ldots P_n$. (FC, 5)
7. The statement "God exists" is formally true. (DEF, 6)

The justification for the elimination premise follows from the definition of the notion of eminent containment[13] and the hierarchy principle. EC asserts that a content-property ø is contained eminently in a substance s only if there is a property P corresponding to ø such that P is contained in s and P is at a higher level of reality than ø. But in the case where ø is the property *infinite-beinghood*, the hierarchy principle asserts that a being possessing this property is at the highest possible level, hence there is no property P, hence the content property of infinite-beinghood cannot be contained eminently in s,[14] where s is any substance. QED.

Let us now replace premise 2 of the archetype argument with its underlying, equivalent principle, the rule of truth (final version), specified to the content of infinite-beinghood:

(RTF) If I have a clear and distinct idea i of a set of content properties $\emptyset_1 \ldots \emptyset_n$ determining the sense of a singular term t for an individual object, then there is a substance s and there is a set of real properties $P_1 \ldots P_n$ corresponding to the set of content properties $\emptyset_1 \ldots \emptyset_n$ such that $\emptyset_1 \ldots \emptyset_n$ are contained formally or eminently in s and $P_1 \ldots P_n$ are the objects of i.

By doing so we get an instance of Descartes's general pattern of necessary existential reasoning, which I reproduce here for convenience:

The General Pattern of Necessary Existential Reasoning

1. Assume that t is a constant term or definite description and that there is a set of content properties $\emptyset_1 \ldots \emptyset_n$ determining the sense of t.
2. Assume that I have a clear and distinct idea of $\emptyset_1 \ldots \emptyset_n$.

Then we can reason as follows:

3. There is a substance s such that $\emptyset_1 \ldots \emptyset_n$ are contained formally or eminently in s. (RTF, 1,2)
[4. If the content properties $\emptyset_1 \ldots \emptyset_n$ are contained eminently in s then they are not identical with the corresponding real properties. (EC, 2)]
5. If the content properties $\emptyset_1 \ldots \emptyset_n$ are contained formally in s there is a set of real properties $P_1 \ldots P_n$ such that $P_1 \ldots P_n$ are identical with the corresponding content properties and s exemplifies $P_1 \ldots P_n$. (FC, 2)
6. Necessarily $\emptyset_1 \ldots \emptyset_n$ are not contained eminently in s. (EP)
7. Necessarily, $\emptyset_1 \ldots \emptyset_n$ are contained formally in s. (3, 6)
8. There is a set of real properties $P_1 \ldots P_n$ such that $P_1 \ldots P_n$ are necessarily identical with the corresponding content properties and s exemplifies $P_1 \ldots P_n$. (5, 7)
9. A sentence, "t necessarily exists," is formally true. (DEF, 8)

I take this result to show that we can consistently interpret Descartes's main causal proof of the existence of God in light of the fundamentality thesis. The next question is whether Descartes gives any recognition of a commitment to this thesis. There is some indirect evidence that he does.

Ontological Doctrine in Causal Clothing

Notice that when Descartes speaks of the idea of God in the passage quoted earlier from paragraph 10 (AT VII, 45; CSM II, 31) he gives a *causal characterization* to the status of this idea, but when he speaks of the idea of God as a "true idea" (an idea of a real entity) (AT VII, 46; CSM II, 31–32) he gives an *intentional characterization* of the idea by means of specifying the ontological status of the object of the idea.

The official taxonomy of kinds of ideas introduced earlier in Meditation III (AT VII, 37–38; CSM II, 26) divides ideas into three classes: those that "derive from my own nature" (*innate ideas*); those that "come from things located outside me" (*adventitious ideas*); and those that are "my own invention" (*invented ideas*). This is evidently a causal system of classification, but it introduces the following difficulty in understanding Descartes's account of the idea of God. Descartes certainly regards this idea as an innate idea, hence, by the official taxonomic description, as one derived from my own nature. And yet Descartes seems to deny this outright in his proof of God's existence in paragraph 10. The relevant sentences are these:

> [T]he more carefully I concentrate on them, the *less possible it seems that they* [the idea I have of them] *could have originated from me alone.* So from what has been said it must be concluded that God necessarily exists. (AT VII, 45; CSM II, 31; my emphasis; my interpolation)

If the objective reality of the idea of God could not have originated from me alone, does this mean that the idea of God is partly innate and partly adventitious? Presumably not. But where, then, does the idea of God fit in the official taxonomy? It must still fall within the category of innate ideas—that much is certain—but with the category described not in terms of the origin of the idea but in terms of an ontological characterization of its objects introduced in a letter to Mersenne of 1641:

> I use the word 'idea' to mean everything which can be in our thought, and I distinguish three kinds. Some are adventitious, such as the idea we commonly have *of the sun*; others are constructed or factitious, in which class we can put the idea which the astronomers construct of the sun by their reasoning; and others are innate, such as the idea of God, mind, body, triangle, and *in general all those which represent true immutable and eternal essences.* (AT III, 382; *Letters*, 104; emphasis at end is mine)

Notice that only constructed ideas are given an essentially causal definition; the others are described in terms of the ontological category of their objects, not their causes. Regarding the text from Meditation III, it appears that Descartes has shifted from the causal description of innateness present in the passage quoted from paragraph 10 to the ontological description present in the following passage from paragraph 13:

Nor can it be said that this idea of God is perhaps materially false and so could have come from nothing. . . . On the contrary, it is utterly clear and distinct, and contains in itself more objective reality than any other idea. . . . This idea of a supremely perfect and infinite being is, I say, true in the highest degree; for although perhaps one can imagine that such a being does not exist, it cannot be supposed that the idea of such a being represents something unreal, as I said with regard to the idea of cold. (AT VII, 46; CSM II, 31)

What the phrase "could have come from nothing" means in this passage is that the idea of God could fail to have a positive content (objective reality), namely, could "represent something unreal." Descartes is saying in this passage that this is not possible, that the idea of God must represent something real. The something real is not the actual existence of God but, as the passage quoted previously from the letter to Mersenne of 1641 indicates, it is the immutable essence of God, the property of *infinite-beinghood*. This doctrine is an ontological doctrine expressed in causal terminology ("could have come from nothing"). The operative category for the idea of God is still that of innate ideas, but the latter is now understood ontologically rather than in the straightforward causal sense of ideas that have originated within me.

With the idea of God now classified by the ontological category of its object, Descartes reorients what heretofore looks like a purely causal argument for God's existence in the direction of an argument that employs a major premise that even looks like the rule of truth (see emphasized lines in the passage quoted below) and, as such, exemplifies the general pattern of existential reasoning. This reorientated argument occurs in paragraph 13:

It does not matter that I do not grasp the infinite, or that there are countless additional attributes of God which I cannot in any way grasp, and perhaps cannot even reach in my thought; for it is in the nature of the infinite not to be grasped by a finite being like myself. It is enough that I understand the infinite, and that I judge that *all the attributes which I clearly perceive and know to imply some perfection — and perhaps countless others of which I am ignorant — are present in God either formally or eminently*. (AT VII 46; CSM II, 32; my emphasis)

Notice that the emphasized passage is a statement of the major premise, the rule of truth, of Descartes's general pattern of existential reasoning. Descartes makes an easy and unacknowledged transition between this pattern of reasoning and the archetype argument — a pattern of reasoning employing the general qualitative causal principle (GQCP) — a fact that lends support to the idea that both the rule of truth and the GQCP were regarded by Descartes as equivalent.

3.4 The Relation between the Causal Argument and the Ontological Argument

The ontological argument is given officially in Meditation V. There is also an extensive discussion of the ontological argument in the First Replies. There Descartes distinguishes between the two ways of proving God's existence, by means of his effects and by means of his essence (AT VII 120; CSM II, 85). My thesis in this section will be that both the causal and the ontological proofs are derived from the same underlying proof structure and that important elements of one method are established by Descartes only in the context of the other method. (This is not to say that they are exactly the same in all respects—that would be to fly in the face of an explicit assertion to the contrary.) The role of eminent containment in the ontological proof is vouchsafed in the letter to Mersenne of March 1642 (AT III, 502; *Letters*, 132) but the only place where Descartes gives a detailed discussion of the role of this concept in the proof of God's existence is in the archetype argument of Meditation III.

In the same portion of the First Replies where Descartes distinguishes the two proof methods, he also considers St. Thomas Aquinas's proof for God's existence from the premise that the word "God" is to be defined as "that than which nothing greater can be conceived." Descartes objects to this definition on the grounds that "because a word conveys something, that thing is not therefore shown to be true" (AT VII 115; CSM II, 83). He might also have objected on the grounds that this definition implies that there is no being greater than the greatest being we can conceive, an implication that makes our powers of conception equal to the nature of God. This Descartes clearly means to deny.[15] What Descartes does assert is that

existence belongs to the concept of a supremely perfect being just as much as three sides belong to the concept of a triangle; and this point can be understood without adequate knowledge of God. (AT VII 114; CSM II, 82)

He does not, however, think that the concept of necessary existence is simply one element in a complex idea that we have constructed:

So we shall come to understand that necessary existence is contained in the idea of a supremely powerful being, not by any fiction of the intellect, but because it belongs to the true and immutable nature of such a being that it exists. (AT VII, 119; CSM II, 85)

A demonstration that necessary existence belongs to the true and immutable nature of God (an ontological proof of God's necessary existence) will be an a priori proof beginning with the assumption that we possess a clear and distinct idea of God and employing a version of the rule of truth to reach the conclusion that God necessarily exists.[16] The only general pattern of proof capable of meeting these conditions is the general pattern of necessary existential reasoning. Applied to the clear and distinct idea of God the proof looks like this:

An Ontological Proof of God's Necessary Existence

1. I have a clear and distinct idea (of God) with the objective reality of *infinite-beinghood*.
2. There is a substance s such that *infinite-beinghood* is a set of content properties contained formally or eminently in s. (RTF, 1)
[3. If the content properties $\phi_1 \ldots \phi_n$ are contained eminently in s then they are not identical with the corresponding real properties. (EC)]

4. If *infinite-beinghood* is contained formally in *s* then there is a set of real properties $P_1 \ldots P_n$ such that $P_1 \ldots P_n$ are identical with *infinite-beinghood* and *s* exemplifies $P_1 \ldots P_n$. (FC)
5. Necessarily, *infinite-beinghood is* not contained eminently in *s*. (EP)
6. Necessarily, *infinite-beinghood* is contained formally in *s*. (2, 5)
7. There is a set of real properties $P_1 \ldots P_n$ such that $P_1 \ldots P_n$ are necessarily identical with *infinite-beinghood* and *s* exemplifies $P_1 \ldots P_n$. (4, 6)
8. The sentence "Necessarily, God exists" is formally true. (DEF, 7)

This proof is identical with the archetype causal argument save for the replacement there of the rule of truth (premise 2) with its causal equivalent, the GQCP. And so, although the point appears not to be always recognized by Descartes, the two methods for proving God's existence in the *Meditations* are driven by the same underlying theory of existential inference. Both rest on alternative formulations of the same major premise, the rule of truth, and both embody the same general pattern of reasoning.

I now consider whether the second major existential proof of the *Meditations*, that of the existence of the material world, can also be seen as conforming to this pattern.

3.5 The Causal Principle and the Proof of the External World in Meditation VI

An Overview

There is some independent textual evidence that Descartes sees one fundamental pattern of reasoning underlying all of our knowledge of existence. It comes in a portion of the Second Replies:

> Axiom IV. Whatever reality or perfection there is in a thing is present either formally or eminently in its first and adequate cause.

> Axiom V. It follows from this that the objective reality of our ideas needs a cause which contains this reality not merely objectively but formally or eminently. *It should be noted that this axiom is one which we must necessarily accept, since on it depends our knowledge of all things, whether they are perceivable by the senses or not.* How do we know, for example, that the sky exists? Because we see it? But this "seeing" does not affect the mind except insofar as it is an idea—I mean an idea which resides in the mind itself, not an image depicted in the corporeal imagination. Now the only reason why we can use this idea as a basis for the judgement that the sky exists is that every idea must have a really existing cause of its objective reality; and in this case we judge that the cause is the sky itself. And we make similar judgements in other cases. (AT VII, 165; CSM II, 116–117; my emphasis)

In this passage Descartes seems to be claiming that the explanatory account of the qualitatively specific content of our ideas is to be governed by a causal principle requiring that the same item that exists objectively in the idea also exist formally or eminently in the cause. This is not the minimal at-least-as-much principle mentioned in the official causal proof of God's existence in Meditation III but is, rather, the preexistence principle, and its scope extends quite generally to all ideas with objective realities, even ideas of ordinary objects arising from the senses, in this case, the sky.

But does the principle not extend too generally? Descartes can surely not mean that we know the sky exists based solely on the premises that we have an idea of the sky and that we have the causal principle of Axiom V. To render this suggestion consistent with the Cartesian epistemological programme, we need to interpret this passage in the same way we interpreted the "two suns" passage from the First Replies;[17] we need to look through the apparent subject matter of this idea, the sky, to the properties comprising its individual concept, and treat those as the objects to which the causal principle applies. Since the only content properties that Descartes will accept are geometrical properties—he means to exclude properties of light, color, heat, and so on,—when the causal principle is applied to ideas of ordinary objects perceived through the senses, it should be interpreted as applying only to geometrical content properties. But even thus restricted the causal principle might seem too broad in its application, since the properties that comprise the individual concept of the sun are *specific* properties and we may presume that Descartes does not think that the causal principle allows us to infer the formal existence of those properties simply from the premise that we have those ideas and from the causal principle of Axiom V. However, with respect to *general* geometrical properties, for example, extension in general, we might well expect to prove the formal reality of this property by means of the causal principle. Indeed, the next item on Descartes's philosophical agenda is the proof of the external world.

The proof of the external world certainly relies on causal concepts. Notice, however, that the causal concepts mentioned Axiom V apply to the objective reality of our ideas specifically, and it is only the archetype and levels arguments that employ this conception of causality. Descartes does not, however, show us how to use the causal principle to prove the existence of any being other than God. This is unfortunate, because Descartes's official discussion of the proof in Meditation VI leaves it especially unclear how that proof can be satisfactorily construed on the pattern of either of these arguments.

Descartes sets the context for this proof in Meditation VI by drawing a distinction between an active faculty and a passive faculty of sense experience (AT VII, 79: CSM II, 55). The former is the intellect and has already been described by Descartes as a self-subsisting substance with which he "as a whole" could be identified; the latter is "a faculty for receiving and recognizing the ideas of sensible objects." The essential distinguishing characteristic of passivity is then used to argue that the causes of these ideas cannot be in the purely "intellectual me" since, if they were I would have control over them but, as it happens, "the ideas in question are produced without my cooperation and even against my will." The whole passage reads as follows (passage A):

> Now there is in me a passive faculty of sensory perception, that is, a faculty for receiving and recognizing the ideas of sensible objects; but I could not make use of it unless there was also an active faculty, either in me or in something else, which produced or brought about these ideas. (AT V II, 79: CSM II 55)

Descartes goes on to say (passage B):

> So the only alternative is that it is in another substance distinct from me—*a substance which contains either formally or eminently all the reality which exists objectively in the ideas produced by this faculty.* . . . This substance is either a body, that is, a corporeal nature, in which case it will contain formally <and in fact> everything which is to be found objectively <or representatively> in the ideas; or else it will be God, or some creature more noble than a body, in which case it will contain eminently whatever is to be found in the ideas. (AT VII, 79; CSM II 55; my emphasis)

The italicized portion of passage B suggests that the causal principle applied to the objective realities of ideas will in fact be operative in this proof. Passage A taken together with B suggests that ideas of sensible objects possess objective realities and that the latter will figure in the proof as the effects from which Descartes will reason to the existence of the material world as the cause. However, to accomplish this Descartes goes on to mention the possibility that the causes of my ideas (of sensible objects) contain their objective reality only "eminently," observing that this possibility must be eliminated if I am not to be deceived in my belief in the existence of the material world (passage C):

> But since God is not a deceiver, it is quite clear that he does not transmit the ideas to me either directly from himself, or indirectly, via some creature which contains the objective reality of the ideas not formally but only eminently. (AT VII, 79; CSM II, 55)

The elimination is effected by a draft on God's benevolence (passage D):

> For God has given me no faculty at all for recognizing any such source for these ideas; on the contrary, he has given me a great propensity to believe that they are produced by corporeal things. So I do not see how God could be understood to be anything but a deceiver if the ideas were transmitted from a source other than corporeal things. It follows that corporeal things exist. (AT VII, 79–80; CSM II, 55)

The pattern of reasoning present in passages B and C is apparently similar to that which we found operating in the main causal argument for God's existence in Meditation III. But just as we wondered whether the causal principle should be taken in its quantitative or in its qualitative form there, so we wonder how the principle should be taken here. Corresponding to our choice of principles there is a choice of arguments: if we take the quantitative principle we get a version of the levels argument; if we take the qualitative principle we get a version of the archetype argument.

First I consider what the proof of the external world looks like on a quantitative/levels reading due to Gueroult[18] and argue that it faces serious difficulties. Next I consider a qualitative reading modeled on our reconstruction of the archetype proof of the existence of God developed earlier in this chapter and argue that it too faces difficulties. Since these are the only two ways in which a causal argument for the external world can be constructed from the set of causal principles that Descartes has available, I conclude that proof of the external world in Meditation VI possesses serious defects. I then suggest that these defects are traceable to fundamental deficiencies in Descartes's account of the role of imagination in the exhibition of corporeal properties, a role that is unduly restrictive. Finally, I suggest that Descartes seems to assign a less restrictive role to the imagination in the *Principles* I, 71, arguing that he there countenances in addition to the intellectual intuition of corporeal properties a special form of concrete intuition. This new kind of intuition is ideally suited to remove the deficiencies with the proof of the external world in Meditation VI, had Descartes made use of it there. In the final stage of my discussion I show that the structure of the proof of the external world in *Principles* II, 1 (and the difference between that proof and the proof in Meditation VI) is nicely accounted for if we assume that Descartes had the notion of the concrete intuition of corporeal properties implicitly in mind when he developed it.

The Quantitative Reading Due to Gueroult

Gueroult offers an eight-step reconstruction of the argument of which elements five and six are of primary importance to our case.[19]

> The fifth element is constituted by the recall of the principle of causality defined according to the formula of *Meditation III*: there is necessarily a quantity of formal reality in the cause that is at least equal to the quantity of objective reality in the idea. We therefore reach a second conclusion: this activity foreign to myself must either be *God* or a *substance nobler than body*, in which case it is an eminent cause, or it must be *body itself*, in which case it is a formal cause.
>
> The sixth element is constituted by the appeal to *nature*, meaning to the presence in us of an instinctive and irresistible inclination to believe that the cause is body. If this inclination is veracious, body exists; and that will be the third and final conclusion.[20]

It is clear from his description of the fifth element that Gueroult interprets the causal principle quantitatively. He does so apparently because he takes the main causal argument of Meditation III to be a version of the levels argument. I, of course, disagree with this, but the suggestion that it is a levels argument rather than some other form of the causal principle that is operative here in the proof of the external world should be assessed on its own merits. Gueroult's reconstruction of Descartes's argument assumes that the degree of objective reality of our idea of God is at a maximum in the ontological hierarchy. "In the present case, on the other hand," he argues, "the objective reality of the idea is at a *minimum*, since it is normal for sensible ideas to be at the extremes of being and nothingness, with respect to their representative content."[21]

Combining the claim that sensory ideas have a degree of objective reality at or close to the minimum with a quantitative version of the causal principle leads Gueroult to conclude that the cause of sensory ideas can be virtually anything:

> [W]e are referred to the full multitude of possible causes between the *minimum* and the *maximum*, and we have no means of determining in this fashion which is the real cause. . . . [T]he soul can be conceived as one of these possible eminent causes.[22]

The chief and, I think, fatal difficulty with this reading is not so much that it relies on a quantitative version of the causal principle but that it sees that principle as doing almost no work in the proof. We know from the outset of this argument that the cause of an idea of an object, or of anything else, must be either a mental, physical, or divine substance or a mode thereof. Unlike the case with the idea of God, where the infinite nature of its objective reality allowed even a quantitative reading of the causal principle to eliminate important alternatives, no such work is done by a quantitative causal principle in this proof.

Indeed *none* of the elements prior to 6 seem to play an essential role in the argument as construed here. All rests on the sixth element: we have a strong inclination to believe in the external world; God is not a deceiver, hence God sees to it that our belief inclination is true. But if this is how Descartes sees the proof why write passages A, B, and C? Why not simply begin and end the argument with passage D? Above all, why say in the Second Replies that all knowledge depends on the causal principle? The existence of this conundrum serves as a fatal objection to the quantitative reading of the causal principle in the proof of the external world in Meditation VI. I now turn to the alternative.

The Case for a Qualitative Reading

The conundrum just mentioned is an inevitable consequence of two interpretive assumptions: (1) the assumption that Descartes assigns to sensory ideas a degree of objective reality at or close to the minimum and (2) the assumption that the causal principle operative in the proof is quantitative. The only escape from it is to abandon one of the assumptions. There are three powerful reasons for abandoning at least the second.

The first is that in the most general statement of the role of the causal principle in existential proofs, that in the Second Replies, the formulation of that principle invites a quantificational reading characteristic of the preexistence principle, one of the qualitative principles.

The second is that in passage B of the Meditation VI proof Descartes describes the cause in the following way: either "it contains formally *everything* which is to be found objectively in the ideas," or else it "will contain eminently *whatever* is to be found in the ideas" (my emphasis), formulations suggesting an underlying quantificational structure characteristic of the qualitative principles.

Third, passages B and C suggest a proof that has important structural similarities with the archetype causal proof of the existence of God,[23] namely, passage B corresponds to premise 2, passage C corresponds to premise 4 (the elimination premise), and to line 8 corresponds the conclusion—*corporeal things exist*. The elimination premise in the present application is itself derived from passage D, the assertion that God is not a deceiver.

Since I have argued previously that Cartesian archetype causal proofs are simply variants of Cartesian general existential proofs, the hypothesis that the proof of the external world is fundamentally an archetype proof is equivalent to the hypothesis that the proof is an instance of the general pattern of existential reasoning.

Seeing the structure of Descartes's proof of the external world in this light is attractive, not only because it will allow us to avoid the exegetical conundrum presented by Gueroult's proposal but because it reveals a high degree of systematicity and generality to Cartesian epistemological method. There are, however, two very serious obstacles to our accepting this picture. These are the facts that (1) in passage A Descartes makes it clear that the ideas to which he intends to apply his theory of existential reasoning are ideas that derive from sense experience and that (2) elsewhere in the *Meditations* Descartes seems to say about such ideas that they do not represent anything real. This is the first of Gueroult's two assumptions collectively responsible for the conundrum we were hoping to escape. Our plan was to escape by abandoning the second of his assumptions—the assumption that the kind of causal principle at issue is quantitative—but we now see that we can do so only by abandoning the first assumption (that the objective reality of sensory ideas is minimal). It is therefore crucial that we take a closer look at the latter assumption.

The chief text in the *Meditations* bearing on the question of the representational power of sensible ideas lies in Meditation III where Descartes asserts that ideas of "light and colours, sounds, smells, tastes, heat and cold and the other tactile qualities" either represent "non-things" or, if they represent something, what they represent has a degree of reality "so extremely slight that I cannot even distinguish it from a non-thing" (AT VII, 44; CSM II, 30). In virtue of this representational deficiency Descartes characterizes these ideas as "materially false." If the "ideas of sensible things" of passage A are the materially false ideas of Meditation III, then the interpretation of the proof of the external world just proposed, whatever its other attractions, is doomed. For that interpretation requires that the ideas of sensible things present content properties to the mind—precisely what materially false ideas of the senses fail to do. There is, moreover, one very important independent reason for thinking that Descartes cannot be treating ideas of sensible objects as a subclass of materially false ideas. Materially false ideas are ideas of sensory qualities, colors, sound, heat, and cold, but if we are to make any sense at all of how passage B interacts with the general qualitative causal principle—as we must on the present hypothesis—the ideas of sensible objects must be taken as ideas whose content properties are corporeal properties, geometrical properties implying extension.[24] These Descartes certainly does not treat as materially false, regarding them, rather, as clear and distinct ideas.[25]

If we now assume that it is clear and distinct ideas of geometrical properties, and only such properties, that serve as the basis for Descartes's proof of the material world, we can represent that proof as an instance of the general causal pattern of existential reasoning:

The Proof of the External World in Meditation VI

1. I have a clear and distinct idea of a set of geometrical content properties $\emptyset_1 \ldots \emptyset_n$ determining the sense of the term "matter." This set of properties will henceforth be called *essential material properties.* (Assumption)
2. My having a clear and distinct idea i of the set of *essential material content-properties* M is causally explained by there being a substance s and there being a set of real properties $P_1 \ldots P_n$ corresponding to m such that M is contained formally or eminently in s and $P_1 \ldots P_n$ are the objects of i. (GQCP)

3. There is a substance s and there is a set of real properties $P_1 \ldots P_n$ corresponding to M (*essential material properties*) such that M is contained formally or eminently in s. (GQCP, 1)
4. M is not contained eminently in s. (The elimination premise)
5. M is contained formally in s. (3, 4)
6. There is a set of real properties $P_1 \ldots P_n$ such that $P_1 \ldots P_n$ are identical with the corresponding members of M and s exemplifies $P_1 \ldots P_n$. (FC, 5)
7. The statement "The material world exists" is formally true. (DEF, 6)

The difficulty with this proof comes in the elimination premise. Descartes certainly asserts this premise. He does so on the grounds of a "great propensity to believe that *they* are produced by corporeal things" (AT VII, 79–80; CSM II, 55; my emphasis). The term "they" refers to "these ideas" considered objectively. Viewed in this light the premise asserts that we have a great propensity to believe that the corporeal content properties presented by these ideas are caused by corporeal objects. The difficulty with this premise is that the only kind of ideas presenting corporeal content officially allowed by the doctrine of the *Meditations* are intellectual ideas whose objects are the immutable essences introduced in Meditation V (AT VII, 64; CSM II, 44). However, I have argued[26] that these ideas *are* eminently contained in a substance, namely, in my mind. It transpires, therefore, that "these ideas" are not, after all, the kind of clear and distinct ideas of geometrical properties Descartes needs for his proof of the external world in Meditation VI. But they also cannot be the kind of materially false ideas of the senses he countenances in Meditation III. What else can they be? Given the theoretical possibilities which Descartes officially allows in the *Meditations* the answer has to be *Nothing*!

Concrete Intuition of Corporeal Properties

If we were not restricted to the official possibilities mentioned above, it would be possible to break the destructive dilemma that the proof of the external world of Meditation VI faces by allowing for a notion of clear and distinct sensory awareness of corporeal objects that does not amount to an intellectual intuition of corporeal essences eminently contained within the mind but, rather, that amounts to a nonintellectual intuition of corporeal properties formally contained in matter. Descartes often speaks about *sensations* of color, light, heat, and so on. Unfortunately, he never speaks of sensations of size, shape, and so on. We can of course understand why he would never speak of size, shape, and so on, as *being sensations*, namely, as being modes of mind, but why does he not speak of *sensations of* those qualities? Some have argued that this is because he does not countenance any mode of sensory experience of primary qualities, allowing only for intellectual awareness of such qualities,[27] but, I shall make the case in the next chapter,[28] that this is not so. Part of that case draws upon a text from *Principles* I, 71, wherein Descartes makes an important distinction between sensations "which do not represent anything located outside our thought" and thoughts that present external objects to mind:

[T]he mind perceived sizes, shapes, motions and so on, which were presented to it not as sensations but as things, or modes of things, existing (or at least capable of existing) outside thought. (AT VIIIA, 35; CSMI, 219)

Since "presenting" things to the mind is a way of making things cognitively accessible to the mind, and things are made accessible to the mind in Cartesian philosophy only through the good offices of a "true" (viz., not materially false) idea, when Descartes speaks here of geometrical qualities being presented "as things" (rather than "as sensations") we have the makings of a doctrine that there is a class of true ideas that are *sensory presentations of corporeal objects*. But this doctrine is given in the *Principles* not the *Meditations*, and it would be anachronistic to posit its operations in the proof of the external world that occurs in Meditation VI.

There is, however, another proof of the external world that occurs in the *Principles* (*Principles* II, 1) shortly after *Principles* I, 71. It would not of course be anachronistic to see the notion of a (true) sensory presentation of corporeal properties at work in this proof and, thus, legitimate to at least consider whether the structure of that proof contains the general qualitative causal principle and, thus, conforms to the pattern by means of which existential claims are in general to be demonstrated.

3.6 The Proof of the External World in *Principles* II, 1

The central passage in the proof is this:

> For we have a clear understanding of this matter as something that is quite different from God and from ourselves or our mind; and *we appear to see clearly that the idea of it comes to us from things located outside ourselves, which it wholly resembles.* (AT VIIIA, 40–41; CSM I, 223; my emphasis)

In the first clause of this passage Descartes says that the nature of matter is something concerning which we have a clear understanding. Descartes says much the same in Meditation VI:

> [I]n many cases the grasp of the senses is obscure and confused. But at least they possess all the properties which I clearly and distinctly understand, that is, all those which, viewed in general terms, are comprised within the subject matter of pure mathematics. (AT VII, 80; CSM II, 55)

There is, however, an important difference between the role of clear ideas in the order of argument in Meditation VI and the role played in the order of argument in *Principles* II, 1.[29] In the first argument, the existence of the corporeal world is derived *before* an express reference to clear and distinct ideas is made; clear and distinct ideas do not appear as premises in the derivation.[30] In the second proof, it appears that the clarity[31] of our grasp of the source of our ideas as "different from God and from ourselves or our mind" and the apparently clear vision we have of the resemblance of the cause of our idea of the external world with the idea itself do appear as premises for the conclusion. Moreover, the claim that we have a natural propensity to believe in the external world and the general doctrine of the teachings of nature in which that claim appears to be embedded are important elements in the Meditation VI proof.[32] These elements are altogether missing from the proof in *Principles* II, 1.

These differences are sufficiently central that they indicate that the two proofs have fundamentally different structures: the Meditation VI proof rests on a natural inclination to believe in a corporeal world;[33] the proof in *Principles* II, 1, does not.

A central element of the proof in *Principles* II, 1, involves the notion of sensory awareness:

> But we have sensory awareness of, or rather as a result of sensory stimulation we have a clear and distinct perception of, some kind of matter, which is extended in length, breadth and depth, and has various differently shaped and variously moving parts which give rise to our various sensations of colours, smells, pain and so on. (AT VIIIA, 40; CSM I, 223)

Clear and distinct perception is a species of intuitive awareness of properties that has come into cognitive focus by an application of Cartesian method. However, the kind of intuitive awareness at issue in this passage does not appear to be a purely intellectual contemplation of immutable geometrical essences, for, as previously noted, the objects of such contemplation are eminently contained within our own mind and no immediate inference can be made from the eminent containment of a property in one substance to the formal containment of that property in that same or any other substance. But when Descartes says that we "see clearly" that the cause of our ideas (of geometrical properties) "resembles" those ideas (and setting aside the concern about the possibility that God is a deceiver), he appears to say that there is an immediate inference from our clear and distinct awareness of the geometrical properties to the formal existence of "something extended in length, breadth and depth."

Descartes clearly does not intend that the *particular form* that our sense experience of the external world takes is a concrete intuition in the sense being developed here, for particular corporeal experiences are regarded by Descartes as subject to a "high degree of doubt and uncertainty" (AT VII, 80; CSM II 55).

However, if we take only the most general aspects of corporeal objects—*that they are extended*—to be presented by concrete intuition, then such images give an entirely accurate picture of the nature of its remote objects—entities in the world external to the brain—as well as its immediate objects—corporeal images within the brain. My proposal, then, is that the object of immediate concrete intuition is the *general property of being actually extended*[34] and the substance that formally contains this property is the brain. Perhaps we can regard this intuition as an innate feature of our sensory awareness left by our Creator to enable us to know clearly and distinctly that the world of extended things exists.

If this is Descartes's intention, then I suggest that he may be here introducing a new kind of intuitive awareness, one distinct from both sensory awareness of secondary qualities and intellectual intuition of geometrical immutable essences. Like sensory intuition but unlike intellectual intuition, this new form of intuition gives an immediate inference to the formal containment of the intuited properties. Like intellectual intuition but unlike sensory intuition, this new form of intuition is a "true idea," for it tells us the nature of the substance formally containing the intuited properties, namely, "all the properties which we clearly perceive to belong to an extended thing." He then adds, "And it is this extended thing that we call 'body' or 'matter.'" This new form of intuition is, thus, both concrete and true. In these respects it is most like that paradigm of intuitive awareness, the inner awareness of ourselves.

With this new form of concrete intuitive awareness at his disposal Descartes can formulate a varient of the general rule of truth that leads immediately to the desired conclusion.

The Rule of Truth for Concrete Intuition (RTCI)

If I have concrete intuitive awareness of $P_1 \ldots P_n$, then there exists a substance s such that s possesses $P_1 \ldots P_n$ formally.

If we now assume that this intuitional awareness has been "noticed" in the appropriate way and thus amounts to a clear and distinct idea, we can represent the general pattern of reasoning at issue for concrete intuitive awareness as follows:

Inference D

1. I have a clear and distinct concrete perception of $P_1 \ldots P_n$. (Assumption)
2. I have a concrete intuitive awareness of $P_1 \ldots P_n$. (DEF, 1)

Therefore,
3. There exists a substance s such that s possesses $P_1 \ldots P_n$ formally. (RTCI, 2)

Inference D can be compared to the general pattern of existential reasoning that Descartes employs in his proofs of God's existence. Inference D clearly departs from this pattern in the omission from the rule of truth of the disjunction of formal with eminent containment. The difference is that in the more general pattern of reasoning the intuitional premise supplies intellectual intuition and intellectual intuition does not entail the actuality of its object. Actuality is achieved only with an additional step provided by the elimination premise. In the case of inference D the intuitional premise is much stronger: it asserts that we have concrete intuition of certain properties, a form of intuition that by itself entails the actuality of its object. It is difficult to say whether Descartes actually had such an idea in mind when he wrote the proof in *Principles* II, 1, but if he did, it would account for the absence of an elimination premise from the proof. It would also avoid the dilemma afflicting the proof in Meditation VI. I propose, therefore, to impute to the proof of the external world in *Principles* II, 1, a structure corresponding to inference D.

Instantiating the variables $P_1 \ldots P_n$ in inference D with the properties *depth in extension*, *length in extension*, and *breadth in extension* yields the following reconstruction:

The Proof of the External World from Clear and Distinct
Concrete Ideas (*Principles* II, 1)

1. I have a clear and distinct concrete perception of the properties *depth in extension, length in extension,* and *breadth in extension.* (Assumption)
2. I have a concrete intuitive awareness of the properties *depth in extension, length in extension,* and *breadth in extension.* (DEF, 1)
3. There exists a substance *s* such that *s* possesses the properties *depth in extension, length in extension,* and *breadth in extension* formally. (RTCI, 2)
4. There exists a substance we call "matter" or "body." (DEF, 3)

A number of questions remain.

There is, first, an important element of the proof that I have not reflected in this reconstruction, namely, the role of God as a nondeceiver. In connection with my analysis of two previous texts from Meditation III and the Second Replies in chapter I,[35] I claimed that intuitive awareness of propositions is not a possible candidate for error. The possibility of erroneous judgments concerning intuitive knowledge enters only in the form of an erroneous judgment whether a given form of awareness that I think is intuitive awareness is actually so. It is at this point that some assurance is needed that we are not subject to deception from any source, including of course, that of a deceiving God. There is some evidence that Descartes sees the problem here in a similar way for he says that "we *appear* to see clearly that the idea of it [the material world] comes to us from things located outside ourselves, which it wholly resembles." The next sentence then reads: "And we have·already noted that it is quite inconsistent with the nature of God that he should be a deceiver" (AT VIIIA, 41; CSM I, 223). On this interpretation, the possibility "already noted" that God himself might be producing the idea of the geometrical properties would show that I did not, after all, possess concrete, intuitive awareness of these properties but only thought I did.

There is, then, a consistent interpretation of the proof of the external world in *Principles* II, 1, which sees Descartes relying upon a notion of the concrete, true intuitive awareness of geometrical properties.

There is also the question of how, using Cartesian method, we are to establish that we are in a state of concrete intuitional awareness of geometrical properties. The method I described in chapter 1[36] is a partly phenomenological method. It requires that we consider a range of phenomenologically indiscernible possible situations in light of the assumption that if two situations, s_1 and s_2 are phenomenologically indiscernible then in each situation there is a form of intuitive awareness directed to the same object type. This method was applied most explicitly and clearly by Descartes in the "piece of wax" discussion in Meditation II. It will be recalled that in that discussion Descartes speaks of both colors and shapes as the proper objects of perception. It is true that he describes the mode of perception there as intellectual, to distinguish it from sensory or physiological modes of perception, but even in that text there is evidence of a distinction between the mental scrutiny of the properties of wax in general and of this particular piece of wax in particular (AT VII, 31; CSM II, 21). I suggest that the latter is afforded through the kind of concrete intuitive awareness of geometrical properties apparently at issue in *Principles* II, 1.

There is, however, a significant difficulty in finding broad textual support for the idea that Descartes assigns a phenomenological dimension to the concrete intuitive awareness of geometrical properties. I conclude this chapter with an explanation for this difficulty and an assessment of its significance for the line of interpretation I have just been advancing.

3.7 Descartes's Ambivalence toward the Senses

In *Principles* II, 1, Descartes sees an intimate connection between concrete intuitive awareness and sensory experience. (He is even tempted to call it a form of sensory awareness of the material world.) What he has in mind, I think, is that this form of awareness is present within our ordinary perceptual consciousness as the phenomenological dimension of our sense experience of primary qualities. Now this suggestion will seem most implausible to students of Cartesian thought not because it is intuitively implausible that there is a phenomenological dimension to our experience of primary qualities—things look round as surely as they look red— but because it seems that Descartes never countenances this dimension in his philosophical writings on sense perception. This impression is largely, though not exactly, accurate. Descartes does, however, have a good deal to say about this dimension in his empirical writings on sense perception. There he develops a powerful and, within the limits of empirical knowledge in his day, a plausible account of the physical, physiological, and psychological mechanisms underlying the phenomenological dimension of our experience of primary qualities.

If I am right about this, there remains the question why this account is so hard to find in his philosophical writings. The answer has two parts. The first is that within Descartes's taxonomy of cognitive faculties, the kind of concrete, intuitive awareness we are seeking belongs to the faculty of *imagination* rather than to either the faculties of *sense* or *intellect*. The second is that, overall, Descartes is ambivalent about the value of the imagination to epistemology. In the *Meditations* he takes a uniformly negative view. Nevertheless, there are places where he seems to relent somewhat, including the following passage from a letter to Princess Elizabeth of June 28, 1643:

> The soul can be conceived by pure intellect; the body (i.e. extension, shape, and movement) can likewise be known by pure intellect, but much better by intellect aided by imagination. (AT III, 690; *Letters*, 141)

In the next chapter I begin to build the case for a phenomenological interpretation of the Cartesian notion of concrete intuitive awareness by looking at Descartes's account of the imagination. In chapter 6 I look at the evidence that Descartes sees a positive epistemic role for the sense experience of primary qualities in the theory of natural knowledge. There (section 6.4) I reconsider the proofs of the external world in Meditation VI and *Principles* II, 1, from the perspective of these results and offer an assessment of their relative merits.

I conclude this section with a conjecture on the sources of Descartes's ambivalence about the philosophical importance of ideas of the imagination. The conjecture is that it is underwritten by fear—the fear that if the phenomenology of the experience of primary qualities (ideas of the imagination) were to be a form of concrete intuitive awareness, then it might be plausible to argue that other aspects of the phenomenology of our sense experience should also be elevated to the status of concrete intuitive awareness. In particular, I think that Descartes feared that he might have to accept that the phenomenological fusion of primary and secondary qualities is also a form of concrete intuitive awareness of a world in which secondary and primary qualities are *ontologically* fused, that is, of a world in which secondary qualities are modes of extension. This conception of the physical world is not, of course, consistent with Descartes's austere mechanistic physics, but it is consistent with "the manifest image" of the external world, an Aristotelian image whose grip on the imagination Descartes is constantly struggling to offset. It is because of this, I think, that Descartes has gone to such lengths[37] to suppress reference to the phenomenology of the sense experience of primary qualities and to disparage the epistemic value of sense experience in general.

It is difficult to directly establish the truth of this conjecture about Descartes's underlying motives and, if true, to fully trace its effects. However, if it *is* true, that would show that Descartes has a fundamental metaphysical interest in discrediting the representational and epistemological credentials of only a *certain range* of sensory experience—that responsible for the phenomenological fusion of primary and secondary qualities. This would leave room for the concrete intuitive awareness of primary qualities identified here.

Objections and Replies

In *Principles* I, 30, Descartes says,

> And as for our senses, if we notice anything here that is clear and distinct, no matter whether we are awake or asleep, then provided we separate it from what is confused and obscure we will easily recognize—whatever the thing in question—which are the aspects that may be regarded as true. (AT VIIIA, 17; CSM I, 203)

If my interpretation is correct, Descartes maintains that I have a clear and distinct idea of actual extension, a fact which allows us to infer by means of the rule of truth for concrete intuition that there exists an actual corporeal world. But Descartes says here that clear and distinct ideas give us the truth about sensory matters even when I am asleep. But does not the conjunction of these two claims yield the consequence that even in sleep I have concrete intuition of actual corporeal properties, namely, those contained in the brain? And does not Descartes deny that dreaming necessarily involves the brain?

My reply is that the conjunction of these claims does have this consequence but that Descartes does not deny that dreaming necessarily involves the brain. On the contrary, he accepts that the imagination (to which faculty dreaming belongs) bears an intimate relation to the body and that this fact provides the basis for a proof that material things exist:

The conclusion that material things exist is also suggested by the faculty of imagination, which I am aware of using when I turn my mind to material things. For when I give more attentive consideration to what imagination is, it seems to be nothing else but an application of the cognitive faculty to a body which is intimately present to it, and which therefore exists. (AT VII, 71–72; CSM II, 50)

The "intimacy" suggested in this passage is not the relation of contingent causality between mind and body but the much stronger, necessary relation of concrete intuition — an idea proper to the imagination *is nothing but* the intimate presence of a body (viz., a corporeal image in the brain) to the cognitive faculty. (By contrast, the relationship between the ideas proper to the intellect and corporeal images *is* a contingent, causal relationship.) Of course, early in the *Meditations* Descartes had seemed to deny that there is a necessary relationship between dreams (ideas proper to the imagination) and the body:

Suppose then that I am dreaming, and that these particulars — that my eyes are open, that I am moving my head and stretching out my hands — are not true. Perhaps, indeed, I do not even have such hands or such a body at all. (Meditation I: AT VII, 19; CSM II, 13)

But I take Descartes's observation that "perhaps" I lack a body to be an *epistemic* possibility, a possibility that Descartes cannot rule out for certain on the basis of what he is entitled to believe at that stage of his meditations. This does not imply a denial that (first-order) dreaming[38] depends on the body.

Descartes also expresses related doubts in a passage from Meditation VI itself occurring just a bit later than the one quoted above:

And I can easily understand that, if there does exist some body to which the mind is so joined that it can apply itself to contemplate it, as it were, whenever it pleases, then it may possibly be this very body that enables me to imagine corporeal things. . . . But this is only a probability. (AT VII, 73; CSM II, 51)

I take it that the term "probability" in this passage refers not to the connection between imagination and the body but to the state of Descartes's theoretical opinion of that connection, which, I take it, is that the connection is one of necessary dependence. However, Descartes also says that

despite a careful and comprehensive investigation, I do not yet see how the distinct idea of corporeal nature which I find in my imagination can provide any basis for a necessary inference that some body exists. (AT VII, 73; CSM II, 51)

He does not see this because he does not see how to take the nonabstract/nonintellectual idea of corporeal nature, namely, that found in his imagination, to be a *clear and* distinct idea. However, he seems to have found how to do so in the *Principles* since he there asserts that all distinct ideas are clear ideas,[39] having already asserted in the present passage that ideas of the imagination are distinct. His insight is to regard the primary quality dimension of sense experience as a "clear idea" (genuine intuition) of actualized corporeal properties. Since all forms of (first-order) experience due to the imagination necessarily have this dimension, the imagination does provide a "basis for a necessary inference that some body exists."

Appendix A: Alternative Accounts of Descartes's Notion of Eminent Containment

I consider two alternative accounts of Descartes's notion of eminent containment. The first is due to Clatterbaugh,[40] the second to O'Neill.[41] The central concept of interest to us in Clatterbaugh's account is given in the second of two "sufficient conditions for an adequate similarity between cause and effect":

> (II) A substance, x, has at least as much reality as a substance, y, with respect to a reality, P, where x is a cause and y's being P is its effect, if P formally or objectively inheres in y, and Q formally inheres in x, and P and Q are the same kind of property which admits of degree and Q is that property to a greater degree than P. In this case x eminently contains P.[42]

Clatterbaugh offers the example of one stone containing a great deal of heat and transfering some, but not all, of that heat to another stone.[43] In this case the heat in the second stone is of a lesser degree than the heat in the first stone, thus, by (II), the heat in the second stone is *eminently contained* in the heat of the first. Unfortunately, as Clatterbaugh notes,[44] there is a class of cases in Descartes's "more metaphysical writings" that escape this analysis, namely, those in Meditation III where Descartes says that the properties of corporeal things "might be contained in me eminently." In these cases the notion of eminent containment does not seem to be a containment of an effect property in a cause property, as in the case of the transfer of heat from one substance to another, but a quite different notion, used in the Cartesian theory of the ontological and epistemological status of properties and essences. O' Neill observes that Descartes never explicitly employs the notion of eminent containment in cases like that of the heat transfer, reserving that notion for cases like those in Meditation III. When he does use the notion it is always to "present us with something which is of a higher order, in the ontological scale, than the substance in which the effect inheres."[45]

O'Neill's own suggestion for an analysis of eminent containment is given as follows:

> The property ø is eminently contained in X if and only if: ø is not formally contained in X; X is an entity displaying a greater degree of relative independence than any possible Y which could contain ø formally (i.e., is higher up in the ontological hierarchy than any such Y); and X has the power to bring about the existence of ø.

She defines *formal containment* as follows:

> The property ø-of-n degrees is formally contained in X if and only if X contains at least n degrees of ø.[46]

Curiously, there is little similarity between her definitions and those offered by Descartes, which I reproduce for purposes of comparison:

> Whatever exists in the objects of our ideas in a way which exactly corresponds to our perception of it is said to exist *formally* in those objects.
>   Something is said to exist *eminently* in an object when, although it does not exactly correspond to our perception of it, its greatness is such that it can fill the role of that which does so correspond. (AT VII, 161; CSM II, 114)

The dissimilarities are fundamentally three. (1) Descartes's definitions make essential reference to the way properties are perceived; O'Neill's omit any such reference. (2) The degree of reality ("its greatness") mentioned in Descartes's definition is a property of the property ("something") eminently contained in an object; that mentioned in O'Neill's definition is a property of the object. (3) O'Neill makes essential reference in her definition to the existence of a causal power on the part of the object to bring about the existence of the eminently contained property; no such reference is made in Descartes's definition. With apparent differences as dramatic as these between O'Neill's account and these central Cartesian texts, we are naturally curious to find out what evidence O'Neill might be able to marshall for her account.

Part of O'Neill's evidence concerns those cases which, she correctly observes, Clatterbaugh's account failed to accommodate. These are the cases in which Descartes speculated that the properties of corporeal substances might be eminently contained in me. But if we now apply her definition to this case, letting X be my mind and Y be corporeal properties, we find it implying that my mind contains corporeal properties eminently just in case my mind "has the power to bring about the existence of corporeal properties. Whatever else Descartes may think about this subject, he does not think this.

Another part of her case rests on a reading of several passages from Suarez, including the following:

> This is not to say that, formally speaking and according to an exact definition, to contain things eminently is [just] to be able to create [efficere] them. For I distinguish these two things by reason, and I believe the following causal inference to be true: "It is able to create them *because* it contains them eminently". Rather, I explicate this containment by means of its relation to its effect, since I cannot present this notion in a clearer way.[47]

Recall that O'Neill explains the possibility of eminent containment in terms of the primitive notion of a causal power whereas, I have argued in section 3.2 (the fundamentality thesis), with Descartes the procedure is the reverse—he explains the possibility of causal power in terms of the notions of (formal and) eminent containment. This also appears to be Suarez's procedure. In any case, I note that it is unclear how much fidelity to any particular Scholastic doctrine we should attribute to Descartes's pronouncements even when they are couched in Scholastic terminology.

For all of these reasons I believe that O'Neill's interpretation cannot be accepted.

Appendix B: Inadequacy versus Misperception in our Idea of God

Before proceeding I need to consider a prima facie difficulty. In a well-known passage Descartes says that although I cannot "grasp the infinite" I can "understand it," an obscure distinction that Descartes makes in several places. (See the letter to Mersenne of 27 May, 1630: AT I, 151; *Letters*, 15.) Whatever this distinction amounts to, it implies that attributes of God are greater than our grasp of them. Since the proof of God's existence requires that God's essential properties, *infinite-beinghood*, not be contained eminently in God, this would be a problem for my interpretation if, but only if, that implication entails that the content attributes of God must be contained eminently in God. Does it entail this? Consider again the definition of the notions of formal and eminent containment in the Second Replies:

> Whatever exists in the objects of our ideas in a way which exactly corresponds to our perception of it is said to exist *formally* in those objects. Something is said to exist *eminently* in an object when, although it does not exactly correspond to our perception of it, its greatness is such that it can fill the role of that which does so correspond. (AT VII, 161; CSM II, 114)

The only general solution to this problem is to find some way of defining the content properties of God so that although our grasp of them is inadequate, they do not fail to "exactly correspond" to our perception of them. Let us suppose that the difference between inadequacy and failure to exactly correspond is that the latter, unlike the former, implies some kind of *misperception* of the nature of the content properties.[48] With our perception of geometrical properties as mathematical *possibilia*, for example, it seems that this can reasonably be categorized as a case of misperception. That is why I maintained that mathematical properties are eminently contained in their ground (namely, our minds). In the case of our grasp of God's perfections, however, Descartes seems to regard the deficiency as a case of our perception failing to encompass the whole of its object rather than misperceiving the nature of the object, a point he seems to be making in the following passage from the First Replies:

> But in the case of the thing itself which is infinite, although our understanding is positive, it is not adequate, that is to say, we do not have a complete grasp of everything in it that is capable of being understood. When we look at the sea, our vision does not encompass its entirety, nor do we measure out its enormous vastness; but we are still said to "see" it. (AT VII, 113; CSM II, 81)

What we "see" is only part of what there is, but what we see of it is not misperceived.

FOUR

The Sense Experience of Primary Qualities

4.1 Some Background

In Rule 12 of the *Rules for the Direction of the Mind*[1] Descartes provides a concise and unusually systematic account of the important cognitive and perceptual capacities of man as he then saw them. Though Descartes's thinking on these matters will change and become more complex in his later works, important aspects of the early account survive in the later accounts, and important aspects of the later doctrines can be better understood by seeing their antecedents in the earlier work.

In the *Rules for the Direction of the Mind* Descartes regards the understanding as a "single power" relating passively or actively to four different objects. It *imagines* when applied to a part of the brain called the corporeal imagination (phantasia) in order to construct mathematical figures in brain material; it can engage in *sense perception* of objects by being directed to the corporeal imagination and a part of the brain called the "common sense" (the receiver of sensory impressions from the outer senses); it can *remember* objects by being directed to a part of the brain containing traces of previous activities; it can have purely *intellectual understanding* when applied to its own special objects (intellectual simple natures) (AT X, 415–416; CSM I, 42).

When the intellect has thoughts of shape, extension, and motion inhering in bodies, the object of these thoughts are not the intellect's own special objects but actual material configurations in the brain. In subsequent parts of the *Rules for the Direction of the Mind* Descartes hopes to ground mathematical method in the mind's capacity to scrutinize, manipulate, and generalize from these material configurations. Because of the logical intimacy between our thought of bodily properties and shapes in the brain, Descartes says, if I judge that a certain shape is not moving, I shall say that my thought is in some way composed of shape and rest. (AT X, 419–420; CSM I, 45)

There is an interesting similarity between this doctrine and a doctrine of Aristotle's regarding the relation between thought and its object: "[A]ctual knowledge is identical with its object."[2]

We shall discover other similarities as well. It will, therefore, be useful to have a brief sketch of the basic Aristotelian theory of perceptual awareness[3] and of the Scholastic doctrine of intentional species[4] into which the former evolved available to us before we enter into the main task of this chapter.

The Aristotelian account of interest to us is an "act-object" theory of perceptual acts such as seeing, hearing, smelling, and so on. These were treated by Aristotle as relational acts of immediate awareness directed at images of qualities ("sensible forms") present in the corresponding sense organs or a central repository, "the common sense."[5] These acts are differentiated from one another by being directed at different qualities "proper" to the kind of act in question.[6] Thus acts of vision are thought of as immediate awarenesses of color present in the sense organs, acts of hearing are thought of immediate as awarenesses of sounds located in the body, and so on. Just as acts of awareness are classified as "seeing" and "hearing" because they are directed to colors and sounds, so sense organs are classified as "eyes" and "ears" because they are thought to be the locations in which the colors and sounds are present in the body. Some qualities are perceived by more than one organ, namely, qualities of size, shape, and other "primary qualities." Because they are common to several senses, they cannot be taken as the *differentia* among acts of perception, that task being exclusively assigned to the "proper objects."

In its crude form the Aristotelian theory postulates a simple kind of "transmission" of these qualities (qualities understood as *forms*)[7] from their location in physical objects to a location in the sense organs and the "common sense." However, as theorizing about these matters became more sophisticated in the case of vision especially, it became clear that the awareness of primary qualities had to be due to the intervention of the cognitive power in the form of some kind of inference carried out on initial physical registrations of these qualities. The "proper objects of the senses" remained more or less as they had been for Aristotle, present in the body in a special category of more or less physical stuff known as "visual spirits."[8]

The general outline of this account was essentially in place in the writings of Alhazan (c. 965–1039), whose work established a paradigm influencing theorists into the seventeenth century, among the most prominent of whom was Kepler. Kepler, writing in the period just prior to Descartes,[9] was able to revise the geometrical optics of this paradigm, though he seemed in important respects to accept its ontology of secondary qualities. In the *Rules* it appears that Descartes accepted this same paradigm, but in subsequent work, he revised the ontology of secondary qualities and, drawing upon Keplerian optics, made important contributions to the theory of the inferential processes underlying the perception of primary qualities.

Throughout his work Descartes accepted the basic Aristotelian analysis of perceptual awareness[10] if not its ontology.

The theory of intentional species is a sophisticated theory of perception and intentionality that has its classical expression in the writing of St Thomas Aquinas.[11] Its roots are Aristotelian. The theory postulates that the qualities ("forms") of external objects are transmitted to the sense organs or other parts of the brain not in their original form but as "sensible species," where they become the objects of the cognitive power. Surprising though it may seem in light of his later views on this subject, some commentators[12] suggest that in the *Rules* Descartes himself accepted, if not the theory itself with all of its Scholastic underpinnings, at least some of its central elements.

To be sure, Descartes's views on intentionality underwent a transformation by the time of the mature theory of ideas. He certainly reworked his theory of mathematical objects, revising the class of the intellect's own objects (the "simple natures") from one that excluded mathematical objects to one that included them. Many other aspects of theory were reworked as well. However, we will also find that some of the mature doctrines are surprisingly conservative transformations of these earlier doctrines effected under the pressure of new methodological needs and changed metaphysical commitments.[13]

Evidence of these changed commitments appears quite dramatically in the first sentence of the *Treatise on Light*. Descartes writes:

> The subject that I propose to deal with in this treatise is light, and the first point I want to draw to your attention is that there may be a difference between the sensation we have of light (i.e. the idea of light which is formed in our imagination by the mediation of our eyes) and what it is in the objects that produces this sensation within us (i.e. what it is in a flame or the sun that we call by the name 'light'). (AT XI, 3; CSM I, 81)

It is hard to date this work precisely, but it appears to have been written somewhere between 1629 and 1633, though published only posthumously. In any case it was written after the *Rules* and seems to mark a clear departure from that work in its express rejection of the doctrine that the apparent extended form of the experience of color (light) is a literal form in extended matter.[14] Though it is a matter of speculation why Descartes altered his view at this time, we know that Galileo published the *Assayer* in 1623, a work in which he gave expression to what is more or less the modern distinction between "primary" and "secondary" qualities. Descartes may have been reading the *Assayer* around 1630, and, if he was, his views may have changed as a result of Galileo's influence.[15] In any case, change they did.

In the *Optics* (AT VI, 112; CSM I, 165) and in the Sixth Replies (AT VII, 441–444; CSM II, 297–299) Descartes devotes much energy to demolishing the theory of intentional species as a theory of intentionality, replacing it with what is, in essential outline, his mature theory of ideas. This part of his program is relatively well known and relatively well understood.[16] On the other hand, his theory of the sense experience of primary qualities is relatively unknown and, I believe, not well understood.

4.2 The Account of Sense Experience of Primary Qualities in Mature Cartesian Philosophy

Is There an Account?

Objects can appear to have primary qualities no less than secondary qualities,[17] a fact well recognized by Descartes in his treatment of perception in the *Rules*: (passage A):

> [N]othing is more readily perceivable by the senses than shape, for it can be touched as well as seen. . . . [T]he concept of shape is so simple and common that it is involved in everything perceivable by the senses. Take colour, for example: whatever you may suppose colour to be, you will not deny that it is extended and consequently has shape. (AT X, 413: CSM I, 40–41)

His treatment of perception not only recognizes this fact but provides the theoretical framework of *direct realism* to explain it. In the sense in which I propose to use it, *direct realism*[18] is a doctrine with two main elements. (1) it postulates that thoughts are a cognitive act with two components, the content of the perceptual act itself and the objects (at which the act is directed), and (2) it explains how thoughts get their contents. The explanation is that the nature of the objects determines the nature of the content of the thought. In the case of Descartes's theory, the object is the presence of properties. Evidence that Descartes's view in the *Rules* contains these elements comes from a number of texts. For example, the first element seems to be present in a text where Descartes is describing the functions of the "spiritual power" (passage B):

> It is one single power, whether it receives figures from the 'common sense' [a part of the brain] at the same time as does the corporeal imagination, or applies itself to those which are preserved in memory. . . . [W]hen applying itself along with imagination to the "common" sense", it is said to see, touch, etc. (AT VI, 416; CSM I, 42; my interpolation)

This passage should be read in conjunction with other passages, in which Descartes is discussing those "simple natures . . . which are recognized to be present only in bodies—such as shape, extension, and motion." These, he says, "are purely material" (AT VI, 419; CSM I, 45). Moreover, the contents of thoughts that take material simple natures as objects seem to depend on the objects themselves:

> Thus, if I judge that a certain shape is not moving, I shall say that my thought is in some way composed of shape and rest; and similarly in other cases. (AT VI, 420; CSM I, 45)

This reflects the second element of direct realism.

According to the formal/epistemic interpretation of Descartes's mature theory of true ideas (viz., those possessing objective reality) given in chapter 2 section 2.7, true (clear and distinct) ideas are awareness relations among a person x, a set of real; properties $P_1 \ldots P_n$ and a set of content properties comprising the form F in which $P_1 \ldots P_n$ are presented to the mind of x. Moreover, as I have argued in chapter 3, section 3.2 Descartes's commitment to the causal principle for the objective reality (content) of ideas explains the content. These components of the mature theory also satisfy the description of the two elements of direct realism. Thus, in both the early and the mature works, Cartesian cognitions share important stuctural properties.

A central difference between the two accounts regards the metaphysical status of the objects of geometrical thought: in the early account they can be only material; in the mature account they can also be intellectual. In light of the pressures at work in the dissolution of Descartes's project of the *Rules for the Direction of the Mind* it is not surprising to see some adjustment of the metaphysics of sense experience in his mature work. What is perhaps surprising in light of this expectation is the degree to which the theoretical apparatus of direct realism remains in force throughout Descartes's mature period. For example, it is to be found in the official Second Replies' definition of "idea" (AT VII, 161; CSM II, 113) and in the *Conversation with Burman*, which is itself offered as a clarification of the theory of sense experience of Meditation VI. The similarity between the passage from *Conversation with Burman* (below) and passage B quoted above is especially striking:

> When external objects act on my senses, they print on them an idea, or rather a figure, of themselves; and when the mind attends to these images imprinted on the gland in this way, it is said to have sensory perceptions. (AT V, 162; CSM III, 344)

If the same theoretical apparatus introduced to explain facts that Descartes regarded as intuitively obvious in his early theory of perception is present in his later theory of perception, it seems reasonable to infer that he accepts the existence of those same facts in his later theory. The facts in question are those mentioned in passage A: the centrality of primary qualities in perceptual experience.

Moreover, there are a number of passages in Descartes's mature writings on perception, both empirical and philosophical, that seem to bear out this expectation. Thus, Descartes speaks of the "outward forms" of the piece of wax (Meditation II: AT VII, 32; CSM II, 22), forms that the context suggests contain primary qualities and are presented to us by sense perception rather than the intellect. He speaks of "the garments under which corporeal substance appears [*paraître*] to us" in the French version of Meditation III (AT IX, 33; CSM II, 31, n.1). Optics VI is replete with references to the size and shape with which objects "appear" [forms of *paraître* and *apparaître*] to us, a choice of verb which seems to indicate a contrast between sensory experience and knowledge [*connaissance*: AT VI, 134; Alquié I, 704] or opinion [*opinion*: AT VI, 140; Alquié I, 710] or the act of judging [*juger*: AT VI, 140; Alquié, 710]. In *Passions* I, 24, Descartes says that pains are felt [*sentis*] "as being in our limbs rather than as being in objects outside us" (AT XI, 346–347; CSM I, 337). *Principles* I, 69, contains the observation: "It is true that when we see a body we are just as certain of its existence in virtue of its having a visible [*visible*] colour as we are in virtue of its having a visible [*visible*] shape" (AT VIIIA, 34; CSM I, 218).

Nevertheless, many careful and sympathetic commentators on Descartes have simply denied that he has an account of the sense experience of primary qualities.[19] The core of their case rests on the contrast Descartes draws in his mature writings between sensations and the perception of primary qualities. This contrast is drawn in terms of the list of examples of the objects of sensations—heat, light, color, and so on—a list that never includes primary qualities.[20] It is drawn in terms of a distinction between the clarity and distinctness of ideas of primary qualities and the confusion and obscurity of sensations of secondary qualities, a distinction that is full of the implication that the former is due to a purely intellectual mode of awareness of primary qualities.[21] It is drawn in terms of a distinction between the "grade" (degree) of rational involvement in the production of sensations versus that involved in the production of perception of primary qualities: with the former there is no involvement; with the latter there is great involvement.[22] These contrasts are consistently drawn throughout Descartes's mature writings.

The impression that Descartes means to treat the perception of primary qualities as a purely intellectual affair is reinforced by a text in Meditation II where Descartes says that sense experience of all kinds is simply a form of "thinking" (AT VII, 29; CSM II, 19). Here, however, I suggest caution. If there is any useful support for the intellectualist doctrine in this text we need to know that thinking is a purely intellectual operation for Descartes. I have observed already[23] that Descartes seems to employ *two* notions of sense perception, a "restricted" notion that is a purely intellectual matter and a broader notion which is not. The restricted notion was introduced for special purposes in Meditation II having to do with the argument that the mind is a "complete thing," but it is the broader notion in which I am interested for present purposes. Moreover, when we go to the official definition of "thought" in the Second Replies we find that thought is defined as "all the operations of the will, the intellect, the imagination and the senses" (AT VII, 160; CSM II, 113). This reference to "operations" is a reference to Cartesian faculty psychology. For an account of the operations of the faculty of sense we should turn to the Sixth Replies where we find that the faculty of sense is explained as the faculty whose operations, properly construed, yield "sensations of colour, heat light, etc.," entities described by Descartes as "second grade" rather than "third grade," precisely in order to deny any involvement of the intellect (AT VII, 437–438; CSM II, 294–295). If we take this chain of texts all together we find that they have no tendency whatsoever to show that sense experiences (in the broad sense) are *purely* intellectual.[24]

Nevertheless, the evidence that remains still powerfully supports the intellectualist reading. There is, thus, powerful evidence on both sides. To reach an overall judgment on this matter therefore requires that we balance exegetical evidence for and against each hypothesis. My own view is that the evidence we have considered so far decides the case in favor of the sensuous hypothesis, largely on the grounds that evidence in favor of it is more direct and depends less on background assumptions about how various contrasts should be taken than is the case with its competitor.

This decision leaves us with two important questions: (1) Where in the official Cartesian taxonomy of ideas is the sensuous perception of primary qualities to be found? (2) Once found, why was it so hard to find? My answer to the first question is that the Cartesian home for the sense experience of primary qualities is not in the category of operations of the senses but in the category of operations of the imagination. My answer to the second question follows from my answer to the first: the account of the sense experience of primary qualities is hard to find because we have been looking for it in the wrong place.

The Case for Locating the Account of the Sense Experience of Primary Qualities in the Theory of Imagination

When we look to some of the texts where we would expect to find an account of the metaphysical category of the sense experience of primary qualities, we are disappointed. For example, when we turn to the taxonomy of "grades of sensory response" in the Sixth Replies we find that none of the three grades provides a clearly suitable home (AT VII, 436–440; CSM II, 294–295). The first grade is purely physiological; the second grade is mental and phenomenological, but its list of items includes only secondary qualities like color, heat, and so on; and the third grade is characterized as comprising judgments based purely on the intellect, also apparently unsuitable as the home for ideas with phenomenological dimensions.

There are several strategies available to an interpreter otherwise convinced of the existence of a Cartesian account of the sense experience of primary qualities.

For example, Epstein and Hatfield[25] regard Descartes as accepting a version of the "sensory core" theory of perception. The sensory core is a mental correlate of two-dimensional retinal images or their projection into the brain. In the Cartesian version the sensory core is something of which we can in principle become conscious and, according to Epstein and Hatfield, finds a home in the second grade of sensory response. This theory also countenances a distinction between the sensory core and the sensory experience of the three-dimensional world. This experience is dependent on experience of the four primary qualities (size, shape, distance, and direction) produced by the psychophysical procedures described in the *Optics* (to which we are referred by Descartes in the present text) as being third-grade sensory responses. The reference to "intellect" is thus seen by them as a reference not to special intellectual *objects* of our ideas but to the *method* used in producing sensory ideas. (In order to accommodate ideas of mathematical qualities with special intellectual objects, Hatfield appeals in a later paper to a neo-Platonic interpretation of innate ideas.)[26] Epstein and Hatfield thus find a home for sensory experience of primary qualities in both second and third grades of sensory response. My own interpretation is a variation on theirs.

Unfortunately, the textual case for attributing this view to Descartes is at best ambiguous. The only evidence Epstein and Hatfield cite for assigning at least some primary qualities (those in the sensory core) to the second grade is this passage from the Sixth Replies:

> [T]hough my judgement that there is a staff situated without me, which judgement results from the sensation of colour by which I am affected, and likewise my reasoning from the extension of that colour, its boundaries, and its position *relatively to the parts of the brain* to the size, shape and distance of the said staff, are vulgarly assigned to sense, and are consequently here referred to the third grade of sensation, they clearly depend on the understanding alone.[27]

A better source of textual support lies elsewhere, in those places where Descartes is discussing the imagination.

In Meditation VI (AT VII, 71; CSM II, 51) Descartes characterizes the imagination as "probably" depending in a special way on the corporeal imagination. It is true, of course, that in the "three-grades" text Descartes is not talking about the faculty of imagination, and in the Meditation VI text Descartes is not talking about the faculty of sense, at least not in *the narrow sense* in which he sometimes speaks of this faculty. He may, however, be talking about it in the broad sense of interest to us.[28]

For Descartes the imagination is a faculty that performs two distinct functions. The function that he most consistently recognizes is the *creative* function, the act of imagining (in the ordinary sense) figures or nonexistent objects. The other, not consistently recognized, is its function as the faculty responsible for computations involving ideas of primary qualities. For example, in the *Optics* VI, Descartes describes the use made by the perceptual system of natural geometry as "an act of the imagination," indicating that the results of this act are "contained in the imagination" (AT IX B, 138; CSM I, 170). On the other hand, in the *Conversation with Burman* Descartes does not give any play to the second role for the imagination:

> The difference between perception and imagination is thus really just this, that in perception the images are imprinted by external objects which are actually present, whilst in imagination the images are imprinted by the mind without any external objects, and with the windows shut, as it were. (AT V, 162; CSM III, 345)

We shall see in detail below that the perception of primary qualities is dependent on inferential processes involving cognitive premises — that is why the perception of these qualities is called "third grade" rather than "second grade." It is clear that these procedures match neither of the two procedures described in the passage just quoted. They are not simply a matter of imprinting a shape conveyed from the sense organs directly onto the brain, nor are they acts of the creative imagination performed "with the windows shut." They are acts with elements satisfying each description. It thus appears that Descartes's description of perception in this passage is an oversimplification of the theory he actually proposes in *Optics* VI.

There is evidence from the details of that theory (see section 4.3) that the mental processes of perceptual inference affect the brain just as much as the brain affects mental processes. Though this is a direction of causation not countenanced in the passage from the *Conversation with Burman*, there is little doubt that on matters of the psychophysics of vision the *Optics* is canonical. Moreover, it may be that Descartes's tendency to abstract from theoretical details in his metaphysical discussion of sense perception[29] has left him with an inadequate taxonomic basis within which to describe those details in places like the Sixth Replies and Burman's text.

To obtain a more adequate taxonomic basis we need to look to the *Optics* and earlier writings for evidence of the brain location of the effects of perceptual inference. Though the textual evidence indicates some confusion on this issue, on balance, it seems to favor the "corporeal imagination" rather than the "common sense."[30] (The common sense is that part of the brain which is the direct recipient of first-grade sensory effects whose *immediate* phenomenological effects seem to be restricted to sensations of color, light, etc.) As Descartes affirms in the *Treatise of Man*, the corporeal imagination (the "phantasy") is a separate structure:

> Now among these figures, it is not those imprinted on the organs of external sense, or on the internal surface of the brain, but only those which are traced in the spirits

on the surface of gland H where the seat of the imagination *and* 'common' sense is located which should be taken to be ideas. (AT XI, 176–177; Hall, 86; my emphasis)

The clearest evidence that in his empirical theory of sense perception Descartes countenances a direct connection between the common sense and the corporeal imagination comes in *Rules* 12:

> [T]he 'common' sense functions like a seal, fashioning in the phantasy or imagination, as if in wax, the same figures or ideas which come, pure and without body, from the external senses. The phantasy is a genuine part of the body, and is large enough to allow different parts of it to take on many different figures and, generally, to retain them for some time; in which case it is to be identified with what we call "memory." (AT X, 414; CSM I 41–42)

If we read this passage in connection with that quoted from *Optics* VI (AT IX,138; CSM I, 170), we may infer that the reference to what is "contained in the imagination" is a reference to memory traces in the *corporeal imagination*. Moreover, this passage indicates that the information initially received in the common sense is transmitted, automatically and intact, to the corporeal imagination. This procedure clearly does not fit the description of imagination as a "windows shut" operation, but it might fit as part of the "act of the imagination" involved in perceptual inference.

Some further evidence that the physiological basis of the phenomenology of extension is in the imagination can also be found in Meditation II in a passage from AT VII, 32 (CSM II, 21). This is the passage in which Descartes speaks of the "outward forms" of objects, forms that clearly include shape. Though Descartes does not say that the perception of outward form is due to the imagination, we may infer that it is from two facts about the context: (1) that in this passage Descartes is contrasting the power of the intellect to know the essences of things with the power of the imagination and (2) that it is not the intellect that presents the mind with outward forms. The passage runs as follows:

> So let us proceed, and consider on which occasion my perception of the wax was more perfect and evident. Was it when I first looked at it, and believed I knew it by my external senses, or at least by what they call the 'common sense'—that is, *the power of the imagination*. Or is my knowledge more perfect now? (AT VII, 32; CSM II, 21–22; my emphasis)

If this is in fact Descartes's view he would see an account of the sense experience of primary qualities as occurring within the theory of the imagination proper rather than the theory of the senses proper. My own proposal supplements Descartes's account of the three-grades taxonomy of response to sensory stimuli by the faculty of sense with a parallel account of three grades of response to perceptual stimuli by the faculty of imagination.

The ordering principle orders perceptual responses according to increasing amounts of involvement by the mind in the etiology of these responses.[31] I will suppose that the first grade involves no contribution by the mind, being purely neurophysiological. The second grade involves the mind as one of the relata in the relation of mind-body union subserving sensory experience but is not causally mediated by reasoning. The third grade divides into two parts. The first (3a) involves processes of reasoning in the production of sense experience, the second (3b) involves reasoning in a reflective activity directed to sense experiences of grades 2 or 3a.

The distinction between responses attributable to the faculty of sense and those attributed to the faculty of imagination is drawn in terms of the objects of the ideas produced by each faculty. In the case of the senses, the objects of awareness are secondary qualities—color, light, heat, sound; in the case of the imagination the objects of awareness are primary qualities (*Optics* VI: AT VI, 130; CSM I, 167).

In a similar way we can draw a distinction between the faculty of intellect and these others: the former has its own special objects, which are taken by Descartes to be immutable essences differing from the concrete realizations proper to the faculty of imagination. My proposal allows that awareness of these abstract entities can be occasioned by perceptual stimuli in accord with either the second- or third-grade causal paradigm.

Finally, in my proposal, perceptual responses of grades 2 and 3a proper to both the faculty of sense and the faculty of imagination are experiential (phenomenological) responses; those occurring at grade 3b do not produce experiential results but are directed to propositions (the subject of judgments) in one of two ways: either they comprise a derivation of propositional content from the non-propositional objects proper to each faculty or they comprise reasoning about the propositions thus derived.

The case that I have made in this section has been largely taxonomic and somewhat conjectural. As a test of the conjecture, I now turn to Descartes's empirical writings on perception to see how the theory of the sense experience of primary qualities contained in these conjectures is actually carried out.

4.3 Descartes's Empirical Theory of the Sense Experience of Primary Qualities

An Inconsistent Quartet of Propositions?

It is clear from Descartes's earliest views on perception in the *Rules for the Direction of the Mind*[32] as well as his later views in the *Optics*[33] and the Sixth Replies that Descartes sees a fundamental role for reason in the formation of perceptual judgments concerning size, shape, distance, and location. It is also clear that Descartes thinks that men and animals have perceptual mechanisms built into the brain that do not depend on reasoning and that these mechanisms are sufficient to account for all animal behavior and all human behavior that is shared with animals.[34]

The difficulty in reconciling these two doctrines comes into focus when we try to render the following quartet of propositions consistent:

1. Reason determines judgments about the size, shape, distance, and location of objects in man's immediate environment.
2. Animals must have some mechanism for calculating and representing the size, shape, distance, and location of objects in their immediate environment for us to explain their movement in that environment.

3. Only mechanical brain processes and not reason are required to explain the movement of animals in their environment.
4. All of man's bodily movements save for rational speech can be accounted for by the same automatic processes postulated for similar movements of animals.

It follows from propositions 2 and 3 that the kind of representation and calculation of shape, size, distance, and location possessed by animals must be *corporeal*; it follows from this corollary together with 4 that humans must also have mechanisms of corporeal representation and calculation of those properties. The problem is to see how Descartes might hope to reconcile this conclusion with the doctrine expressed in proposition 1. The only interpretation that renders all four propositions jointly consistent is one that postulates for Descartes *two* mechanisms for generating representations of size, shape, distance, and location in man: reason generates intellectual representations, and brain mechanisms generate corporeal representations. Of course it may be that Descartes's views on these matters are not consistent and cannot be rendered consistent without abandoning some fundamental aspects of his theory of man and nature. Let us see.

In the Sixth Replies Descartes makes the following claim:

> I have demonstrated in the *Optics* how size, distance and shape can be perceived by reasoning alone, which works out any one feature from the other features. (AT VII 438; CSM II, 295)

In the *Optics* Descartes is concerned to give an account of *human* perception, the perception of beings with *minds*.[35] As such his interest in the purely physiological mechanisms underlying perception is somewhat secondary to his interest in providing an explanation for the way in which such mechanisms influence the formation of perceptions, both sensory and intellectual. However, the *Treatise of Man* is declared to be a treatise on the purely corporeal mechanisms of the body and we might therefore expect that it would give us insight into how Descartes drew the line between perceptual inference and perceptual mechanisms. Of special interest to us is how Descartes proposed to explain the perceptual mechanisms registering the qualities of shape, size, position, and direction. Since animals must surely somehow register these properties in order to behave as they do, Descartes must surely have a purely mechanistic account in the *Treatise on Man* of how this registration occurs.

The Treatise on Man

I think that Descartes does in fact have at least the materials for such an account in the *Treatise on Man*.[36] Strangely, however, it does not occur, or does not fully occur, in the official place where Descartes talks about the perception of mathematical qualities; for his discussion there, as in the *Optics*, is a discussion of how the *soul* has perception of these qualities. For three of these qualities—direction, shape, and distance—Descartes's explanation of the soul's perception of them clearly postulates a physiological representation, but for size it does not.

This is how it stands for the first three.[37] In the case of *direction*, it appears that the physical arrangement of the nerves or animal spirits in the brain is correlated with the direction in which the eye is pointed at objects affecting it; in the case of *shape* the physiological representation is the retinal image; and in the case of *distance*, it is the shape of the lens and the degree of blurriness of the retinal image. However, in the case of *size*, Descartes does not provide any physiological representation, saying that size is "known . . . simply through [the mind's] knowledge of the distance and position of all points thereof" (AT XI, 160; Hall, 62).

If this account were allowed to stand, then it seems that Descartes makes no provision for animals having perceptual registration of size, something that Descartes surely cannot intend. It soon transpires, however, that this account will not be left to stand, for Descartes soon claims that the physiological representation of those qualities accessible to the mind are ultimately focused as "figures" produced on the surface of the pineal gland. These "figures" seem to consist in the flow of animal spirits directed by the structure of tube openings and closings on the surface of the gland. Descartes lists the "figures" as

> not only things that somehow represent the position of the edges and surfaces of objects [that is, their shape], but also everything which, *as indicated above*, can cause the soul to sense movement, size, distance, colours, sounds, odors, and other such qualities. (AT XI 176; Hall, 85; my emphasis)

The reader will note that "size" appears on this list but only as something the *soul* senses "as indicated above," namely, as inferred from the other physically registered primary qualities. It is not clear from this list by itself whether Descartes supposes that there is a separate pineal gland representation for size in addition to representations of the other qualities, but I can find no evidence in the *Treatise* that he did. Indeed, one has to work hard to find the pineal representations for *the other qualities*, but it appears that *shape* is represented by the shape of the pineal representation of the retinal image (AT XI 176; Hall, 85); *direction* from a member is represented by the orientation of points on the surface of the pineal gland ("each point corresponds to a direction towards which these members can be turned" AT XI 183; Hall, 94); and *distance* from a member is represented by the inverse of the distance of a point on the surface of the gland from the center of the brain (AT 183; Hall, 94). Once again there is no mention of objective size as a quality having a distinct physiological representation.[38] How, then, do we explain the behavior of animals that seems to depend on their possessing some sense of size of objects in their environment?

One possible answer depends on a distinction between a genuine computational process and a simulation of same. Following Cummins[39] we can explain a genuine computational process as follows. First we presuppose a system specifying logical operations like addition or inference on logical items like numbers or sentences. Then we identify a physical system as *computational* when it takes inputs and generates outputs such that the inputs and outputs can be treated as discrete representations of logical items and, when so treated, the set of inputs and outputs satisfies a given logical operation. For example, we can treat a physical system as a computational device for addition if we can treat its inputs as representations of numbers, if we can treat its outputs as representations of numbers, and if the input-output set of number representations satisfies the addition operation.

We can of course build machines that count as addition computers by the definition just offered. It is also in principle possible to build a machine that is not an addition computer in the sense defined but which *simulates* one. An example of such a machine would be one that takes as inputs states that can be treated as number representations and produces a "behavior" of printing out the right answer for an addition operation with those inputs, but which does not have a discrete representation of the sum itself as a state of its internal workings. We can call such a machine a *computational simulation system*.[40]

Since animals clearly do act as if they were somehow aware of the objective size of objects in their environment, Descartes must recognize the existence of some computation-like process providing the physiological basis for this behavior and a computation simulation would seem to serve Descartes's purposes here as well as a genuine computational process.

Perhaps the story goes somewhat as follows. Suppose we want to explain why one animal flees from another animal of the same species that is much bigger than itself. Part of the explanation must be that the first animal registers the second as bigger than itself. Since a retinal image of a given size paired with a long distance can be treated as representative of a relatively large-sized object compared with the objective size represented by the same-size retinal image paired with a short distance, we can imagine a machine in which the former pair would cause a movement of flight in the direction opposite to that of the large animal but the latter would not. Because there are no discrete states representative of the objective sizes, this system counts only as a computational simulation, thus allowing Descartes to explain the behavior of animals in response to objective size *as if* it were to be explained in the same way we explain the behavior of humans in response to objective size, without the former explanation implying the existence of minds or the existence of a separate "figure" in the brain representing objective size.

It is fairly clear that Descartes's account of perception in the *Treatise of Man* is somewhat muddled on the matter of precisely which operations of the human faculty of sense are to be provided purely physiological counterparts to serve as the basis for animal behavior. Nevertheless, Descartes insists that the registration of objective size is a cognitive registration. Why? We shall see in the *Optics* that Descartes insists on an essential cognitive link in the chain of causes producing the human sense experience of objective size. Perhaps Descartes's insistence in the *Treatise of Man* that the perception of size is an act of the soul is an anticipation of this doctrine.

The Optics

In several pages in the Sixth Discourse of the *Optics* (AT VI, 134–141; CSM I, 169–172) Descartes lays out a theory of the psychophysical processes generative of perception of the four basic primary qualities. These processes seem to consist of either a "natural institution," namely, a noninferential causal connection between a physiological registration and a second-grade perceptual response of the imagination or a geometrical inference ("surveyor's reasoning": AT VI, 138; CSM I, 170) employing innate geometrical principles and other information as perceptual algorithms yielding third-grade (3a) responses of the imagination. These algorithms appear to be regarded by Descartes as innate features of the psychophysical system.

The set of processes seem to be ascribed a recursive structure that generates an initial level of mental outputs by natural institution from physiological inputs. For example, regarding position (direction relative to our limbs):

> Our knowledge of it [position] does not depend on any image, nor on any action coming from the object, but solely on the position of the tiny parts of the brain where the nerves originate. For this position changes ever so slightly each time there is a change in the position of the limbs in which the nerves are embedded. Thus it is *ordained by nature* to enable the soul [to know the position of things]. (AT VI, 134; CSM I, 169; my emphasis)

From an initial level of physiological responses (grade 1 responses) and naturally instituted psychological responses (grade 2 responses) the system then generates higher levels of mental outputs (grade 3a or b responses) recursively from certain other assumptions:

> Concerning the manner is which we see the size and shape of objects . . . we judge their size by the knowledge or opinion we have of their distance, compared with the size of the images they imprint on the back of the eye — and not simply by the size of these images. (AT VI, 140; CSM I, 172)

However, when the eye converges on an object "at infinity" the perceptual system can no longer determine specific values that reliably vary with distance so it enters an arbitrary assumption that the object is "one or two hundred feet away." This functions as a "default assumption" in further applications of the perceptual algorithms by the perceptual system:

> [I]f one is looking at an object at all far away, there is also hardly any variation in the angles between the line joining the two eyes (or two positions of the same eye) and the lines from the eye to the object. As a consequence even our 'common' sense seems incapable of receiving in itself the idea of a distance greater than approximately one or two hundred feet. . . . [In] the case of the moon and the sun . . . they normally appear to us as at most only one or two feet in diameter. . . . [This] happens . . . because we cannot conceive them as more than one or two hundred feet away, and consequently their diameters cannot appear to us to be more than one or two feet. (AT VI, 144; CSM I, 173)

There is some ambiguity about how to distribute outputs and inputs described in these texts over the categories of grade 2 and 3 sensory responses. Sometimes Descartes speaks of the size things "appear to us" (e.g., AT VI, 144; CSM I, 173). In other places he speaks of our "knowledge or opinion" of the primary qualities both as a premise to be used in the surveyor's reasoning (AT VI, 140; CSM I, 172) and as a result of other psychophysical processes (AT VI, 135; CSM I, 169). Finally, he speaks of our ability to "imagine distance if not actually to see it" (AT VI, 139; CSM I, 172) and of our inability to "conceive" of objects being more than one or two hundred feet away. (This is how Descartes expresses the "default assumptions" mentioned in the previous paragraph.) My policy will be to treat what we "know," "opine," "imagine," and "conceive" as perceptual responses of the intellect, responses that are conceptual rather than experiential, occurring at grade 3b and to treat what "appears" to us as experiential, occurring at grades 2 or 3a.

My interest in this portion of *Optics* VI is to determine whether Descartes recognizes rational inference as a causal influence on the way in which primary qualities appear to us. On the outcome of this question hangs the justification for distinguishing within the phenomenological grade between grade 2 and grade 3a responses of the imagination. In light of the policy about how to interpret "appears," it is clear from the passage just quoted above that the size which the sun appears to have is causally dependent on reasoning, namely, a response of grade 3a. In the case of appearances arising by natural institutions (see the first of the passages quoted above) they should be regarded as responses of grade 2.

There may, however, still remain some doubts about whether Descartes's conception of appearances should be taken, as I have taken it, in the experiential (qualitative) sense. Despite the contrast Descartes appears to draw between conceptual attitudes such as knowledge and opinion about the way things are and experiential states of the way things appear, can Descartes nevertheless be read as interpreting the concept of the way things look *conceptually*, perhaps as a tendency to believe that things are a certain way? The answer, I believe, is that he cannot be read this way. There are two principle reasons that I would offer for this. (1) Descartes denies that the corporeal imagination influences the will and asserts that tendencies to believe something are properties of the will:

> Now we may distinguish two kinds of movement produced in the [pineal] gland by the spirits. Movements of the first kind represent to the soul these objects which stimulate the senses, or the impression occurring in the brain; and they have no influence on the will. Movements of the second kind, which do have an influence on the will, cause the passions or the bodily movements which accompany the passions. (*The Passions of the Soul* I, 47: AT XI, 365; CSM I, 346)

(2) Some of the phenomena for which he provides a theoretical explanation are described in terms of a conception of appearance that does not naturally lend itself to a conceptualist interpretation. A good example of this comes in Descartes's treatment of size constancy.

Size constancy is a feature of the way things appear to us, specifically, a feature of the way in which apparent size varies with the parameters of distance and size of the retinal images, not just with the size of the retinal image itself. A modern source describes the phenomenon this way:

> As the object increases in distance its image in the eye will correspondingly shrink — just as for a camera. But (and this is easily checked for oneself) as the viewed object recedes it does not appear to shrink anything like as much as the optical halving of the retinal image with each doubling of its distance. It normally *looks* almost the same size over a wide range of distances. This is due to a perceptual compensation called "size constancy scaling."[41]

The phenomenon of size constancy, thus described, must be regarded as a property of the qualitative aspect of the way the object looks rather than a property of our beliefs about the object since, although a familiar object like one's hand is described as *looking* progessively smaller as it is moved away from our eye (though not in proportion to the shrinking of the size of the retinal image), we do not believe (or tend to believe) that our hand *is* getting smaller as it is moved away from our eye.

That there is such a phenomenon, says Descartes,

> is sufficiently obvious from the fact that the images imprinted by objects very close to us are a hundred times bigger than those imprinted by objects ten times farther away, and yet they do not make us see the objects a hundred times larger; instead they make the object look almost the same size, at least if their distance does not deceive us. (AT VI, 140; CSM I, 172)

Notice that in this description, the effect of the distance parameter is not to yield an appearance that is identical with the objective size we believe the object to have, since apparent size does diminish somewhat and objective size not at all. This is why the reference in this passage to how the objects looks should be read qualitatively rather than conceptually.

Size constancy requires the application of perceptual algorithms to the information provided by the size of the retinal image as well as information provided by other physiological mechanisms, for example, variations in the shape of the lens and variations in the angle of convergence of the eye (assuming that the object is closer than one or two hundred feet). We have yet to see the details of how this mechanism works.

Descartes's commitment to direct realism—a doctrine explaining the content of our perceptual ideas—requires that changes in the way things appear to us are due to changes in that part of the brain toward which the mind is directed in these cases, namely, the corporeal imagination. There is, however, some difficulty in seeing how the details work here in light of the presence in the brain of two structures, the corporeal imagination and the common sense, both of which play a role in the physiological determination of perception.

Now consider the difference between what happens in this mechanism in the case where an object is perceived close to us and the case in which it is perceived ten times farther away. In order to account for the approximate constancy of perceived size, we must suppose (1) that in both cases the structure toward which the mind is directed in the corporeal imagination retains approximately the same size. Descartes also says (2) that the size of the retinal image is one hundred times bigger in the first case than in the second. We also have it (3) that "the 'common' sense functions like a seal, fashioning in the phantasy or imagination, as if in wax, the same figures or ideas which come, pure and without body, from the external senses" (Rule 12: AT X, 414; CSM I, 41–42). It appears that these three propositions require that the relevant structures in the corporeal imagination in the two cases both are and are not the same size.

This conundrum arises because we have not taken fully into account the complexity that Descartes sees in the interplay between the corporeal imagination, the common sense, and the mind. The complexity is perhaps best seen in a text from *Rules* 12:[42]

> [The cognitive power] receives figures from the 'common' sense at the same time as does the corporeal imagination, or it applies itself to those which are preserved in

the memory, or forms new ones which so preoccupy the imagination that it is often in no position to receive ideas from the 'common sense' at the same time. . . . In all these functions the cognitive power is sometimes active, sometimes passive; sometimes resembling the seal, sometimes the wax. (AT XI, 415; CSM I, 42)

I infer from this description that the (small) physiological registration of the retinal image in the second case must be altered upon its arrival in the corporeal imagination. *If* this is done by an activity of the cognitive power, it must be an act of trigonometric reasoning employing the assumption present in the second case that the object is ten times more distant than it is in the first case.

Because of its relative constancy under changes to the retinal image, the corporeal image of the distant object can be regarded as a physiological registration of objective size, though one relatively less accurate than the responses of grade 3b comprising conceptual knowledge of objective size. Because of its production as a result of inference,[43] this image can also be regarded as a kind of physiological *hypothesis* concerning the objective size of its causes. I will regard this explanation as a paradigm for other psychophysical explanations of sense experiences involving primary qualities including, as we shall see in the next section, those connected with "referred sensations."

If my reconstruction of the details of the mechanism postulated by Descartes for producing size constancy is accepted, there still is some doubt about whether the output of this mechanism is a grade 2 or a grade 3a response. Grade 3a responses require the active intervention of reasoning, an act of the cognitive power. The doubt arises because there is nothing in Descartes's description of the case nor in the details of our reconstruction requiring that it is the activity of the *mind* that intervenes in the corporeal imagination to effect the changes postulated a couple of paragraphs back. Descartes evidently believes this, but there are sufficient physiological sources of information available in the Cartesian account that a purely physiological computation mechanism might very well suffice also. This possibility suggests the need for a sub-division within grade 2 sensory responses. If a response employs physiological computation mechanisms simulating geometrical inference, it will be assigned to grade 2b. All other responses of grade 2 will be assigned to grade 2a. Descartes needs to provide an additional argument that some perceptual responses require the active intervention of reasoning. The puzzle is to see what that argument might be.

This puzzle is the same as one we uncovered in our discussion (in the preceding section) of the *Treatise on Man*. What had seemed puzzling there was *why* Descartes should insist that the process generating objective size registration in humans (if such there is) can only be a mental act rather than a computational act carried out by the physiological machine. The puzzle arose because Descartes's advertised purpose in writing that portion of the *Treatise on Man* which we are studying (and which is the only portion to have been published) is to provide a theory of the perceptual system that humans share with animals, and, although Descartes regards animals as having no minds, there is as much behavioral evidence for thinking that animals have some kind of registration of perceived objective size as there is for thinking that humans do. Descartes's general explanation for why humans have minds but animals do not is that minds are needed to explain the former's capacity for articulate, spontaneous speech.[44] However, and whatever merits it may have for the intended *explanandum*, this *explanans* does not explain for the case of *perceptual* processes why we should attribute mental computational processes to humans while not attributing such processes to animals.

There is however an empirical argument available from the Cartesian treatment in the *Optics* of a class of phenomena we have yet to consider that provides some justification for seeing in human sensory responses a role for reason and understanding that might not be required for an empirically adequate treatment of animal sensory responses. The phenomena I have in mind are perceptual illusions, and the example I propose to consider is Descartes's treatment of the "moon illusion," well known in modern treatments of perception:[45]

> [W]e can notice their distance [the distance of the moon and the sun on the horizon] more easily [than the distance of the moon and the sun in the sky] because there are various objects between them and our eyes. And, by measuring them with their instruments, the astronomers prove clearly that they appear larger at one time than at another not because they are seen to subtend a greater angle, but because they are judged to be farther way. It follows that the axiom of the ancient optics — which says that the apparent size of objects is proportional to the size of the angle of vision — is not always true. (AT VI, 145; CSM I, 174)

If my general description of the paradigm explanation is correct, the difference in the way the sun or moon look on the horizon compared to the way they look high in the sky is due to a difference in the way in which their respective images are extended in the corporeal imagination. Again, these differences in brain extension require a physiological registration of size different from either the retinal image itself or its reproduction in the "common sense."

A crucial part of Descartes's explanation of these differences is that we "notice" the distance more when the moon is on the horizon (and looks bigger) than we do when the moon is high in the sky (and looks smaller). This noticing is itself due to our noticing objects we know to be large (trees, tall buildings, etc.) that yet look small lying between us and the moon. These facts lead us to infer that the moon must be very far away indeed when observed under these conditions, an inference that we are not inclined to make when the moon is viewed under normal conditions. In this case, *unlike the basic case of size constancy*, the specification of the distance parameter in the algorithm used to compute objective size is not one that can be explained in terms of the purely physiological registration of distance since, *ex hypothesis*, the distance information derived from convergence and accomodative mechanisms is essentially the same in both cases: the distance is "at infinity." What else is needed is a cognitive registration of distance obtained by, and registered in the objects of, the understanding. This registration in turn interacts with the size of the visual angle (or the idea of same naturally instituted) and the algorithm to generate a physiological registration of apparent objective size.

Perhaps Descartes could now justify his denial of cognitive processing to animals both on the methodological grounds that explaining perceptual illusions without appeal to genuinely mental processes would be simply too cumbersome and on the empirical grounds that animals betray no behavioral evidence requiring us to think that they are subject to the appropriate kinds of illusions.

One final observation: the *causal role* in the generation of sense experiences that we have apparently just found for reasoning (grade 3a responses) needs to be distinguished from the *critical role* that Descartes sees for reasoning in the formation of grade 3b sensory responses to perceptual circumstances. For example, in the Sixth Replies, reasoning is cited as the explanation of how we overcome the impulsive tendency to judge that a stick looking bent in water really is bent (AT VII, 438–439; CSM II, 295–296). In this case reason's job is to critically evaluate the relative reliability of judgments made (impulsively) on the basis of the way things look. What distinguishes the critical role of reason in these contexts from its causal role in the contexts discussed here is that the former function subsequent to the generation of sense experiences, the latter function as part of the generation process itself.

The theory that we have just examined counts as an *empirical* theory of the perception of primary qualities, in part because it gives an account of what *causes* sense experience of primary qualities rather than an account of what sense experience *is*. The latter falls within the domain of philosophical theories of perception. Descartes, of course, has a philosophical theory of sensations of color, light, heat, and so on. This theory is quite explicit and can be found in various places in Descartes's philosophical writings. I have been making the case in this chapter that Descartes also recognizes the existence of sense experiences of primary qualities. There must, therefore, be some account of the nature of these experiences within the relevant philosophical doctrine, namely, within the mature theory of ideas. I propose to orient ourselves for the search for this account by giving some initial consideration to Descartes's theory of referred sensations in the *Passions of the Soul*, a late work in which philosophical and empirical considerations are melded together.

4.4 Referred Sensations

The Doctrine in The Passions of the Soul

In *The Passions of the Soul* Descartes divides the functions of the soul into the class of volitions (actions which we "experience . . . as proceeding directly from our soul and as seeming to depend on it alone") and the class of passions ("perceptions or modes of knowledge") (sec. 17: AT XI, 342; CSM I, 335). Passions are then further subdivided into those that are caused by the soul and those those that are caused by the body. In the latter category are the three classes of passions of interest to us (sec. 25: AT I, 349; CSM I, 337–338). Thus in section 23, which is headed with the words "The perceptions we refer to objects outside us," Descartes says "[W]e refer these sensations to the subjects we suppose to be their causes in such a way that we think we see the torch itself and hear the bell"; in section 24 he speaks of our referring sensations of pain to various parts of the body; and in section 25 he identifies those perceptions we "refer only to the soul" as "those whose effects we feel as being in the soul itself," for example, joy, anger, and the like.[46]

The distinctions between kinds of referred passion that Descartes marks here seem to be phenomenological: it is not said here that we "judge" [*juger*] that pain is in our limbs rather than in external objects but that pains are felt [*sentis*] "as being in our limbs and not as being in objects outside us."[47] On the other hand, Descartes clearly does countenance some connection between referred sensations and judgments in his remark just quoted that the nature of referred visual sensations somehow influences us to "think that we see the torch itself." I take this reference to "seeing the torch itself" to be an indication that Descartes sees common sense committed to a version of commonsense realism.[48] The causal explanation for these phenomenological distinctions appears to rely on the psychophysical mechanism of referral. Before considering the empirical details and philosophical significance of the doctrine of referred sensations in *Principles* I, 71, I briefly consider the doctrine as it appears in the *Meditations*.

The Doctrine in the Meditations

In Meditation III Descartes says that some ideas admit of error and some do not: those that do are judgments, acts of the will affirming contents provided by perception,

> And the chief and most common mistake which is to be found here consists in my judging that the ideas which are in me resemble, or conform to, things located outside me. Of course, if I considered just the ideas themselves simply as modes of my thought, without *referring* them to anything else, they could scarcely give me material for error. (AT VII, 37; CSM II, 26; my emphasis)

The notion of referral at issue here seems to be a cognitive act that is somehow responsible for my making errors about the external world. The errors in question have something to do with a naive view that the world resembles my sensory experience, and the *me* in question appears to be an adult person acting unreflectively in response to that experience. The notion of referral at issue here I shall call "mature referral."

Yet if we turn to the discussion of referral in *Principles* I, 71 (see passage quoted in the next subsection, below), we find Descartes speaking of infants rather than adults engaged in an erroneous application of the resemblance principle, an error connected later in this same discussion with the notion of referral. This notion of referral I shall call "immature referral."

We also find there the claim that prior to the intervention of infantile reasoning there was a separation of sensations of color and the sense experience of primary qualities. Since our mature sense experience is of a phenomenological fusion of colors and primary qualities, Descartes's claim seems to have the startling corollary that infantile cognitive acts are causally responsible for the phenomenological form taken by adult sense experience. Though Descartes does not say that the "fused" form of sense experience is responsible for the mistakes of common sense, it seems clear that it is this feature of sense experience that gives commonsense realism its great intuitive power, and it will be my working hypothesis that this is the feature of sense experience that provides the "material for error" of which Descartes speaks in Meditation III.

In the view which I take of this notion, the "material for error" of the senses prompts adults to make mistaken judgments about the objects of the senses; it does not itself consist in the mistake. Descartes must therefore explain how the mistake arises, namely, what psychological processes are at work in generating it, and he must also explain *what the mistake consists in*. The first explanation must draw upon Descartes's theory of doxastic inclinations and the second draws upon much of the apparatus of Descartes's official theory of ideas. My own discussion of these aspects of what I will call Descartes's "error theory"[49] must therefore await my discussion of these other elements of the Cartesian program.[50] I now turn to a reconstruction of Descartes's empirical theory of immature referral suggested by texts from *Principles* I, 71.

The Doctrine of Referred Sensations in Principles I, 71

Referred sensations are sensations in what I shall call *extensional form*. Those referred to the body are *felt as if they are located in the body*, those referred to the world external to the body *appear to be located in the world external to the body*. It will be recalled from the previous subsection that Descartes seems to explain the difference between the two kinds of referred sensations by supposing that we make a hypothesis about the location in the external environment of the cause of a given sensation. Since we have available to us a detailed account of the psychophysical explanation giving rise to these hypotheses, I propose to see if we might extend that explanation to the phenomenon of referred sensations.

The location of the source of a sensory stimulation relative to the eye is a function of the parameters of direction and distance of the source from the eye, and we have seen that Descartes countenances purely mechanical registrations of these parameters. However, it is important to note that the physiological mechanisms underlying the second-grade perception of primary properties—position, distance, size, and shape—are quite different from those underlying the second-grade sensations of secondary qualities:

> All the qualities which we perceive in the objects of sight can be reduced to six principle ones: light, colour, position, distance, size and shape. First, regarding light and colour (the only qualities belonging properly to the sense of sight), we must suppose our soul to be of such a nature that what makes it have the sensation of light is the *force of the movements* taking place in the regions of the brain where the optic nerve-fibres originate, and what makes it have the sensation of colour is *the manner of these movements*. (AT VI, 130; CSM I, 167; my emphasis)

Neither force nor manner of movement are cited by Descartes as physiological bases for perception of the four primary qualities. There is, therefore, no fundamental reason issuing from physiology or the causal principle requiring that the four primary qualities be experienced in a phenomenological fusion with the two secondary qualities. And yet in adult sensory experience this is how they are experienced.

The explanation that I propose is an extension of the basic empirical theory as described previously and some rather scanty materials occurring in a discussion of referred sensations in the *Principles*, part I, article 71 (AT VIIIA, 35; CSM I, 219), and surrounding passages. The themes taken up there seem to reflect the discussion in the *Passions*, though with an important twist. The twist is that in this article from the *Principles* Descartes sees the hypothesizing at work in referral as occurring at an early stage in developmental psychology.[51] Descartes here describes the (childhood) mind as "attributing" sensations to those external objects that it took to cause the sensations. Though Descartes does not say in this passage why the mind does this, he makes repeated references in surrounding passages to the principle that causes must resemble their effects.

Of course Descartes does not accept this principle but appears to think it holds an irresistible attraction for children. (It is the resemblance principle that constitutes the "preconceived opinions" to which the title of the article refers.)[52] I suggest that Descartes treated this principle as a cognitive assumption in the psychophysical process of referring sensations to external objects. This process seems to involve actual, dated "stages." The following passages are taken from Article 71 (passage A):

> [T]he mind that was attached to the body began to notice that the objects of . . . pursuit and avoidance had an existence outside itself. And it attributed to them not only sizes, shapes, motions and the like, which it perceived as things or modes of things, but also tastes, smells, and so on, the sensations of which were, it realized, produced by the objects in question.

Prior to this stage (passage B),

> the mind had various sensations . . . namely what we call sensations of tastes, smells, sounds, heat, cold, light, colour and so on—sensations which do not represent anything located outside our thought. At the same time the mind perceived sizes, shapes, motions and so on, which were presented to it not as sensations but as things, or modes of things, existing (or at least capable of existing) outside thought.

These passages suggests that children experience the world quite differently from adults, experiencing the world of physical objects as not phenomenologically fused with (what turn out to be) sensations of color, heat, and so on. We have yet to see how, in detail, that mechanism works.

Perhaps the story goes somewhat as follows. In the case of sensations referred only to the soul, the corresponding physiological states do not get transmitted to regions of the corporeal imagination representing their causes, since no such representations have been constructed. The result is an emotion, a passion that is not experienced as located anywhere. In the case of sensations referred to bodies "we" (i.e., the psychophysical mechanism) first establish a hypothesis about the location of the cause of the sensation. Sometimes the hypothesis will locate the cause in the environment external to us, sometimes it will locate it within our bodies. (These two possibilities are described in *Passions* I, 23, 24, respectively.) Second, the mechanism concretely represents these locations in a brain "map" (in the corporeal imagination), which serves to represent locations of objects including our own body in the environment. Third, the physiological machinery "refers" (i.e., duplicates) the physiological state s corresponding to a given sensation in the common sense, namely, a state of force and manner of motion, to the appropriate external location l by transmitting s-type information from the common sense to the place in the corporeal imagination representing l. Finally the mind directs itself to the appropriate place in the brain map, the result of which is the creation of a sense experience with the appropriately fused phenomenological characteristics.

Why should the perceptual system perform this complex act of physiological referral? Perhaps it does so under the influence of the resemblance principle, operating here as an assumption of the perceptual system analogous to the other empirical assumptions required to yield grade 3a perceptions of the external environment. This suggestion treats immature referral as a process whereby the physiological system hypothesizes the way the world must be if the resemblance principle were true. Since Descartes thinks that this principle is not true, he regards the experienced world (the world of commonsense realism) as an illusion, an illusion to be explained in terms of the kind of complex interactions between the three grades of sensory response so fruitfully exploited in the *Optics* to explain illusions of a more mundane variety. The difference is one of complexity: in the present case interaction occurs not only within the domain of objects of the imagination but between those objects and the objects proper to the faculty of sense.

Descartes's empirical theory of the material for error provided by the senses serves several purposes within the Cartesian project. For one thing, it serves to confirm the overall empirical theory of perception, for if Descartes can successfully explain how and why things go wrong in the perceptual system, he can have more confidence in his explanation of how and why things go right.

It is also important because it helps to buttress the philosophical case against his Aristotelian opponents. If Descartes can show that there exists a plausible psychophysical hypothesis that can explain how their conception of the world (a development of commonsense realism) can seem obviously true to them even while it is false, this provides an alternative to the Aristotelian explanation that commonsense realism seems obviously true because it is true.

To serve these purposes, Descartes must develop a theory of the material for error of the senses that does not simply beg the question against the Aristotelians. This means deriving the theory of error from within a psychophysical theory that has at least some independent measure of support. Bringing the theory of the material for error within the general empirical theory of perceptual illusion has just this effect.

4.5 Imaginal Images

In chapter 3 I cited passage B[53] (quoted in section 4.4) as one of the few places where Descartes seems to endorse the idea that sensory experience can "present" corporeal objects to the mind (by means of sense experience of geometrical properties). Ordinarily, Descartes seems to regard geometrical properties as perceived only though intellectual contemplation. That something else may be afoot in passages A and B here is indicated partly by the fact that it is *the mind attached to the body* rather than the intellect by itself that is the subject of the perceptions and partly by the fact that Descartes denies that geometrical properties are presented as sensations. There would be no point in making this denial if such properties were simply the immutable essences contemplated by the pure intellect.

There is a good deal of independent evidence that Descartes sees a special cognitive relation between the mind and the brain. This evidence shows up in those texts where Descartes speaks of the brain as an object which the mind "contemplates," to which the mind is "directed" and similar concepts that look to be in the same general neighbourhood of the concept of intuitive awareness. These texts are scattered throughout Descartes's philosophical writings, from the early work of the *Rules*[54] to the *Meditations*.[55]

But a passage from *Conversation with Burman* (quoted in section 3.2) is especially striking:

> When external objects act on my senses, they print on them an idea, or rather a figure, of themselves; and when the mind *attends to* these images on the gland in this way, it is said to perceive. (AT V, 162; CSMK III, 344; my emphasis)

The mind that "attends to theses images" is the mind attached to the body, the same mind that Descartes is discussing in passage A from *Principles* I, 71. As I have argued previously in this chapter, Descartes generally takes this act to occur within the precincts of the imagination. It appears, therefore, that the presentations of corporeal objects under discussion in *Principles* I, 71, are awarenesses proper to the faculty of imagination. I shall call such awarenesses *imaginal images*.

There are some places in which Descartes acknowledges an important role for the imagination in our knowledge of the external world:

> The soul can be conceived only by pure intellect; the body (i.e. extension, shape and movement) can likewise be known by pure intellect, but *much better by intellect aided by imagination*. (AT III, 690; *Letters*, 141; my emphasis)

However, in general, the epistemic function of the imagination is not one that Descartes is at much pains to emphasize, going out of his way in the *Meditations* to deny any significant role to that faculty either in knowing the nature[56] or the existence[57] of the material world. Nevertheless, as I have argued[58] on both systematic and exegetical grounds, in his proof of the existence of the material world in *Principles* II, 1, Descartes appears to be relying on the existence of a class of perceptions that have the logical properties of concrete intuitions of geometrical properties, and the only likely candidates for this class of perceptions are the imaginal images of *Principles* I, 71.

Concrete intuitions are awarenesses of properties that entail the formal containment of the properties in some actual substance. Awarenesses (clear and distinct ideas) are relations among persons x, properties P, and the form ϕ in which the properties are presented to the mind of x. The general rule of truth connects awarenesses of properties with the containment of those properties in a substance:

The General Rule of Truth (Final Version) (RTF*)

If I have a clear and distinct idea i with objective reality $\phi_1 \ldots \phi_n$ comprising the individual sense of t, then there is a substance s and there is a set of real properties $P_1 \ldots P_n$ corresponding to the set of content properties $\emptyset_1 \ldots \emptyset_n$ such that $P_1 \ldots P_n$ are contained formally or eminently in s and $P_1 \ldots P_n$ are objects of i.

In the *special case* of concrete intuitive awareness the content properties and the object properties are the same, resulting in a version of the rule of truth that can be expressed as follows:

The Rule of Truth for Concrete Intuition

If have intuitive awareness of $P_1 \ldots P_n$, then there exists a substance x such that x possesses $P_1 \ldots P_n$ formally.

My proposal is that imaginal images are concrete intuitions of geometrical properties in this sense. For purposes of grounding the proof of the external world in *Principles* II, 1, we need only assume that the object properties of imaginal images are very general properties—breadth, depth, length, and extension-in-general are the properties Descartes mentions in the proof. Later I will consider the possibility of extending the class of imaginal images to *particular* geometrical properties.[59] Since on this reading imaginal images entail both the existence of bodies and the existence of minds, it follows that imaginal images fall within that special domain of the union of mind and body, a fact which is indicated by the phenomenologically sensuous way in which imaginal images present their objects to our minds.[60]

If imaginal images are needed in Cartesian epistemology, they are also needed to ground the Cartesian phenomenology of sense experience. I have contended in the previous section that the phenomenology of sense experiences has for Descartes a primary-quality dimension as well as a secondary-quality dimension—things can look extended in a phenomenological sense just as they can look colored.

It is clear that in his mature writings Descartes does not allow that colors have an extended form, for colors are sensations[61] and sensations certainly lack extended form. (Sensations are a species of acts of thought and "acts of thought have nothing in common with corporeal acts, and thought, which is the common concept under which they fall, is different in kind from extension" [Third Replies: AT VII, 176; CSM II, 124].) We cannot, therefore, account for the phenomenological fusion of color and shape by supposing that shape is the form of color or vice versa. We might, however, be able to account for their fusion by supposing that color is a mode of imaginal images, the sensory perception of shape due to mind-body union. A "mode" in Cartesian terminology is a nonessential property (form) of the basic attributes of mind (thought), of bodies (extension) or of mind-body union.[62] I say "nonessential" because sensory perceptions of shape are the imaginal images of *Principles* I, 71, and Descartes suggests in that passage that imaginal images and sensations of color (and sounds, etc.) are not phenomenologically fused in early infancy. As we have seen the fusion occurs as a result of the operations of "referral," the psychophysical mechanism also responsible for most of the errors of common sense.

In making the case that Descartes countenances a true, concrete idea of geometrical properties, I have assumed that Descartes countenances a qualitative presence of such properties in consciousness. The text from *Principles* I, 71, has formed an important part of my evidence for this. However, Ann MacKenzie takes this same text as evidence that Descartes denies this very contention, denying, in her words, that "mechanical properties are exhibited in consciousness by means of qualia."[63]

MacKenzie's case focuses on the text we have called passage B, arguing as follows: "Since a qualitative counterpart of a sensible mechanical property would not be capable of existing outside thought, this passage seems to imply that mechanical properties are not presented to the mind by means of qualia."[64] If we translate MacKenzie's notion of a "qualitative counterpart of a mechanical property" into the theory of concrete intuition we get the notion of a mechanical property being the *object* of concrete intuition. Thus understood, there is no reason to accept the premise of MacKenzie's: the geometrical objects of concrete intution certainly would be capable of existing outside thought: they would not, indeed, be capable of existing anywhere else.

Underlying MacKenzie's claim is the assumption that by "sensation" Descartes must have meant what contemporary philosophers mean by "qualia," that is, anything presented in a phenomenologically sensuous manner to the mind.[65] This, I think, is a mistake. Sensations, for Descartes, are essentially modes of mind or of a mind-body relationship. When Descartes speaks of things not being presented *as sensations*, as he does in passage B, he means that they do not appear as modes of a mental substance; correlatively, speaking of things that are presented as sensations, he means that things do appear as a mode of a mental substance. I take "appear" here to occur in a phenomenological rather than in an epistemic sense, since Descartes concludes this passage by saying that we are not yet "aware of the difference between things and sensations." (The awareness at issue in this phrase must be the epistemic awareness that develops only later in the cognitive evolution of the child, a process that Descartes goes on to describe in detail subsequently in the passage.) This does not entail that Descartes is denying a phenomenologically sensuous dimension to our perception of sizes and shapes. On the contrary, when Descartes denies that sizes and shapes are presented as sensations, as he does in passage B, I take him to be affirming that they are presented (in a phenomenological sense) as modes of a material substance.

FIVE

The Perceptual Representation of Ordinary Objects

5.1 Descartes's Theory of Natural Signs: The Constitutive versus the Minimalist Interpretation

In the previous chapter I developed a taxonomy of Descartes's theory of perceptual responses that divided perceptual responses into those proper to the faculty of sense—sensations of color, heat, and so on—and those proper to the faculty of imagination—experiences of size, shape, and other primary qualities. I also appealed to differences in the causes of these experiences to produce four subcategories corresponding to the "three grades of sensory response" introduced in the Sixth Replies. The first level, grade 1, is a purely physiological response; the second level, grade 2, is a phenomenological response causally unmediated by inference; the third level, grade 3a, is a phenomenological response causally mediated by inference; and a fourth level, grade 3b, is the intellectual response resulting from reflective reasoning applied to responses of the second or third grade.

In Meditation III, however, Descartes introduces another taxonomy of ideas:

> Among my ideas, some appear to be innate, some to be adventitious, and others to have been invented by me. My understanding of what a thing is, what truth is, and what a thought is, seems to derive simply from my own nature. But my hearing a noise, as I now do, or seeing the sun, or feeling the fire, comes from things which are located outside me, or so I have hitherto judged. Lastly, sirens, hippogriffs and the like are my own invention. But perhaps all my ideas may be thought of as adventitious, or they may all be innate, or all made up; for as yet I have not clearly perceived their true origin. (AT VII, 37–38; CSM II, 26)

I shall call this the "philosophical taxonomy of ideas" to contrast it with the "empirical taxonomy of perceptual responses" previously developed.

Though it is clear that the categories in the philosophical taxonomy are related to those in the empirical taxonomy, it is also appears that these are not simply the same categories under different descriptions. Consider one of Descartes's standard examples of an apparently adventitious idea, the idea of the sun. Of principal significance is the fact that the sun is *an object*, an object which, from the commonsense point of view of the Third Meditation, possesses both primary and secondary qualities. Consequently, the commonsense *idea* of the sun is an idea that apparently represents a material object with both primary and secondary qualities. This introduces an element into the discussion of apparently adventitious ideas not present in the discussion of the empirical taxonomy.

In Meditation I Descartes says that we form "all the images of things, whether true or false, that occur in our thought" from a class that includes:

> corporeal nature in general, and its extension; the shape of extended things; the quantity, or size and number of these things; the place in which they may exist, the time through which they may endure, and so on. (AT VII, 20; CSM II, 14)

We have yet to consider how these simple natures comprise images of ordinary physical objects. There seem to be two main possibilities, corresponding to the distinction between theories determining reference by means of an individuating sense or description and theories determining reference by a causal or other "naturalistic" relation between word and object. There are elements of each position in Descartes's writings. The first is reflected in the philosophical theory of truth we explored in chapters 1 and 2, in which *reference*, insofar as Descartes has such a notion, is determined through the exemplification of properties comprising individual senses. The second is reflected in some of Descartes's empirical writing where he relies on a theory of "natural signs":

> Words, as you well know, bear no resemblance to the things they signify, and yet they make us think of these things. . . . Now if words, which signify nothing except by human convention make us think of things to which they bear no resemblance, then why could nature not also have established some sign which would make us have the sensation of light, even if the sign contained nothing in itself which is similar to this sensation? Is it not thus that nature has established laughter and tears, to make us read joy and sadness on the faces of men? (AT XI, 3; CSM I, 81)

It is also reflected in those writings , chiefly in *Optics* IV, where he speaks of the ability of corporeal images arising from perceptual processes to represent objects in the environment causally responsible for them. With these images Descartes "note[s] that the problem is to know simply how they can enable the soul to have sensory perceptions of all the various qualities of the objects to which they correspond—not to know how they can resemble these objects" (AT VI 113; CSM I, 166). Descartes seems to make the same point about the theory of natural signs in the *Treatise on Light*: "[It] is our mind which represents to us the idea of light each time our eye is affected by the action which signifies it" (AT XI, 4; CSM I, 81).

I have discussed many of the passages in which Descartes discusses natural signs previously[1] although with a somewhat different purpose. There my purpose was to explore the significance of the Cartesian analogy of ideas to images, here I propose to see whether the naturalistic notion of signification is partly constitutive of, or merely causally related to, the Cartesian notion of the representation of ordinary physical objects.

Any theory of natural signs postulates some item that carries natural information about objects in the environment. It is not in dispute whether Descartes employs a theory of natural signs in this sense. However, it is important to distinguish between theories that employ natural signs to *explain causally* how contents (re)presented to the mind by other means come to be in general reliable indicators of the truth, and theories that employ natural signs in the *definition* of perceptual (re)presentation. Any theory of perceptual (re)presentation employing natural signs must at least accomplish the first task. I shall call a theory that *at most* attempts the first task a *minimal theory of natural signs*. I shall call a theory that attempts the definitional task a *constitutive theory of natural signs*.[2]

There is strong evidence that Descartes does not regard natural signification as constitutive of his basic notion of (re)presentation. Consider, for example, the passage from Meditation I quoted earlier in this chapter in which it is simple natures that are said to be responsible for the mind's capacity to form "images of things." Lest we are in doubt that Descartes means to exclude "corporeal images" from the class of images of things, Descartes expressly says that he does mean to exclude them in a passage from the definition of *idea* in the Second Replies:

> Indeed, insofar as these images are in the corporeal imagination, that is, are depicted in some part of the brain, I do not call them 'ideas' at all; I call them 'ideas' only insofar as they give form to the mind itself, when it is directed toward that part of the brain. (AT VII, 160; CSM II, 113)

I have argued in chapter 2, section 2.8, that ideas are the chief means by which contents are presented to the mind and that the point of saying that ideas are like images is to ascribe this property to ideas. In denying that corporeal images are ideas, Descartes is therefore telling us that corporeal images are not among the primary vehicles of (re)presentation. So Descartes does not adhere to a constitutive theory of natural signs. The Cartesian constitutive theory of the representation of ordinary physical objects is the individuating-sense theory: our ideas refer to those physical objects that uniquely exemplify them. But why, then, does Descartes speak of corporeal *images* at all? He does so, I believe, because even in a minimal theory of natural signs, corporeal images contribute to making physical objects accessible as a content to cognition.

To see this, note that unless the sets of properties that (real) ideas present to the mind are true of an actual object in the environment, the individual sense that those sets comprise will not refer to that object and that object will thus remain inaccessible to cognitive action. Note also that corporeal images are naturally correlated with certain environmental properties that standardly cause them and with certain ideas which they cause. For example, Descartes regards the pineal gland registration of the direction in which the eyes are pointed as both being caused by a stimulus object lying in that direction and as causing the mind to perceive the simple nature corresponding to that direction. What makes it reasonable to describe a corporeal image as making a physical object accessible to the mind on a certain perceptual occasion consists in the fact that the corporeal image is *causally respon-*

sible for (but not constitutive of) the fact that the individual sense is true of that object on that occasion.

Consider again the list of items comprising our images of external objects: "corporeal nature in general, and its extension; the shape of extended things; the quantity, or size and number of these things; the place in which they may exist, the time through which they may endure, and so on" (AT VII, 20; CSM II, 14).

Notice that no mention is made of sensory qualities.[3] This appears to mean that the power of an idea to represent something lies exclusively in either the ideas of the imagination or those of the intellect.

There is, of course, more to the commonsense idea of the sun than the idea of an object with purely primary qualities: the sun is also hot and yellow. However, some difficulty attends to seeing how Descartes proposes to incorporate these properties into the idea of the sun, for he does not mention color and heat in the list of ideas with representational power. Lest we think this a simple oversight on his part, we see from a corresponding passage in *Principles* I, 71, that it is not:

> [T]he mind had various sensations . . . what we call the sensations of tastes, smells, sounds, heat, cold, light, colours and so on—sensations which do not represent anything located outside our thought. At the same time the mind perceived sizes, shapes, motions and so on, which were presented to it not as sensations but as things, or modes of things, existing (or at least capable of existing) outside thought. (AT VIIIA, 35; CSM I, 219)

If the sensations of color and heat do not represent "anything outside thought," how can they contribute to the ability of an apparently adventitious idea to represent an object "outside thought" having those properties? The answer is that they contribute to the content of apparently adventitious ideas, not in virtue of some representative function, since they have none,[4] but by way of the special cognitive act Descartes calls "referral":

> [W]e refer these sensations [the sound of a bell and the light of a torch] to the subjects we suppose to be their causes in such a way that *we think we see the torch itself* and hear the bell and not that we have sensory perception merely of movements coming from these objects. (*Passions* I, 23: AT XI, 346; CSM I, 337; my emphasis)

As the emphasized phrase indicates, it is a *judgment* that the act of referring produces. The central thesis that I will be defending in the remainder of this chapter is this: what plays the role in the Cartesian system of representations of commonsense objects possessing both primary and secondary qualities is not an (image-like) idea—an entity falling within the passive faculty of perception/intellect—but a judgment arising from referred sensations—an entity falling within the province of the will.

Moreover, this class of judgments (*referral judgments* as I shall call them) is identified by Descartes as a chief source of the errors of common sense:

> And the chief and most common mistake which is to be found here consists in my judging that the ideas which are in me resemble, or conform to, things located outside me. Of course, if I considered the ideas themselves simply as modes of my thought, without referring them to anything else, they could scarcely give me any material for error. (AT VII, 37; CSM II, 26)

I will focus my defence of this thesis on a consideration of the following two questions. What is the nature of referral judgments? And why do we make them?

5.2 Referral Judgments: What are They?

A paradigm Cartesian judgment takes a propositional object derived from clear and distinct ideas in accord with the rule of truth. The objects of referral judgments are not propositions; nor is there any indication that, whatever status these objects possess, they are derived by means of the rule of truth from the clear and distinct perception of immutable essences. On the contrary, referral judgments take ideas of secondary qualities, heat, cold, color, and so on, ideas that Descartes characterizes a bit later in Meditation III as "obscure," "confused," and "materially false" (AT VII, 44; CSM II, 30). Whatever these descriptions mean, it is very clear that Descartes intends by their use to contrast such ideas with those of geometrical properties. These properties are proper objects of intuitive awareness and can form the basis for propositional judgment. Although Descartes will eventually countenance sensory qualities among those that can be the objects of intuitive awareness,[5] in Meditation III they have no such status. Referral judgments concern such properties and, thus, fail to fit the Cartesian paradigm for acts of judgment.

How, then, are we to understand these acts? The only clue that Descartes provides us in Meditation III is that the belief that ideas "resemble" their effects is somehow responsible for acts of referral judgment. There seem to be two ways in which resemblance might figure in an account of referral judgments: (1) by way of explaining the nature of referral judgments, and (2) by explaining what causes us to make referral judgments. In the case of the process of *immature referral* (the empirical process responsible for the phenomenological characteristics of our experience of ordinary physical objects described in the previous chapter),[6] I claimed that the concept of resemblance plays a causal role in the process, namely, that of a hypothesis assumed by the perceptual system. However, in the case of *mature referral* at issue in the present discussion the situation is different. Here the concept of resemblance plays a constituting rather than a causal role. What it constitutes is the notion of a referral judgment.

Throughout his writings, Descartes makes use of several notions of resemblance. One is a theoretical postulate we make regarding the resemblance of ideas with their causes.[7] As I shall understand it, in its *causal/explanatory use* resemblance functions as a general premise in an inference from the nature of our ideas to the nature of the things that produce them. Sometimes this principle is used preconsciously as in immature referral, sometimes it is used consciously as a theoretical principle that presupposes an awareness of ideas *as ideas*. In addition to this causal/explanatory use, there seem to be at least three other uses for the notion of resemblance, each related to the other in important ways.

The Scholastic Use. Just after noting in the Third Meditation that he thinks that "this sensation or idea of heat comes to me from something other than myself," Descartes adds, "And the most obvious judgement for me to make is that the thing in question *transmits* to me its own likeness rather than something else" (AT VII,

38; CSM, II, 26; my emphasis). I have emphasized "transmits" to indicate that Descartes conceives of this as the theoretical error embodied in the Scholastic doctrine of the transmission of intentional species. Because this use commits to a specific proposal about causal mechanisms preserving the purported resemblance between ideas and their sources, it should be distinguished from the broader causal/explanatory use.

The Verisimilitude Use. To mark the end of his initial consideration of resemblance reasoning in the Third Meditation, Descartes considers the lack of resemblance between our two ideas of the suns (AT VII, 39; CSM II, 27). The point of discussion is that the "idea" I have of the sun derived "from the senses" is very inaccurate in comparison with that derived from astronomical reasoning. In this case "idea" seems to mean "judgment" and "from the senses" refers to the physiological and computational processes described in the Sixth Discourse of the *Optics*. This point is much obscured by Descartes terminology: he uses "resembles" where he means to speak of degree of verisimilitude.

The De Re *Use.* In the Sixth Meditation Descartes offers some examples of judgments that are "ill considered":

> Cases in point are the belief that any space in which nothing is occurring to stimulate my senses must be empty; or that the heat in a body is something exactly resembling the idea of heat which is in me; or that when a body is white or green, the selfsame whiteness or greenness which I perceive through my senses is present in the body. (AT VII, 82; CSM II, 56–57)

In this passage the juxtaposition of "resemblance" in the second clause with the claim embodied in the third, suggests that Descartes sees an easy slippage between one formulation and the other. Given this context it looks as if resemblance for color should consist in the presence of the "self-same whiteness or greenness" both as what I see and as what exists in the body itself. Thus interpreted, the belief that there is a "resemblance" between the colors I see and the colors in objects that I see is *constituted by* the composite belief that color qualities are both immediate objects of perception and properties of physical objects.

Of course Descartes thinks that the immediate objects of sensory perception are ideas and that colors, conceived as immediate objects of perception, are sensations, or aspects of sensations but this is a philosophically sophisticated view that Descartes does not seem to attribute to naive subjects. If we treat the naive belief in a purely representational way, that is as a *de dicto* belief that colors in bodies resemble colors in sensations, we are forced to attribute this philosophically sophisticated view to naive subjects. However, if we treat the naive belief as the *de re* belief—*colours are in fact modes of sensation but philosophically naive people believe of colors that they are modes of objects immediately seen by them* —we avoid this attribution.

I suggest that the same kind of *de re* cognition is involved in the passage from *Passions* I, 23, serving as my chief textual source[8] for the notion of referral judgments:

> [W]e *refer these sensations to the causes we suppose to be their subjects in such a way that we suppose we see the torch itself* . . . and not that we have sensory perception merely of movements coming from these objects. (AT XI, 346; CSM I, 337; my emphasis)

To test the merits of this suggestion consider how the passage reads with the italicized phrase in the previous passage replaced by an explicitly *de re* formulation (in brackets) of the same judgment as follows:

> [Colors (e.g., flame colors) are in fact a set of modes of sensation M but philosophically naive people believe of M that they are a set of properties of an object x (e.g., a torch) such that x is both an immediate object of sensory perception and a cause of that sensory perception,] and not that we have sensory perception merely of movements coming from these objects. (AT XI, 346; CSM I, 337; my interpolation)

If I have Descartes right here, he is suggesting that referral judgments are a special class of judgments distinguished from paradigm judgments by their logical properties. Referral judgments are relational acts of the will capable of falsehood but not truth, holding between sensations and objects we believe to be the causes of those sensations. Paradigm judgments are relational acts of the will capable of truth but not falsehood, directed to propositions known intuitively. Although I shall have a bit more to say later[9] about how referral judgments fit into other aspects of the Cartesian theory of ideas, I shall assume that we now have at least a rough idea of what referral judgments are. In the next section I propose to consider why we make them.

However, before turning to that question I need to say a bit more about Descartes's philosophical taxonomy of ideas. In particular, I wish to clarify the nature of, and the relationship between, adventitious ideas, apparently adventitious ideas and innate ideas.

An adventitious idea is one that is "foreign to me and coming from outside" (French text: AT IX, 29; Alquié II, 434) and a "prime example" of an apparently adventitious idea is the idea of the sun:

> For example, there are two different ideas of the sun which I find within in me. One of them, which is acquired as it were from the senses and which is a prime example of an idea I reckon to come from an external source, makes the sun appear very small. The other idea is based on astronomical reasoning. (Meditation III: AT VII, 39; CSM II, 27)

I have been speaking here of *apparently* adventitious ideas because Descartes is careful not to say that there are any *genuine* adventitious ideas. What he says, rather, is simply this: "But perhaps all my ideas may be thought of as adventitious, or they may all be innate, or all made up; for as yet I have not clearly perceived their true origin" (Meditation III: AT VII, 38; CSM II, 26). A reader of this passage will naturally expect Descartes to say which particular ideas fall genuinely into which particular categories and which merely seem to fall there. Yet what is Descartes's account and where does he give it? My proposal about the content of Descartes's account has two parts. (1) What Descartes calls "adventitious ideas" of ordinary objects are not passive effects of the faculties involved in perception—hence not, *strictly speaking*, ideas at all[10]—but are referral judgments (effects of the will engaging in a special cognitive activity) that we fail to recognize as such. (2) Once we recognize referral judgments for what they are, we can separate the passive from the active elements of those judgments. The passive elements can be divided into the class of ideas—ideas in the strict sense—of particular sensory qualities like color, sound, heat, and cold—and the class of particular geometrical qualities. Both classes of ideas are innate, not adventitious. However, we take them to be adventitious for various reasons to be discussed in section 5.3.

Descartes poses the question of how ideas are to be correctly classified early in Meditation III. He does not, however, give a very clear or comprehensive answer to this question anywhere in the *Meditations*. What he does say is confined mainly to the following passage from later in Meditation III.

> Such ideas obviously do not require me to posit a source distinct from myself. For on the one hand, if they are false, that is, represent non-things, I know by the natural light that they arise from nothing—that is, they are in me only because of a deficiency and lack of perfection in my nature. If on the other hand they are true, then since the reality which they represent is so extremely slight that I cannot even distinguish it from a non-thing, I do not see why they cannot have originated from myself. (AT VII, 44; CSM II, 30)

The class of ideas of which Descartes is speaking here includes "light and colours, sounds, smells, tastes, heat and cold and the other tactile qualities" (AT VII 43; CSM II, 30). If the ideas on this list come from myself then they are not adventitious ideas. A partial answer to Descartes's question has thus been provided.

There of course remains the question of how we are to understand the reasons offered by Descartes in support of this answer. The argument comes in the form of a dilemma, and I shall not consider the second horn until chapter 7. The first horn assumes that these ideas are in me "because of a deficiency and lack of perfection in my nature." Descartes waits until Meditation IV to give his account of the nature of human imperfection:

> Next, when I look more closely at myself and inquire into the nature of my errors (for these are the only evidence of some imperfection in me), I notice that they depend on two concurrent causes, namely on the faculty of knowledge which is in me, and on the faculty of choice or freedom of the will; that is, they depend on both the intellect and the will simultaneously. Now all that the intellect does is to enable me to perceive the ideas [French edition: without affirming or denying anything] which are subjects for possible judgements; and when regarded strictly in this light, it turns out to contain no error in the proper sense of that term. (AT VII, 56; CSM II, 39; my interpolation; AT IX, 45; Alquié II, 459)

In this passage Descartes says that the only deficiencies that exist in relation to ideas arise from the will, that is, from the faculty of judgment. If we compare this passage with passages from early in Meditation III,

> Now as far as ideas are concerned, provided they are considered solely in themselves and I do not refer them to anything else, they cannot strictly speaking be false. (AT VII, 37; CSM II, 26)

and

> [T]he chief and most common mistake which is to be found here consists in my judging that the ideas which are in me resemble, or conform, to things located out-

side me. Of course if I considered just the ideas themselves simply as modes of my thought, without referring them to anything else, they could scarcely give me any material for error. (AT VII, 37; CSM II, 26)

The second of these passages is one that I quoted before to initiate a discussion leading to the result that referral judgments are a special class of *de re* cognitions. What we have from the other passages is the claim, given the first horn of the dilemma, that ideas of color, sound, smell, and so on, are in me because they are deficencies and deficiencies are located only in acts of judgment. This gives the result that this class of "ideas" is not genuinely a class of ideas at all but rather a class of judgments. The similarity in content of the two sets of passages suggests that this class of judgments is identical with the class of referral judgments.

For example, the apparently adventitious idea of heat embodies a referral judgment that heat is a single property type that exists as both something immediately present to consciousness (as the sensation of heat) and as a mode of an external object. Since Descartes thinks that sensory qualities could not satisfy these conditions, he takes the objects of the apparently adventitious idea of heat to be impossible. It is somewhat in this sense that I take Descartes's claim in Meditation III that ideas of heat are "non-things," "chimerical things that cannot exist" (CSM II, 30: AT VII, 43).

That we choose to make such judgments is a defect of our will, correctable in principle by those who choose to follow Cartesian method to its ultimate conclusion embodied in the mechanistic theory of nature.[11] Yet even those people who have yet to reach this conclusion can still avoid error by restricting the content of their belief about sensory qualities to what we shall call the *content-neutral description*, "the things, whatever they may turn out to be, which are the source of our sensations" (*Principles* I, 70: CSM I, 218; AT VIIIA, 35). Like the erroneous, apparently adventitious idea of heat, the content-neutral idea of heat is a functional compound of various other categories of idea, but unlike the apparently adventitious idea, it is neither confused nor false. It is unconfused because it is not a *de re* ascription of sensations to objects but is a reflective judgment *de dicto* taking as its object a proper intellectual proposition functionally describing the causes of sensations. It is not false because it veridically expresses a minimal content appropriate to the measure of epistemic caution that we should adopt when in the preliminary stages of rational inquiry.

It is important to note, however, that although the topic-neutral description of the causes of sensations seems to be regarded by Descartes as a nonconfused conception of heat, it still contrasts with the idea of heat as a simple perceptual response. The former is a grade 3b response; the latter is a grade 2 response.

There are, thus at least *three* conceptions of heat and other secondary qualities present in Descartes' taxonomic schemes. The confused conception is clearly not a legitimate one, its objects are "chimerical things that cannot exist." What of the other two? Does Descartes think that colours are functional, content-neutral states of the external world or does he think that are content-specific properties of minds or of mental states? I take these questions up in a later chapter.[12]

There is some independent evidence for the claim that apparently adventitious ideas of the senses are a special form of judgment. Consider, for example a letter to Mersenne of July 16, 1641:

> [A]ll those [ideas] which involve no negation or affirmation are innate; because the sense organs do not bring us anything which is like the idea which arises in us at their stimulus, and so this idea must have been in us before. (AT III, 414; *Letters*, 108)[13]

I will take it that ideas that *do* involve affirmation or negation are some kind of judgment, states of mind that are at least partially acts of the will, not simply passive responses of the senses. Here Descartes seems to bifurcate ideas into those that do not involve affirmation or negation and those that do. The former he calls "innate"; he has no name for the latter. However, if we employ the terminology from the tripartite taxonomy of Meditation III, it seems that the latter class of ideas must be the same as the class of ideas that are either invented or adventitious. Moreover, the reference to what "the sense organs bring us" suggests that Descartes is thinking here of apparently adventitious ideas as the contrast class for innate ideas, thus as the class of ideas that involve some element of judgment.

In the passage just quoted from the letter to Mersenne it seems that Descartes does not mean to exclude ideas of the senses in general from the class of innate ideas ("this idea must have been in us before"). Since the perceptual responses of grades 2 and 3a from both the faculties of sense and imagination are ideas of the senses and yet are not constituted by judgments of any kind, such responses do not appear to be excluded from the class of innate ideas. So, perhaps, we can find here a home for perceptual responses.

To summarize the claims made to date in this section: Descartes sees a fundamental difference within the theory of sensory ideas between ideas of the senses that are judgment laden and those that are not, and he sees the latter coinciding with the class of innate ideas.

Further evidence for these propositions is to be found in a passage from *Comments on a Certain Broadsheet*:

> [T]here is nothing in our ideas which is not innate to the mind or the faculty of thinking, with the sole exception of those circumstances which relate to experience, such as the fact that *we judge* that this or that idea which we now have immediately before our mind refers to a certain thing situated outside us. (AT VIIIB, 358–359; CSM I, 304; my emphasis)

A bit later Descartes argues:

> [N]either the motions themselves nor the figures arising from them are conceived by us exactly as they occur in the sense organs, as I have explained at length in my *Optics*. Hence it follows that the very ideas of the motions themselves and of the figures are innate in us. The ideas of pain, colours, sounds and the like must be all the more innate if, on the occasion of certain corporeal motions, our mind is to be capable of representing them to itself, for there is no similarity between these ideas and the corporeal motions. (AT VIIIB, 359; CSM I, 304)

In this passage Descartes declines to treat both ideas of primary qualities and ideas of secondary qualities as adventitious on the grounds that the patterns transmitted through the physical media are not the same as the qualities which become the objects of our ideas. This suggests that Descartes is thinking of adventitious ideas

(ideas that "come from outside us") as the *species* countenanced by Scholastic theories of perception, and Descartes has theoretical reasons grounded in his mechanistic philosophy for rejecting these theories.

The net effect of this on the classification of ideas is as follows. Cognitions of sensory qualities come in two main varieties: those that are purely passive responses to sensory stimulation (sensations) and those that are the *de re* cognitive acts by means of which the first are referred to their external causes. The former *seem* to be adventitious (seem to come from outside us) because of the misleading effects of this quasijudgmental act, but they are in fact innate. Although the proximate causes of the latter (the referral judgments) lie within the faculty of will and the faculty of sensation, hence lie within us, the remote causes are circumstances "which relate to experience," and we may infer that Descartes regards such cognitions as genuinely adventitious.

Some direct textual confirmation for this conclusion comes from a passage in the *Conversation with Burman* where Descartes is responding to Burman's impression that in the passages from the *Broadsheet* that we have just been considering Descartes was advancing the view that all ideas are innate. As a result of this impression Burman then asked: "Does it then follow that the mystery of the Trinity, for example, is innate?" Descartes replied as follows:

> The author does not say that all ideas are innate in him. He says there are also some which are adventitious, for example the idea he has of the town of Leiden or Alkmaar. Secondly, even though the idea of the Trinity is not innate in us to the extent of giving us an express representation of the Trinity, none the less *the elements and rudiments of the idea are innate in us,* as we have an innate idea of God, the number 3, and so on. (AT V, 165; CSM III, 347; my emphasis)

In this passage Descartes says that ideas of ordinary physical objects (e.g., towns) are adventitious, while the elements of those ideas (ideas of their qualities) are innate in us. This provides confirmation for the view offered in this chapter that Cartesian ideas of ordinary objects are complex ideas composed in part of referral judgments and that the latter are *de re* cognitions that are in turn composed of innate elements from the faculty of sensation. Descartes also maintains that external events are salient (though partial and remote) components of the etiology of referral judgments. These two things together imply the doctrine reported in this passage, namely, that such cognitions are adventitious.

In Meditation III Descartes had posed the question "But perhaps all my ideas may be thought of as adventitious, or they may all be innate, or all made up." In the *Broadsheet* he provides his answer: all elemental (basic) ideas of the faculty of perception (passions) are innate; all ideas involving referral judgments (attributable in part to the faculty of will) are adventitious.[14] The latter fall into two categories: those that are basic acts of referral judgments (ideas of ordinary sensible *qualities*) and those that are compounds of the first (ideas of ordinary physical *substances*).

However, because Descartes generally declines to use the term "innate idea" for any but intellectual ideas, I shall respect that usage by speaking of ideas that are innate in the narrow sense — these are intellectual ideas — and ideas that are innate in the broad sense — these are ideas that are uninfected with judgment and not compounded from other ideas. The result is the following taxonomic scheme of items that Descartes generally refers to as "ideas."

The Cartesian Taxonomy of Ideas

A. Innate Ideas

A1. In the broad sense:
   (a) Sensations. These are basic grade 2 and grade 3a perceptual responses of the faculty of sense.
   (b) Sensory experiences of the four basic primary qualities. These are grade 2 and grade 3a perceptual responses of the faculty of imagination.

A2. In the narrow sense: These are clear and distinct ideas of the intellect, both propositional and non-propositional.

B. Adventitious Ideas: These are regarded by Descartes as a form of *de re* judgment ("referral judgments") about the objects perceived by the senses combining elements of the faculty of judgment with elements from the category of basic ideas to yield a "confused" idea (a cross-categorial hybrid entity) whose real nature is misunderstood by ordinary folk. They come in two varieties:

B1. Basic referral judgments about a given sensation x. These comprise Descartes's analysis of the commonsense conception of the quality x.

B2. Compounds of referral judgments and other ideas. These comprise Descartes's analysis of the commonsense conception of ordinary physical substances.

C. Cousins of Adventitious Ideas

C1. Apparently adventitious ideas.
There is also a class of apparently adventitious ideas. This is the class of ideas that seem to come from outside us but do not. This class coincides with the class of innate ideas of the senses and the imagination but with the additional explanation that we think they come from outside us because of the misleading effects of basic referral judgments.

C2. Theory-neutral descriptions.
Theory-neutral descriptions of the causes of our sensations are also about sensations. However, because they do not create the illusion of "seeming to come from outside us" but are simply cautious definite descriptions, they do not fall into the class of apparently adventitious ideas; because they are not referral judgments they do not fall into the class of adventitious ideas. They are, simply, proper Cartesian judgments about sensations falling into category E.1 below.

D. Invented Ideas: These are ideas, other than those already mentioned in (B), which are compounded by the creative imagination from other ideas.

E. Actions of the will other than those already mentioned in (B):

E1. Judgments.

E2. Volitions.

5.3 Referral Judgments: Why Do We Make Them?

Descartes maintains that our ordinary unphilosophically tutored view of the world is commonsense realism, a view expressed by referral judgements affirming de re of colors and other sensory qualities that they are properties of extended stuff. Descartes regards this view as radically mistaken. Nevertheless, he owes us an account of why we come to hold it in the first place.

An obvious candidate for this account is suggested in the following passage from Meditation III, which we have already seen:

> And the chief and most common mistake which is to be found here consists in my judging that the ideas which are in me *resemble*, or conform, to things located outside me. Of course if I considered just the ideas themselves as modes of my thought, without referring them to anything else, they could scarcely give me material for error. (AT VII, 37; CSM II, 26; my emphasis)

The suggestion is that we refer our sensations to their external causes because we accept a certain *theory* about the causes of our sensations: the causes of our sensations must "resemble" (i.e., share the same sensory property with) our sensations. There is, however, one crucial difficulty with this suggestion: Descartes says that the mistake "consists in" the resemblance claim, not that the mistake is caused by the resemblance claim. It therefore is reasonable to treat this occurrence of resemblance not as an expression of the causal/explanatory use but as an expression of the *de re* use.

Moreover, Descartes expressly tells us what the explanation is for this error and it is not a theoretical principle:

> But the chief question at this point concerns the ideas which I take to be derived from things existing outside me: *what is my reason for thinking that they resemble these things? Nature has apparently taught me to think this.* (AT VII, 38; CSM II, 26; my emphasis)

Descartes is here treating the resemblance claim as the *explanandum* not the *explanans* and the *explanans* is that "nature has apparently taught me to think this." When Descartes does mention reliance on a *principle* of resemblance as one of the explanations for such cognitions, the principle is the Scholastic principle that "the thing in question transmits to me its own likeness rather than something else" (AT VII, 38; CSM II, 26). It is not plausible to suppose that express reliance on this principle is a part of the psychology of commonsense realism, though Descartes clearly thought that it did form part of the psychology of the Scholastic theoreticians whom Descartes seems to have regarded as his chief opponents in matters of perceptual theory.[15] In any case, it is an apparent teaching of nature rather than this principle which Descartes offers as an explanation.

Reading "apparently a teaching of nature" for "an apparent teaching of nature," I now consider the merits of attributing to Descartes the view that that it is apparently a teaching of nature that creates a tendency within common sense to believe in naive realism. There is evidence in Rule 12 of the *Rules for the Direction of the Mind* that Descartes regards psychological explanations relying on principles like the Scholastic one just discussed as falling into a different category from psychological explanations relying on teachings of nature. There Descartes identifies three basic kinds of causes of belief formation: "impulse," "conjecture," and "deduction" (AT X, 424; CSM I, 27).[16] Conjectures are probable reasonings from general principles that are not intuitively evident, as Descartes would surely regard any version of the resemblance principle. Descartes is thus *contrasting* natural inclination ("impulse") with reliance on the resemblance principle as possible candidates for the explanation of our tendency to make erroneous referral judgements.

It appears from this that in the Meditation III text that we have been looking at Descartes must be explaining the tendency to make erroneous judgments as a natural inclination to make such judgments.[17] It also appears that Descartes is referring to the same concept of a teaching of nature in Meditation III that appears in Meditation VI, for the contrast with what is known by the light of nature is clearly present in both places:

> When I say 'Nature taught me to think this', all I mean is that a spontaneous impulse leads me to believe it, not that its truth has been revealed to me by some natural light. (Meditation III: AT VII, 38; CSM II, 26–27)

> But at least they possess all the properties which I clearly and distinctly understand, that is, all those which, viewed in general terms, are comprised within the subject matter of pure mathematics. . . . What of the other aspects of corporeal things? . . . Indeed, there is no doubt that everything that I am taught by nature contains some truth. (Meditation VI: AT VII, 80; CSM II, 55–56)

Yet in Meditation III Descartes sees teachings of nature in a purely negative light, for "they were pushing me in the wrong direction" (AT VII, 39; CSM II, 27); in Meditation VI teachings of nature are seen quite positively. A resolution of this tension comes from a text a bit later in Meditation VI, where Descartes speaks of a class of "things which I may *appear* to have been taught by nature, but which in reality I acquired not from nature but from a habit of making ill-considered judgements" (AT VII, 82; CSM II, 56; my emphasis). Referral judgments fall into this class, a class disjoint from (actual) teachings of nature. Descartes's position in Meditation III, then, must be that a merely apparent teaching of nature (something that appears to be a teaching of nature, but is not), is responsible for our commonsense realist beliefs. What might this something be?

One suggestion comes from Margaret Wilson.[18] Her view is that in the *Meditations* Descartes sees the "material for error" (the causes of our erroneous judgments) as an intrinsic feature of sensory ideas.[19] Though this aspect of her interpretation of the theory of representation in the *Meditations* has received some criticism[20] she is surely right in her supposition that Descartes sees something in the nature of the sensations we refer to external objects as responsible for the fact that we do so refer them. Wilson goes on to identify the intrinsic feature of ideas responsible for referral as providing a *positive inclination* to make erroneous judgments. However, there is a passage in the *Passions of the Soul* where Descartes seems to imply the absence of such an influence:

> Now we may distinguish two kinds of movement produced in the [pineal] gland by the [corporeal] spirits. Movements of the first kind represent to the soul the objects which stimulate the sense, or the impressions occurring in the brain; *and they have no influence on the will.* Movements of the second kind, which do have an influence on the will, cause the passions or the bodily movements which accompany the passions. As to the first, although they often hinder the actions of the soul, or are hindered by them, yet since they are not directly opposed to these actions, we observe no conflict between them. (AT XI, 365; CSM I, 346; my emphasis)

The "movements" (in the brain) that "represent to the soul the objects which stimulate the sense" perform this function by causing apparently adventitious ideas in the mind, a category of ideas that provide the subject for mature referral judgments in the manner described previously. It is the explanation for our tendency to make such judgments that we are currently seeking, and I take this passage to say that the corporeal imagination does not provide it. Actions of the corporeal imagination do, however, "hinder the actions of the soul."

It is somewhat mysterious how the operations of the corporeal imagination might hinder the soul, but the only plausible candidate in the general vicinity is the mechanism of "immature referral" described in chapter 4, section 4.3. It will be recalled that this mechanism produced the fusion of sensory and spatial properties characteristic of the phenomenology of the "referred" sense experiences of adult human beings.

It is obvious to me that awareness of the fusion property of sense experience is at least partially responsible for the strong tendency to commonsense realism present in our ordinary system of beliefs.[21] Since none of the other likely Cartesian candidates for a causal explanation of this tendency—resemblance reasoning, natural disposition—are actually accepted by Descartes, it seems reasonable to postulate that Descartes accepted the obvious explanation.

It is not easy to see, however, just how Descartes thought the explanation would work. I have just rejected suggestions that in Descartes's mature philosophy there is a direct disposition to form such beliefs. This leaves us with only the alternative of postulating some kind of indirect influence. Descartes offers a variety of suggestions and hints in variety of places about what such influences might be, but in general they involve mistaken assessments on the part of untutored people about the nature of sense experience and an "ill considered" inference grounded on this assessment to the erroneous judgment. Like the reliance on a principle of resemblance in infantile reasoning about the causes of sensations, mistaken assessments of the nature of sense experience are theoretical mistakes, but unlike those infantile errors they are mistakes made by more conceptually advanced folk not about the causes of sense experience but about their epistemic, representational and metaphysical status.

I see Descartes invoking two major categories of explanation.

Category 1. There is a class of explanations that Descartes discusses in Meditation III under the rubric of the *material falsity of ideas of the senses* (AT VII, 43; CSM II, 29). We will see in chapter 7 that there are in fact two different properties tangled up under the rubric of "material falsity," both having to do with deficiencies with the representational function of sensory ideas. Associated with each property is an explanation why we think that sensory qualities might genuinely be modes of extended matter.

The first explanation has to do with confusing a mode of perception with a "real quality." The second explanation affirms that the very nature of sensuous modes of awareness *obscures* the ultimate metaphysical nature of their proper objects. This is not so much a confusion which we are positively encouraged to make by phenomenology but a rash judgment we are permitted to make by phenomenology; it amounts to a general mistake about the metaphysical category to which the objects of sensuous awareness (second- and third-grade responses) ultimately belong.

Partly because of the complexities of Descartes's doctrines of material falsity and partly for reasons of strategy that will emerge later, I will postpone consideration of this doctrine until chapter 7. I devote the remainder of the present chapter to a discussion of the second category of explanations.

Category 2. We confuse the phenomenology of colors appearing in extensional form with a natural noninferential tendency to affirm that there is an object in the environment consisting of colors in extended form. (This is a confusion of phenomenological content with a natural inclination.)

To see how this may arise, notice that when a painting or photograph puts us in mind of a scene it does not force us to affirm that the scene is real, but it makes us ready to adopt an attitude of affirmation toward its content. There is, however, some difficulty in how we should describe this "readiness." (1) We could describe it simply as a matter of the picture's presenting its content to our faculty of judgment but without supplying any positive inclination to affirm the content: we see the picture, and we are moved for some other reason to adopt an affirmation attitude toward it and say, "That's how things are," where "that" demonstrates the picture. (2) We could describe it as providing us with a *positive inclination* to affirm the content provided by the picture. To be sure, such an inclination is normally overridden as a result of contraindications in the environment, for example, the frame surrounding a picture hanging on a wall, but it is there nonetheless and reveals itself when these counterindications are masked.

In the *Rules for the Direction of the Mind* Descartes regards ideas in the corporeal imagination as providing an "impulse" to belief formation, thus accepting description 2.[22] However, we have just seen that by the time Descartes wrote the *Passions of the Soul* he would reject description 2. He thus came to regard ideas as constraining *what* we affirm or deny or place in suspension but not as influencing us to adopt one of these attitudes.

It may be, however, that we *think* that sensory ideas influence our judgment because *we confuse* their role in providing apparent subjects for judgment—a constraint on what we can affirm—with their role in providing a positive impulse to engage in an act of judgment. This is how Descartes puts this possibility in a letter to Princess Elizabeth (October 6, 1645):

> Sometimes also people confuse the inclinations or habits which dispose to a certain passion with the passion itself, though the two are easy to distinguish. (AT II, 312; *Letters*, 179)

Perhaps some similar confusion is what Descartes has in mind in Meditation III when, soon after introducing the doctrine that all ideas are "as it were images of things," he says of commonsense realist judgments: "Nature has *apparently* taught me to think this" (AT VII, 38, CSM 26).[23]

This confusion provides "material for error" in the following way: the confusion initially leads us to think that we have a natural inclination to make judgments with commonsense realist contents from which we infer that such a judgment must have prima facie warrant. Believing ourselves, therefore, to be naturally justified in accepting naive realism, we naturally proceed to accept it.

The Theory of
Natural Knowledge

6.1 Introduction

I have just finished making the case that Descartes does not treat our commonsense tendency to believe in naive realism as a natural inclination (a "teaching of nature") but, rather, regards it as one of a family of "ill considered judgments" influenced in various ways by the phenomenological fusion of primary and secondary qualities in our sense experience of the external world. Descartes's account of these judgments comprises an "error theory" of the senses, and, despite some misleading indications in Meditation III, this theory is quite distinct from Descartes's theory of the "teachings of nature." I now turn to a consideration of that theory, first by looking at its antecedents in the theory of cognitive impulses in the *Rules for the Direction of the Mind* (section 6.2) and then by looking at the mature theory as presented in the *Meditations* and *The Passions of the Soul* (section 6.3).

In this chapter I also propose to tie up some loose ends related to the theory of natural inclinations left over from previous chapters. In chapter 3 I argued that although natural inclinations play a key role in the proof of the external world in Meditation VI, they seem to be absent from the corresponding proof in *Principles* II, 1. In section 6.4 I suggest an explanation for this. In chapter 4 I developed an account of Descartes's empirical theory of the sense perception of particular primary qualities. That theory is reasonably explicit about how *ideas* of particular primary qualities are produced, but ideas are not beliefs and Descartes owes us an account of how the latter arise from the former. Since Cartesian beliefs are dispositions to affirm ideas and the theory of teachings of nature is a theory of doxastic inclinations, it is possible that the latter contains the account we are looking for. I explore this possibility in section 6.5.

Teachings of nature play a relatively unheralded but apparently important, positive role in the epistemology of the *Meditations*. This role is summarily described in Meditation VI (AT VII 8off.; CSM II, 55ff.). As described there, the function of teachings of nature is to explain how we can have some measure of justification for believing an important range of propositions not of such a high status as to be certified by the method of clear and distinct ideas and yet not so lowly as to amount to no more than ill-considered judgments. Among these are the following: (1) "that I have a body," (2) "that I am not merely present in my body as a sailor is present in a ship," and (3) "that various other bodies exist in the vicinity of my body."[1] Mattern has argued that even (4), that body in general exists, is itself counted by Descartes as a teaching of nature.[2] So a good deal hangs on Descartes's ability to justify his postulation of this category of proposition.

The reader will recall that one of my objectives in this part of the book is to confirm that sense experience is involved in Cartesian epistemology in a positive way[3] and to develop an account of the details of that involvement that supports a "concrete intuition" interpretation of Descartes's proof of the external world.[4] It is therefore now relevant to note that there seems to be a correlation between sense experience and each of the four teachings of nature just given. In the case of (1) and (3) their objects—my body and bodies in the vicinity of my body respectively—correspond to the two classes of referred sensations discussed in *Passions* I, 23, 24, respectively; in the case of (2) Descartes says that nature teaches these propositions "by these sensations of pain, hunger, thirst and so on" (AT VII, 81; CSM II, 56); and in the case of (4) Descartes says that the source of our belief in this proposition is closely associated with "a faculty for receiving and recognizing the ideas of sensible objects" (AT VII, 79; CSM II, 55). But what is the connection? Is it that intrinsic features of sense experience provide the natural instrument by means of which we learn the truth of all of these propositions, as Descartes apparently asserts to be the case specifically with (2)? Or are the intrinsic features of sense experience essentially dispensible from the story, being only accidently associated with an innate disposition placed in us by nature (i.e., God) to affirm the truth of these propositions when stimulated by sense experience?

There is evidence that Descartes could have maintained the first account for at least some of his examples but I will argue that he ultimately maintains the second for all but example 2. The argument has four stages. (1) I describe the progress of Descartes's thinking about cognitive dispositions from its nonepistemic phase in the *Rules for the Direction of the Mind* to its incarnation as a natural epistemology in the *Meditations*. (2) I show that Descartes has a theory of natural knowledge regarding those things that are beneficial or harmful to the body that is based on intrinsic features of our sensory experience. This theory takes the form of a set of defeasible warrant principles linking sense experience with beliefs about practical propositions. The latter comprise resistible natural inclinations to act in certain ways related to the welfare of ourselves as embodied creatures. (3) I show how this account can be used as a possible model for a theory of natural perceptual knowledge regarding sample propositions like 1, 3 and 4. (4) Finally, I consider the exegetical case for attributing this model to each of the other three examples proposed by Descartes.

6.2 The Account of Cognitive Impulse in the *Rules* for the Direction of the Mind

In explaining in Rule 12 how we come to know "composite natures," Descartes describes three causes of belief formation: impulse, conjecture, and deduction (AT X, 424–425; CSM I, 46–48).

Though Descartes is mainly interested in the last of these three, he also gives an informative account of the first two. Belief formation, he says,

> is a case of composition through impulse when, in forming judgments about things, our mind leads us to believe something, not because good reasons convince us of it, but simply because we are caused to believe it, either by some superior power, or by our free will, or by a disposition of the corporeal imagination. (AT X, 424; CSM I, 47)

The method of conjecture appears to be the method of inference from general principles not certified by the method of intuition and deduction. The latter is the highest rational method, the canons of which Descartes is attempting to provide elsewhere in this work.

Descartes offers as an example of someone forming a composite belief a man afflicted with jaundice who comes to believe that all the things he sees are yellow. Descartes attributes this belief to two sources: "what his corporeal imagination presents to him" and "the assumption he is making of his own account, *viz.*, that the colour looks yellow not owing to any defect of vision but because the things he sees really are yellow" (AT X, 423; CSM 47). It appears that the first source corresponds to impulse (a "disposition of the corporeal imagination") and the second to conjecture.

Descartes is at some pains in the paragraph in which he presents the jaundice example to caution the intellect that it should "not judge that the imagination faithfully represents the objects of the senses, or that the senses take on the true shapes of things, or in short that external things always are just as they appear to be" (AT X, 423; CSM I, 47). This observation does not, however, deny a role to the imagination in belief formation but simply injects a natural caution in our impulse to judge that things are as they are presented to us by the imagination.

There is much in common between the account of the structure of sense experience in the *Rules* and in the later works. Aside from a twist that metaphysical considerations have placed on the categorial structure of sense experience in the later accounts, both remain remarkably similar in their recognition of an intimate relation between the extensional form of sense experience and the extended form of the matter in the corporeal imagination that subserves sense experience. There is, however, one very significant difference between the ways in which the two accounts see the corporeal imagination and its phenomenal correlates influencing judgment and belief formation. We can best see this by comparing the following passage from the *Passions* with the passage quoted above from the *Rules*:

> Now, we may distinguish two kinds of movement produced in the [pineal] gland by the [corporeal] spirits. Movements of the first kind represent to the soul the objects which stimulate the senses, or the impressions occurring in the brain; *and they have no influence on the will*. Movements of the second kind, which do influence the

will, cause the passions or the bodily movements which accompany the passions. (AT XI, 365; CSM I, 346; my emphasis)

The reference to "influence on the will" in this passage is a reference to acts of judgment by the will.[5] Interpreted in light of this, this passage says that the corporeal imagination does not influence judgment, contradicting the passage quoted from the *Rules for the Direction of the Mind*.

Of course finding apparent inconsistency between isolated passages written at opposite ends of Descartes's philosophical career need not in general have much significance, but in this case I believe that the inconsistency heralds a profound change in the relation Descartes was to see between psychology and epistemology.

6.3 The Mature Theory of Natural Reasons

Reasons of Goodness

There is not much in the way of a perceptual epistemology in the *Rules for the Direction of the Mind*. There, Descartes's interest in perception seems to lie in its structural and causal dimensions; Descartes's interest in epistemology seems to be in the form it takes as the method of intuition and deduction. What we can say about the epistemic properties of cognitive impulses in the *Rules for the Direction of the Mind* is largely negative: they are not based on reasons, and they do not confer any epistemic standing on the beliefs they occasion. However, epistemic failings do not prevent impulses from having causal effects on the mind. There is, thus, an essential separation in the *Rules for the Direction of the Mind* between psychology and epistemology. This is not the case in the *Meditations*.

Briefly, this is how things go there. All doxastic influences on the mind involve the perception that the causes of our actions involve good reasons for those actions. Since Descartes will claim that the sense experiences subserved by the corporeal imagination cannot be perceived as good reasons, they cannot influence the will noninferentially and hence cannot play the same role in Descartes's psychology of *The Passions of the Soul* and other mature works that impulses from the corporeal imagination play in the psychology of the *Rules for the Direction of the Mind*.

On the other hand, Descartes does think that some "passions" do influence the will and must, therefore, possess epistemic credentials not possessed by sense experiences. That Descartes is committed to such an asymmetry between the epistemic standing of different kinds of passions (in the "broad sense" of passion) is the main point of interest for Descartes in the passage quoted from *The Passions of the Soul* near the end of the last section.

In Meditation IV Descartes denies that judgments are determined by anything, indicating that they are acts of a free will. These acts are acts of affirming, denying, or suspending of judgment directed to ideas. Ideas are provided to the will by the intellect but the intellect by itself does not have beliefs nor does it make judgments.

This is not to say, however, that the will acts without explanation or reason when it makes a cognitive decision. Descartes's account of this postulates *inclinations of the will* as the property that explains why the will acts as it does with regard to a given idea but explains it in such a way "that we do not feel we are determined by an external force."[6] I take it that the inclination to act in a certain way is itself caused by one of two other factors,

> either because I clearly understand that *reasons* of truth and goodness point that way, or because of a divinely produced disposition of my innermost thoughts. (AT VII, 143; CSM II, 40; my emphasis)

Descartes categorizes the judgments due to the former explanation as "natural knowledge" and those due to the latter as judgments of "divine grace." Within the class of cognitive inclinations produced by natural knowledge Descartes seems to countenance two degrees of strength corresponding to two grades of reasons: *irresistible inclinations* to affirm an idea are produced when the idea is clear and distinct;[7] *resistible inclinations* are produced by other reasons.

We may wonder how to relate the "natural knowledge" of the *Meditations* to the "impulses" of the *Rules for the Direction of the Mind*. One especially relevant example of natural knowledge comes from the Second Replies where Descartes is considering the fact that the "natural instinct" of thirst can mislead us:

> These patients [sufferers of dropsy] have a positive impulse to drink which derives from the nature God has bestowed on the body in order to preserve it; yet this nature does deceive them because on this occasion the drink will have a harmful effect. Nevertheless, this is not inconsistent with the goodness or veracity of God, and I have explained why in the Sixth Meditation. (AT VII, 143; CSM II, 102)

The reference to the Sixth Meditation makes it clear that the impulse in question is a form of natural knowledge (AT VII, 80; CSM II, 55–56). What distinguishes this "impulse" from that mentioned in the *Rules for the Direction of the Mind* is that the former unlike the latter is grounded in a perception of good reasons: thirst is perceived as a reason to think that its object will be good for us. It is this reason which produces the inclination to drink.

It is clear from this passage that the reason that thirst provides is a *fallible* reason, and it is clear from a passage just following this that such a reason could be "corrected by . . . clearer judgments or by means of [another] natural faculty," that is, that such a reason is also *defeasible*. That thirst should be perceived this way is not the result of an inference but is due to "the nature God has bestowed on the body in order to preserve it." We might say that thirst provides a *noninferential warrant* for our choosing to drink. We have seen in the previous chapter that this property of natural inclinations separates genuine teachings of nature from their spurious counterparts.[8] I shall call such reasons "reasons of the passions."

In *The Passions of the Soul* Descartes does not mention the role of reasons in explaining inclinations. His account there distinguishes between *actions* and *passions in the broad sense*. The latter class include subclasses of *perceptions of external objects*, *sensations* (pain, thirst, etc.), and *emotions*. He explains that it is only the latter category that he means to be explaining under the heading "passions of the soul" (AT XI, 345–348; CSM I, 336–338). Consequently he does not offer there a discussion of how sensations influence the will, though we may take his account of the emotions to provide an indication. He says, "the feeling of fear moves the

soul to want to flee" (AT XI, 359; CSM I, 343), the desire to flee being an inclination in the sense of Meditation IV. *The Passions of the Soul* thus suggests that fear
directly causes inclination rather than does so through the perception of reasons to
act as in the doctrine of Meditation IV.

There is, however, reason to think that even in *The Passions of the Soul* Descartes
recognizes the need for reasons to intervene between emotions and inclinations.
For example, in Article 47 Descartes denies that there is any conflict within the
soul:

> For there is within us but one soul, and this soul has within it no diversity of parts:
> it is at once sensitive and rational too, and all its appetites are volitions. It is an error
> to identify the different functions of the soul with persons who play different, usu-
> ally mutually opposed roles — an error which arises simply from our failure to distin-
> guish properly the functions of the soul from those of the body. *It is to the body alone
> that we should attribute everything that can be observed in us to oppose our reason.*
> (AT XI, 365; CSM I, 346; my emphasis)

With the example of the sensation of thirst driving us to drink water when we
know that the water is poisoned, this doctrine entails that the tension we feel is not
to be explained as a struggle between reason and desire. For, if thirst affected the
will directly by simply causing a desire to drink, as in the earlier theory from the
Rules for the Direction of the Mind, rather than by giving it a reason to desire to
drink, then thirst would produce a causal conflict within the soul itself in the example described. This is what Descartes's mature theory does not allow. There is
of course some kind of contrariety present in the soul even on Descartes' mature
account, but it is the rationally resolvable contrariety that a defeasible reason bears
to a potential overriding reason.

We can perhaps summarize Descartes's account of the psychology of natural
inclinations in the following way. Physiological states of the brain produce sensations (passions in the broad sense) of fear, thirst, pain, and so on. These sensations
do not themselves contain motivational components but cause the perception that
their objects are good for us or bad for us; it is this perception that provides the
motivational component inclining the will to action.

Before proceeding I need to say more about two key notions in this account:
that of *perception that p* and that of the *objects* of sensations.

A perception that the object of a sensation is good for us plays a role in Descartes's
psychology as both an effect of perceptual processing and a (nondetermining) rational cause of action. As such, contemporary functionalists might wish to see in
this notion the propositional attitude of *belief*. However, it is important to bear in
mind that perceptions are not judgments for Descartes, and it is judgments that are
the primary bearer of practical, epistemic, and semantic evaluation. We should
therefore be very cautious in regarding Cartesian propositional perceptions as a
species of propositional beliefs notwithstanding the functional characteristics they
share. The notion of the *external object of a sensation* in the context of Descartes's
theory of natural inclination should not be confused with the notion of the *proper
object of intuition* in the context of Descartes's theory of clear and distinct ideas[9]
for Descartes will claim there that sensations do not represent anything external to

the mind[10] and that their objects possess no more than a vanishingly small degree of reality.[11] The notion is, rather, that of a natural sign for an object.

Natural signs[12] involve natural institutions connecting a physical registration of an object with a (mental) idea of it; and the idea is itself a component in the belief that the object of the sensation is good for us or bad for us. Descartes's theory of natural inclinations is, thus, a rational psychology, an account that explains why we act as we do by showing that we are justified in acting as we do. That is why Descartes speaks of the perception of "reasons of goodness or truth" in Meditation IV.

Recall the passage quoted earlier from the Second Replies regarding God's role in creating our bodies with a natural "instinct" of thirst. In making reference to God's role in creating the body Descartes does not suggest that we must first know of God's existence and his role in making all things in order to see that thirst provides us with reason to drink.[13] Rather, the role of God seems to be to provide such reasons with a kind of authority,[14] a basis that explains why someone who follows natural inclination will likely achieve his or her goal (doing something beneficial for the body). This is the source of a distinction within what I will call the *Cartesian structure of natural reasons* between two elements: (1) the principles connecting reasons with inclinations to act (*warrant principles*) and (2) the authority basis for the warrant principles.[15]

Descartes does not make it clear in the passage quoted earlier in this section from the Second Replies (ATVII, 143; CSM II, 102) precisely how God's actions authorize natural reasons, but we have seen in the previous chapter[16] that Descartes postulates a reliable connection between states of the brain registering external conditions and mental states (ideas) that represent those conditions. Natural connections between mind and body of this sort are further described in *Comments on a Certain Broadsheet* as comprising an "innate faculty" (AT VIIIB, 359: CSM I, 304), which is itself said to be due to God's actions and serves as a kind of "signpost" of his nature (AT VIIIB, 366; CSM I, 309). God's role in establishing such natural connections serves to authorize our rationally based inclinations because we can infer from his omnipotence and benevolence that such ideas will reliably reflect whatever truth has been successfully registered by the corporeal mechanisms.

Notwithstanding this, Descartes also allows that such mechanisms may deceive us in abnormal conditions; what God's benevolence seems to assure is that they will not generally do so, and when they occasionally do lead us astray we can correct the mistake by a careful application of rational method, a point Descartes makes indirectly in a passage just following that quoted earlier from the Second Replies:

> In the case of our clearest and most careful judgments, however, this kind of explanation [for error] would not be possible, for if such judgments were false they could not be corrected by any clearer judgments or by means of any other natural faculty. (At VII, 143–144; CSM II, 102–103)

One of the great advantages of a defeasibility theory of justification lies in its ability to explain how, in perceptual contexts, beliefs can be rationally warranted when the agent is unaware that abnormal conditions obtain. The explanation rests on the fact such a theory does not require that the agent first determine that conditions are normal and then infer that some action is justified. We might represent this form of reasoning in the following schema.

Inference E

1. The belief that p is prima facie warranted for S when reason R obtains. (Assumption)
2. Reason R obtains. (Assumption)
3. The belief that p is prima facie warranted for S. (1, 2)
4. There are no defeating reasons[17] against p relative to R known to S. (Assumption)

We may infer

5. The belief that p is warranted *tout court*. (3, 4, definition of warrant *tout court*)

This theory of warrant principles may be contrasted with one requiring that an inference to the warrant *tout court* of an action A for an agent S must involve an assertion that abnormal conditions are absent. Thus we would have to reason as follows:

Inference F

1. The belief that p is warranted (*tout court*) for S when reason R obtains *and* conditions are normal. (Assumption)
2. (a) Reason R obtains *and* (b) conditions are normal. (Assumption)

Therefore

3. The belief that p is warranted (*tout court*) for S. (1, 2)

Descartes does not express his theory of natural reasons in sufficient detail to say conclusively that he would reason in practical contexts in accord with the first pattern of inference, but indications in a letter to Hyperaspistes suggest that he would:

Suppose that a man decided to abstain from all food to the point of starvation, because he was not certain that it was not poisoned, and thought that he was not bound to eat because it was not clearly established that he had the means of keeping alive, and it was better to wait for death by abstaining than to kill himself by eating. Such a man would be rightly regarded as insane and responsible for his own death. Suppose further that he could not obtain any food that was not poisoned, and that his nature was such that fasting was beneficial to him; none the less, *if the food appeared harmless and healthy*, and fasting appeared likely to have its usual harmful effects, he would be bound to eat the food and thus follow the apparently beneficial course of action rather than the actually beneficial one. (AT III, 422; *Letters*, 110; my emphasis)

This is a context in which some prospective set of practical actions—to eat or not to eat the food—is the ultimate object of evaluation; the immediate object of evaluation is a set of possible acts of judgment about the state of the food itself. In saying that the food does not *appear* to be poisoned to this man or that his constitution does not *seem* to be unusual, Descartes is not suggesting that the man has undertaken to establish that normal conditions are in place. Rather, Descartes is suggesting that there is available to the man no apparent evidence that abnormal conditions are in place. Though Descartes does not expressly consider the difference between an inference of the first pattern and that of the second, his formulation suggests that he would choose the first. I propose to take it as at least tentatively established that Descartes's theory of natural reasons assigns warrant to practical judgments in accord with the defeasibility pattern.

Inference E gives the general form of warrant principles in a defeasibility theory of warrant but it does not reflect the fact that the qualitative character of the sensations has a role to play in the Cartesian theory of natural reasons. (It is the qualitative difference between sensations of hunger and sensations of thirst than explains our differential responses to those sensations.) The qualitiative dimension can be incorporated into the theory by means of two definitions. First I define the notion of natural reasons:

Natural Reasons

Subject x has a *natural reason* to affirm that p iff x has a natural inclination to affirm that p, namely, an inclination that does not essentially involve the intervention of acts of reasoning or judgment.

Now I define the notion of a natural *perceptual* reason:

Natural Perceptual Reasons

If x has an natural reason i to affirm that p *and* S is a sense experience, then i is a *natural perceptual reason* to affirm that p *iff* i is causally based on s in a way that essentially involves the qualitative nature of s.

In the case of the example of thirst, the qualitiative character of thirst serves as a cause for the inclination we have to believe the proposition p that the object of the thirst is good for us. Thirst is, thus, a natural perceptual reason R confering prima facie warrant on the practical proposition p. Since p is a proposition about what is beneficial to the body, thirst is a "reason of goodness." I now consider how to extend this epistemic model to "reasons of truth," that is, to a theory of warrant for propositions that are about facts other than those relating to harms and benefits to the body.

Extending the Model to Reasons of Truth

In one of Descartes's examples of a teaching of nature, proposition 2,[18] he says that nature teaches that "I am not present in my body as a sailor is present in his ship by these sensations of pain, hunger, thirst and so on." For nature to teach something by means of sensations is for those sensations to cause an inclination to affirm something without reliance on acts of judgment or reasoning. Although Descartes does not say that sense experience has anything to do with causing the inclinations in propositions 1 and 3, in *Passions* I, 23, 24, Descartes describes a process ("referral") wherein sensations are assigned to one of two categories of extensional form. "Extensional form" is the term I used in chapter 4, section 4.5, to describe the general feature of sense experience responsible for the difference between feeling pain and heat "as being in our limbs and not as being in objects outside us." It is relevant to note that this process assigns two categories of extensional form to sensations: the first assigns the form of externality-to-our-body to sensations like color; the second assigns the form of internality-to-our-body to sensations like pain. The first of these forms corresponds to proposition 3 of teachings of nature, the second to proposition 1.

Moreover, when Descartes introduces proposition 1 he does so by saying, "There is nothing that my own nature teaches me more vividly than that I have a body, and that when I feel pain there is something wrong with the body" (AT VII, 81; FSM II, 56). How does "my own nature" teach me that I have a body if not by the very form in which I experience the sensations which I refer to the body? One exegetical suggestion, then, is that the inclination to believe that we have a body and the inclination to believe that bodies exist external to our bodies is caused by a natural inclination based on sense experiences with an intrinsic nature whose forms can be described as internal to the body and external to the body respectively.

Let us suppose, perhaps counterfactually, that this suggestion is one that Descartes would accept. Teachings of nature are not only psychological principles, they are also *warrant principles* that treat natural inclinations as reasons of goodness or truth. In the case of reasons of truth (if there are such reasons in Cartesian epistemology), the warrant principles could therefore take the following form:

The Warrant Principle for Natural Reasons
of Truth (WPNRT)

If x has a natural inclination to affirm that p, then x is prima facie warranted in affirming that p.

When the inclinations are based on sensory experiences, the corresponding warrant principles give conditions on natural perceptual reasons of truth. They have the following form:

The Warrant Principle for Natural Perceptual
Reasons of Truth (WPNPRT)

If x has a natural perceptual inclination to affirm that p, then x is prima facie perceptually warranted in affirming that p.

Now suppose that we instantiate the perceptual warrant principle in the case of the natural inclination to believe that I have a body (proposition 1). Assuming for the moment that there are no defeating reasons available against the proposition that I have a body, and in keeping with the first pattern of reasoning described above, this yields the conclusion that the belief that I have a body is warranted *tout court*.

More formally, this inference can be represented as follows:

Inference E*

1. If x has a natural perceptual inclination to affirm that p, then x is prima facie perceptually warranted in affirming that p. (WPNPRT)

2. I have a natural perceptual inclination to affirm that I have a body. (assumption)
3. I am prima facie warranted in affirming that I have a body. (1, 2)
4. There is nothing defeating the warrant of the proposition that I have a body. (assumption)

Therefore,

5. I am perceptually warranted *tout court* in believing that I have a body. (3, 4)

If it now be objected that there might be an evil demon subjecting me to delusions about the existence of my own body (a class 2 defeater)[19] Descartes would say that such a possibility cannot be detected by even the most scrupulous application of the method of clear and distinct ideas, hence

> the very fact that God is not a deceiver, and the consequent impossibility of there being any falsity in my opinions which cannot be corrected by some other faculty supplied by God, offers me a sure hope that I can attain the truth even in these matters. (AT VII 80; CSM II, 55–56)

The function of the nondeceiving God in the context of inference E* is to eliminate a potentially powerful class 2 defeater, thus saving premise 4 from falsification.

Does Descartes Accept the Extension of the Model?

Just after Descartes's description of that class of beliefs he calls "ill considered judgments" (AT VII, 82ff.; CSM II, 57ff.), he undertakes to "more accurately define exactly what I mean when I say that I am taught something by nature." In the page or so of discussion that follows Descartes draws a sharp contrast between, on the one hand, practical knowledge to avoid "what induces a feeling of pain" and to "seek out what induces feelings of pleasure, and so on" and, on the other, some putative ability

> to draw any conclusions from these sensory perceptions about things located outside us without waiting until the intellect has examined the matter. For knowledge of the truth about such things seems to belong to the mind alone, not to the combination of mind and body. (AT VII 82–83; CSM II, 57)

He reiterates this point when he says,

> In these cases and in many others I see that I have been in the habit of misusing the order of nature. For the proper purpose of the sensory perceptions given to me by nature is simply to inform the mind of what is beneficial or harmful for the composite of which the mind is a part; and to this extent they are sufficiently clear and distinct. But I misuse them by treating them as reliable touchstones for immediate judgments about the essential nature of the bodies outside us. (AT VII 83; CSM II, 57–58)

This passage says clearly and forcefully that sense experience has no role to play in any knowledge of "factual matters," that is, matters other than those pertaining to the welfare of the body. This implies that whatever natural reasons we have for believing that we have a body (and that there are bodies outside our body), these reasons cannot be natural *perceptual* reasons since the theory of natural perceptual reasons assigns an essential role to the qualitatively intrinsic character of our sensations. Descartes's reason for taking this position are not clearly enunciated here, but one can perhaps be inferred from other things that Descartes has said about the class that "these cases and many others" is supposed to comprise.

One of the central examples from this class of cases concerns the perception of a star:

> [A]lthough a star has no greater effect on my eye than the flame of a small light, that does not mean that there is any real or positive inclination in me to believe that the star is no bigger than the light; I have simply made this judgment from childhood onwards without any rational basis. (AT VII 83; CSM II, 57)

The star example is drawn from the third class of cases that Descartes is discussing in this portion of Meditation VI. The first class is clear and distinct perceptions, the second is teachings of nature, and the third is "ill considered judgments":

> There are, however, many other things which I may appear to have been taught by nature, but which in reality I acquired not from nature but from a habit of making ill considered judgements; . . . Cases in point are . . . when a body is white or green the selfsame whiteness or greenness which I perceive through my senses is present in the body . . . or, finally, *that stars and towers and other distant bodies have the same size and shape which they present to my senses.* (AT VII 82; CSM II, 56–57; my emphasis)

I have argued in chapter 5 that what makes a judgment ill-considered for Descartes is that it is produced by reasoning from false principles. In the case of commonsense realist metaphysics the false principle is that ideas (in the material sense) must resemble their causes, a principle at work in the prototheoretical activities of infants I have called "immature referral."[20] But if I have Descartes right here, then he should also be claiming that the belief that large distant objects are the same size as small near ones is also due to reasoning from false principles. And so he does, but he makes the point in *Optics* VI, not in Meditation VI:

> And if one is looking at an object at all far away, there is also hardly any variation in the angles between the line joining the two eyes (or two positions of the same eye) and the lines from the eyes to the object. As a consequence, even our 'common' sense seems incapable of receiving in itself the idea of a distance greater than approximately one or two hundred feet. This can be verified in the case of the moon and the sun. Although they are among the most distant bodies that we can see and their diameters are to their distances roughly as one to a hundred, they normally appear to us as at most only one or two feet in diameter—although we know very well by reason that they are extremely large and extremely far away. (AT VI, 144; CSM I, 173)

The reasoning that is occurring here seems to depend on the following false principle: *When the angle of convergence of the eyes is at its minimum practical limit, all objects are located two hundred feet from the eye.* Descartes seems to have believed that this principle is simply a default assumption made by the visual system in order to state the value of the distance parameter when no further useful information is available from the convergence angle. This suggests, regarding the inclination to think that a star and a candle are of the same size, that the argument Descartes would offer against treating this inclination as a *natural* inclination is the same as the one he offered against commonsense realism—in both cases the inclinations are based on reasoning from false principles.

The principle that Descartes sees as operating in the case of commonsense realism is the resemblance principle. I have argued previously that commonsense realism emerges as a kind of accidental cognitive product of the role that this principle plays in the referral of our sensations both to the body and to the environment outside the body. This process produces the characteristic phenomenology of two classes of sense experiences, those with internal-to-the body form and those with external-to-the-body forms. Since these are the forms upon which natural perceptual inclinations to believe that I have a body and that there are bodies outside my body would have to depend, the fact that the etiology of these forms depends essentially on reasoning from a false principle entails that the reasons we have for believing that we have a body and that there are bodies outside our body are, to the extent to which they depend on qualitative features of our sense experience, not *natural* reasons in Descartes's sense.

Descartes does maintain that the propensity to have these beliefs is a natural propensity, that is, a propensity that is not based on any act of reasoning. What Descartes is denying is that the natural propensity is caused by the qualitative character of our sense experiences. This propensity would be there regardless of its qualitative character, placed there by the act of a benevolent creator. Of the four examples of natural doxastic propensitites with which we began this chapter there remains only that of the propensity to believe that there are corporeal bodies, simpliciter. Is this a natural perceptual propensity?

Descartes asserts that I have "a great propensity to believe that [ideas of sensible objects] are produced by corporeal things" (AT VII, 79–80; CSM II, 55). This statement does not appear in the official catalog of teachings of nature in Meditation VI but does occur in the proof of the external world, a text occurring just prior to that catalog. We found in an earlier chapter[21] that, although Descartes seems to have intended that that proof fit the pattern of general existential reasoning, it does not do so successfully. Since the notion of a propensity to believe in corporeal objects plays a key role in that argument and since that propensity is expressly directed to ideas of sensible objects, it is natural to ask if the proof at least succeeds in fitting the model of reasoning from natural perceptual inclinations.

6.4 Natural Inclinations and the Proofs of the External World in Meditation VI and *Principles* II, 1

To satisfy the model of natural perceptual epistemology the proof of the external world in Meditation VI would have to have the following structure:

Inference E**

1. If x has a natural perceptual inclination to affirm that p, then x is prima facie perceptually warranted in affirming that p. (WPNPRT)
2. I have a natural perceptual inclination to affirm that there are corporeal bodies. (assumption)
3. I am prima facie warranted in affirming that there are corporeal bodies. (1, 2)
4. There is nothing defeating the warrant of the proposition that there are corporeal bodies. (assumption)

Therefore,

5. I am perceptually warranted *tout court* in believing that there are corporeal bodies. (3, 4)

Premise 2 represents the assumption that the propensity to believe that there are corporeal objects is a result of the fact that our sensations of sensible qualities seem to be presented in some general kind of spatial form. This assumption makes no distinction between a form that is internal to the body and one that is external to the body. Premise 4 also is represented in the text of the argument:

> For God has given me no faculty at all for recognizing any such [noncorporeal] source for these ideas; on the contrary he has given me a great propensity to believe that they are produced by corporeal things. (AT VII, 79–80; CSM II, 55)

Premise 1 is supplied by the normative component of the theory of natural inclinations and (3) is derived from (1) and (2). So, given our assumption of premise 2, the text of the proof of the external world seems to contain all the premises needed for reasoning in accord with natural perceptual warrant principles.

Premise 2 itself amounts to the claim that our propensity to believe that there are corporeal bodies is due to the (intrinsic features of the) appearance of corporeal bodies or, simply put, that we tend to believe that there are corporeal objects because it looks as though there are. But premise 2 is equivalent to the conjunction of the claims (1) that my belief that I have a body is a natural perceptual inclination and (2) that my belief that there are objects outside my body is a natural perceptual inclination. Since Descartes denies both of these claims, he must deny premise (2). This is implicit in the text in Meditation VI in which he declares that knowledge "of the truth about such things seems to belong to the mind alone, not to the combination of mind and body" (AT VII, 82–83; CSM II, 57). The latter, the special preserve of the faculty of imagination, is the source of the extensional form of our sense experience, and in ruling out this faculty as a source of knowledge about the external world, Descartes rules out this possibility. It is, however, still possible for Descartes that the propensity to believe in corporeal objects is a *natural* propensity even if not a natural *perceptual* propensity. For example, he might be treating the fact that ideas of sensible objects "are produced without my cooperation and often even against my will" (AT VII, 79; CSM II, 55) as a property of ideas that is sufficient to trigger the propensity to believe that these ideas are caused by corporeal objects without relying an any qualitatively intrinsic features of those ideas. This would make the propensity to believe in an external world natural but not perceptually natural. But even this much reliance on the theory of natural inclinations in the proof of the external world in Meditation VI is absent from the corresponding proof in *Principles* II, 1. Indeed, in Descartes's only reference to a propensity to believe in the external world he expressly dismisses its epistemological relevance:

> Everyone is quite convinced of the existence of material things. But earlier on we cast doubt on this belief and counted it as one of the preconceived opinions of our childhood. (AT VIIIA, 40; CSM I, 223)

In Meditation VI Descartes also refers to our preconceived opinions, saying that he had "no trouble refuting them."

> For since I apparently had natural impulses towards many things which reason told me to avoid, I reckoned that a great deal of confidence should not be placed in what I was taught by nature. (AT VII, 77; CSM II, 53)

However, a couple of pages later Descartes introduces his doctrine of the teachings of nature, which considerably refurbishes the status of at least some of the opinions produced by these natural impulses. No such refurbishment is attempted in the corresponding passages from *Principles* II, 1. I take this to indicate that Descartes felt some dissatisfaction with the role of natural inclinations in the proof structure of Meditation VI. To see what dissatisfaction Descartes might have had I will draw upon the difference between inclinations that are genuinely natural inclinations and those that masquerade as such.

According to the theory of natural knowledge, the sense perception of those qualities produced by innate psychophysical mechanisms produces a noninferential "natural inclination" to believe that the object of the sensation is good for us or to affirm some ideas as true. From the perspective of an agent engaged in the practical affairs of life, simply acting upon these inclinations yields presumptively warranted judgments. However, not all inclinations to judge are "natural" in the required sense — some are ill considered judgments depending on reasoning from false premises. Descartes appears to think that it is not simply obvious which inclinations are produced by "natural institutions" and which may have their causes in some "ill considered judgment" masquerading as a judgment based on natural reasons. As passages from Meditation III indicate, Descartes appears to think that the possibility of deception on this score is "the chief source of error" into which common sense can fall.[22]

A detailed Cartesian justification for classifying any given doxastic disposition as spurious rather than genuinely natural would appear to require the deployment of a psychophysical theory postulating ill considered judgments at certain *loci* in the causal processes generating the given disposition. However, from the vantage point of Meditation VI it appears that Descartes's development of this theory involves some danger of circularity arising between the two branches of the theory of natural knowledge: Descartes justifies certain elements of the psychophysical theory by appeal to what we are naturally inclined to accept and justifies the claim that certain inclinations count as natural by appeal to the absence of ill considered judgments in the etiology of the inclinations, a postulate of the theory of psychophysics.

Some circularity is probably inevitable in any project of this sort and, in some forms at least, can probably be accepted as benign, but it is clear that Descartes requires that at least some fundamental elements of the psychophysical theory be established independently of appeal to natural inclinations. We might naturally think that among the postulates and presuppositions comprising Descartes's empirical theory of psychophysics the existence of the physical world is one of the fundamental elements. This observation, of course, raises the specter of a vicious circularity arising in Descartes's proof of the external world in Meditation VI.

In the structure of the Meditation VI proof Descartes does say expressly that the kind of sensory perception upon which the proof is premised "are produced without my cooperation and often even against my will" (AT VII, 79; CSM II, 55), a fact that Descartes takes to be established by introspection. Presumably Descartes would claim that the absence of acts of conjectural judgment in the etiology of natural doxastic inclinations is also something that can be established by introspection. Now this claim is, perhaps, reasonable enough for currently occurring acts of the intellect that pass slowly enough to be detected by the introspective powers of an attentive mind. Unfortunately, many of the rash acts of the will that differentiate imitators from genuine natural inclinations either occur too quickly to be detected[23] or have occurred so long ago in our infancy[24] that even Descartes must find it hard to maintain that they are detectable by introspective techniques. Moreover, in the doctrine that sensory ideas can be clear but not distinct, newly introduced in the *Principles*, Descartes seems to accept that we can even be mistaken about whether a given mental event is a judgment (an act of the will) or a sensation (a passion of the intellect). Speaking of the sensation of pain, Descartes writes in *Principles* I, 46:

> [P]eople commonly confuse this perception with an obscure judgment they make concerning the nature of something which they think exists in the painful spot and which they suppose to resemble the sensation of pain; but in fact it is the sensation alone which they perceive clearly. (AT VIIIA, 2; CSM I, 208)

It is perhaps owing to a recognition of these difficulties that the proof that Descartes produces in *Principles* II, 1 seems to proceed without reliance on the doctrine of the teachings of nature. In that proof Descartes mentions only our "clear understanding of this matter [the existence of the material world]" as the basis that activates God's property as a nondeceiving being. Teachings of nature have no role to play in the proof; specifically, they have no role to play in an elimination premise (the premise where Descartes shows that the properties of which we have intuitive awareness are not contained eminently in their grounding substance).

I conclude section 6.4 with a comment on the relative strengths of the two proofs.

An Assessment of the Relative Strengths of the Two Proofs of the External World

Most commentators on Meditation VI give relatively little discussion to the proof of the material world, much more to other issues raised there. Dicker, for example, devotes five and a half pages to the proof, out of forty-six he gives to Meditation VI.[25] This lack of attention is perhaps partly due to his conviction that the structure of the proof is relatively clear and unproblematic—something which I of course dispute—but also to a conviction that the proof is subject to a

> fundamental objection. Descartes' proof of the material world depends crucially on his thesis that there exists a perfect God. That thesis in turn depends on his proofs of the existence of God in *Meditations III* and *V*. Those proofs, however, are unsuccessful.[26]

Assuming for the sake of argument that Dicker is right about the theological proofs, his objection that the proof of the material world "depends crucially" on the theological proofs is sound in the case of Meditation VI but not, I will argue, for the proof in *Principles* II, 1. The difference arises from a difference in the role that divine benevolence plays in the two proofs.

The proof apparatus that Descartes is able to deploy in Meditation VI is incapable by itself of establishing the formal reality of the material world from the only nontheological premise that Descartes allows himself—that corporeal properties are perceived by the intellect alone. What else is required is the doctrine of the teachings of nature. Indeed, when all is said and done the whole force of the proof rests on the conjunction of the following three facts: (1) I have a natural propensity to believe in the existence of a material world; (2) natural propensities are authoritative (likely to be true) if, but only if, a nondeceiving God exists; and (3) a nondeceiving God exists.

In a world without God, there would be just the natural propensity to have this belief and just the degree of warrant attaching to that belief that the warrant principles can assign on their own. But the Cartesian structure of natural reasons includes an *authority basis*, and it takes a positive action on God's part to constitute that basis. The action in question is to arrange the world such that warranted belief amounts to true belief when no rational means exists for detecting the difference:

> [T]he very fact that God is not a deceiver, and the consequent impossibilty of there being any falsity in my opinions which cannot be corrected by some other faculty supplied by God, offers me a sure hope that I can attain the truth even in these matters. Indeed, there is no doubt that everything that I am taught by nature contains some truth. For if nature is considered in its general aspect, then I understand by the term nothing other than God himself, or the ordered system of created things established by God. (AT VII 80; CSM II, 55–56)

In *Principles* II, 1, on the other hand, the force of the proof rests on an inference from the concrete intuition of general corporeal properties to the formal containment of those properties in an actual substance. In a world without God, no essential premise of this proof would be false. It is true that Descartes says in that proof that "if God were himself immediately producing in our mind the idea of such extended matter, or even if he were causing the idea to be produced by something which lacked extension, shape and motion, there would be no way of avoiding the conclusion that he should be regarded as a deceiver" (AT VII, 40–41; CSM I, 223). But this claim does not entail that the *nonexistence of God* would undermine an essential premise of the proof; on the contrary, this claim entails that the *existence of an omnipotent God* creates the possibility of radical deception. This is a problem for Cartesian epistemology that only an appeal to the benevolence of that same God can solve. Of course the problem would not arise in the first place if there were no being capable of this scale of deception, and it appears that the only such being is God.[27] It thus seems that the nonexistence of God would actually serve to enhance the prospects of the proof of the material world in *Principles* II, rather than to undermine them. This is not the case with the proof in Meditation VI.

There is, of course, the possibility that Descartes is mistaken in various of his theoretical beliefs, for example, that he does possess a concrete intuition of corporeal properties and that his general theory of existential reasoning is correct, and so on. Descartes seems to argue that he can set these doubts aside by considering his knowledge of God.[28] So at least in this respect the existence of God would enhance aspects of Descartes's epistemic position in the *Principles* II, 1, proof. The issue that we are raising here is, of course, that of the circle and, without taking any particular stand on its ultimate resolution (by Descartes or by us), it suffices for present purposes to note that the doubts in question are metatheoretical. Though significant, the fact remains that in a world without God these doubts do not entail the falsity of any premise essential to the proof of the material world in *Principles* II, 1.

6.5 Dispositions to Affirm Particular Properties of Corporeal Things

Extending the Model of Natural Perceptual Epistemology to Particular Aspects of Corporeal Things

When Descartes discusses teachings of nature in Meditation VI, there is evidence of some indecisiveness concerning which kinds of judgment are to be included under this rubric. Descartes seems to give his official catalog of teachings of nature in the paragraph beginning with the words "There is nothing that my own nature teaches me more vividly than that I have a body" (AT VII 80; CSM II, 56). This teaching of nature and those that follow in the next two paragraphs are clearly contrasted with the "ill considered judgments" introduced in the first paragraph of AT VII, 82 (CSM II, 56), but they also seem to be contrasted with judgments about "other aspects of corporeal things which are either particular (for example, that the sun is of such a size and shape)" mentioned earlier at AT VII, 80 (CSM II, 55). However, concerning these "other aspects" Descartes says:

> Despite the high degree of doubt and uncertainty involved here, the very fact that God is not a deceiver, and the consequent impossibility of there being any falsity in my opinions which cannot be corrected by some other faculty supplied by God, offers me a sure hope that I can attain the truth even in these matters. Indeed, there is no doubt that everything that I am taught by nature contains some truth. (AT VII, 80; CSM II, 55–56)

Descartes therefore seems to be the position of saying in some places that judgments about particular aspects of corporeal things are teachings of nature and in others that they are not.

At least part of the explanation for this ambivalence about the status of judgments about these "other aspects of corporeal things" may lie in an ambiguity in Descartes's conception of natural inclination. In one sense natural cognitive inclinations are contrasted with cognitive inclinations based on reasoning of any kind, in another, teachings of nature are contrasted with ill-considered judgments. This ambiguity comes into play especially clearly in connection with particular spatial properties of corporeal things seen nearby.

As we have seen in a previous chapter,[29] the perception of these properties occurs at different grades in a recursive procedure of perceptual information processing. The first grade is a purely physiological level with no inferential or phenomenological dimensions. The second is the grade where phenomenology appears but without any cognitive-inferential components in the etiology. The third grade (3a) is also phenomenological but does include inference in its etiology. The fourth grade (3b) is a rational level without sensuous phenomenology, whose etiology is fully penetrated by reason in all its employments. The second grades (2a & b) are the lowest of interest to us, and perception on this level is generated by a "natural institution," it is thus "natural" in the first sense, whereas at the third grade (3a) perceptions are produced by inferential processes and are thus *not* "natural" in the first sense. Nevertheless, some of these inferential processes are governed by information from physiological perceptual systems plus geometrical principles and other perceptual algorithms that Descartes seems to regard as "natural," that is, innate.[30] These are cases where the eyes converge on nearby objects. In other cases the perceptual system adds an arbitrary "default assumption" that Descartes would regard as an ill considered judgment. But even with a naturalism of this kind, judgments we are disposed to make about particular spatial properties do not meet the conditions of a natural *perceptual* epistemology because the latter requires that our inclinations be causally based on qualitative features of our sense experience of particular spatial properties; Descartes is quite explicit that such features do not influence our judgments. His ultimate motivation for taking this view is that the qualitative character of our experience of primary qualities is blended with the qualitative character of an experience of colors and other secondary qualities comprising overall causes of error rather than reasons of truth.

My own view is that the qualitative character of our experiences of particular primary qualities does provide reasons, both psychological and esoteric, for making judgments about the existence of objects possessing particular primary qualities and that Descartes has the theoretical resources to account for this. What I deny is that those resources are to be found within his theory of natural reasons.

In the Sixth Replies Descartes characterizes the third grade of sensory responses as "judgments" based, he says, on "rational inferences" (AT VII, 438; CSM II, 295). For details he refers us to the *Optics*. However, when we turn to that work we find that rational inferences are operations on the *qualities* of size, shape, distance, and orientation registered initially in the pineal gland and then represented by perceptions in the mind. He also speaks in that work of knowledge, opinion, and judgment of particular properties but does not explain how these states arise from the perception of those particular properties. We have seen in section 6.2 that in *Rules for the Direction of the Mind* Descartes had no objection to attributing a doxastic disposition directly to the corporeal imagination, but he denies the existence of such dispositions in his mature writing. If we do not look to a theory of natural perceptual inclinations to provide the link between perception and belief there seems to be only one other place to which we can look—the theory of clear and distinct ideas.

In the first three chapters of this book I developed an interpretation of Descartes's theory of clear and distinct ideas according to which a statement ascribing a clear and distinct perception of a set of properties provides a premise in a pattern of reasoning based on the rule of truth. That pattern of reasoning also includes a premise designed to yield the conclusion that the properties are formally contained in a substance by eliminating the possibility that they are eminently contained in a substance. The elimination of this possibility is equivalent for Descartes to the claim that an entity possessing those properties actually exists. The actual applications of this pattern of reasoning are directed to the establishment of metaphysical propositions of general import, namely, the existence of God and the existence of the external world. Nevertheless, in the Second Replies he has said that the causal principle—a principle that, as I have argued,[31] is equivalent to the central premise of the general pattern of existential reasoning countenanced by Descartes[32]—is the basis for "our knowledge of *all* things whether perceivable through the senses or not." The passage continues:

> How do we know, for example, that the sky exists? Because we see it? But this 'seeing' does not affect the mind except insofar as it is an idea—I mean an idea which resides in the mind itself, not an image depicted in the corporeal imagination. Now the only reason why we can use this idea as a basis for the judgment that the sky exists is that every idea must have a really existing cause of its objective reality; and in this case we judge that the cause is the sky itself. And we make similar judgments in other cases. (AT VII, 165; CSM II, 116–117)

The judgment that the sky exists amounts to the judgment that certain particular primary qualities are formally contained in something, and "similar judgments in other cases" presumably also involve ideas of particular primary qualities.

If we are to take Descartes at his word here, then we should be able to reconstruct from the general theory of existential inference a version suitable to generating judgments of particular properties of corporeal objects. My suggestion is that we begin by looking again at the inference from concrete intuition, inference D:

Inference D

1. Suppose that I have a clear and distinct concrete perception of $P_1 \ldots P_n$.
2. I have a concrete intuitive awareness of $P_1 \ldots P_n$. (Def., 1)
Therefore,
3. There exists a substance x such that x possesses $P_1 \ldots P_n$ formally. (2, RTCI)

Suppose that we instantiate inference D with particular spatial properties, for example, the property of being round or the property of being ten feet away. Inference D requires that there must then exist an actual substance with these properties. But what if we are taken in by a perceptual illusion, a dream, or the evil demon? Surely Descartes cannot mean that the perceptual consciousness of particular spatial properties is necessarily veridical. No. But he might maintain this for a subclass of properties, for example, those occurring at the phenomenological grades of perceptual response in what Epstein and Hatfield have called "the sensory core"[33] of ordinary perceptual consciousness.

On their reading, the sensory core is a two-dimensional, phenomenological array of primary properties corresponding to the retinal projection of external objects. The three-dimensional world results from judgment and, according to them,[34] occurs at the third level of perceptual response. I have argued,[35] however, that Descartes seems to distinguish between a phenomenological grade of perceptual responses *caused* by rational processes (and physiological analogues of rational processes) and a nonphenomenological grade of perceptual responses *constituted* by intellectual processes. The former, occurring at grade 3a (and 2b, respectively) comprise the appearances of the three-dimensional world, the latter, occurring at grade 3b, comprise that intellectual understanding of the three-dimensional world, which is occasioned by reflection on appearances produced by the other grades.

Our intellectual understanding of the spatial environment typically includes some numerical measure (a metric) of size, shape, distance, and direction expressed in conventional units—we think of objects as *ten feet* away or as *two feet* across. In *Optics* VI Descartes recognizes the incorporation of conventional measures into perceptual responses.[36] There are not many texts on which to base an interpretation of how Descartes thinks the cognitive system assigns conventional numerical measures, but in his brief discussion in Rule 14 of the *Rules for the Direction of the Mind* he seems to take the basic units as given ("Unity is the common nature which . . . all the things which we are comparing must participate in equally" (AT X, 449; CSM I, 63); other units are to be assigned as needed. While it is difficult to extrapolate anything that one would want to call an explicit theory of measurement from these few remarks, it does seem that the intellect is involved at least in the second stage of the operation. So, and acknowledging that Descartes is not careful in the *Optics*[37] to speak of conventional numerical measures only in connection with operations of the intellect (responses of grade 3b), it is reasonable to suppose that it is the intellect that assigns conventional numerical measures. This is not to say that the structure of the appearance of the three-dimensional world lacks objective properties of *relative* size, shape, orientation, and distance, but it is to say that they lack an *absolute*, conventional numerical measure of those properties. That must be assigned extrinsically by the operations of the intellect. If this is right, then we can regard the three-dimensional appearances produced at grade 3a (and 2b) of perceptual responses as a sensory core relative to the intellectual responses of grade 3b.

Suppose, then, that we allow Descartes to identify in this way a class of properties in the *three-dimensional* sensory core of a given perception and restrict inference D to that core of properties. I shall call the version of inference D restricted in this way *inference D**.

Inference D* (The Sensory Core Restricted Version)

1. I have a clear and distinct concrete perception of sensory core properties $P_1 \ldots P_n$. (Assumption)
2. I have a concrete intuitive awareness of $P_1 \ldots P_n$. (Def., 1)

Therefore,

3. There exists a substance x such that x possesses $P_1 \ldots P_n$ formally.
   (RTCT, 2)

Inference D* requires that there must be an actual substance that actually possesses each member of the set $P_1 \ldots P_n$. This conclusion does not fall foul of the obvious problems resulting from illusions and so on that arose for the unrestricted version of D, since these problems arose only when the ostensible objects of the illusion are metrically specific with regard to size, shape, distance, and direction. For example, if we think that we perceive an object ten feet away, then it is not guaranteed that there is a formal (actual) home for such an object in the environment. On the other hand, we can always find a formal home for the restricted sensory core properties—in the brain, if nowhere else—since the lack of metric specificity of sensory core properties leaves the environmental location of their instantiation essentially undetermined.

Inference D* can, thus, be seen as getting us from the perception of a restricted range of real primary properties to the formal containment of these properties somewhere. Supplementary reasoning begins to refine this picture in the face of difficulties. It does so not by denying that the properties in question are actually exemplified by a subject, but by finding a new subject. For example, if we find it hard to maintain that the properties experienced in a dream are located in subjects in the public spatial environment, we postulate a private spatial environment, presumably in the brain, to serve as the subject of these properties. The total set of inferences—inference D* and the supplementary sets—occurs within the grade 3b of perceptual response and produces the knowledge of particular aspects of corporeal things that Descartes mentions in the passage from the Second Replies. Before concluding this story let me issue a disclaimer. This story is one, it seems to me, that Descartes could have told from the resources available within his empirical theory of perception and his general theory of existential reasoning. Attributing it to Descartes has the advantage of accounting for perceptual judgments in terms of basic elements of his epistemology and yet not committing him to a doctrine of natural inclinations of the imagination. This in turn satisfies the declaration of Meditation VI that all knowledge, including that of particular things, belongs to the mind alone, not to the union of the mind and the body. Whether this story is one that Descartes actually did tell, or intended to tell, is something that my exegetical arguments by themselves leave indeterminate.

Appendix A: The Cartesian Circle and the Theory of Natural Knowledge

It may be that a structure analogous to the Cartesian structure of natural reasons is also operating in the theory of intuitive reasons (clear and distinct ideas). If so it can provide another possible way of dissolving the problem of the Cartesian circle.[38] I have maintained above (chapter 1, section 1.4) that Descartes employs a psychological criterion for determining when an idea is clear and distinct. It can be formally expressed as follows:

The Criterion of Psychological Certainty
for Clear and Distinct Ideas

If I have an irresistible inclination to affirm that I perceive a property P in the face of all reasons to doubt that I do, then I am warranted in believing that I have a clear and distinct idea of P.

This conditional statement is a warrant principle in what we might call the *Cartesian structure of intuitive reasons*, corresponding to the first element of the Cartesian structure of natural reasons. If we now ask for an explanation why this principle should give true results, Descartes's answer must be that *otherwise God would be a deceiver*.

This answer can be treated as providing the second element in a Cartesian structure of intuitive reasons. The question naturally arises how we know that God exists and whether a determination of the answer can be made in a noncircular way. If it is required that we can apply the warrant principle (the first element of the structure) to prove that I have genuine intuitive awareness of divine properties only after determining that God exists (a precondition for satisfying the second element), then a vicious circle certainly arises. But if we allow that the warrant principle can be applied first, then there is no vicious circularity. In analyzing Cartesian epistemology as a two-part structure of reasons, we treat the authorizing role of God as an *explanation* for the reliability of the warrant principle. The existence of this explanation contributes to the overall coherence of Cartesian epistemology, hence to its systematic virtues, but does so without incurring a vicious and unnecessary circle of justification. Viewed in this light, Cartesian epistemology has some of the features—and some of the virtues—of Sellarsian epistemology.[39]

The Janus-Faced Theory of Ideas of the Senses

7.1 The Cartesian Regulatory Ideal

The central purpose of this book is to present an argument for the existence within Cartesian epistemology of a division of labor between the senses and the intellect, which might be put as follows:

> Intellectual awareness is transparent to the nature of its objects, or at least it can be made so by proper applications of Cartesian method. Sensory awareness is intrinsically opaque to the nature of its objects. Since any systematic body of scientific knowledge worthy of the name must contain clear descriptions of ultimate metaphysical categories and clear decisions about which objects fall in which categories, the intellect is an indispensable part of scientific method. Sensory awareness is transparent to the actuality of its objects, or can be made so by proper applications of Descartes's method. Intellectual awareness is intrinsically opaque to the actuality of its objects (excepting the self and God). Since any systematic body of knowledge worthy of the name must make clear decisions about which objects actually exist and which do not, the senses are also an indispensable part of Descartes's method.

Descartes's commitment to the division of labor between the senses and the intellect embodied in this ideal emerges slowly from the epistemology of the *Meditations*, attaining at best a tentative status in the proof of the external world of *Principles* II, 1, and, I shall argue, in the doctrine of the clear but not distinct ideas of the senses of *Principles* I, 46ff. This commitment is never stated clearly even in this latter work but operates, as I propose to see it, as a regulatory ideal guiding the progress of Descartes's thinking about epistemology.

Nevertheless, for Descartes, sensory experience will always remain a Janus-faced notion. In the *Meditations* Descartes generally emphasizes the negative aspects of sense experience, attempting to show that ideas of the senses are obscure and confused, ideas to be avoided by the intellect rather than squarely countenanced. In this chapter I shall take up this negative case in the form of a consideration of Descartes's theory of the errors caused by the senses—Descartes's error theory, as I called it in chapter 4 (section 4.4). In this chapter I shall also take up the positive case, arguing that not only does Descartes eventually develop a more balanced treatment of ideas of sense in the *Principles* but that the seeds for this development lie in the very same properties of obscurity and confusion of ideas of the senses that lie at the heart of the negative doctrine of the *Meditations*.

An error theory is a theory offered by a philosopher as part of a project to overturn a system of commonly held beliefs. The theory consists of an explanation of how those beliefs could be systematically false and yet held by people with rational and sense-perceptual capabilites that are not systematically unreliable. Cartesian error theory proposes to achieve this result by locating a small set of mistaken beliefs at crucial nodes in the inferential scaffolding sustaining commonsense epistemology and metaphysics. Because the mistakes are small in number (though large in effect), because they concern matters over which we exercise free choice and because they arise in circumstances where the interaction between reason and the senses puts us at a considerable risk of confusion, the existence of these mistakes does not entail the existence of systematic unreliability in reason and the senses.

One of the main contentions to be defended in this chapter is that the main locus of Descartes's critique of the senses lies with Cartesian error theory rather than Cartesian epistemology. What I mean by this is that the features of the senses that Descartes employs in his critique are generally used as components in a psychological explanation of why we believe what we do, given that we are mistaken, rather than as premises in an argument proving that we *are* mistaken. There is, however, one important exception to this general practice and that concerns the use Descartes makes of dreaming in Meditation I—it does supply a premise in an essentially epistemic argument.

One of the other main contentions defended in this chapter is that Descartes has a positive epistemology of the senses and, moreover, that it evolves from a dialectic undertaken between the epistemology and the error theory. The key transition in this dialectic is from the claim that ideas of the senses are obscure, a thesis that is developed from Descartes's theory of the material falsity of ideas of the senses, to the claim that there can be clear but not distinct ideas of the senses. The foundational text for Descartes's doctrine of the material falsity of ideas of the senses occurs in Meditation III. I now turn to a detailed consideration of this text.

7.2 The Doctrine of the Material Falsity of Ideas of the Senses in Meditation III

Several pages after introducing the "new method" of considering ideas, Descartes discusses a defect in our ideas of "light and colours, sounds, smells, taste, heat and cold and the other tactile qualities," explaining that

[1] I think of these only in a very confused and obscure way, to the extent that I do not even know whether they are true or false, that is whether the ideas I have of them are ideas of real things or of non-things [French version: chimerical things which cannot exist]. [2] For although, as I have noted before, falsity in the strict sense, or formal falsity, can occur only in judgements, there is another kind of falsity, material falsity, which occurs in ideas, when they represent non-things as things. [3] For example, the ideas which I have of heat and cold contain so little clarity and distinctness that they do not enable me to tell whether cold is merely the absence of heat or vice versa, or whether both of them are real qualities, or neither is. [4] And since there can be no ideas which are not as it were of things [French version: And since ideas, being like images, must in each case appear to us to represent something], if it is true that cold is nothing but the absence of heat, the idea which represents it to me as something real and positive deserves to be called false; and the same goes for other ideas of this kind. (AT VII, 43–44; CSM II, 30; the reference numbers are my interpolations)

In chapter 5[1] I considered in detail only one explanation afforded by Cartesian error theory: confusing the phenomenological content of sense experience with a natural inclination to refer sensations to their causes in the external environment. On that interpretation the referral of sensations is a hybrid act from the Cartesian psychological zoo combining the action of judging with the passion of sensing. Insofar as it is a judgment, it is a false judgment concerning entities that are in fact modes of mind or mind-body relations (sensations) to the effect that they are modes of material substances. Insofar as it is an idea, it is a defective idea, embodying the property of material falsity.

The property of material falsity is distinguished by Descartes (in sentence 2) from the notion of falsity in judgments ("formal falsity"). An idea is materially false if (a) it fails to (re)present[2] a real thing (res) and (b) it somehow mis(re)presents something that is not a real thing as a real thing. (This same property seems also at issue in the French interpolation in sentence 4.) I shall call the first property the *non(re)presentation property* and the second the *mis(re)presentation property*. In sentences 1 and 3 however, a different property of ideas seems to be intimated, one having less do with a capacity for mis(re)presentation than with (c) an *obscurity* of sensory ideas concerning which (re)presentational status they actually possess.

Though I claim that Descartes regards all three kinds of defects as distinct, he also seems to regard them as all closely associated with the property of material falsity. (The association with [a] is made in [2], with [b] in [2] and [4], and with [c] in [3].)[3] We can account for these associations if we regard the notion of material falsity as having generic and specific senses. The specific sense is given in (2), comprising (a) and (b). Following Wells,[4] I propose that we think of material falsity in the generic sense as a notion of unfaithfulness to a functional paradigm. Materially false ideas are, thus, like false friends: both fail to properly fulfill the function of their office.

For Descartes, the "function" of an idea seems to be determined by reference to the function of paradigm ideas, and for Descartes, intellectual ideas are paradigm ideas. In the model that I have proposed,[5] intellectual ideas have the structure of a three-place relation between the intellect, an object, namely, a property, and the objective reality (form) with which that object is presented to the intellect through the good office of the idea. Failing to present a real object to the mind—property *a*, the non(re)presentational property—is one clear way in which an idea might fall short of its paradigmatic function. Another is for an idea with the right ontological form to fail to *reveal* essential features of the object. This can occur in two ways— as a misrepresentation of the real nature of the objects (property *b*) or as an indeterminacy (vagueness) in what we perceive of the object by means of our awareness of it, (property *c*).

This means, I take it, that the ideas of sense that suffer from generic material falsity are not quasi-judgmental referred sensations, but are the innate ideas of sense[6] themselves that somehow fail to present their objects as they really are, namely, as forms of sensory awareness. This is one important way in which the innate ideas of the senses are inferior to the basic ideas of the other faculties.

It must be admitted that these distinctions do not leap out of this text, a text that seems, in the main, to be a jumble of the three. Rather, the distinctions must be introduced as hypothetical readings of Descartes's intentions supported in part by other texts and in part by inference from the contrast Descartes evidently means to draw between proper ideas and those that embody the generic defect of "material falsity." In the remainder of this chapter I develop an interpretation of the three species of material falsity, beginning with the property of non(re)presentation.

7.3 The Non(re)presentational Property

In the passage from Meditation III quoted in the previous section Descartes says, among other things, that ideas of sense represent nothing real. He says much the same in *Principles* I, 71.[7] This is the property I have called the non(re)presentational property, and it marks one of the main differences between ideas of sense (ideas of colors, sounds, heat, and cold) and ideas of geometrical properties.

In *Principles* I, 69, Descartes makes it clear that we know those things that are "referred to the senses" ("colours, pains and the like") in quite a different way than we know "magnitude and figure." One of the most striking features of ideas of geometrical properties lies in the number and richness of theorems that can be derived a priori from a small axiomatic basis and the high degree of logical interconnectedness holding among them. For example, the idea of triangularity is logically connected to the idea that the sum of the interior angles is 180 degrees, an idea that is connected to the sum of angles between parallel lines and intersecting perpendiculars, which idea is in turn connected to a great many others. Ideas of colors, heat, cold, sound, and so on, on the other hand, seem not to be systematically related to one another in this way. The number of general principles governing such ideas is few, seem not to be connected with one another, and are not in general derivable a priori from first principles. We might then suppose that primary qualities are "better known" because any given mathematical property can be inferred from others, something made possible by the logical interconnectedness of such properties.

If this is how Descartes is seeing the differences between ideas of sense and ideas of geometrical properties in the material falsity text from Meditation III, then the discussion of privations in sentence 3 of that text is made intelligible. There, Descartes says that the ideas of heat and cold have such little clarity and distinctness that "thcy do not enable me to tell whether cold is merely the absence of heat or vice versa." Why can't we determine which is the positive and which the negative property by simply *analyzing* them down to their simple notions and then seeing which is to be analyzed in terms of which? This method is, after all, Descartes's preferred method, one used before in the Meditations to clarify the logical structure of certain concepts. We might speculate that the reason Descartes does not use the method of analysis on the ideas of heat and cold is that they have no complex structure to be analyzed: they are both "simple ideas" existing in a logical vacuum. The same holds true of all ideas of sense. Descartes does not, however, claim in this text that *geometrical* properties are subject to these same difficulties, that is, that there are any difficulties about determining which geometrical properties are positive qualities and which are privations of same. We might explain this fact by saying (in the formal mode) that the system of ideas of geometrical properties constitutes a hierarchy of primitive terms, definitions, axioms, and postulates such that we can determine definitively whether a given geometrical property is a "privation" of another—for example, curvature might prove to be a privation of straightness, or vice versa.[8]

This contrast between ideas of sense and ideas of geometrical properties is a contrast drawn in terms of degrees of logical interconnectness among different ideas in each field. The contrast with which we began the section is one drawn in terms of degrees of the power to represent reality. The first contrast concerns the contents of the ideas with which we perceive objects; the second concerns the metaphysical status of the contents. The fact that these two contrasts are so closely intertwined in the Meditation III text suggests that Descartes sees a close connection between them.

To see what the connection might be, suppose that Descartes is reasoning hypothetically as follows: *If a given mode of perception (intellectual, sensory, etc.,) were to put us in contact with a set of real entities, it would put us implicitly in contact with them all, a fact that we should be able to discover by looking around in the logical environment.* ("Looking around" here means using the method of intuitive inference.) We can now use this fact in an argument to the best explanation—the *realist argument* as I shall call it—to establish that a given kind of perception does, or does not, put us in touch with a set of real entities.

If we look around in the logical environment of a given idea and find a rich set of other ideas, we might naturally surmise that this is because these ideas are revealing a rich structure of real things. Descartes appears to employ an argument of this kind in Meditation V, to the effect that the objects of mathematical ideas are real things:

> When, for example, I imagine a triangle, even if perhaps no such figure exists, or has ever existed, anywhere outside my thought, there is still a determinate nature, or essence, or form of the triangle which is immutable and eternal, and not invented by me or dependent on my mind. This is clear from the fact that various properties can be demonstrated of the triangle, for example that its three angles equal two right angles, that its greatest side subtends its greatest angle and the like; and since these

properties are ones which I now clearly recognize whether I want to or not, even if I never thought of them at all when I previously imagined the triangle, it follows that they cannot have been invented by me. (AT VII, 64; CSM II, 44–45)

If, on the other hand, when we use a particular mode of perception and find a vacuum in the logical space surrounding its contents, then we conclude either that the contents are not real things or that the mode of perception is unclear (inadequate to reveal its contents accurately). In claiming in *Principles* I, 69 (as I read it), that ideas of colors and other sensible qualities are not embedded in a rich set of logical interconnections, Descartes is claiming to find just such a logical vacuum surrounding particular ideas of sensible qualities.[9] Where the perception of sensible qualities is clear (explicitly allowed for in the *Principles*[10] but not in the *Meditations*), the conclusion to be drawn by disjunctive syllogism is that such ideas do not put us in touch with an underlying system of real entities. This, I take it, is why Descartes says later in the *Principles* that ideas of the senses "do not, except occasionally and accidently, show us what external bodies are like in themselves."[11]

Returning at last to the material-falsity text from Meditation III we might imagine that Descartes had the logical interconnection property of geometrical properties in mind when he drew there the contrast between ideas of geometrical qualities and ideas of sensible qualities on the privation issue (sentence 3), and was using this contrast to justify drawing (in 2) the contrast between these classes of ideas on the issue of the reality of their objects. On this reconstruction, Descartes reasons thus: the inability to tell whether heat is a privation of cold or vice versa is an indication of an absence of logical interconnections between ideas of heat and cold; the latter provides evidence by means of the realism argument that such ideas fail to present any reality to the intellect.

7.4 Material Falsity as Mis(re)presentation

We have just seen Descartes's case that the objects of sensory awareness — colors, sounds, heat and cold — are not in Descartes's technical sense, "real things" of any kind. This is why Descartes describes ideas of the senses as non(re)presentational, materially false in the sense that it fails to (re)present a real thing (*res*). But ideas of the senses are also described as mis(re)presentational, and it is puzzling how an idea that does not represent something real can mis(re)represent anything.[12]

Descartes often speaks meaningfully about colors, sounds, and so on. There must, then, be some legitimate sense in which colors, sounds, and so on are objects presented to the intellect by acts of sensing. But colors, sounds, and so on are modally dependent on real things; they are not real things themselves. The puzzle, then is to see how these things could be *objects* of ideas even though they are not *real things*. Perhaps Descartes thinks that ideas play a formative role here, acting as a kind of "lens" focusing cognitive attention on various items, real things and modes of real things alike, thereby making them into subjects for judgment? Perhaps this is why Descartes ascribes to sensory ideas that most basic of all (re)presentational properties, being "as it were an image of things." (This property is introduced in sentence 4 in the passage quoted at the outset of section 7.2.)[13]

I propose to accept these suggestions and to see Descartes as claiming that ideas of the senses present something, somehow, to the mind, even though they present no real attributes of any real substance. But why then does Descartes speak of such ideas as (re)presenting "non-things as things," namely, as *mis(re)presentations*, the second variant of material falsity? One possibility is that Descartes means to be speaking of the fact that our (referral) judgments comprise a class of false beliefs. But the kind of falsity at issue in judgments (including referral judgments) is *formal falsity*, and Descartes is at pains in the passage from Meditation III to contrast formal falsity with material falsity.

The key to interpreting Descartes correctly here depends on the fact that there seem to be *two* kinds of real things serving as putative objects of sensory ideas, Cartesian real things and another kind. An indication of what this other kind might be is given in the *Conversation with Burman*:

> For example: I may consider the idea of colour, and say that it is a thing or a quality; or I may say that the colour itself, which is represented by the idea, is something of this kind. For example, I may say that whiteness is a colour; and even if I do not refer this idea to anything outside myself—even if I do not say or suppose that there is any white thing—I may still make a mistake in the abstract with regard to whiteness itself and its nature or the idea I have of it. (AT V, 152; CSM III, 337)

What this seems to mean is that we take whiteness (actually presented as a *logical subject* for referral judgment) to be a *metaphysical subject*, a quasi-substantial entity that is more than mere mode of substances.[14] Though it is a matter of speculation precisely how to understand this quasi substantiality, in the Sixth Replies Descartes seems to connect this idea with the Scholastic notion of a "real quality" or "substantial form" (AT VII, 441, 443; CSM II, 297, 298). These qualities have turned up before in *Optics* IV as the "images transmitted by objects to the brain" postulated by "our philosophers" (AT VI, 112; CSM I, 165). Notice, however, that "our philosophers" go beyond the basic error of treating whiteness as a quasi-substantial entity for they additionally "refer" this entity to the external environment in what is a highly theoretical account.[15] But how, then, does Descartes understand quasi-substantial whiteness *before* it gets dressed up in Scholastic garb?

Perhaps we can get a clue from the following passage from *Rules for the Direction of the Mind* 12:

> Take colour for example: whatever you may suppose colour to be, you will not deny that it is extended [*qu'elle soit étendue*] and consequently has shape [*qu'elle soit figurée*]. (AT X, 413; CSM I, 40–41; the interpolations from the French text [Alquié I, 137] are mine.)

In speaking of colors as being extended and shaped, Descartes is thinking of colors as "material causes" in Aristotle's sense, as quasi substances possessing forms. It is a short step from this view to the view that it is simply obvious that the ordinary objects of common sense comprise colored matter in spatial form. I shall call such entities "Aristotelian objects" and assume that Descartes found the possibility that the real world consisted of such objects plausible, even attractive, at the time he was writing this passage. In any case, there is an evident contrast between the view

Descartes took when he wrote this passage and the view he took when he wrote the passage quoted above from the *Conversation with Burman*. Indeed, it would seem not too far amiss to suppose that the "I" making the mistake about colors referred to in the latter passage is Descartes himself writing in the *Rules for the Direction of the Mind*. But why did Descartes make this mistake?

The answer that the text of Meditation III suggests is that the error is somehow grounded in the *imagio* property, the property of ideas that creates objects of thought out of formal aspects of reality by focusing these aspects into a content that cognition can act upon. In the case of sensory ideas these objects are logical subjects of referral judging, and we may surmise that the source of our error lies in taking a logical subject for a metaphysical subject , that is, for a real thing.

However, the passage from Rule 12 suggests a somewhat less metaphysically sophisticated error. It suggests that we take colors to be quasi-substantial qualities because sense experience presents them to us that way. Descartes makes this point explicitly in the Sixth Replies: "But surely the only reason why people have thought that accidents exist is that they have supposed that they are perceived by the senses" (AT VII, 434; CSM II, 293). In a passage at *Principles* I, 71, entitled "The chief cause of error arises from the pre-conceived opinions of childhood," Descartes describes the cause of error as a series of mistaken inferences. I reproduce this text, which we have seen several times before, for convenience:

> [T]he mind had various sensations of tastes, smells, sounds, heat, cold, light, colours, and so on—sensations which do not represent anything located outside our thought. At the same time the mind perceived sizes, shapes, motions and so on, which were presented to it not as sensations but as things or modes of things existing,. (or at least capable of existing) outside thought, although it was not yet aware of the difference between things and sensations. (AT VIIIA, 35; CSM I, 219)

Notice that Descartes is quite express in his declaration that sensations (i.e., sensations proper) "do not represent" objects external to the mind, though he does not deny that the combination of sensation and the presentation of modes of external things represents something, claiming only that these two elements are to be regarded as distinct. In this passage the distinction appears to be a "real distinction"[16] for us in early childhood prior to the reconfiguration of the corporeal imagination that will produce the fusion of form and matter in mature sense experience.[17]

The strong explanation of error that Descartes envisages here seems to develop in three stages:

1. After earlier childhood we confuse the representational component of our sense experience (imaginal images) with its phenomenological accompaniment (sensations proper), thinking that the latter is somehow essential to the former.

2. We regard the form of imaginal images as reliably presenting the nature of their objects. We thus regard these objects as having the nature of extended objects external to the mind.

3. Because of error 1 we also come to regard sensations as having the power to reliably present an additional dimension of the nature of external objects, namely, to present them as extended objects with secondary qualities.

The chain of reasoning comprises another basis for the "ill considered judgements" that Descartes so roundly and so often condemns in his writings on commonsense perception. Although these transitions of thought are based on mistakes, they are nonetheless rational inferences embodying Descartes strong program of rational psychology. In addition, these inferences are driven by the phenomenological fusion of secondary and primary qualities present in Descartes's doctrine of referred sensations, thus embodying Descartes's doctrine of the material for error provided by sense experience.

But there is more to the story of the errors of common sense than is mentioned here. Descartes suggests elsewhere that the common view is not only that we perceive Aristotelian objects through sense experience but that we perceive them as such *clearly and distinctly*:

> For all of us have from our early childhood, judged that all the objects of our sense-perception are things existing outside our minds and closely resembling[18] our sensations, i.e. the perceptions that we had of them. Thus, on seeing a colour, for example, we supposed we were seeing a thing located outside us which closely resembled the idea of colour that we experienced within us at the time. And this was something that because of our habit of making such judgements, *we thought we saw clearly and distinctly—so much so that we took it for something certain and indubitable.* (AT VIIIA, 32; CSM I, 216; my emphasis.)

I take this passage from the *Principles* to show that mistaken beliefs about what is clear and distinct form one of the main bases for the prediliction of common sense to believe in a world of Aristotelian objects. We have seen in an earlier chapter[19] that Descartes considered and then rejected the idea that the phenomenological fusion of color and extension creates a natural inclination to believe that objects in the physical world are Aristotelian objects. However, we *think* that there is such an inclination, thus causing us to fall into the error. We think this because of certain confusions and mistakes that we make. One such mistake is that we we confuse content with inclination. Another mistake is the one at issue here: we suppose that ordinary sense experience comprises direct intuitive awareness ("clear and distinct" perception) of Aristotelian objects. Descartes of course rejects this supposition, but we are entitled to ask what resources he has available to show that it is false.

7.5 Descartes's Case against Treating Ordinary Sense Experience as a Form of Concrete Intuitive Awareness of Aristotelian Objects

If the sense experience of ordinary physical objects comprises genuine intuitive awareness of those objects, then the sense experiences of ordinary objects are subject to some version of the rule of truth. All versions of the rule presuppose that there are some properties that are the immediate object of some kind of intuitive awareness. In the case of *concrete intuitive awareness* the rule requires that there be an actual substance that formally contains those properties; in the case of *ab-*

stract intuitive awareness the rule requires that there be an actual substance that contains those properties eminently. The notion of *formal* and *eminent* containment of properties are Descartes's theoretical representations of what we would ordinarily express as, respectively, the *actual* or *merely possible* existence of the objects exemplifying those properties.[20]

If we now adopt the language of actual and merely possible objects of awareness, we can say that any genuine *concrete intuitive awareness* is necessarily of actual not merely possible objects. The principle affirming this is a form of Descartes's rule of truth for concrete intuition,[21] and if we stipulate that Aristotelian objects are the immediate objects of the relevant form of concrete intuition, we have what I shall call the *Aristotelian rule of truth* (ART).

If someone wishes to show that a given candidate for a concrete intuitive awareness-type *I* is not a genuine case of intuitive awareness, one way to do so would be to show that some tokens of *I* fail to have actual objects. Formally, the structure of this argument can be represented as follows:

The Nonentailment Argument against Concrete
Intuitiveness (Schematic)

1. If *I* is a genuine case of intuitive awareness then necessarily, all tokens of *I* have actual objects. (ART)
2. It is not the case that necessarily, all tokens of *I* have actual objects. (assumption)

Therefore,

3. It is not the case that *I* is a genuine case of intuitive awareness. (1, 2)

I now argue that Descartes may have been employing an argument of this form in Meditation I against the Aristotelian rule of truth.

In Meditation I Descartes carries out a program to "detach" us from the senses. One of the key elements of this program is, of course, the argument about dreaming. In Meditation I Descartes seems to use this argument to create doubts about the confidence that we ordinarily possess in the truth of the deliverances of the senses:

> Reason now leads me to think that I should hold back my assent from opinions which are not completely certain and indubitable just as carefully as I do from those which are patently false. (AT VII, 18; CSM II, 12)

This injunction seems irrationally harsh.[22] If I have on some occasions found that my friend Sam lies to me, does that mean that I should assume that he always lies? Of course not. But unless I make this unwarranted inference, are there any circumstances in which I should treat a randomly selected utterance of Sam's, which I have no special reason to believe to be false, as if I *knew* it to be false? The answer is yes: I should treat such an utterance as false if my knowledge of even one occasion on which Sam utters a deliberate falsehood effectively undermines the *rational methods* that I have been using to affirm the truth of his utterances in the majority of cases. Suppose, for example, that the only method I had been using to determine whether Sam spoke the truth was to infer that he did from the assumption

Everything Sam says is true. This is a rule of truth; even one example of something Sam says that is not true refutes it. Then, but only then, would it be prudent to "hold back my assent" in all the cases "just as carefully" as I would do if I knew them to be false.

In the sentences of Meditation I immediately following the one just quoted, Descartes says that his goal is to "go straight for the basic principles on which all my former beliefs rested." The first principle that Descartes offers as an example is this: "Whatever I have up until now accepted as most true I have acquired either from the senses of through the senses" (AT VII, 18; CSM II, 12). This is also a rule of truth; even one example of something "acquired through the senses" that is not true refutes it. There is, in fact, a sequence of rules of truth that Descartes introduces in the paragraphs leading up the dream argument and a sequence of corresponding counterexamples.[23] So Descartes thinks that we are all in the same position vis-à-vis what the senses tell us as we were vis-à-vis Sam in my analogy.

In Meditation I Descartes represents these rules of truth as one of our preconceived opinions, the origins of which are obscure. However, writing retrospectively in Meditation III about these opinions, Descartes says this:

> But there was something else which I used to assert, and which through habitual belief *I thought I perceived clearly,* although I did not in fact do so. This was that there were things outside me which were the sources of my ideas *and which resembled them in all respects.* Here was my mistake. (AT VII, 35; CSM II, 25; my emphasis)

This passage makes essentially the same point as the one made in the passage quoted from *Principles* I, 66: our belief in a world of Aristotelian objects is due to a mistaken belief about the kind of awareness (clear and distinct) constituted by ordinary sense experience. If we are to find a previous meditation in which Descartes identifies this error, it must surely be Meditation I; and if we are to locate a precise text in which he does so, I suggest that it is those in which he discusses the commonsense, empiricist rules of truth. Now Descartes does not identify the rule of truth introduced in Meditation I expressly in this passage from Meditation III, but it is difficult to see what other texts he could have in mind, and I shall suppose that it is in fact these.

In characterizing his former opinion to be that the commonsense rules of truth were *clearly perceived* Descartes introduces the idea that the rules of truth discussed in Meditation I are not simply the untutored assumptions of common sense but are instances of what I have called the "Aristotelian rule of truth," which Descartes himself was once tempted to employ and which he now is determined to overthrow.

How does Descartes go about doing this? He does so by arguing explicitly, first, that for every token *o* of an ordinary sense perception-type there is a token *d* of a dream experience-type such that *o* and *d* are qualitatively indiscernible ("I see plainly that there are never any sure signs by means of which being awake can be distinguished from being asleep" (AT VII 19; CSM II, 13)) and, second, that the objects of *d* are not necessarily actual ("Suppose then that I am dreaming and that these particulars—that my eyes are open, that I am moving my head and stretching out my hands—are not true" (ATV II 19; CSM II, 13). The principle of phenomenological indiscernibility (PPI) implies that the class of tokens of an act-type of intuitive awareness is closed under the relation of qualitative indiscernibility. I have earlier argued (chapter 1, section 1.8) that Descartes implicitly relies on PPI in his discussion of the hats and coats example of Meditation II. If we now add PPI to the two propositions explicitly defended by Descartes, we have the makings of an argument against the Aristotelian rule of truth.

> The Nonentailment Argument against the Aristotelian
> Rule of Truth (Inference G)
>
> 1. If any ordinary sense experience-type T is a genuine case of concrete intuition, then necessarily all tokens of T have actual objects. (ART, PPI)
> 2. Some tokens of T are not actual (e.g., when I am dreaming). (Assumption)
> 3. It is false that necessarily all tokens of T have actual objects. (2)
> *Therefore,*
> 4. It is not the case that any ordinary sense experience-type T is a genuine case of concrete intuition. (3, 1)

This comprises Descartes's argument against the existence of the Aristotelian rule of truth and, thus, against one of the main reasons that Aristotelians might offer for the truth of their metaphysical view of the world.

But Descartes is not content with showing just this: he also seeks to show that the objects of ordinary sense experience are *not even possible objects,* a much more demanding task than the one we have just considered. This result, first intimated but not defended (at least not in a form that I can detect) in the discussion of material falsity in the French text of Meditation III — the text where he says that the objects of the ideas of the senses are "chimerical things that cannot exist" (AT IX, 34; Alquié II, 442) — is stated and defended in *Principles* IV.

7.6 Descartes's Argument that Aristotelian Objects Are Inconceivable (The Causal Argument)

When Descartes says that the objects of ideas of the senses cannot exist, we naturally wonder what sort of impossibility he has in mind here. Wilson suggests that it is a conceptual impossibility that derives from what Descartes "ultimately wants to say" about the nature of the material world, namely,

> Because the sensation [of cold], like all 'thoughts' comes to us *tanquam rei imagio* we refer it to the realm of things, take it to tell us about things. In fact, however, all that there is in the realm of things to 'correspond to' this sensation is just the chain of (geometrically describable) events that precede and give rise to the occurrence of the sensation in the human mind. (This is all there *can* be: all that is distinctly conceivable.)[24]

Although I have earlier rejected Wilson's account of why we refer sensations to "the realm of things,"[25] she seems to me to be quite right to look to the postulates of Descartes's mechanistic conception of the physical world as containing the basis for his deeming the objects of ideas of the senses—which I am taking here to be Aristotelian objects—to be impossible. But her explanation of why these postulates make these objects impossible is incomplete, for asserting that the only conceivable *causal processes* are mechanistic processes does not by itself show that Aristotelian *objects* are inconceivable.

Perhaps we can supply the missing steps as follows. It is reasonable to suppose that for any state of affairs that could be realized, there is a theory that could be true countenancing it. Moreover, it is a reasonable methodological principle (which I shall call *MP*) to require of any theory sufficiently comprehensive and coherent to be a serious candidate for truth that the theory explain (make comprehensible to us) *how we can know* the basic structure of the world it describes. If Descartes could show that the comprehensive "Aristotelian theory," namely, the theory providing the theoretical framework for countenancing Aristotelian objects, fails to satisfy this principle, then he would have a case for claiming that that Aristotelian objects, in the sense just explained, are inconceivable.

Garber also has developed an account of Descartes's case against his opponents.[26] He construes Descartes's target as the Scholastic doctrine that physical bodies have "little souls," mind-like forms that explain why these bodies behave in the ways that they do, for example, why they fall toward the center of the earth. Garber's main text for this is from the Sixth Replies (AT VII, 441ff.; CSM II, 297). There is, however, another set of texts from *Principles* IV (which Garber does not consider) in which Descartes seems to supply an argument more along the lines I have suggested. For example, there is this text from *Principles* IV, 198:

> Now we understand very well how the different size, shape and motion of the particles of one body can produce various local motions in another body. But there is no way of understanding how these same attributes (size, shape and motion) can produce something else whose nature is quite different from their own—like the substantial forms and real qualities which many [philosophers] suppose to inhere in things; and we cannot understand how these qualities or forms could have the power to produce local motions in other bodies. (AT VIIIA, 322; CSM I, 285)

His proof in that article should be read in light of article 203, where Descartes reminds us that he has a set of clear and distinct ideas of what a material world must be like—it must satisfy "the principles of geometry and mechanics"—and article 206, where he tells us that the only way in which we can have awareness of external objects is through causal processes satisfying those same principles. It is also in article 206 that Descartes infers the absolute impossibility of an alternative account:

> [T]here are some matters, even in relation to the things in nature, which we regard as absolutely, and more than just morally certain. [French version: Absolute certainty arises when we believe that it is wholly impossible that something should be otherwise than we judge it to be.] ... Mathematical demonstrations have this kind of certainty, as does the knowledge that material things exist; ... [The absolute certainty of this proposition] will be especially appreciated if it is properly understood that we can have no sensory awareness of external objects unless these objects produce some local motion in our nerves; and that the fixed stars, owing to their enor-

mous distance from us, cannot produce such motion unless there is also some motion occurring both in them and also throughout the entire intervening part of the heavens. (AT VIIIA, 328; CSM I, 290)

What is claimed here to be absolutely certain, and hence necessary, is both the unconditional statement that "material things exist" and the conditional principle that we can have sensory awareness of external objects only if the world satisfies a certain mechanistic conception of causation. This text appears to express a mechanisic version of the methodological principle MP mentioned at the outset, "the mechanistic principle" as I shall call it, and to commit Descartes to its status as a necessary truth.

One thing this necessity claim might mean is that the principle is conceptually necessary—we believe that denying the truth of the idea is absolutely impossible. Descartes seems to at least sometimes view our belief in the absolute impossibility of an idea as a matter of our conception of the denial of the idea involving a contradiction. Speaking in connection with his doctrine that God could bring about even things we think are impossible, he says:

> I would not dare to say that God cannot bring it about that there is a mountain without a valley, or that one and two should not be three; but I only say that he has endowed me with such a mind that it is not possible for me to conceive a mountain without a valley, or an aggregate of one and two which is not three, etc., and that such things involve a *contradiction* in my conception. (Letter to Arnauld, July 29, 1648: AT V, 267; *Letters*, 236–237; my emphasis)

There is, however, another way in which we might understand the conceptual necessity of the mechanistic principle: take it as a constraint on our ability to *understand how* things can be rather than as a constraint on our ability to *conceive that* they can be.

These possibilities are not the same.[27] For an intuitive example we might consider looking at a sealed light bulb and seeing a mouse rolling around inside: I may be unable to comprehend how it could be there (since I cannot comprehend how it got in there), but must accept that it could be there since I know that it is there.

For a Cartesian example, we might consider the following passage from a letter to Mersenne. Speaking of God's power to create the eternal truths he writes:

> I say that I *know* this, not that I can *conceive or comprehend it*; because it is possible to know that God is infinite and all powerful although our soul, being finite, cannot comprehend or conceive Him. In the same way we can touch a mountain with our hands but we cannot put our arms around it as we could put them around a tree or something else not too large for them. To comprehend something is to embrace it in one's thought; to know something is to touch it with one's thought. (Letter to Mersenne, May 27, 1630: AT I, 151; *Letters*, 15; my emphasis)

I infer from this example that Descartes accepts that comprehensional impossibility does not imply unknowability. (Call this the *nonentailment thesis*.)[28]

In both of these examples I have said that certain things are incomprehensible. But how do we know this? Is it perhaps due to our own lack of imaginative ability or to insufficient time and effort spent imagining? It seems best to say about the mouse-in-the-light case that the incomprehensibility is not *absolute* but only relative to the intellectual efforts we have made to date and to our own particular intellectual limitations. It is plain that we should not seek to rest very much on what is incomprehensible in this relative way. There is, however, good reason to think that the special nature of Descartes's Meditation III proof of God's existence requires a notion of *absolute incomprehensibility*, for it is only if we could not have created the idea whose objective reality presents God to us from our own finite conceptions that the proof can succeed.[29] To ensure that this central premise is true Descartes had to have some means of ensuring that there were some absolute limits to what the human mind could comprehend.

I suggest that the means Descartes employed was a *criterion of (absolute) comprehensibility* consisting of a subclass of clear and distinct ideas. I shall call such ideas *comprehensibility canons*. I also suggest that the causal principle from article 206 is a comprehensibility canon governing the nature of causal processes. (Call this the "causal-comprehensibility assumption": CCA) In this sense a clear and distinct idea amounts to an a priori recipe for deciding among candidate causal explanations those that describe processes of which Descartes can say he understands how they work and those that do not describe such processes. The former then serve as the set of possible hypotheses subject to further reasoning. A comprehensibility canon does not, however, amount to a canon of conceptual necessity, a property of propositions whose opposite seems contradictory.

It is important to remark that since Descartes allows that we *know* with clarity and distinctness that God has incomprehensible properties, including incomprehensible causal powers, Descartes must allow that we can have rationally decisive grounds for believing in things whose existence violates the comprehensibility canons, both of which are drawn from the set of ideas Descartes characterizes as "clear and distinct." I can now state the following as a methodological corollary of the nonentailment thesis:

Methodological Corollary of the Nonentailment Thesis

It must be possible for us to have rationally decisive grounds of the highest possible order, that is, grounds amounting to clear and distinct ideas, that a proposition *p* is true and, therefore, absolutely possible even though *p* violates a comprehensibility canon.

My interest in the methodological corollary lies in its effect on the causal argument for the impossibility of Aristotelian objects. A simple form of this argument can represented formally as follows:

The Causal Argument for the Impossibility of Aristotelian
Objects (Inference H)

1. If Aristotelian objects are possible, then it is possible to know of their existence. (MP)
2. If it is possible to know of their existence, then there must be a suitable kind of causal process connecting perceivers and Aristotelian objects that satisfies the causal comprehensibility canons. (CCA)

3. There is no suitable causal process satisfying the comprehensibility canons. (Assumption)

Hence,

4. Aristotelian objects are impossible. (1, 2, 3)

The methodological corollary shows that premise 2 of this argument is inconsistent with a central tenent of Cartesian epistemology.

Descartes has at least one card left to play: he can say that God would not have created a world of Aristotelian objects, because, as a benevolent being, God would not have placed in our minds comprehensibility canons that do not truly characterize the natural order. Since God's nature is necessary to God, perhaps Descartes can still claim that Aristotelian objects are impossible. Unfortunately, this reply is also inconsistent with the methodological corollory, a doctrine needed in the proof of God's existence itself. This reply thus fails, and with it fails Descartes's attempt to prove that a world of Aristotelian objects is impossible.[30]

7.7 The Methodological Corollary and the Mind-Body Problem

The motivation for introducing the methodological corollary and its paradigm application has thus far been drawn from Descartes's discussion of God. There are, however, places where it looks as if Descartes is employing this corollary even in matters concerning the finite natural order. One of these places is in a well-known letter to Princess Elizabeth. In this letter Descartes maintains that we have clear knowledge of mind-body union:

> [W]hat belongs to the union of the soul and the body can be known only obscurely by pure intellect or by intellect aided by imagination, but it can be known very clearly by the senses. That is why people who never philosophize and use only their senses have no doubt that the soul moves the body and that the body acts on the soul. (AT III, 690; *Letters*, 141)

Earlier in this same letter Descartes observes:

> I distinguished [in a previous letter] three kinds of primitive ideas or notions each of which is known in its own proper manner and not by comparison with any other: i.e. the notion of soul, the notion of body, and the notion of the union between soul and body. (AT III, 690; *Letters*, 140)

The difficulty is that it is not clear how to reconcile Descartes's claim in this passage that our understanding of mind-body union is a "primitive notion," "known in its own proper manner," with the claim from the first quoted passage that mind-body union is known only obscurely by the intellect. Since the intellect is the faculty responsible for understanding things, this sounds very like the claim that mind-body union is virtually incomprehensible.[31]

There is, it should be noted, a difference for Descartes between mind-body union and mind-body interaction: the latter would obtain even if the mind were "in the body like a pilot is in a ship" (Meditation VI: AT VII, 81; SM II, 56). But mind-body union involves more than simply causal interaction between two distinct substances: it comprises a "substantial union" between the mind and the body.[32] Much has been written on these problems and the need to keep them distinct, but for our purposes the central points are these:

1. Descartes says that the notion of mind-body union is epistemically basic.
2. Descartes says that mind-body union is virtually incomprehensible.

Bedeau has noted that this tension can be resolved by supposing that Descartes accepts what I have called "the nonentailment principle," a principle that allows Descartes to jointly affirm points 1 and 2 without contradiction.[33] While this is certainly part of the resolution of the tension, it still leaves us with the need to explain how, in the Cartesian theory of ideas, something can be known and yet not understood.

A clue to the explanation lies in the fact that our knowledge of mind-body union is said to be "by the senses," not by the intellect and in the fact that the intellect, not the senses, is said to be the faculty which "understands" things. (Meditation II: AT VII, 34; CSM II, 22). The explanation I shall propose has two components. (a) I see Descartes assigning to the senses a power to provide a sensory (re)presentation of mind-body union that, in the terminology of *Principles* I, 46, becomes the subject of "clear but not distinct" perception. (b) I see the incomprehensibility of the notion of mind-body union as lying in its nondistinctness to the intellect, and the nondistinctness to the intellect as lying in the inability (or great difficulty) the intellect has in placing mind-body union within the official Cartesian set of metaphysical categories. The fact that mind-body union is clear (first component) explains why point 1 is true; the fact that it is nondistinct (second component) explains why point 2 can be true at the same time.

The first component is a reflection of Descartes's doctrine that the senses can provide concrete intuitive awareness of certain things and thus can be brought within a special version of the rule of truth The second is a reflection of Descartes's doctrine that the senses fail to reveal the metaphysical category to which their objects belong. This failure amounts, in the terminology of Meditation III, to a kind of "obscurity" in the ideas of sense that comprises a third sense in which ideas of the senses are materially false. (The first two senses are discussed in sections 7.3 and 7.4, respectively.)

7.8 Material Falsity as Obscurity: Sense 3

One piece of textual evidence for construing obscurity as a distinct variant of material falsity comes from the passage from Meditation III quoted at the outset of this chapter. Another comes from Descartes's reply to Arnauld's objections written in response to this passage. (In both places, Descartes's exposition is so unclear that determining his underlying intentions must remain a speculative enterprise.)

Arnauld had made a fundamental objection to Descartes's claim that ideas of sensory qualities can be materially false. (AT VII, 206–208; CSM II, 145–146) That objection can be put in the form of a dilemma that I shall call "Arnauld's Dilemma."

Arnauld's Dilemma

1. Either cold is a privation or it is not. (In this case it is said to be a positive entity.)
2. Either our idea of cold is an idea of a privation or it is not. (In this case it is an idea of a positive entity.)
3. Assume that our idea of cold is an idea of a privation. If so, and if cold is in fact a privation, then our idea of cold is true, not false, in that respect. If cold is in fact not a privation, then what we have been calling "our idea of cold" is not in fact an idea of cold.
4. Assume that our idea of cold is an idea of a positive entity. If so, and if cold is in fact a positive entity, then our idea of cold is true, not false, in that respect. If cold is in fact a privation, then what we have been calling "our idea of cold" is not in fact an idea of cold.

Hence,

5. It cannot be that something which is in fact an idea of cold be false.

Descartes gives his own enthymatic formulation of Arnauld's dilemma in the following words: "[I]f it [the idea of cold] represents an absence, he says, it is true; and if it represents a positive entity it is not the idea of cold" (AT VII, 234; CSM II, 164). In response to this Descartes notes only that he agrees. I take it that Descartes is not indicating agreement with Arnauld's conclusion—the idea of cold cannot be a materially false idea—but rather with Arnauld's premises.

Since Descartes has already indicated agreement with the conditional statements themselves, he must be objecting to the assumptions, (1) that cold is an idea of a positive entity *and* (2) that cold is an idea of a privation. But since Descartes seems to regard these categories as exhaustive of the possible natures of cold, Descartes must be saying that the idea of cold fails to present the nature of cold to the intellect *whatever that nature may be*. Descartes does not seem to be giving expression here to the idea that cold misrepresents that nature, that is, that the idea of cold is materially false in the specific sense, but rather to the idea that cold presents its object in an epistemically indeterminate way, obscures it in a way appropriate to the generic notion of material falsity.

Descartes moves further in this direction in the sentences immediately following the one in which he gives his cryptic rebuttal of Arnauld's dilemma:

[1] [M]y only reason for calling the idea 'materially false' is that, *owing to the fact that it is obscure and confused, I am unable to judge whether or not what it represents to me is something positive which exists outside of my sensation.* And hence [2] I may be led to judge that it is something positive though in fact it may be an absence.

Hence in asking what is the cause of the positive objective being which, in my view, is responsible for the idea being materially false, my critic has raised an improper question. For [3a] I do not claim that an idea's material falsity results from some positive entity; [3b] it arises solely from the obscurity of the idea—although [3c] this does have something positive as its underlying subject, namely the actual sensation involved. Now this positive entity exists in me, in so far as I am something real. But [4] the obscurity of the idea is the only thing that leads me to judge that the idea of the sensation of cold represents some object called 'cold' which is located outside me; and [5] this obscurity in the idea does not have a real cause but arises simply from the fact that my nature is not perfect in all respects. (AT VII, 234–235; CSM II, 164; my reference numbers; my emphasis.)

My interpretation pivots on one central fact about the passage. The fact is that the property of obscurity and confusion is introduced (in claim 1) to explain *why* we make erroneous judgments about the nature of cold (claims 2, 3b, 4). This fact seem to me to rule out the possibility that Descartes is treating materially false ideas as formally false referral judgments since material falsity is cited in the passage as an *explanation* for the formally false judgment about cold. On the other hand, this same fact lends positive support to the possibility that he is giving expression to the doctrine that material falsity is the property of obscurity (sense 3 of material falsity; see section 7.2), a suggestion reinforced by the clear terminological emphasis on "obscure" in most of this passage.

Though the apparent shift in focus from the *Meditations* to the Reply is easy to miss, if it is occurring at all, I am not alone in noticing that something is afoot in the Reply not evident in the *Meditations*: Wilson[34] too has noticed a change. She argues that Descartes began to abandon the doctrine of material falsity (as she has conceived it) under pressure from Arnauld's objection, completing the task by proposing a different doctrine of ideas of sensory qualities in the *Principles*. As Wilson describes the ultimate result of the exchange between Descartes and Arnauld, Descartes begins somewhat confusedly to give up the idea that there is intrinsic to sensory ideas a representational character responsible for our positive inclination to think that they represent real things when they do not, replacing it with the idea that there is only a "weak" explanation, that is, an explanation for how, in the circumstances, an "opportunity" to commit error arises rather than how the circumstances are causally sufficient for an error to arise. This is the obscurity property of ideas of the senses. To support her interpretation she cites claim 3 from the passage quoted above.[35]

To see what Wilson might have in mind here and to help give further definition to my own statement of the obscurity doctrine, it will be useful to illustrate the difference between a "weak" explanation" for error and a "strong" one by the following pair of cases:

(A) If we look out our window at dusk and see obscurely a human figure in the garden below who is in fact male but presents an appearance compatible with being either a male or a female, we might say that the perception of the figure presents us with an opportunity to make a mistake, though the perception by itself does not *positively incline us to get it wrong*. We might of course still make an erroneous judgment, but if we do, the explanation for our doing so will be extraneous to the perception itself, lying perhaps in a mistaken inference from the assumptions that the person in the garden is the upstairs tenant and that that person is a woman.

(B) This proposal should be distinguished from one assigning to obscurity the role of a misleading indicator. Thus if we see a man in broad daylight standing close before us disguised in female clothing, there is a sense in which we are mislead by that perception itself to make a mistake.

When Descartes says that he cannot determine *whether* a false idea exhibits one kind of object or another (claim 1, above) he is like the person in the first case who "obscurely sees" an object and makes a mistaken judgment about its nature based on reasoning from an uncertain premise. The perceptual obscurity present in this case permits but does not positively mislead us to make mistakes. The notion of obscurity as a permissive cause of error therefore introduces a novel kind of error explanation.

The difficulty that Wilson finds with this new story of Descartes is that it leaves the positive source of error unexplained: sensations are now not clearly seen as falsely clothed with representational character , but merely seen in such an obscure way that we can't tell what representational properties they may possess. Her view is that Descartes waits until the *Principles* to offer his account of the positive source of error. She does not, however, seem to pause very long over the notion of obscurity itself, dismissing its importance to Descartes's argument and moving quickly to focus on the positive explanations for error in the *Principles*.

My own view is that Wilson is essentially right to see Descartes's concern with material falsity in Meditation III coming into focus as a concern with obscurity in the Reply. I also think that she is right to look forward to the first part of the *Principles* to seek further development of this conception and of the "new" positive source of our errors. However, I think that she is mistaken to dismiss the significance of the notion of obscurity for Descartes's ultimate position in the *Principles*. Just because that notion embodies a concept of *permitting* error rather than figuring as an element in a sufficient causal explanation of error, this defect must be seen as one that is somehow internal to ideas—a kind of inherent *vagueness*—rather than a defect attributable to will or intellect.

The doctrine of the obscurity of the ideas of the senses in the *Meditations* and in the Reply to Arnauld undergoes a transformation in the *Principles*. It becomes, I am about to argue, the doctrine that sensory awareness can be *clear but not distinct*.

7.9 From Obscure Ideas of the Senses to Clear and Distinct Ideas of the Senses

From Obscure Ideas to Clear but not Distinct Ideas

Descartes claims in *Principles* I, 46, that we can have perceptions of sensations that are clear without being distinct. He offers as an example pain:

> For example, when someone feels an intense pain, the perception he has of it is indeed very clear, but is not always distinct. For, people commonly confuse this perception with an obscure judgement they make concerning the nature of something which they think exists in the painful spot and which they suppose to resemble the sensation of pain. (AT VIIIA, 22; CSM I, 208)

Few commentators lavish much attention on trying to interpret this doctrine or to relate it to the other things Descartes says about clear and distinct ideas. Ashworth concludes that any account of clear and distinct ideas that seeks to provide a unified treatment incorporating this doctrine is "unlikely to be reliable."[36] Markie takes the view that Descartes's texts "simply do not give us enough to go on"[37] in constructing an interpretation that relies on a notion of clarity separated from that of distinctness. In fact, however, there is a good deal to go on—less than we would like, probably not enough to provide the basis for a definitive interpretation, but enough to point an enterprising interpreter in the right direction.

For one thing, there are several tolerably clear texts dealing with this matter, one of which I have just quoted, several more of which I quote below. For another, and despite all of the scholarly grumbling, Descartes's basic intention seem clear enough: he wants to say that when we feel a pain it is clear that we do so, though in locating the pain literally in a part of our body, we rashly make a *judgment* that goes beyond what the perception of the pain by itself presents us with, a judgment that Descartes takes to be false. The truth of the matter, according to Descartes, is that the pain is a sensation in the mind.[38]

In calling the perception of pain *clear* I have taken Descartes to mean that pain is the object of a form of awareness in which the quality of painfulness is immediately present to the mind. Part of the evidence for this comes in the preceding section where Descartes defines clear perception thus: "I call a perception "clear" when it is present and accessible to the attentive mind" (AT VIIIA, 22; CSM I, 207).

Notice that Descartes does not here speak of the object of the clear perception, pain in the present example, as being present and accessible to the mind, but of "it", namely, the perception itself. This does not, however, mean that Descartes takes the perception of pain *rather than* the pain itself to be present to the mind, for Descartes takes pains to be properties of perceptions. This point is obscured by the fact that pain is also an object of perception and Descartes is not always careful in his terminology to distinguish between these two things.

Sometimes Descartes speaks of color and pain as *being* sensations. He does so, for example in *Principles* I, 68:

> In order to distinguish what is clear in this connection from what is obscure, we must be very careful to note that pain and colour and so on are clearly and distinctly perceived when they are regarded merely as sensations or thoughts. (AT VIIIA, 33; CSM I, 217)

And elsewhere as well, for example, in the Sixth Replies:

> But colours, smells, tastes and so on, are, I observed, merely certain sensations which exist in my thought, and are as different from bodies as pain is different from the shape and motion of the weapon which produces it. (AT VII, 440; CSM II, 297)

This formulation treats sensations as a natural kind to which colors and pains belong as members. This is not, however, his usual way of expressing the relationship between sensations and their objects. Normally he speaks of "sensations *of* colour," a formulation that expresses an act-object relationship.

Both of these formulations express Cartesian doctrine. The first expresses Descartes's doctrine that pains, colors, and so on, are modes of a mental stuff (or an irreducible mind-body relation), and it is this doctrine that we should see in the passage just quoted. The second formulation expresses the doctrine that the intellect is presented with these modes through a special cognitive relation I claim to be a kind of concrete intuition. We thus should interpret the doctrine that ideas of pain become distinct when we regard them "as sensations" as the doctrine that the intellect produces distinct ideas of the objects of concrete sensory intuition when it arrives at a true understanding of the nature of these objects. This, of course, is a task that only the intellect in its theoretical employment can carry out.

In the foregoing I have assumed that colors and other such qualities are treated by Descartes as of a piece with pains, all are qualities of mind or a mind-body relation rather than qualities of external objects or states. Although the positive exegetical evidence for this assumption is significant—some of which I have just cited from *Principles* I, 68, and the Sixth Replies—there is also evidence that points in a contrary direction.

First I will review some of the positive evidence.

Descartes *clearly* thinks that pains and other passions referred to the body are really in the mind (see *Principles* I, 46), and yet he generally lists colors and other such qualities referred to the world external to the body together with those in the former category. (In addition to the texts cited above and below, see the important text in the Sixth Replies: AT VII, 437; CSM II, 294.)

Moreover, in *Principles* I, 71, Descartes speaks of "what we call the sensations of tastes, smells, sounds, heat, cold, light, colours and so on—sensations which do not represent anything located outside our thought" (AT VIIIA, 35; CSM I, 219). The point to note in this passage is that it is the *objects* of sensation—what sensations (re)present to us—that are characterized as not "located outside thought."

Furthermore, speaking about "the nature of light and heat and all other sensible qualities" in a letter to Chanut[39] Descartes says, "I presuppose that these qualities are only in our senses, like pleasure and pain." Again, the point is that it is the *qualities* not just the sensations that are "in our senses."

These passages seem to me to be decisive on the question of the ontological category of colors and other sensory qualities—they belong to the category of things dependent on mind, not matter. Nevertheless, there is a class of passages that seem to indicate that Descartes takes colors and other qualities referred to external objects as in fact modes of those objects rather than modes of mind. The following passage from *Principles* I, 70, is representative:

> It is clear, then, that when we say that we perceive colours in objects, this is really just the same as saying that we perceive something in the objects whose nature we do not know, but which produces in us a certain very clear and vivid sensation which we call the sensation of colour. (AT VIIIA, 34; CSM I, 218)

What is characteristic of these passages, and there are many of them in the Cartesian corpus,[40] is that Descartes speaks in the "formal mode" of what common folk mean (should mean?) when they say that colors are "in objects." Descartes contrasts this conception of color with color as the immediate object of sensory awareness. Thus he says later in the same article:

> [W]e easily fall into the error of judging that what is called colour in objects is something exactly like the colour of which we have sensory awareness. (AT VIIIA, 34–35; CSM I, 218)

Though in this and similar passages Descartes does not say that the material-process-cautiously-described conception of color is an illegitimate conception, in describing this view always in the formal mode—"what is *called* colour"—(my emphasis), he seems to suggest that color thus described is not *really* a legitimate sense of color at all. Whether this is his suggestion or not, it is clear that he does regard "the colour of which we have sensory awareness" as color in a sense that is both legitimate and different from "what is called colour in objects." It is this sense that I take to be fundamental.

Returning now to the main path, a clear perception of pain is the obvious presence of the quality of pain to the mind. There is philological evidence from *Principles* I, 66, that Descartes regarded the obvious presence of pain (and other sensory qualities) as an intuition in his technical sense. This is the English text:

> [Sensations] may be clearly perceived provided we take great care in our judgements concerning them to include no more than what is strictly contained in our perceptions—no more than that of which we have inner awareness. (AT VIIIA, 32; CSM I, 216)

The French text expresses the concept of inner awareness with the words *connaissance intérieur*; the Latin by the words *intime conscii*. These are special terms that Descartes uses to express a special notion of *consciousness* distinct from the broader notions of *thought* and *perception* expressed in other terms.[41] I argued in chapter I that these are the terms that Descartes uses characteristically to express his technical notion of intuition. For example, he uses the French term *la connaissance* to express the idea of an intuitive awareness ("inner awareness") of our thought and existence in a passage from the Sixth Replies that we have discussed before (I reproduce it here for convenience):

> This inner awareness of one's thought and existence is so innate in all men that, although we may pretend that we do not have it if we are overwhelmed by preconceived opinions and pay more attention to words than to their meanings, we cannot in fact fail to have it. Thus when anyone notices that he is thinking and that it follows from this that he exists, even though he may never before have asked what thought is or what existence is, he still cannot fail to have sufficient knowledge of them both to satisfy himself in this regard. (Sixth Replies: AT VII, 422; CSM II, 285)

This text indicates that inner awareness may not always be clearly identified as such. When it *is* identified as such we have what Descartes would call in the *Meditations* a *clear and distinct idea*. In the text from *Principles* I, 68, Descartes seems to have a similar idea in mind when he speaks of including in our *clear ideas* "no more than that of which we have inner awareness." Notice that here Descartes speaks of an idea that is clear simpliciter, not clear and distinct.[42]

Descartes does not explicitly introduce the distinction between ideas that are clear and those that are clear and distinct ideas in the *Meditations* and appears to treat the words "clear and distinct" as semantically noncomposite in that work. Introducing the notion of clear but not distinct ideas in *Principles* I, 46, amounts to a significant refinement of doctrine in which the notion of a clear idea of sensation in the *Principles* seems to be equivalent to the fused notion of clear and distinct ideas in the *Meditations*. (I consider in the next section what a distinct idea of sensations might be.)

In Meditation III Descartes introduces the rule of truth. I argued in chapter 1 that the rule of truth is a general principle that governs the transition from intuitional awareness of the presence of properties to knowledge that the properties are contained in a substance. I also argued in chapter 1 that the rule of truth takes on a special form in the case of the intuitive cogito. One central difference between the general rule and the special rule is that, in the latter, the content of intuitional awareness is a property *as actualized*, whereas in the former the content of intuitional awareness is of the "presence" of a property (or set of properties) *where presence does not entail actualization.*

In the case of the intuitive awareness of sensory qualities the question naturally arises whether Descartes countenances a principle analogous to one of the preceding. In seeking such a principle we face a number of constraints, of which one is paramount: "sensory perceptions . . . do not, except occasionally and accidently, show us what external bodies are like in themselves" *(Principles* II, 3: AT VIIIA, 41–42; CSM I, 224). In fact, Descartes seems to offer this constraint in an even stronger form in Meditation III, where he asserts that sense perception either represents "non-things" or represents a reality "so extremely slight that I cannot even distinguish it from a non-thing" (AT VII, 44; CSM II, 30).[43] Both of the other principles *do* show us what substances are "like in themselves." In this respect a principle applied to intuitive awareness of sensory properties will be different from the other two.

There is, however, one important respect in which intuitive awareness of a sensory quality is like the intuitive awareness of ones own thought and existence—in both cases the awareness is awareness of a property not merely possibly but actually exemplified. In such circumstances the intuitive awareness of a sensory quality is unlike the case of (intellectual) intuitive awareness. We might express the comparison between these three modes of intuitive awareness summarily by saying that intellectual intuition gives us the nature but not the actuality of its object, sensory intuition gives us the actuality but not the nature of its object, and intuitions of our own mental states give us both the nature and the actuality its object. That is why the last mode is taken by Descartes as a paradigm for the others.

My conjecture is that the principle that we are seeking will turn out to be a specialized rule of truth that has the implication that the qualities of which we have intuitive awareness are actually exemplified in something but does not imply what the nature of the something is. We know, however, that if the something were a substance, then a property actually exemplifed in that substance would contain an implication about what that substance was like in itself. So I take it as a corollary from this that the bearer of sensory qualities whose existence is affirmed by the specialized rule of truth must not be a substance. The proposed rule can thus be formally put as follows:

The Specialized Rule of Truth for Sensory Awareness
(SRTSA)

If have intuitional awareness of the presence of sensory qualities $P_1 \ldots P_n$ then there exists an entity x[44] such that x is not a substance but x actually exemplifies $P_1 \ldots P_n$.

The specialized rule of truth applies to clearly perceived sensations, not clearly and distinctly perceived sensations. However, it is also possible for us to have clearly *and distinctly* perceived sensations:

> [I]n order to distinguish in this connection what is clear from what is obscure we must be careful to note that pain and colour and so on are clearly and distinctly perceived when they are regarded merely as sensations or thoughts. (*Principles* I, 68: AT VIIIA, 37; CSM I, 217)

The central difference between clear perception and clear and distinct perception that is brought to light by the second of these passages is that the objects of the intuitive awareness, "pain, colour and so on," are *identified* ("regarded") as what they are, namely, "sensations." Locating these objects in the category of sensations is locating them within their proper *metaphysical category*, just the thing we fail to do when we have an idea of pain that is clear but not distinct.

But what is Descartes's argument that pains and colors do in fact fall into this category? It is, after all, very tempting to think that both of these properties, but color especially, are "out there," are, that is, modes of extended rather than mental substance. I consider Descartes's answer to this question next in the context of a discussion of Descartes's general theory of inference.

From Clear but not Distinct to Clear and Distinct Ideas of Sensory Qualities

Descartes treats logic (the theory of valid inference) in several places. He treats it most explicitly under the rubric of the method of intuition and deduction in the *Rules for the Direction of the Mind*. I treated Descartes's theory of intuitive inference extensively in chapter 1 and will return to it again in the epilogue. However, it will be useful to have a brief summary of the main points available here.

"Intuition," Descartes says, is "the conception of a clear and attentive mind, which is so easy and distinct that there can be no room for doubt about what we are understanding" (AT X, 368; CSM I, 14). Descartes distinguishes intuition from deduction, characterizing the latter as "a continuous and uninterrupted movement of thought in which each individual proposition is clearly intuited" (AT X, 369; CSM I, 15). This way of putting the distinction suggests that inference falls exclusively within the province of deduction, but Descartes makes it clear that this is not so:

> Take for example, the inference that 2 plus 2 equals 3 plus 1: not only must we intuitively perceive that 2 plus 2 make 4, and that 3 plus 1 make 4 but also that the original proposition follows necessarily from the other two. (CSM I, 15; AT X, 369)

In order to infer one thing from another we need to intuit a necessary connection between the two things. The kind of inference in question is *immediate inference*, so called because it derives the presence of one property from that of another without the mediation of a general principle. Inferences that rely on general principles in addition to particular propositions are called *syllogisms* in classical logic, and I take Descartes's technical notion of deduction to include only immediate inference.

To take an example of intuitive inference from the domain of geometry: if I begin with an intuition of the property of triangularity, I may then see that this property necessarily implies the property of figuredness and that this in turn implies extension and that extension is an essential attribute of material substance. Notice that the latter implication concerns the metaphysical-type to which extension belongs: it belongs to material substance.

There is an important contrast between this case and the case with sensory qualities. We have intuitive awareness of the presence of colors, pains, and other sensory qualities, just as we do with the presence of geometrical properties, but we do not seem to have intuitive knowledge of the metaphysical status of sensory qualities. This is so because there does not seem to be a series of immediate inferences that we can make from an initial intuition of the presence of a color to the idea that the color is a second-order property of ideas, hence a property of immaterial substance. I take this claim to be the same as, or a near cousin to, the doctrine of the obscurity of ideas of the senses in the *Meditations*. (What is missing from the latter work is any recognition that ideas of the senses share with ideas of geometrical objects the property of *clarity*.)

The lack of connectedness between ideas of colors (and other sensory qualities) and ideas expressing the metaphysical type of colours (and other sensory qualities) can be seen as a reflection of the general lack of logical connectedness that distinguishes ideas of sensory qualities in general from ideas of geometrical qualities.[45] Descartes expresses this difference by calling ideas of the senses *indistinct* while calling ideas of geometrical properties *distinct*.

If I have Descartes right on this, we would expect to find that he employs in the *Principles* an alternative method for determining the metaphysical type of sensory qualities. Some evidence for this appears in a letter to Chanut of 1649:

> [I]t must be remembered, while reading this book [the *Principles*], that although I consider nothing in bodies except their sizes, their shapes, and the movement of their parts, I claim nonetheless to explain the nature of light and heat and all other sensible qualities; because I presuppose that these qualities are only in our senses, like pleasure and pain, and not in the objects which we feel, in which there are only certain shapes and movements which cause the sensations called light, heat, etc. *This I did not explain and prove until the end of the fourth part*; nonetheless it is useful to know and observe it from the beginning of the book, so as to understand it better. (AT V, 289; *Letters*, 246; my emphasis)

Descartes describes light and heat in two ways in this passage, as "sensible qualities" and as "sensations." In light of my account of the senses in the previous sections of this chapter I take the latter to be the act of sensory awareness, the former to be the objects of those acts. Notice that Descartes describes these objects as "qualities," evidently meaning by that not the "real qualities" of Scholastic theory — none such exist on the Cartesian scheme of things — but the items which Descartes claims to be able to "explain" at the end of the *Principles*. If we now turn to the relevant texts, especially *Principles* IV, 198, we find various arguments drawn from Cartesian mechanistic science, some empirical, some a priori, the general thrust of which is to show that postulating colors and other such properties as real qualities in extended matter is inconsistent with an intelligible story of our ability to causally inter-act with such entities. (This story is the causal argument discussed earlier in this chapter.)[46] Although the overall argument for this conclusion can probably be treated as deductive in our sense, it is fairly clear that it cannot be treated as an application of intuitional inference in the strict sense.

Showing that the argument is deductive in a broad sense requires showing that its conclusion can be inferred from within Descartes's synthetic method.[47] It is here that the specialized rule of truth for sensory qualities might prove its mettle.

This specialized rule of truth is the first principle of what I shall call "Cartesian sensory foundationalism," a species of Descartes's general synthetic method of proof applied to sensory qualities concretely intuited. Once this principle has been ap-plied to yield the knowledge that something other than a substance exemplifies this property, it then becomes a matter of choosing the correct ontological status for this entity from among a set of possible candidates consistent with the a priori con-straints. We can represent this pattern of reasoning as follows:

The Inferential Structure of Cartesian Sensory
Foundationalism (Inference I)

1. I have a clear and distinct idea of sensory qualities $P_1 \ldots P_n$. (Assump-tion)
2. There exists an entity y such that y is not a substance but y actually exemplifies $P_1 \ldots P_n$. (SRTSA, 1)
3. There exists a set of logically possible entity types for y of which only one, *mode of mind*, is consistent with the a priori constraints. (Assump-tion)

Therefore,

4. $P_1 \ldots P_n$ are properties of modes of mind.

I now consider two objections to the thesis that Descartes subscribes (or would subscribe) to this pattern of reasoning. The first can be put in the form of a charge that an inconsistent quartet of propositions can be constructed from the premises in this pattern of inference together with other central tenets of Cartesian episte-mology. The first two members of the proposed quartet describe the epistemic situ-ation of a knower prior to invoking premise 3 in inference I:

1. I know that a given sensible quality x is actually exemplified.
2. I do not yet know that x is exemplified in a mental entity.

The third asserts a metaphysical principle:

3. Necessarily, if a given sensible quality is actually exemplified, then it is exemplifed in a mental entity.

The fourth describes an epistemic principle:

4. If S knows that p and p entails q, then S knows that q.

Statements 1, 3 and 4 taken together entail the negation of 2.

Drestske has called statement 4 the "Penetration Principle"[48]; I shall call it the "general penetration principle." My interest is not whether the general penetration principle is true but whether Descartes was committed to it. If he was, the present context gives us grounds for thinking either that Descartes's theory of sensory foundationalism (as represented by inference I) is inconsistent or that I have misrepresented Descartes's theory.

Fortunately, both of these alternatives can be avoided. I first observe that the general penetration principle should be distinguished from the following variation: "If S knows that p and S *knows* that p entails that q, then S knows that q." (The italicized phrase is what distinguishes the two principles.) This is an epistemic version of the penetration principle (EVPP) and it seems clear that Descartes is committed to EVPP. However, EVPP is consistent with propositions 1 and 2, for the circumstance in which a person would naturally be said to know, for example, that they feel pain but not know that they are thereby perceiving a quality of mind (or a mind-body relation) is just the circumstance in which the second conjunct in the antecedent of EVPP fails to hold, namely, the one in which we would fail to know that feeling a pain entails that I am feeling a mode of mental rather than extended substance.

We can, therefore, set aside the charge that Cartesian foundationalism rests on the inconsistent quartet of propositions, 1 to 4.

The second objection, due to Maull, is that sense experience is "in no sense an epistemological foundation for Descartes."[49] She appears to derive this conclusion from an intepretation of *Principles* I, 46, according to which *both* clarity and distinctness are properties of sensations rather than judgments:

> We confuse what is a judgement- for example that the rose is red- with the mere sensation of red, and accord the former the clearness and distinctness that is characteristic only of the latter.[50]

Her central text is *Principles* I, 46, where Descartes explains that when we have a clear but not distinct perception of pain "we confuse this perception with an obscure judgement concerning the nature of something which exists in the painful spot." Maull takes this as a rejection of the proposal that clear perception of sensations provides a foundational basis for sense certainty. However, this objection fails to take proper cognizance of Descartes's theory of judgment: *referral* judgments do not themselves create propositional contents but are acts of will directed toward the contents of sensations. The fact that Descartes says in this passage that we confuse sensations with obscure judgments should not, therefore, be regarded as a denial that *basic sensory awareness* provides propositional contents for *proper* judgments. The confusion in question is that of taking a referral judgment for the *sensation* itself.

My interpretation of Cartesian foundationalism is driven by the central thesis that Descartes must allow that we can know that some things exist without first having to know the ultimate metaphysical status of the things. I have focused mainly on texts from the *Principles* to establish this thesis, but there is evidence of this doctrine in other places as well. Consider, for example, this passage from a letter to Princess Elizabeth quoted before:

The soul can be conceived only by pure intellect; the body (i.e. extension, shape, and movement) can likewise be known by pure intellect but much better by intellect aided by imagination; and finally what belongs to the union of the soul and the body can be known only obscurely by pure intellect or by intellect aided by the imagination but it can be known very clearly by the senses. (AT III, 690; *Letters*, 141)

Note that Descartes speaks here of "clear" knowledge not of "distinct" knowledge of mind-body union. Descartes does not explain what sort of clear knowledge the senses give us regarding the union between mind and body, but the context of discussion suggests it is the knowledge *that such a relationship exists*. He also does not explain what the obscurity of the intellect's grasp consists in, but the context is again suggestive: it consists in a lack of understanding of *the nature* (metaphysical category) of that relationship. The idea appears to be that we are certain that there exists an intimate mind-body relationship on the basis of sense experience, but we are not certain what that relationship consists of. This is an uncertainty relating to metaphysical category and therefore amounts to a lack of distinctness in the idea of mind-body union in precisely the sense explicated above.

This is one of the few places Descartes will see a positive advantage to sense experience over intellect, one of the few places where any positive epistemic role is explicitly assigned to the senses.

Epilogue

Two of my stated goals in this book[1] have been to show that Cartesian epistemology has more power and plausibility overall than contemporary philosophers are willing to admit, and to defend Descartes's rule of truth.[2] I have attempted to do the second of these things by showing, first, that Descartes has a single underlying theory of existential reasoning—reasoning from the contents of our thoughts to the existence of things outside our thoughts—that is simple, comprehensive and, within the broad outline of foundational epistemology, can meet a variety of objections traditionally brought against it, and, second, that the rule of truth provides the main premise for the general theory of existential reasoning. One can certainly wonder whether I have been successful in either of these enterprises, but if I have, then I would also claim that Cartesian theory is a useful model for solving some of the more intractable problems that have been identified for foundational epistemology by recent critics.

Consider, for example, the following problem raised by BonJour.[3] BonJour supposes that foundational epistemology comprises a set of rules or principles—*warrant principles* as I term them—asserting conditions under which we are epistemically justified in believing the contents of certain propositions but which do not, in general, assert conditions entailing the truth of those propositions. (Those that assert such conditions are *rules of truth*.) What makes a set of warrant principles foundational in my sense is that the conditions specify items other than beliefs or relations to beliefs as grounds of justification. BonJour wonders how we could go about vindicating a certain choice of warrant principles, finding that we could do so only if we could establish by some informative and noncircular means that someone applying the warrant principles correctly is likely to achieve the truth. Since warrant principles are not rules of truth (in the sense explained above), the vindication must proceed by way of a nondeductive argument based on premises that themselves need to be justified. Justifying these premises, argues BonJour, will inevitably lead away from foundationalism and toward coherentism.[4] Since I am convinced that the foundationalist's only decisive response is to replace the warrant principle approach with a rule-of-truth approach like that provided by Cartesian epistemology, I see Cartesian epistemology providing an important tool to contemporary epistemologists concerned to defend the merits of foundationalism.

But there is more to Cartesian epistemology than the rule of truth; there are also methods (accounts of how rules of truth are to be discovered, justified, and employed) and a methodology (a theory of what different kinds of methods there are and why some are to be preferred to others). An overall appraisal of the merits of Cartesian epistemology, the kind required to determine whether my first objective has been achieved, requires a discussion not only of the first-order epistemic principles but also of the methods associated with the use of these principles. It is in the doctrine of method no less than in the rule of truth that Descartes has a major contribution to make to contemporary epistemology.

In the *Rules for the Direction of the Mind* Descartes identifies intuition as a source of knowledge of both individual simple natures and necessary relations holding between simple natures. In both cases there is the need to identify and distinguish simple natures from the other things with which they might be confused (things like impulsive and conjectural judgments) and to do the same for necessary relations. In addition to this, there is the need to decide which of the multitude of necessary relations already identified are useful for the theoretical problem at hand, thus helping us to draw useful deductions. To satisfy both of these needs Descartes introduces a two-part doctrine of method summarized in the synopsis of Rule 5:

> The whole method consists entirely in the ordering and arranging of the objects on which we must concentrate our mind's eye if we are to discover some truth. We shall be following this method exactly if we first reduce complicated and obscure propositions step by step to simpler ones, and then, starting with the intuition of the simplest ones of all, try to ascend through the same steps to a knowledge of all the rest. (AT X, 379; CSM I, 20)

Essentially the same description is given in the second and third (of four) rules of method enumerated in the *Discourse on Method* (AT VI, 18; CSM I, 120).

The first part of this method (corresponding to the first need) was known traditionally as the *method of resolution,* the second (corresponding to the second need) as the *method of composition.* The pair of terms *analysis/synthesis* was also sometimes used in a roughly synonymous way.[5] Although Descartes does not employ the first pair of terms officially as names of these elements of the method, he does employ the terms "synthesis" and "analysis" in an important passage in the Second Replies (AT VII, 155ff.; CSM II, 110ff.). There is, however, a potential for confusion here, since he does not use them to delineate the traditional distinction between analysis (the method of resolution) and synthesis (the method of composition). Rather, the method of analysis seems to comprehend both resolution and composition. The case for this rests on two main premises: (1) that the method of analysis is the method of the *Meditations* and (2) that the method of the Meditations comprehends both resolution and composition.[6] Following Schouls[7] I will distinguish between the traditional conception of synthesis as the act which is guided by the method of composition (this is the act of deduction), and Descartes's more specialized conception of synthesis as a method of exposition of a body of knowledge. The latter is equivalent to the notion of synthetic method operating in the Second Replies.

In this passage Descartes characterizes each method in several ways. Analysis is said (1) to "show the true way in which the thing in question was discovered methodically," the effect of which on a reader (2) is that "he will make the thing his own and understand it just as perfectly as if he had understood it himself." Unfortunately, (3) "this method contains nothing to compel belief in an argumentative or inattentive reader." Synthesis is said (1) to proceed in the manner of traditional geometrical proofs, employing "a long series of definitions, postulates, axioms and theorems," and (2) to "compel assent" in a reader "however argumentative or stubborn he may be" because the conclusion is implicitly contained in the premises. Unfortunately, (3) arguments constructed by this method fail "to engage the minds of those who are eager to learn, since it does not show how the thing in question was discovered." Both synthesis and analysis share a common feature (4) regarding the order of presentation: "It consists simply of this. The items which are put forward first must be known entirely without the aid of what comes later."

Elsewhere, in Rule 10 of the *The Rules for the Direction of the Mind*, Descartes (5) characterizes the difference between syllogistic reasoning and intuitive inference in terms that suggest the modern distinction between semantic and syntactic proof: "They [the dialecticians] prescribe certain forms of reasoning in which the conclusions follow with such irresistible necessity that if our reason relies on them, even though it takes, as it were, a rest from considering a particular inference clearly and attentively, it can nevertheless draw a conclusion which is certain simply in virtue of the form" (AT X, 405–406; CSM I, 36). When reason is not on holiday, it infers one thing from another because it understands the content of the two propositions; when it goes on holiday, it relies simply on the syntactic features of the sentences expressing the propositions to draw its inferences.

Although it is not easy to distill these various comments into a set of necessary and sufficient conditions defining each method, the central logical difference between the two can perhaps be put as follows. Once the basic intuitions have been identified, the drawing of conclusions within the method of analysis is deductive in the modern sense and involves immediate inferences whose validity cannot be defined purely syntactically. Once the basic intuitions have been identified, the drawing of conclusions within the method of synthesis is also deductive in the modern sense but is presented in a form whose validity can be given a syntactic definition. This typically will entail that the reasoning be presented in a form that contains universally quantified definitions, postulates, and axioms, as well as various particular propositions serving as initial conditions allowing for the derivation of other particular propositions.

There are, thus, things to be said both for and against each method, although analysis is plainly the one that Descartes finds "most satisfying." There appear to be three chief reasons for this.[8]

First, Descartes makes it clear elsewhere that universal generalizations are not self-justifying but require derivation from intuitions of particular natures—it is in these particular natures that we see the general truths.[9] Therefore, the synthetic method, typically dependent on universally general premises, is itself dependent on the analytic method.

Second, the method of synthesis is not a method of discovery; it does not show how the propositions represented by a synthetic exposition have been discovered.

The third reason, related to the second, is that the synthetic method produces compelled assent in a contrary-minded opponent, that is, one who initially disputes a statement but who subsequently sees that the statement necessarily follows from a set of premises the individual members of which he or she cannot see how to refute. The state of mind that such a person is in is reluctant acquiescence, not conviction. To achieve the latter this person needs to follow the method of analysis. Since the identification of intuitional contents and the derivation of consequences therefrom occur with the aid of the methods of resolution and composition, respectively, and since these methods occur within the analytic method, the analytic method yields a happy coincidence between those things that are true (i.e., those things that can be derived by the rule of truth from intuitions) and those things that are the contents of beliefs that are most enduring in the face of objections. If we now identify the concept of epistemically justified belief with belief that is stable in the face of objections, we have established a connection between epistemic justification and truth. Finding a way of establishing this connection—the "truth connection" as BonJour has called it[10]—is a difficult matter since it requires threading the narrow passage between reductionism (the reduction of truth to justification) and coherentism. There are of course some philosophers who advocate reductionism,[11] and many that advocate coherentism, but such plausibility as these views attain seems to me to derive at least in part from the absence of a good alternative method for establishing the truth connection.

There are of course some other alternatives on the market that I have not yet mentioned, for example, Quine's naturalized epistemology, various forms of epistemological externalism, various forms of contextualism and pragmatism, as well as feminist analyses.[12] Let me say a little here about the relation between Cartesian epistemology and the first two. I will have something to say about the relation between Cartesian epistemology and both Foley's egocentric epistemology and Rorty's pragmatism in the concluding paragraphs.

Quinean naturalized epistemology[13] is characterized by at least the following four theses, two historical, two systematic: (1) traditional philosophy sees the philosophical problem of skepticism arising prior (logically) to science (specifically the sciences of optics, neurophysiology and cognition); (2) traditional philosophy maintains that the solution to this problem requires the construction of a theory of knowledge prior (logically) to the construction of a theory of science; (3) the traditional characterization of the problem and (4) of the solution are both mistaken. Advocates of naturalized epistemology no doubt identify Cartesian epistemology with the tradition mentioned in theses 1 and 2 but, although I am not going to suggest that Cartesian epistemology and Quinean naturalized epistemology are entirely compatible with each other, there is much more similarity between them than is generally suspected. This is partly because, I believe, science relies on doctrines of method that themselves require something that looks a good deal like traditional a priori philosophizing and partly because in some of Descartes's later writings the account of the epistemology of the senses in both its critical and constructive aspects owes much to cognitive science. This is reflected in the prominent role of an error theory in the later articles of *Principles* I. (This role was first described in previous chapters[14] and a possible role for it in foundational epistemology will be discussed more generally below.)

Epistemological externalism[15] has some plausibility as an analysis of the ordinary concept of knowledge, but it fails to provide much in the way of a method for discovering novel truths or of resolving disputes between argumentative and stubborn opponents—the two chief tasks of Cartesian epistemology.

I have claimed above that if the first-order epistemology does not rest on a rule of truth, then the truth connection must be established empirically, and if this is so, then there is no hope for an alternative to coherentism. However, even if first-order foundationalism does rest on a rule of truth, there is still the danger that the case to be made for the existence of the rule of truth and for the existence of the conditions of its applicability will lead to coherentism at the second level—the level of philosophical theory—if not the first. This is why a thoroughgoing foundationalist needs a noncoherentist philosophical method[16] and if Descartes's method of analysis can deliver as promised, it provides such a method. Since successfully establishing the truth connection is among the principle requirements of foundational epistemology, one can see why Descartes regarded his method of analysis with such satisfaction.

There is, however, an important obstacle to accepting that the method of analysis can deliver as promised. Descartes informs us that the analytic method is especially important in metaphysics because, in contrast to geometry, "there is nothing which causes so much effort as making our perception of the primary notions clear and distinct" (AT VII, 157; CSM II, 111). The primary notions in question here are the simple natures and the general truths that can be derived from them. In chapter 1, I argued that the analytic method employs the raising of doubts about whether what we ordinarily think we see is what we actually see, together with the principle of phenomenological indiscernibility to identify the immediate objects of consciousness.[17] Call this the *classificatory use of doubt*.

The classificatory use of doubt should be distinguished from the *method of doubt proper*.[18] The method of doubt proper also employs the raising of doubts to achieve philosophical objectives, but in this case the objectives are epistemological rather than metaphysical. The method gets its paradigmatic employment in the case of the dream argument and the paradigm argument.[19] In the former case the method shows that there are (as yet) undefeated epistemic reasons for doubting the existence of a world outside our ideas; in the latter it shows that there are no undefeated epistemic reasons for doubting either that we are thinking or that we exist. In Meditation III Descartes says that the application of the method of doubt proper to the cogito is the paradigm for establishing the certainty of all propositions.

The classificatory employment of doubt presupposes the prior adoption of a scheme of classifying ideas and is part of Descartes's program of establishing the epistemic credentials of his theory of mind.[20] This in turn requires a method for establishing epistemic credentials in general, the only positive paradigm of which offered by Descartes is the application of the method of doubt proper to the cogito. If the epistemic credentials of these presuppositions are established anywhere in the *Meditations*, they are established at the beginning of Meditation III, but—and this is the obstacle to accepting Descartes's claim for the autonomy of the analytic method—it is a task that cannot reasonably be seen as an application of this paradigm. What this task requires is the development of a complex, philosophical theory—complete with all of the usual ontological and metaphysical baggage—described within a well-structured system of classification. To describe such a system requires a powerful expository tool, and it is the synthetic rather than the analytic method that provides the most powerful available. This is why my own method of exposition has generally relied on the representation or reconstruction of important Cartesian arguments in the synthetic manner, that is, in the form of definitions, principles and proofs expressed in the language of modern deductive logic.[21]

Descartes himself seems to recognize the need [in Meditation III] for a transition from the analytic method of *Meditations* I and II to a method in which the synthetic exposition is given prominence, a transition that pivots on his introduction of the rule of truth: "So now I seem to be able to lay it down as a general rule that whatever I perceive clearly and distinctly is true." This is a principle, a universally general statement that would serve as a premise in a synthetic form of reasoning. The synthetic form of exposition continues in Meditation III with the development of a scheme for classifying ideas and subsequent arguments that depend on this classification.[22]

In addition to making for systematic exposition of a complex philosophical system, a synthetic presentation of reasoning can help with an assessment of the truth of the system by removing one important class of doubts, doubts about whether a certain proposition really does follow from an assumed set of premises. (In this respect a system with a formal definition of validity is superior to one that depends on intuitions of consequence relations.) With this doubt removed we are then free to concentrate on a single kind of problem: *Is the class of premises true?* Even here the synthetic method provides some help since it requires us to specify which of a (usually rather small) set of statements we must designate as untrue in case we are unprepared to accept the conclusion.

Notwithstanding this, it must be acknowledged that the synthetic exposition of a philosophical system is not sufficient to secure for its consequences either truth or stable conviction. An opponent convinced of the falsity of a conclusion that has been deduced in a synthetic manner from a set of apparently true premises is quite entitled to treat the deduction as a *reductio* of those premises. Whether someone will wish to exercise this right depends on several factors, including the comparative systematic virtues of a system of statements that implies truth of the premises and of the conclusion compared to one that implies the falsity of the conclusion and the falsity of at least some of the premises. But systematic virtues are, from the epistemic point of view, soft virtues, hard to connect to truth and somewhat in the eye of the beholder. In the end, there really is no effective epistemic objection to people who find a conclusion so abhorrent that they are unwilling to countenance it, come what may. That is why, I presume, Descartes has made his preferred and basic method one designed to convert rather than silence his opponents.

This is, I think, a sensible objective for a philosophical method. Unfortunately, the method of doubt proper does not seem to me to achieve this objective. This is because in its paradigmatic application to my thought and my existence there are no doubters; where there are doubters—as, for example, there are on the question whether we have a clear and distinct idea of God—the paradigm fails to produce the desired result—conversion to Cartesianism.

This is not, however, the end of the road for a Cartesian epistemology designed for this purpose: there is at least one other method that Descartes occasionally employs to convince his opponents. This method, not employed in the *Meditations*, shows up implicitly in those places in the *Principles* where Descartes is discussing the errors of sensory-based judgments into which his (chronologically mature but intellectually youthful) opponents habitually fall.[23] In its objectives and structure this method is a version of the analytic method, but, although possessing some similarities to the method of doubt proper—they both are methods that permit the maintenance of a belief unless there is a reason to doubt it—the new method has a different conception of what counts as a reason for doubt, and is better suited to serve as an adjunct to theories presented in the synthetic manner. I conclude with a brief discussion of this method which I shall call the *method of error explanations*.

In Meditation I Descartes sets out to "detach us from the senses" by means of various devices having to do with demons, dreamers, and deceiving deities. There is a very large literature on how these devices can be read as arguments undermining ordinary perception-based knowledge claims. These arguments are the classical skeptical arguments with which we are all familiar and are often seen as Descartes's main legacy to epistemology. Despite this, and without intending to mimimize the interest of these arguments by doing so, I have had little to say about Cartesian skepticism as it is usually understood.[24] This is because I believe that a precise understanding of the nature of Descartes's critique of the senses requires seeing it as directed against a rather special opponent, namely one who thinks that ordinary sense perception amounts to a concrete intuition that directly reveals a physical world embodying both primary and secondary qualities. From the perspective of this critique the classical arguments prove either too much or too little. If they show that we can have no perceptual knowledge of the physical world, then they prove too much (since Descartes believes that we have perceptual knowledge of the physical world); if they fail to show this, then they prove too little (since they provide no basis for drawing the kind of ontological distinction betwen primary and secondary qualities that Descartes intends to establish with his critique of the senses).

The case for this interpretation rests on those texts where Descartes says that his opponents (and he himself in his earlier days) took sense experience to be clear perception.[25] Discrediting this position is the way in which Descartes detaches us from the senses, and he discredits it in two ways. First, he employs the case of dreaming to show that ordinary sense experience lacks certain logical properties required for it to be a case of clear perception (intuition).[26] Second, he employs a class of psychological explanations designed to show why, given the falsity of naive realism, folk should be so tempted by it.[27]

These psychological explanations are obscure, presented in various versions in different places and rather speculative even by the standards of a cognitive science still in its infancy. Yet, for all that, I think that Descartes's employment of these explanations is of more importance—both for his interests and those of subsequent philosophy—than the standard arguments for skepticism. For, what in the end makes us ready to contemplate seriously the possibility that an intuitively compelling view is false is not a bizarre skeptical alternative to that view but the existence of a convincing explanation drawn from a plausible theory of cognition why, given that the view is false, we are so certain that it is true.

A convincing explanation of this sort will generally propose that the falsity of our initial convictions arises because we think that we have a clear and distinct idea of something, a mistake that arises not because we are irrational or stupid but because of some misapprehension or mistaken assumption that has crept into our underlying thought processes. It is to this end that Descartes employs the class of explanations that I collectively call his "error theory." An error theory, in this sense, is a powerful tool in the inventory of revisionary philosophers, more powerful, I think, than a priori epistemological arguments, and it is a tool we owe to Descartes. (Dennett seems to have rediscovered it in his book *Consciousness Explained*,[28] where he puts it to use discrediting Cartesian philosophy of mind.)

To take a mundane example, suppose that I have a very clear and distinct (in the ordinary sense) recollection of a recent philosophical conversation with my next-door neighbor, whom I have known for years and who has no interest in philosophy. However, when I next see her, she denies having participated in the conversation altogether. If I accept this, then I am bound to wonder if my cognitive faculties are in even greater decline than I had formerly thought, something I am naturally reluctant to believe. If, however, she also informs me that her identical twin sister was in town on the day in question, then I am at least likely to have an open mind about whether it really was she with whom I was having the conversation. Suppose, further, that she also informs me that her sister is a philosophy professor who likes to talk about philosophy with the next-door neighbors. Since the possibility that it was my neighbor's sister to whom I was speaking provides a better explanation for the fact that the conversation was philosophical than the possibility that it was my neighbor herself to whom I was speaking, I am now likely to become persuaded that my initial recollection was mistaken, however clear and distinct it may have once seemed.

In the case where an initial conviction is based on a belief that we have immediate perceptual awareness of a given fact, our reluctance to abandon the conviction in the face of contrary evidence unsupported by an error explanation may be arising from the fact that the price of admitting error is too high—it is the price of taking seriously the possibility that our most basic cognitive and perceptual mechanisms may be unreliable. Being in this situation presents us with a predicament—one having affinities with the predicament in which Descartes' finds himself when contemplating the madmen of Meditation I (AT VII, 18–19; CSM II, 13).

A similar predicament afflicts anyone who faces a challenge to views that they regard as intuitively obvious. Intuitive obviousness is an important concept in contemporary analytical philosophical method—it provides the primary data on which analytical philosophers construct their theories—and yet the nature of this concept and the justification of the role it plays are matters of great obscurity. In Meditation IV Descartes offers a criterion of clear and distinct ideas—"a great light in the intellect was followed by a great inclination in the will" (AT VII, 59; CSM II, 41). The great inclination in the will is a strong conviction; the great light in the intellect is a clear and distinct idea (intuitive access to a fact recognized as such); and the connection between the two is causal. This suggests a Cartesian account of intuitive obviousness that runs somewhat as follows: we classify those deep convictions we have concerning a proposition p as intuitively obvious when we think that the cause of the conviction that p is an immediate cognitive access to the fact that p. A corollary of this account, taken in conjunction with the error-theoretic method, is that we should be willing to abandon in the face of an opponent's objections something we regard as intuitively obvious only when a convincing error explanation is available. If this account is correct then we can both justify treating intuitive obviousness as a datum for philosophical theorizing—we take this property to be an indicator of direct cognitive access to a certain state of affairs—and also account for the great resilience of claims to intuitive obviousness in the case of objections—convincing error explanations are very difficult to provide.

It should be noted, however, that providing an error explanation for an initial conviction in the obvious truth of a proposition is not by itself *sufficient* inducement to change that conviction. Error explanations are hypothetical explanations drawn in terms of a theoretical framework assumed for the sake of argument, and the fact that such explanations are forthcoming does not in general provide a sufficient reason for us to abandon things we think are obviously true. For example, skeptical scenarios (evil demons, brains in vats, etc.) can be regarded as possible error explanations for our conviction that there are external objects, and yet we are not psychologically disposed to abandon this conviction simply on the basis of these scenarios alone.[29] What else is needed is a good independent argument.

Generalizing from these examples, we can say what makes us disposed to abandon a view once held with great certainty is the combination of a good argument establishing an alternative to the view together with a convincing error explanation.[30] This is a psychological principle useful for securing an abiding conversion of one's opponents.

Now consider a more philosophical example closer in spirit to Descartes's own argument against the Aristotelian realists. The example is Zeno's paradox known as "The Arrow." For our purposes the following representation will serve:

1. If anything is moving during a time interval T then it is moving at any arbitrary instant of time t in T. (Assumption)
2. If something is moving at an arbitrary instant of time t then either it is moving in the place where it is at t or it is moving in the place where it is not at t. (Assumption)
3. It is not moving in the place where it is at t. (Assumption)
4. It is not moving in the place where it is not at t. (Assumption)
5. It is not moving at t. (2, 3, 4, logic)
   Therefore,
6. It is not the case that anything is moving during a time interval T. (1, 5, logic)

The argument presents a paradox. The premises taken individually seem to be true and yet the conclusion seems certainly false. After all, we think that we can simply see things moving during time intervals. Moreover, if we have studied logic we realize that we are within our *logical* rights to treat the argument as a reductio of its premise set in the presence of the assumption that its conclusion is false. Of course because the conclusion is entailed by a set of premises that are individually plausible, we also have some reason to think that the conclusion is true and so are bound to wonder whether we are within our *epistemic* rights to simply treat the argument as a reductio. Settling this question is no easy matter, but I suggest that if a proponent of Zeno's argument can find a persuasive error-explanation for our conviction that we see (are immediately acquainted with the fact of) things moving, then we would not be acting in an epistemically responsible manner if we were to treat the argument this way.

For example, Zeno might point to the fact that discrete events involving no moving object can give rise to the appearance of movement if the events are sequenced close enough together in space and time. Thus a sequence of bulbs lighting up on a billboard can give rise to the illusion that letters are moving across the billboard when no such thing is happening. To be effective, this explanation must appeal to hypotheses about perceptual and cognitive mechanisms for which there is independent evidence. However, once this is in place, there are now at least the makings of a plausible causal explanation for our conviction that we see things moving that does not make essential use of the fact of motion. This does not, of course, establish by itself that we do not see things moving, but it does remove from our set of epistemically responsible choices that of simply treating the argument as a reductio of its premises. If we are now to be in a position to responsibly treat the argument as unsound, we need to examine those premises in detail and find some independent reason for rejecting them.

Consider one final case. Here we imagine a utilitarian arguing from utilitarian principles that there will be cases in which it is right for the state to punish a person for committing a crime which the state knows the person did not commit. Some opponents of utilitarianism will treat this argument simply as a reductio of utilitarian principles on the grounds that it is obvious to them that punishing innocent people is never the right thing to do. Whether this is an acceptable strategy depends (in part) on the availability of an error explanation for this conviction. If the utilitarian can provide the makings of a plausible psychological explanation why we should think that it is wrong to punish innocent people that makes no causally essential use of its being wrong to punish innocent people, then the reductio strategy would, I think, be epistemically irresponsible. Otherwise, the reductio strategy is permissible.

Generalizing from these cases, I would propose the following principle as a part of theory of epistemic obligations: if we expect our opponents to revise their convictions, we are obliged to provide not only an argument for the falsity of those convictions but also an error explanation. Correlatively, our opponents have a right to retain their convictions unless we meet both of these conditions. Of course what applies to others also applies to ourselves: we cannot ask ourselves to abandon our convictions unless we meet the same obligations. This gives rise to a form of methodological conservatism that is just the reverse of what is implied by the method of doubt proper.

It is true that this account gives authority to each individual epistemic agent to decide when a proposed error explanation is convincing, and there will undoubtedly be cases in which there is disagreement between contending parties about whether this is so. In this case neither party will be violating their epistemic duties by sticking to their initial positions. I do not take this to be a disadvantage of this account, since a good theory of epistemic method should be psychologically realistic and should, therefore, allow for the possibility of irresolvable differences of opinion arising between responsible epistemic agents as much as it allows for the possibility of convergence of opinion.

More formally, the proposal (which I shall call the *Cartesian error-theoretic maxim*) might be put as follows:

The Cartesian Error-Theoretic Maxim

If I am a responsible epistemic agent acting in accord with the Cartesian method of error theory I may continue to believe any proposition p which I now regard as obviously true unless (1) I have encountered a suitably powerful proof with a conclusion that implies not-p and (2) I have encountered a convincing error explanation associated with the proof mentioned in (1).

In assessing the merits of this maxim in the face of some possible objections[31] it is important to recall the context in which the method was first introduced: I regard something p as obviously true, and you set about to overturn that belief by giving me a powerful argument in the synthetic manner, that is, a deductive argument based on premises that seem individually plausible and to which I have no immediate objections. This is what is meant by the words "suitably powerful argument" in clause (1) of the maxim. However, and this is an important part of the dialectical context, I continue to think that p is true even though I have heard the argument and am disconcerted by it. Accordingly, I am considered employing the gambit, *one person's modus ponens is another's modus tollens*. So the question really is this. *Should I be convinced by this argument or should I invoke the gambit?* Against this background it would be damagingly circular to gloss "suitably powerful" as "actually convincing." But this is not how these words should be taken—the characterization given above does not presuppose anything about whether, in the final analysis, I am convinced. Indeed, the present proposal is that I should *not* be convinced by such an argument by itself but only if I am also convinced that there is an explanation for why p seems obvious to me in terms consistent with the premises of the alternative argument, hence consistent with the falsity of p.[32]

A method employing both arguments and error explanations has elements of the method of doubt and of the synthetic method and yet has advantages over each taken individually. As part of a theory of rational belief formation or change of belief, the method of doubt gives too much weight to the existence of bizarre alternative possibilities and too little to the existence of strong initial convictions. As part of a theory of rational belief formation or change of belief the synthetic method gives too much weight to initial convictions (in the truth of the premises of a deductive proof) and too little guidance for changing these convictions in the teeth of unpalatable consequences. A theory combining arguments and error explanations avoids these deficiencies. Moreover, because a convincing error explanation needs to be offered in the context of a convincing error theory, and an error theory is a psychophysical theory with all of the theoretical and empirical apparatus that goes with it, someone employing this method is constrained to have a coherent and systematic world view that takes into account epistemology, metaphysics, and natural science.[33] And this, it seems to me, is an embodiment of the Sellarsian ideal of philosophy.

I conclude with a few objections and replies.

In his recent book *Working Without a Net*, Richard Foley characterizes the Cartesian project as "Janus-faced."[34] "The aim," writes Foley, "is to find a method that is subjectively persuasive, thereby making it invulnerable to intellectual self-criticism, and objectively reliable, thereby putting us in a good position to have knowledge. This is a conjunction of claims that must be rejected." (The former aim is part of what Foley calls "egocentric rationality"; the latter is part of an objective, externalist account of rationality.) Descartes's mistake was in endorsing "one method with two aspects, an egocentric one and an objective one," the corrective for which is to "see two projects, and in doing epistemology we must choose between them."

Foley has delineated a very useful general conception of rationality, one that is defined in terms of three main parameters—an objective, a set of cognitive resources, and a perspective. One species of rationality is egocentric rationality, and Foley is quite right to see the importance of this notion for Cartesian epistemology. We should remember, however, that one of Descartes's central objectives was to provide an epistemology that would facilitate not only his own attainment of egocentric rationality but also that of others, his opponents included. This objective is reflected in Descartes's preference for the analytic method and his reliance on a method of error-explanations.

Foley's case for seeing a single method in Cartesian epistemology rests on the assumption that at the heart of Cartesian epistemology is a principle asserting a necessary connection between the indubitable and the true.[35] However, if I have Descartes right, this is not an entirely accurate portrayal, for the Cartesian rule of truth asserts a necessary connection between a content of immediate awareness and the truth of a proposition ascribing that content to a subject. This is the objective part of the program. It differs from recent externalist accounts of knowledge both because it asserts that the subjective end of the truth connection is immediate awarenesses of content-properties, non-doxastic states that contrast with the propositional attitudes of belief or degrees of belief posited by contemporary externalists, and also because the connection is necessary (a rule of truth) rather than logically contingent. In Cartesian epistemology, immediate awarenesses are not Janus-faced entities looking simultaneously in contrary directions but are, rather, entities which serve as both objects and subjects. They are the objects of indubitable but not infallible identification, and they are the subjects of a metaphysically necessary principle that entails foundational truths.

The indubitability of a proposition in Foley's sense presupposes that there will emerge upon careful reflection an egocentrically satisfying and stable set of beliefs to which the proposition in question will belong. Now, I do not think (nor does Descartes) that even the most careful epistemic conduct can *guarantee* the existence of a set of beliefs that is stable and satisfying in the long run—what careful epistemic conduct can guarantee is immunity against the charge of epistemic irresponsibility. Notwithstanding this, the *goal* of egocentric epistemic rationality must still be the production of a set of stable and satisfying beliefs. Be that as it may, the connection between indubitability and truth is not that the former entails the latter, since, as noted in the previous paragraph, the procedures which Descartes employs to identify immediate awarenesses are fallible, but rather that no set of beliefs which Descartes would regard as egocentrically satisfying and stable would fail to include a rule of truth. This is not a stipulation but a prediction.

So Foley is wrong to say that in principle we must choose between egocentric rationality and objective truth as the outcomes attainable by an epistemic method. Indeed, Foley acknowledges that an epistemology countenancing immediate awarenesses is one (the only one) which could attain these outcomes. However, he notes,

> [I]t is also an epistemology that few are willing to take seriously anymore. But if not, we must give up the idea that epistemology is in the business of giving fundamental intellectual advice. For that matter, we must give up the whole idea that there is advice to be had. . . .[36]

These warnings are pretty dire, and if they are indeed consequences of not taking seriously epistemologies which countenance immediate awarenesses, perhaps it is again time to take them seriously. In any case, Foley thinks that Cartesian epistemology suffers from the "conceit" of thinking that "the method of doubt provides advice to inquirers that is at once both useful and fundamental."[37] His case for this claim takes the form of a dilemma, "either it [the method] presupposes that philosopher-scientists can make determinations of a sort that the recommendation says is fundamental or it is misdirected advice or perhaps both,"[38] applied to two cases.

In the first case:

> we interpret Descartes as offering . . . objective advice. He is telling philosophers to believe just those propositions that are clear and distinct. . . . [T]he question of whether something is really clear and distinct in this sense becomes one of the fundamental issues about which they will want advice.

Reply: The point is one Descartes himself insists upon (see the Fifth Replies: AT VII, 361–363; CSM II, 250) but also insists that he has provided the advice (see the following reply to the next horn).

In the second case:

> [I]f we interpret Descartes as telling philosopher-scientists to believe just those propositions whose truth they cannot doubt when they bring them clearly to mind, then

the advice faces both difficulties. First, it is not fundamental enough. It need not be immediately obvious to philosopher-scientists just what is indubitable for them and what isn't. They can thus have questions about that which the advice says is fundamental to their being rational, and these will be questions that the advice cannot help them answer.

Reply: But Descartes's advice is not to simply "intuit" what is indubitable but, rather, to arrive at a stable and satisfying set of beliefs by means of various methods including the method of intuition and deduction, the classificatory use of doubt, the method of doubt proper, the method of error explanation, and the synthetic method of geometrical-style deductive argument.

Second, the advice is misdirected. It is advice that looks inward rather than outward. Insofar as the goal of philosopher-scientists is to conduct theoretical inquiry in an absolutely secure manner, their interest is to find propositions that cannot be false rather than ones that cannot be doubted.

Reply: If we replace "cannot be doubted" in this passage with the objective of egocentric rationality (obtaining a stable and satisfying set of beliefs), and if we distinguish between ultimately desirable outcomes and ultimate objectives,[39] I am not sure that egocentric rationality is not, after all, the ultimate objective of philosopher-scientists. It is, in any case, my ultimate objective, and was, I think, Descartes's as well.[40]

But Foley does not think that egocentric rationality should be a primary motivation; it is "shallower" and more "narcissistic" than the goal of truth.

To see why, consider two inquirers. The first is motivated by a desire to know the truth. This prompts her to be thorough and careful in her inquiries, and as a result she believes that which is egocentrically rational for her. The second is motivated by a desire to avoid intellectual self-condemnation. This prompts him to be thorough and careful in his inquiries, and as a result he believes that which is egocentrically rational for him. The result is the same in each case: each is egocentrically rational. Nevertheless, we are more likely to look askance at his intellectual motivation than hers. His motivation seems shallower, more self-indulgent.[41]

Reply: Leibnitz's God did not create absolute space and time, because to do so would create a problem that even God (a perfect being bound by the principle of sufficient reason) could not solve: why locate the actual universe here rather than there in absolute space and time?[42] Having as our ultimate objective the attainment of truth in addition to the attainment of stable and satisfying beliefs creates a problem that we (even if we were perfect practitioners of epistemic method) could not solve: how to know that the first goal has been attained in addition to the second. The solution to this problem is simply not to have the first goal. (This is not to say that we do not want to secure truth as an outcome; it is to say that we do not set it as a goal.) If avoiding goals that are such that we cannot tell whether we have attained them is a form of self-indulgence, then so be it.

Finally, Foley notes that

even if being rational were your principal intellectual goal, it is a goal that is best sought indirectly. . . . Trying very hard to be rational ordinarily isn't a good way to become rational. A better way is to try very hard to believe truths and not to believe falsehoods.

Reply: Trying to believe truths and to avoid falsehoods is a deliberate activity that requires a first-order method of distinguishing between the two. Not all methods of doing something are equally successful, so we will want to have a second-order way of telling which methods of distinguishing truth from falsehood succeed. To assess whether something is in general successful requires seeing whether it achieves a specified objective. In the case of a first-order epistemic method, its success or failure should be ascertainable noncircularly, i.e., without employing the method itself. Since the only objective the attainment of which could be verified in a non-circular way is the kind of subjective satisfaction characteristic of egocentric rationality, and since we are free to assess our methods in terms of objectives which we stipulate (as long as they are epistemically significant), we should stipulate egocentric rationality as the objective of our first-order methods. Moreover, because Cartesian theory identifies immediate awarenesses by means of criteria entailing egocentric rationality, and because immediate awarenesses entail fundamental truths, the achievement of egocentric rationality is a likely means (indeed, the only likely means) of coming to believe fundamental truths.

At the end of *Philosophy and the Mirror of Nature* Richard Rorty writes:

> If we see knowing not as having an essence, to be described by scientists or philosophers, but rather as a right, by current standards, to believe, then we are well on the way to seeing *conversation* as the ultimate context within which knowledge is to be understood. Our focus shifts from the relation between human beings and the objects of their inquiry to the relation between alternative standards of justification, and from there to the actual changes in those standards which make up intellectual history.[43]

There is not much that Descartes need disagree with here, except for the implication of the first sentence that conversations have to be carried out with other people and the implication of the second sentence that there are no standards of responsibility common to human epistemic agents. What Descartes would add, I think, is that a specification of the right to have certain beliefs is not independent of an explanation of how we come to have those beliefs. If a convincing account of this can be made within a theory committed to the falsity of those beliefs, then the right is defeated. This is the leading idea behind the Cartesian method of error explanation.

The argument of *Philosophy and the Mirror of Nature* can itself be viewed as an extended application of this method, directed against the belief that human cognition provides reliable access to aspects of nature as they really are in themselves. If successful, this argument should convince us that this belief has arisen from causes not including its own truth. The question is whether it does convince us. The answer to this question, whatever it may be, provides an irreducible element of facticity against which Rorty's theoretical claims must ultimately be tested. This question is, moreover, one that each of us must answer for ourselves, preferably in a condition of reflective solitude not unlike that which comes in the early morning just after we have finished dreaming and just before we must again face the insistent demands of the world.

Appendix A: The Cogito: Syllogism or Immediate Inference

(In what follows my thinking has been much influenced by Stephen Gaukroger.)[44]

Perhaps Descartes's clearest argument for claiming that syllogistic reasoning is redundant is made in Rule 11 of the *Rules for the Direction of the Mind*:

> But to make it even clearer that the aforementioned art of reasoning [syllogistic reasoning] contributes nothing whatever to knowledge of the truth, we should realize that, on the basis of their method, dialecticians are unable to formulate a syllogism with a true conclusion unless they are already in possession of the substance of the conclusion, i.e. unless they have previous knowledge of the very truth deduced in the syllogism. (AT X, 406; CSM I, 36–37)

Suppose we consider a simple mathematical syllogism:

1. All squares are rectangles.
2. This is a square.
Hence,
3. This is a rectangle.

As argued previously (chapter 1, section 1.2), basic intuitions are of properties and of relations between properties, specifically the relation of determinability. In the present example what we can intuit is the state of affairs that squareness is a determination of rectangularity. I take Descartes to be claiming that the truth of (1) can be demonstrated if (and only if) we already have seen that squareness is a determination of rectangularity. How otherwise could we prove the general statement if not by seeing necessary relations holding between the properties it ascribes by means of its subject and predicate terms? The only alternative is a proof by enumeration. A proof from an enumeration of a class of objects already containing the object in question in (2) presupposes that we already possess "knowledge of the very truth deduced in the syllogism," namely, (3). However, proof by an enumeration of objects in a class not containing this object will not establish the truth of (1) in the full generality needed for it to serve as a premise in a valid derivation of (3).

But while having intuitions of determinability relations between properties is necessary for us to see that the corresponding general propositions are true, having them does not seem to be sufficient. What else we need to see is that if the property of squareness is a determination of the property of rectangularity then it is necessary that anything that possesses the first property also possesses the second. This latter proposition, (1), is what we had to prove. The seeing in question here is a deduction that does not depend on a general premise antecedently established. The inference is, thus, a nonsyllogistic act that falls within the definition of the analytic method. So far, so good for Descartes's claim in the Second Replies that analysis is epistemically prior to (the general premises involved in) synthetic forms of reasoning.

There is, however, a difficulty with Descartes's claim, made in Rule 11, to show that syllogistic reasoning—reasoning employing a general premise like (1)—is *entirely* otiose. The difficulty is that the epistemic dependence of (1) on particular intuitions about relations between particular *properties* does not entail that (3), a proposition about a particular *individual* having a certain property, can be derived validly without reliance on (1). We cannot, for example, simply derive (3) from (2) by an immediate inference, since the only basis for an immediate inference in the Cartesian system is relational intuition, and relational intuition does not in general yield propositions ascribing properties to particular, concrete individuals. It seems to me, therefore, that the use of syllogistic reasoning in Descartes's mature writings is not simply a matter of convenience, contributing "nothing whatever to knowledge of the truth" about particular objects.

If I am right about this general point, then it helps to explain a puzzle about Descartes's reply to Burman in the passage that I quoted at the end of chapter 1, section 1.6. There Descartes said both that "the major premise comes first, namely because it is presupposed and prior" and also that "we do not separate out these general propositions from the particular instances; rather it is in the particular instances that we think of them" (AT V, 147; CSMK III, 333). The major premise in question here is "whatever thinks exists," and Descartes asserts that it is known prior to the inference "I think therefore I am" for the reason that "it is in reality prior to my inference and my inference depends on it."

To begin to see how to resolve the puzzle, recall that the conclusion of this inference is "I am," a statement whose nominal form ascribes a property (existence) to an individual (me). This makes the inference parallel in form to the inference from (1), and (2) to (3). Since, I have maintained, in Cartesian logic inferences with conclusions of this form must depend on general premises (and are therefore syllogistic), this would explain why Descartes insists on the logical priority of "whatever thinks, exists."

However, as I have also maintained in chapter 2, section 2.2, statements apparently ascribing the existence property to individuals are merely surface formulations to be replaced by existentially quantified statements of the form: "there is a substance s such that s formally contains a property P." When the cogito is logically reconstructed in terms of this replacement, we have what I call the "intuitive cogito," an argument resting on the substance-attribute principle (see chapter 1, section 1.6). The substance-attribute principle, as I have formulated it, is the (implicitly) universally quantified statement, "If a property P is actualized, then there exists an actual substance s such that s exemplifies P." Notice, however, that the domain of the initial quantifier is the set of properties, not the set of individual objects. As such, Descartes would regard this principle as known by induction from "particular instances"; that is, from cases in which P is specified to particular properties including, for example, the property of thinking-belonging-to-myself. In this circumstance, the general principle really is dispensable for inference and, for any specified actualized property P, we can immediately infer that there is a substance exemplifying P. In the case of the argument of the intuitive cogito, this means that the transition from line 3 ("There is the two-level property *actualized thinking belonging to me*") to line 4 ("There exists an actual substance s such that s exemplifies the two-level property *thinking belonging to me*") can take the form of an immediate inference.

I suggest that it is this, the logically perspicuous formulation of the cogito, that should be taken as the subject of Descartes's well-known words in the Second Set of Replies:

> When someone says "I am thinking, therefore I am or exist" he does not deduce existence from thought by means of a syllogism, but recognizes it as something self-evident by a simple intuition of the mind. This is clear from the fact that if he were deducing it by means of a syllogism, he would have to have had previous knowledge of the major premise "Everything which thinks is, or exists"; yet in fact he learns it from experiencing in his own case that it is impossible that he should think without existing. (AT VII 140; CSM II, 100)

Notes

Preface

S. Stich, *The Fragmentation of Reason* (Cambridge, Mass.: MIT Press, 1990), 1–3.

Introduction

1. B. Williams, *Descartes: The Project of Pure Inquiry* (London: Penguin, 1990). Hereafter, Williams, *Descartes*.
2. This passage occurs in the Synopsis of the *Meditations*: AT VII, 12; CSM II, 9.
3. Part 6: AT VI, 63ff; CSM I, 143ff.
4. See the *Meteorology* (Olscamp, 332– 335)
5. D. Garber, (*"Semel in vita*: The Scientific Background to Descartes' *Meditations*," in A. Rorty, [ed.], *Essays on Descartes'* "*Meditations*" [Berkeley: University of California Press, 1986], 81–117); M. Wilson ("Skepticism without Indubitability," *Journal of Philosophy* 81 [1984]: 537–544); and H. Caton, (*The Origin of Subjectivity* [New Haven: Yale University Press, 1973], esp. 68ff.) are recent commentators who see Descartes's motivations in the *Meditations* in a similar light. Hereafter, Rorty (ed.), *Essays*; Garber, *"Semel in vita"*; Caton, *Subjectivity*.
6. In the correspondence there is more direct evidence for this interpretation. See the letter to Mersenne of January, 1641 (AT III, 297–298; *Letters*, 94), quoted in Garber, "*Semel in vita*," 82. In this letter Descartes also makes it clear that he wishes to keep this motivation from his readers, a fact that explains the somewhat circumstantial nature of the case one is forced to make for this interpretation.
7. W. Sellars, "Philosophy and the Scientific Image of Man," in *Science, Perception and Reality* (London: Routledge, 1963): 1–40.
8. Here "matter" is used in the sense of "material cause," what something is made of. See *Physics* II, 3. Here and in what follows my text for Aristotle is *The Basic Works of Aristotle*, ed. Richard McKeon. (New York: Random House, 1966). The references are to the standard Bekker pagination.
9. For recent commentators expressing varying degrees of scepticism, see Margaret D. Wilson, *Descartes* (London: Routledge and Kegan Paul, 1978), 203–204 (hereafter: Wil-

son, *Descartes*); and R. Arbini, "Did Descartes Have a Philosophical Theory of Sense Experience?" *Journal of the History of Philosophy* 21 (1983): 317–337. An exception to this trend is Gueroult who describes Descartes as accepting a sensory "given." See M. Gueroult, *Descartes' Philosophy Interpreted According to the Order of Reasons*, vol. I: *The Soul and God*, and vol. II: *The Soul and the Body*, ed. and trans. Roger Ariew (Minneapolis: University of Minnesota Press, 1985), 35ff. hereafter, Gueroult, *Descartes*, vols. I and II.

10. See Garber, "*Semel in vita*," and L. Loeb, "Is There Radical Dissimulation in Descartes' *Meditations*?" in Rorty (ed.), *Essays*; 243–270.

11. See, e.g., P. Markie, *Descartes' Gambit* (Ithaca: Cornell University Press, 1986), 106.

Chapter 1

1. For a useful discussion of different versions see E. Sosa, "The Raft and the Pyramid," *Midwest Studies in Philosophy* 5 (1980): 3–25.

2. Two seminal critiques are those of Sellars and Quinton. See W. Sellars, "Empiricism and the Philosophy of Mind," in *Science, Perception and Reality*, 127–196; A. Quinton, "The Problem of Perception," in R. Schwartz, (ed.), *Perceiving, Sensing and Knowing* (New York: Anchor, 1965), 497–526.

3. These concepts are drawn from R. Audi, *The Structure of Justification* (Cambridge: Cambridge University Press, 1993): 167–169 hereafter; Audi, *Justification*.

4. There is also this passage: "Many people do not know what they believe, since believing something and knowing that one believes it are different acts of thinking and the one often occurs without the other" (AT V, 23; CSM I, 122).

5. *The Passions of the Soul* I, 17: AT VII, 342; CSM II, 335.

6. *Comments on a Certain Broadsheet* (AT VIIIB, 363; CSM I, 307). However, compare Meditation III: AT VII, 37; CSM II, 26.

7. See W. P. Alston, *Epistemic Justification* (Ithaca: Cornell, 1989), the chapter entitled "The Deontological Conception of Epistemic Justification," sec. 2, 115–152.

8. "I shall do this until the weight of preconceived opinion is counterbalanced" (Meditation I: AT VII, 22; CSM II, 15).

9. The term is due to P. Markie, *Descartes' Gambit* (Ithaca: Cornell University Press, 1986), 33. Hereafter, Markie, *Gambit*.

10. Ibid., 34.

11. See, e.g., the Second Replies: AT VII, 141–142; CSM II, 100, quoted in sect. 1.3.

12. H&R II, 39.

13. CSM II, 101.

14. See H. Frankfurt, *Demons, Dreamers, and Madmen* (Indianapolis: Bobbs-Merrill, 1970), 132 (hereafter, Frankfurt, *Demons*). See also M. D. Wilson, *Descartes* (London: Routledge and Kegan Paul, 1978), 141.

15. He also appears to say this a couple of paragraphs later in Meditation III at AT VII, 37; CSM II, 26.

16. Frankfurt, *Demons*, 134.

17. I say "may not" because it is unclear from Frankfurt's account whether his notion of epistemic certainty entails psychological certainty. I assume that it does. (However, the present difficulty applies to Frankfurt's account only if the entailment holds.)

18. Markie, *Gambit*, 157ff.

19. Ibid., 153.

20. Ibid., 75. There is indeed an impressive list of items offered by Descartes as objects of intuition, each one of which seems to be a proposition in the logical sense: "Thus everyone can mentally intuit that he exists, that he is thinking, that a triangle is bounded by

three lines and a sphere by a single surface, and the like" (AT X 368; CSM I, 14). Notice however, that aside from the first two propositions which concern the rather special subject matter of the cogito, the other two propositions cited are *universally general* propositions about geometrical objects and Descartes does not think that general propositions are epistemically primary on the grounds that they are derived from intuitions of particular instances. (See the *Conversation with Burman*: AT V, 147; CSM K III, 333.) This suggests that such examples should be used with caution as evidence for treating Descartes as a thoroughgoing proposition theorist. Similar remarks apply to the list of "common notions" that Descartes gives in Rule 12 (AT X, 419; CSM I, 45). In showing how the general case is to be derived from the particular instance, we are led to the doctrine that in primary applications, the objects of intuitions are properties rather than propositions. For some more details see the appendix to the epilogue at the end of this book.

21. Ibid., 73ff.

22. Frederick Van De Pitt, "Intuition and Judgment in Descartes' Theory of Truth," *Journal of the History of Philosophy* 26 (1988): 446–466.

23. Quoted on 466. The passage is from AT X, 424; CSM I, 48.

24. See especially AT X, 423–424; CSM I, 47.

25. Descartes very often used the Latin *propositio* in connection with the object of intuition, a term translated by Cottingham as "proposition." The term does, however, have a more general meaning along the lines of *that which is put forth*, i.e., a "proposal," and this is how Van De Pitt translates the term (457, n. 19). It might make sense to think of an item that is nonpropositional in the logical sense as still a setting forth of something.

26. This useful phrase is due to Peter Schouls. See Schouls, *The Imposition of Method* (Oxford: Clarendon Press, 1981), 36. Hereafter, Schouls, *Method*.

27. Some indication of the relation in question is given in the following passage from the *Principles*: "[E]ach substance has one principle property which constitutes its nature and essence, and to which all its other properties are referred. Thus extension in length, breadth and depth constitutes the nature of corporeal substance and thought constitutes the nature of thinking substance. Everything else which can be attributed to body presupposes extension" (*Principles* I, 53: AT VIIIA, 25; CSM I, 210).

The kind of presupposition relation that Descartes has in mind here seems to be either (1) that which a determinate property bears to a determinable property or (2) that which the ground-floor attributes of extension and thought bear to a substance. It is relations of this type that comprise the content of relational intuitions. The former underlies the first type of deduction, the latter the second.

For example, if I intuit the simple nature of squareness I also intuit the relational property of squareness being a determinate form of rectangularity. This way of describing things suggests that the objects of relational intuition are, strictly speaking, states of affairs involving the obtaining of a relational property rather than the relational property all by itself. (Thanks to Jodi Graham for this.) This result may be extended to nonrelational intuition by describing its objects as, e.g., the *presence of squareness*. Similarily in the case of other properties. Because these strict formulations are somewhat cumbersome, I will generally speak more loosely of properties and relations simpliciter as the objects of intuition but ask that the meaning be taken as in the strict sense. (Descartes sometimes speaks in this strict way, e.g., in *Principles* I, 52: "[I]f we perceive the presence of some attribute, we can infer that there must also be present an existing thing or substance to which it may be attributed" (AT VIIIA, 25; CSM I, 210); but often he does not.)

28. Other causes are "impulse" and "conjecture." These are causes of composition that generate unreliable propositions.

29. See the text quoted later in this section from Rule 14 (AT X, 444; CSM I, 60).

30. Schouls argues (1) that all forms of cognition involving a composition in Descartes' technical sense are due to deduction and vice versa and (2) that all forms of cognition involving composition possess vulnerability to error. ("[J]udgement involves composition or deduction, and any beliefs obtained in this way are still dubitable," *Method*, 130. I take the "or" here to be appositive.) I take neither of these claims to be correct. Regarding (1), Rule 12 asserts that some forms of composition are not due to deduction—they are due to impulse or conjecture. (See note 28.) Regarding (2), I note that the results of impulse and conjecture are propositions of class 2. These are, of course, vulnerable to error but not because they are composite per se but because they are a defective composite not generated in accord with the rule that requires a match between inference and logical consequence. In the text of Meditation III to which Schouls directs his remarks, the defective composite is the cognition that results from referring our sensations to things outside our minds. These correspond to class 2 propositions. Corresponding to class 1 propositions is the class of instances of the rule of truth. Both are classes of cognitions that count as composite in the sense of the *Rules for the Direction of the Mind*. However only those of class (2) are vulnerable to error. There is, of course, always the second-order question of whether we have correctly classified an object of consciousness, and the question does generate an irreducible level of doubt that attaches to the process of deduction. However, this kind of doubt attaches especially to cognitions we might be tempted to classify as intuitions, thus placing *both* intuitions and deductions in the sphere of what is doubtful for reasons of classification.

31. Establishing that the rule of truth in Meditation III should be identified with the principle quoted from *Principles* I, 52, and with the doctrine from Rule 12 is not a trivial matter. The task is carried out in section 1.6.

32. Descartes's notion of substance-as-subject corresponds approximately to a conjunction of the first two explications of Descartes's notion of substance offered recently by Markie. See P. Markie, "Descartes' Concepts of Substance," in J. Cottingham, (ed.), *Reason, Will and Sensation* (Oxford: Clarendon Press, 1994), 63–88. Hereafter, Markie, "Descartes' Concepts of Substance."

33. *La connaissance* in the French text; *notitia* in the Latin.

34. Cottingham translates this term exclusively as "knowledge." However, since the nature of *scientia* is a technical concept, one that Descartes will explicate a bit later in this passage, and since what is at issue here is whether seventeenth-century dialecticians would apply a certain Latin term, it seems best to leave the original word in the English text and to explicate the nature of the concept it expresses in the commentary.

35. In French the word is *aperçevons*; the Latin word is *advertimus*. Cottingham's translation renders these terms as "we are aware." However, the kind of consciousness at issue here seems to be similar to that conveyed by the words *lorsque quelqu'un aperçoit que il pense* in the French text (AT IX, 225–226; Alquié II, 862) and *Cum itaque quis advertit* in the Latin (AT VII, 422) in a passage from the Sixth Replies. (The passage is quoted near the beginning of section 1.4.) Even Cottingham there renders the original into the English "When anyone notices. . ." This cognitive attitude is clearly distinguished in the Sixth Replies from "inner awareness of our thought" (*la connaissance intérieur/cognitio interna*). Here and in the remainder of this section I am much indebted to Murray Miles. See M. Miles, *Insight and Inference* (unpublished manuscript), chapter 2. (Hereafter, Miles, *I & I*)

36. Cf. F. F. Schmitt, "Why Was Descartes a Foundationalist?" in Rorty (ed.), *Essays on Descartes' "Meditations"* (Berkeley: University of California Press, 1986), 419–512.

37. Cf. Markie, *Gambit*, 161ff.

38. Dicker also seems to take God's role in the validation of the rule of truth to rest on the "'assent-compelling' nature of clear and distinct perceptions" (G. Dicker, G. *Descartes*

(Oxford: Oxford University Press, 1993), 107 (hereafter, Dicker, *Descartes*). He does not, however, agree that the inference from the content of clear and distinct ideas to truth stands independently of appeal to God's benevolence (see 87– 89).

39. I argue for this contention in section 1.4.

40. I discuss Descartes theory of inclinations and God's role in establishing them in ch. 6.

41. The angle brackets are present in the CSM text itself. They represent words appearing only in the French text that the translator thought useful to include.

42. For an interpretation that argues in much the same way for a "negative character" of Descartes's procedure in validating reason and for the ability of the method thus characterized to avoid falling into a vicious circularity, see Frankfurt, *Demons*, 170ff., esp. 174. See also E. M. Curley, *Descartes against the Skeptics* (Cambridge, Mass.: Harvard University Press, 1978), chap. 5.

43. I explore this question in more detail in appendix A to this chapter.

44. In the *Rules for the Direction of the Mind*, Descartes does not countenance a logical gap between intuition, the foundation of mathematical method, and certain knowledge. (*scientia* in the Latin; *science* in the French): "Of all the sciences so far discovered, arithmetic and geometry alone are . . . free from any taint of falsity *or uncertainty*" (Rule 12: AT X, 364 (Latin); Alquié I, 85 (French); CSM I, 13 (English); my emphasis. This indicates the absence in the early work of the concern with hyperbolic doubt so much in evidence in the later works.

45. Alquié II, 586.

46. E.g., R. McRae, "Descartes' Definition of Thought" in R. J. Butler (ed.), *Cartesian Studies* (Oxford: Blackwell, 1972) (hereafter, McRae, "Descartes' Definition"); D. Radner, "Thought and Consciousness in Descartes," *Journal of the History of Philosophy* 26, no. 3 (July 1988): 439–470 (see 440, n.5) (hereafter, Radner, "Consciousness").

47. AT VII, 423; CSM II, 278.

48. McRae, "Descartes' Definition," 68.

49. My interpolation of French terms appears in square brackets. The Latin is *cognitio interna* , not *conscientia*. However, in a similar passage in *The Search for Truth*, Descartes does use *conscientia*. AT X, 523; CSM II, 417. I owe this point to Murray Miles. See Miles, *I & I*, ch. 2, sec. 5.

50. The passage quoted at the beginning of section 1.3 concerns the atheist mathematician.

51. Radner, "Consciousness," 445–446.

52. Reference to first-order intellectual awareness would be redundant in this formulation of the principle, so I have omitted it.

53. See the passage quoted from the Seventh Replies.

54. M. Gueroult, *Descartes' Philosophy Interpreted According to the Order of Reasons*, vol. 1, ed. and trans. R. Ariew (Minneapolis: University of Minnesota Press, 1985), 62. Hereafter, Gueroult, *Descartes I*.

55. Descartes says that the method in question is the method of doubt (Meditation I: AT VII, 22; CSM II, 15).

56. See Frankfurt, *Demons*, 130.

57. Frankfurt, *Demons*, 131–139.

58. Ibid., 138.

59. Gueroult, *Descartes* I, 75.

60. *Ibid.*, 72.

61. Here I am much indebted to Carriero's analysis of Meditation II. J. Carriero. "The Second Meditation and the Essence of the Mind," in Rorty (ed.), *Essays*, 199–223. Hereafter, Carriero, "Second Meditation."

62. Gueroult, *Descartes* I, 78.

63. For a general survey, see J. Cottingham, *Descartes* (Oxford: Blackwell, 1986), 35ff. Hereafter Cottingham, *Descartes*.

64. A version of this has been defended by Markie. See *Gambit*, 166ff.

65. See for example, J. Hintikka, "Cogito Ergo Sum: Inference or Performance," *Philosophical Review* 71 (1962): 3–32.

66. AT VII, 17–18; CSM II, 12.

67. There may seem to be some question about whether I am right about this in light of a remark made just after the passage quoted above: "I am then, in the strict sense, only a thing that thinks." Should it be taken to mean that corporeal properties are excluded from my essence in the strict sense by this argument? Or should it be taken to mean that corporeal properties are excluded from my current *knowledge* of my essence in the strict sense? In his reply to a query made on this point by Gassendi (Gassendi's objection is quoted in CSM II, 276, n.1). Descartes indicates that his remarks should be taken in the second way. This is fortunate, since we have seen that Descartes has not demonstrated the stronger claim in the argument given to this point.

68. This argument is completed only in Meditation VI. However, as my interest is not primarily in Descartes's overall case for dualism, I do not consider the completion of the argument here. See Cottingham, *Descartes*, 111–118, for a good introductory discussion of the main issues in interpreting Descartes's arguments for dualism. See Wilson, *Descartes*, 177ff., for a sophisticated reconstruction of the overall argument, a reconstruction which in the main I accept. See Markie, *Gambit*, for another sophisticated, book-length treatment of this subject from the perspective of contemporary Anglo-American analytical philosophy.

69. In this case, *K* is humankind. See the Fourth Replies: AT VII, 22; CSM II, 157.

70. Descartes offers some fresh argumentation on these issues in the Synopsis of Meditation II at AT VII, 13–14; CSM II, 9–10. See Markie, "Descartes' Concepts of Substance."

71. I am indebted to Carriero for drawing attention to this. Carriero, "Second Meditation," 209.

72. I examine his empirical theory of imagination in chapter 4.

73. The problem with this interpretation is that Descartes soon introduces the possibility that the simple natures can be the subject of mathematical investigation "regardless of whether they really exist in nature or not" (AT VII, 20; CSM II, 14). One possible line of defense is to see this as a reference to the cautious ontological commitments of mathematicians, not to the ontological commitments of Meditation I. For the latter we should look to what a meditator would reasonably believe if he or she were following the order of argument prescribed in the text. What such a person would believe, so the defense goes, is that the simple natures are actually exemplified corporeal properties. (See Frankfurt, *Demons*, chap. 14.) Alternatively, Lennon has argued that when Descartes says that arithmetic and geometry might be true even if the items of the list of simple natures are not actually existent, he means that the principles of these subjects might be true even if there are no corporeal bodies. Lennon adds that Descartes "does not say that they could be true if there is no extension and in fact immediately introduces the doubt of the clear and distinct perceptions of mathematics on the basis of the possible demon who could cause me to have my present perceptions and yet fail to create the earth, heaven, extended thing, magnitude or place. The crucial item in this list is extended thing (*res extensa*)." T. Lennon, *The Battle of the Gods and the Giants* (Princeton: Princeton University Press, 1993), 208. Hereafter, Lennon, *Gods and Giants*.

74. See also the definition of "idea" in the Second Replies (AT VII, 160–161; CSM II, 113); see also Meditation VI for a statement of this same doctrine, although made in a ten-

tative mood due to the continued operation of doubt about the external world (AT VII, 73; CSM II, 51).

75. A difficulty for this interpretation is provided by a text from paragraph 9. In this text we find Descartes explicitly asserting that "even if, as I have supposed, none of the objects of the imagination are real, the power of imagination is something which really exists and is part of my thinking" (AT VII 29; CSM II, 19). This text might suggest that the existence of acts of imagination does not depend on the body unless we recall the distinction between acts of the mind considered materially, viz., as events in the natural order, and acts of the mind considered objectively, viz., as acts taking intentional objects. The fact that acts of imagination in the objective sense do not entail the existence of their intentional objects does not mean that acts of imagination in the material sense do not entail the existence of the brain or other corporeal objects. (For the distinction between mental acts taken materially and mental acts taken objectively, see the Preface to the *Meditations*: AT VII, 8; CSM II, 7.)

76. There are difficulties with this position of Descartes. The French text uses the word "apperçevoir" (Alquié II, 800), the same word Descartes uses in the Sixth Replies to express the property of "noticing" our intuitive awareness of thought and existence. (See the passage quoted in text accompanying note 47. But this concept of awareness seems to have the following logical property: noticing x entails the existence of x. (This is the notion that Radner has called "C2 awareness." See Radner, "Thought and Consciousness," 445–446.) This gives rise to the problem that if dreaming entails the existence of corporeal images contemplated by the mind (as Descartes seems to accept) and if the noticing that I am dreaming entails the existence of dreaming (as he also seems to accept), then noticing dreaming would also seem to entail the existence of corporeal images (something he does not accept).

77. The sufficient condition argument.

78. See the Second Replies (AT VII, 155–159; CSM II, 110–113). See also the epilogue to this book, especially the appendix.

79. See my discussion of Cartesian methodological, below in the epilogue, for more on this.

80. See section 2 of this chapter.

81. This is similar to what what Lewis has called an attitude *de se*. D. Lewis, "Attitudes *De Dicto* and *De Se*," *Philosophical Review* 88 (1979): 523–514. I am indebted to Terry Tomkow for pointing this out. cf. Markie, *Gambit*, chap. 3, esp. 77ff.

82. See the letter to Clovius quoted.

83. For a detailed discussion of how Descartes might have thought the derivation is to be carried out and some related issues, see my methodological discussion in the appendix to the epilogue.

84. For a discussion of objective reality see chapter 2, sections 2.4, 2.5, 2.7, and 2.8; for formal and eminent containment see sections 2.6, 2.7, and the appendix to ch. 3.

85. See chapter 2, section 2.2.

86. See another letter to Mersenne of October 16, 1639 (*Letters*, 65–66; AT II, 587). See also S. Gaukroger, *Cartesian Truth* (Oxford: Clarendon, 1989), 52ff.

87. The passage from Meditation III quoted at the beginning of section 1.7.

88. If Clarke is right to ascribe considerable looseness to Descartes's notion of deduction (especially with the corresponding French, *déduire*) it is possible to describe this process as a genuine kind of Cartesian deduction. See D. Clarke, *Descartes' Philosophy of Science* (Manchester: Manchester University Press, 1982), app. 1, 207–210. Hereafter, Clarke, *Descartes' Science*. It is not, however, the tight kind of deduction warranted by intuition of necessary relations between properties or propositions.

89. Thanks here to Ronald de Sousa.

90. There are some interesting parallels between this method and the method Descartes used in scientific theory construction, e.g., the account of refraction (*Optics* II, AT VI, 93ff.). In each case there is the use of an initial analogy to suggest new principles, the conservative refinement of the new principles, and the use of deductive logic to derive consequences from the new principles. For a discussion of some scientific applications of these aspects of Cartesian method, see Clarke, *Descartes' Science*, chap. 2, esp. 58ff. and chap. 7, esp. 173ff.

If I am right that Descartes moved to the rule of truth in these two intermediate stages, then Descartes has proved the rule on the basis of premises available by the end of Meditation II. There is, however, an apparently contrary text at AT VII, 3; CSM II, 9 in the Synopsis of the *Meditations*: "A further requirement is that we should know that everything that we clearly and distinctly understand is true *in a way which corresponds exactly to our understanding of it*; but it was not possible to prove this before the Fourth Meditation" (my emphasis). If we take this to be a reference to the rule of truth as I have officially formulated it, then it clearly contradicts the contention I have just made. However, the emphasized part of this passage indicates that Descartes is speaking of a different version of the rule of truth, one restricted to cases in which the properties are contained *formally rather than eminently* in the substance. (That this is so follows from the definitions of formal and eminent containment in the Second Replies [AT VII, 161; CSM II, 114]. See also my discussion of this topic in chapter 2, section 2.2, and 2.7.) Why it should be possible to prove this restricted version of the rule only in Meditation IV may be that it is only by the end of Mediation III that Descartes has proved the existence of God. The relevance of God's existence to the proof of the restricted version of the rule of truth is a matter I take up in chapter 3.

91. See section 1.3.

92. This is a point I argue for in chapter 2, section 2.2.

93. See section 1.4.

94. Notice that the same conflation of the role of properties in the theory of understanding (understanding the nature of the wax) with the role of properties in the theory of existential inference (inferring from the colors and shapes to the existence of the wax before us) present in so many of Descartes's discussions of clear and distinct ideas is present here as well.

95. This passage is drawn from a later portion of the argument not of direct interest to us here where Descartes is no longer contrasting ordinary, mistaken conceptions of the objects of sensory perceptual awareness with the correct conception, but where he is contrasting sensory perception itself with intellectual perception. (His purpose is to compare sensory perception unfavorably with intellectual perception.) I mention this passage in order to show that Descartes has been treating the reference to hats and coats as a metaphor for properties, a point relevant to his discussion of the first of the contrasts just mentioned.

96. The end result of this story is essentially the same as that which Descartes reaches in the "simple natures" argument of Meditation I: all acts of perceptual consciousness— dreams or waking experiences—depend on an awareness of simple natures: [A]lthough these general kinds of things—eyes, head, hands, and so on—could be imaginary, it must at least be admitted that certain other even simpler and more universal things are real. These are as it were the real colours from which we form the images of things, whether true or false, that occur in our thought" (AT VII, 20; CSM II, 13–14).

97. Audi, *Justification*.

98. Ibid., chap. 12, 362.

99. Audi's own brand of foundationalism is discussed in other places in *Justification*. See especially the first three chapters.

100. Ibid., chap. 5, 167–170.

101. The suggestion that follows in the text is not explicitly made by Descartes. When challenged about the possibility of a circularity, Descartes' own suggestion about how to avoid it often involves arguing that the role of God lies not in vindicating the rule of clear and distinct ideas itself but in ensuring that our *recollection* of clear and distinct perception is accurate (see the Second Replies, AT VII 140; CSM II, 100). Not all commentators have accepted this reply at face value. See, e.g., Frankfurt, *Demons*, chap. 14; J. Van Cleve, "Foundationalism, Epistemic Principles and the Cartesian Circle," *Philosophical Review* 88 (1979): 55–91; Dicker, *Descartes*, 121ff. For a classic defense of the memory interpretation see W. Doney, "The Cartesian Circle," *Journal of the History of Ideas* 16 (1955): 324–338; for a more recent account that is sympathetic to the memory interpretation, see Cottingham, *Descartes*, 69ff.)

There is, however, at least this much similarity between Descartes's explicit suggestion and mine: in both cases God is needed to give some kind of guarantee that mental acts that we think are clear and distinct on the basis of subjective indications (memory experiences or irresistable inclinations, respectively) are as they seem.

102. This contention is defended in chapter 5, section 5.3.

103. This contention is defended in chapter 2, section 2.3.

Chapter 2

1. E.g., in the definition of substance of the second Set of Replies (AT VII, 161; CSM II 114).

2. E.g., in the ontological argument, the subject of clear ideas is an object, God. (AT VII, 65; CSM II, 45).

3. A slight terminological variant of this argument is offered by G. Dicker in *Descartes* (Oxford: Oxford University Press, 1993), 158.

4. I. Kant, *The Critique of Pure of Reason*, trans. N. K. Smith (New York: St. Martin's, 1965), 500ff. (A592/B620ff.)

5. For a defense of the Meinongian interpretation see A. Kenny, *Descartes* (New York: Random House, 1968), chap. 7, esp. 155.

6. In the definitions given in the Second Replies (AT VII, 161; CSM II, 114), Descartes speaks of properties "existing formally in the objects of our ideas" (*esse formaliter in idearum objectis*). He also uses this idiom in the definition of substance. Generally, however, he speaks of properties being contained (*contineri*). See, e.g., AT VIII, 11; CSM II, 199. In the demonstrations of the propositions he speaks of the existence (*existentia*) of God. It is this concept that I am calling the monadic concept of existence.

7. I note that the Fregian approach applies only in the case where a name of an object (substance) replaces the term "t" in the context "clear and distinct idea of t." When names of properties replace "t" or when the special pattern of inference characteristic of the intuitive cogito is involved, this approach does not apply.

8. See B. Russell, "On Denoting," in R. C. Marsh (ed.), *Logic and Knowledge* (London: Allen and Unwin, 1956), 42ff.

9. Descartes first introduces the official term "formal truth" in Meditation III at AT VII 43; CSM II, 30.

10. A corollory of this is that Descartes's notion of the *possibility* that an object of a certain type might be actual or might exist is explicated by him in terms of the eminent containment of properties in an actual substance, not in terms of the formal containment of an

existence or actuality property in a subset of possible objects (*possibilia*). Since this case itself depends on an interpretation of the notion of eminent containment, an interpretation which requires more background than I have yet put in place, I shall simply issue a promissory note for an argument to be provided later.

11. These brackets are used with the sense of "Quine's corners."

12. See section 2.7.

13. See chapter 3, section 3.3.

14. See C. Normore, "Meaning and Objective Being: Descartes and His Sources," (hereafter, Normore, "Meaning and Objective Being") in A. Rorty (ed.), *Essays on Descartes' "Meditations"* (Berkeley: University of California Press, 1986), 223–241. See 234. Hereafter, Rorty (ed.), *Essays*.

15. This proposal has also been made by Aquila. See R. E. Aquila, "Brentano, Descartes, and Hume on Awareness," *Philosophy and Phenomenological Research* 35 (1974–75): 228–231.

16. Wilson defends a "quasi-Platonic" interpretation of Descartes's theory of ideas; see M. D. Wilson, *Descartes* (London: Routledge and Kegan Paul, 1978), 170–171 (hereafter Wilson, *Descartes*). Wells defends a quite strong Augustinian/Platonic reading of Descartes; see N. J. Wells, "Material Falsity in Descartes, Arnauld and Suarez," *Journal of the History of Philosophy* 22 (1984): 25–50; see 29ff. Others reject that reading entirely in favor of a reading that prefers option 3. E.g., V. Chappell, "The Theory of Ideas," in Rorty (ed.), *Essays*, 177–198; M. Gueroult, *Descartes' Philosophy Interpreted According to the Order of Reasons*, vol. 1, ed. and trans. R. Ariew (Minneapolis: University of Minnesota Press, 1985), 277ff.; S. Nadler, *Arnauld and the Cartesian Philosophy of Ideas* (Princeton: Princeton University Press, 1989). Nadler claims that this is the "standard interpretation" (161). For an intermediate position see N. J. Jolly, *The Light of the Soul* (New York: Oxford University Press, 1990) (hereafter, Jolly, *Light of the Soul*). Jolly argues that option 3 represents Descartes's dominant view but that options 1 and 2 remain as "a residue of an earlier, Augustinian theory of ideas" (22).

17. See W. Sellars, "The Adverbial Theory of the Objects of Sensation," *Metaphilosophy* 6 (1975): 144–160.

18. See note 16.

19. See letter to Hyperaspistes, August 1641 (AT III, 422; *Letters*, 111).

20. The term comes from Wilson, *Descartes*, 171.

21. However, see Jolly, *Light of the Soul* who maintains that the dispositional sense is one that Descartes primarily applies to innate perceptual mechanisms rather than to ideas with contents.

22. E.g. Cottingham. See Cottingham, J. (ed.) *Conversation with Burman* (Oxford: Clarendon, 1976), (xxxii) ff.

23. See the Sixth Replies: "[C]olours, smells, tastes and so on, are, I observed, merely certain sensations which exist in my thought" (AT VII, 440; CSM II, 297).

24. Three central texts in which this contrast is drawn in a way relevant to present concerns are: (1) the text in which the contrast between materially false and true ideas is first introduced in Meditation III (AT VII, 43–44; CSM II 29–30); (2) a second text in Meditation III (AT VII, 46; CSM II, 31–32); and a text from the *Principles* I, 71 (AT VIIIA, 35; CSM I, 218–219).

25. G. A. Berkeley, *Treatise Concerning the Principles of Human Knowledge*, sec. 49, in A. A. Luce and T. E. Jessop (eds.), *The Works of George Berkeley, Bishop of Cloyne*, vol. 2 (London: Nelson, 1948–57).

26. In the Preface to the Reader of the *Meditations* Descartes says that there is an ambiguity in the word "idea": it can be taken materially (as an "operation of the intellect") or

objectively (as "the thing represented by the operation" (AT VII, 8; CSM II, 7). In the present text it is "idea" in the objective sense that is at issue.

27. See chapter 8, section 8.2.

28. See chapter 1, section 1.6; also see the epilogue, for more on this connection.

29. See chapter 3, appendix A.

30. Section 1.7.

31. Chapter 3, appendix A.

32. He does provide a number of examples of eminently contained properties, e.g., the "stone example" in Meditation III (AT VII, 41; CSM II, 28), but none of these examples helps very much with the misperception property. Indeed, other commentators tend to ignore this property, offering interpretations that focus on the greatness property and its role in Descartes's theory of causation. I consider some of these interpretations in chapter 3, appendix A .

33. Calvin Normore suggests that this was an option for Descartes. Normore, "Meaning and Objective Being," 223–242. See 238.

34. It will occur to some readers that there is in fact one very natural candidate for this principle, the causal principle governing the objective reality of our ideas. However, the causal principle also employs a disjunction between formal and eminent containment in its canonical formulation (*Principles* I, 17; AT VIIIA, 11; CSM II, 199) and the same problem would arise for it as for the canonical version of the rule of truth: an independent means of eliminating the possibility of eminent containment is required. If this means can be provided in the one case than it can be provided in the other and the appeal to the causal principle is redundant. Moreover, and more controversially, I also maintain that the causal principle is ultimately a form of the rule of truth, not an additional principle. These matters are taken up in detail in the next chapter.

35. The primary example of this is the proof of God's existence in Meditation III. See chapter 3.

36. This doctrine—often regarded as curious—is first introduced by Descartes in two letters to Mersenne of May 6 and 27, 1630 (AT I, 147: CSMK III, 24–25 and AT I, 151: CSMK III, 25–26. For an attempt to make this doctrine seem less curious, see J. Bennett, "Descartes' Theory of Modality," *Philosophical Review* 103 (1994): 639–667. For further considerations against attributing to Descartes a commitment to unactualized possibilia, based on a reading of the Leibnitz-Arnauld correspondence, see A. Nelson, "Cartesian Actualism in the Leibnitz—Arnauld Correspondence," *Canadian Journal of Philosophy* 23: 675–694.

37. One other alternative answer, proposed recently by Lennon, depends on the claim that what God creates to make the eternal truths true is actual extension in general, that is, matter. See T. Lennon, *The Battle of the Gods and the Giants* (Princeton: Princeton University Press, 1993), 208. In support, Lennon cites a passage from a letter to Mersenne of May 27, 1638, in which Descartes says, "Pour la question, savoir s'il y aurait un espace reél, ainsi que maintenant, en cas que Dieu n'eut rien creé . . . non seulement il n'y aurait point espace, mais même que ces vérités qu'on nomme éternelles . . . ne serais point vérités, si Dieu ne l'avait ainsi établi, ce que je crois vous avoir déjá autrefois écrit" (AT II, 132; Alquié II, 62).

Lennon bases his case on a reading of the phrase, "si Dieu ne l'avait ainsi établi" that sees a reference back to "espace." Alternatively, CSMK III see a reference to "ces vérités qu'on nomme éternelles," translating the second half of the passage to read "not only would there not be any space, but even those truths which are called eternal . . . would not be truths if God had not so established, as I think I wrote you once before" (CSMK III, 103). Whatever the most natural translation (which I take to be the latter), it should be noted that the earlier letters of Descartes to Mersenne that are mentioned in the concluding words of this passage (presumably those of April 15, May 6, and May 27 (AT I, 135ff.; CSMK III, 20ff.) make copious mention of the doctrine of the free creation of the eternal truths by God, whereas they make no mention of space, either as the source of the truth of the eternal truths nor of its creation by God.

38. A draft on God's benevolence would do the job. It is important, however, to distinguish the role of God's benevolence in justifying the assertion that if a material world exists, it must satisfy the laws of mathematics from the role of God's benevolence in justifying the assertion that the material world exists. The latter is an issue I take up in chapter 6, section 6.4.2.

39. A. Kenny, *Descartes* (New York: Random House, 1968), 110–111.

40. Jolly, *Light of the Soul*, 16–17.

41. M. Costa, "What Cartesian Ideas Are Not," *Journal of the History of Philosophy* 21: 237–248. See 342. Hereafter, Costa, "Cartesian Ideas."

42. See the definition for the notion of *eminent* containment (AT VII, 161; CSM II, 114).

43. Cf. J. Yolton, *Perceptual Acquaintance from Descartes to Reed* (Minneapolis: University of Minnesota Press, 1984). Hereafter, Yolton, *Perceptual Acquaintance*.

44. See chapter 4, section 4.1, for discussion of this doctrine as it first appears in Rule 12 of the *Rules of the Direction of the Mind*.

45. See, e.g., Jolly, *Light of the Soul*, 14.

46. See chapter 7 for a fuller discussion of the notion of material falsity.

47. The point can be put more formally by saying that the form of an act of awareness for Descartes is a one-place predicate operator taking the predicate "is aware of object *a*" as an input rather than a two-place operator taking the predicate "is aware of" as input.

48. An alternative procedure is more common. For example, Jolly thinks that the notion of objective reality is the notion of the object of an act of awareness rather than its form. This assumption then drives a convoluted explanation of what Descartes's notion of "ideas in the formal sense" must mean, the main thrust of which seems to be that Descartes is confused (Jolly, *Light of the Soul*, 16–17). However, Yolton, *Perceptual Acquaintance*, 36ff., seems to adopt a reading closer to my own when he insists that the notion of objective reality should be given an "epistemic" rather than an "ontic" reading.

49. Normore, "Meaning and Objective Being," 223–242.

50. See, e.g., H. Caton, *The Origin of Subjectivity* (New Haven: Yale University Press, 1973); Costa, "Cartesian Ideas"; T. Lennon, "Representationalism, Judgment and Perception of Distance: Further to Yolton and McRae," *Dialogue* XIX (March 1980): 151–162; A. MacKenzie, "Descartes on Life and Sense," *Canadian Journal of Philosophy* 19 (1989): 163–192 (hereafter, MacKenzie "Life and Sense"); A. MacKenzie, "Descartes on Sensory Representation: A Study of the Dioptrics," *Canadian Journal of Philosophy*, Supp. Vol. 16 (1990): 109–147 (hereafter MacKenzie, "Sensory Representation). Yolton, *Perceptual Acquaintance*, chap. 1.

51. This point is easier to see if these passages are read in conjunction with comments Descartes makes in the Sixth Reply (AT VII, 438; CSM II, 295).

52. The term is Wilson's (*Descartes*, 102). I am much indebted to her ground-breaking work on the Cartesian theory of ideas.

53. M. B. Bolton, 1986. "Confused and Obscure Ideas of Sense," in Rorty (ed.), 389–406. Bolton sees Descartes as claiming that when naive people employ the resemblance principle they do so in a theoretical or prototheoretical way to advance a (mistaken) theory of representation. One can see how such an interpretation might draw strength from the discussion of corporeal images in the *Optics*.

54. See Normore, "Meaning and Objective Being," 225–226.

Chapter 3

1. AT VII, 165; CSM II, 116–117.

2. D. Radner, "Is There a Problem of Cartesian Interaction?" *Journal of the History of Philosophy* 23 (1985): 35–49 (hereafter, Radner, "Is There a Problem?"). These principles are given on 40–42.

3. See L. Loeb, "Is There a Problem of Cartesian Interactionism?" *Journal of the History of Philosophy* 23 (1985): 227–231.

4. See D. Radner, D. "Descartes' Notion of the Union of Mind and Body," *Journal of the History of Philosophy* 9 (1971): 159–170; J. Broughton and R. Mattern, "Reinterpreting Descartes on the Notion of the Union of Mind and Body," *Journal of the History of Philosophy* 16 (1978): 23–32; R. Richardson, "Union and Interaction of Body and Soul," *Journal of the History of Philosophy* 23 (1985): 221–226; D. Radner, "Is There a Problem?" 35–49.

5. Contemporary discussion of Descartes's notion of eminent containment is wrapped up in a discussion of the causal principle. In appendix A to this chapter, I consider how these reasons have shaped two recent alternative accounts of the notion of eminent containment by Clatterbaugh and O'Neil, arguing that theirs suffer from important deficiencies not present in my own account: K. Clatterbaugh, "Descartes' Causal Likeness Principle," *Philosophical Review* 89 (1980): 379–402; E. O'Neill, "Mind-Body Interaction and Metaphysical Consistency: A Defense of Descartes," *Journal of the History of Philosophy* 25 (1987): 227–245.

6. See C. G. Hempel, *Aspects of Scientific Explanation* (New York: Macmillan, 1965), 367ff. Hempel's thesis is somewhat stronger than this, asserting that all explanations have a *deductive-nomological form*, a characteristic that ensures that reversing the order of an explanation yields a deductive inference.

7. For counterexamples and general criticism of the strong Hempelian thesis, see R. C. Jeffrey, "Statistical Explanation vs. Statistical Inference" and W. Salmon, "Statistical Explanation," both in W. Salmon (ed.), *Statistical Explanation and Statistical Relevance* (Pittsburgh: University of Pittsburgh Press, 1971).

8. It is true that Descartes seems to place his reliance in the proof for God's existence on the weaker, quantitiative causal principle, but I will argue in the next section that this appearance is deceptive.

9. The term "archtype" comes from M. Gueroult. See *Descartes'* I: 126. I am indebted to Gueroult for pointing out the difference between the argument I have called the levels argument and the one I have called the archtype argument. That is not to say that our interpretations of those arguments are the same.

10. An anaphoric term functions like a bound variable in quantification theory.

11. I have argued in the previous chapter that Descartes believes that such content properties actually *are* contained within himself eminently. See chapter 2, sections 2.5. and 2.6.

12. The case for this as Cartesian doctrine has been made in chapter 2, section 2.2.

13. See chapter 2, section 2.7.

14. See this chapter, appendix B.

15. See passages earlier in the Second Replies at AT VII 133ff; CSM II, 81ff.

16. See Meditation V: AT VII 65; CSM II, 45.

17. See chapter 2, section 2.4.

18. Gueroult, *Descartes* II, 62.

19. Elements 1–4 yield the result that the active cause of my sensible ideas lies "in a substance that is different from me."

20. Ibid., 67.

21. Ibid., 62. For a discussion of the merits of the claim that the objective reality of ideas of the senses is at a minimum, see below.

22. Ibid., 67–68.

23. See section 3 of this chapter.

24. Martha Bolton, "Confused and Obscure Ideas of Sense" in A. Rorty (ed.), *Essays on Descartes' "Meditations"* (Berkeley: University of California Press, 1986, 389–403 (hereafter, Rorty (ed.), *Essays*) turns this reasoning to opposite effect, claiming that because Descartes intends to include sensations as "sensible objects", sensations must have objective reality. She argues: "[H]is only reason for thinking that bodies affect our senses depends on the assumption that sense presentations exhibit material things. So, unless ideas of heat, cold, and so forth, do exhibit bodies, no reason for thinking they proceed from bodies has been supplied" (397–398). The second sentence embodies Bolton's assumption that by "sense presentations" Descartes means to include "ideas of heat, cold and so forth." Her claim is that these ideas must be taken to exhibit (represent) material things because there are no other kinds of sensory ideas available to do the job. I take it that the text from *Principles* I, 71 (this is passage B quoted in chapter 4, section 4.3) shows that Bolton is mistaken about this. Cf. Margaret D. Wilson, "Descartes on Sensation," in J. A. Cover, and M. Kulstad (eds.), *Central Theories in Early Modern Philosophy* (Indianapolis: Hackett, 1990), 1–22.

25. "[A]ll the properties which I clearly and distinctly understand . . . are comprised within the subject matter of pure mathematics" (AT VII, 80; CSM II, 55).

26. In chapter 2, section 2.5.

27. E.g., W. Sellars, "Berkeley and Descartes: Reflections on the Theory of Ideas," in P. Machamer and R. Turnbull (eds.), *Studies in Perception* (Columbus: Ohio State University Press, 1978); and MacKenzie, "Descartes on Sensory Representation," 116–120.

28. Chapter 4, section 4.3.

29. See D. Garber, "*Semel in vita*: The Scientific Background to Descartes' *Meditations*," in Rorty (ed.), *Essays*, 115, n. 51. See also D. Garber, *Descartes' Metaphysical Physics* (Chicago: University of Chicago Press, 1992), 72ff. (hereafter, Garber, *Metaphysical Physics*). Garber claims that the proofs are different in substance, the first relying on the notion of natural propensities and not on clear and distinct perception, the latter relying on clear and distinct perception, not on natural propensities. I am indebted to Garber for drawing attention to the apparent differences between the two proofs.

30. If we *impute* their appearances as premises to the proof then we encounter the destructive dilemma discussed in the previous section.

31. I set aside here and in the rest of this chapter the fact that Descartes speaks only of a "clear" rather than a "clear and distinct" understanding. I devote section 7.9 of chapter 7 to exploring the distinction between clear and clear and distinct ideas.

32. I devote chapter 6 to a discussion of these doctrines. See section 6.4 for the relevance of these doctrines to the Meditation VI proof of the external world.

33. See R. Mattern, "Descartes: All Things Which I Conceive Clearly and Distinctly in Corporeal Objects Are in Them," in Rorty (ed.), *Essays*, 473–490. Cf. R. Field, "Descartes' Proof of the Existence of Matter," *Mind* 44 (1985): 244–249.

34. Lennon argues that actually existing extension in general is the object of clear and distinct perception and thus forms the basis for Descartes's proof of the extenal world. In this respect our accounts are in agreement. However, Lennon does not countenance two forms of intuition (clear and distinct perception), one intellectual the other concrete . He therefore sees the proofs in both Meditation VI and *Principles* II, 1 as having the same structure and as depending on the same conception of clear and distinct perception. (See T. Lennon, *The Battle of the Gods and the Giants* (Princeton: Princeton University Press, 1993), 196–197, 208–209.) While this reading certainly has the advantage of parsimony, it

seems to me that in assigning to the intellect the capacity to directly perceive actually (formally) exemplified properties of matter (extension in general) Lennon assigns a capacity that Descartes would assign to the imagination. With the exception of the special case of self-knowledge, I take the intellect to gain access to actuality only through the general pattern of existential reasoning. For more on Lennon's position see the discussion of unactualized possibilities in chapter 2, section 2.6, n. 37.

35. Chapter 1, section 1.3.

36. See chapter 1, section 1.9.

37. See the introduction, 1–6.

38. It is true that in Meditation II Descartes does not invite us to see the objects of sense experience as depending on body in any essential way. But it should be borne in mind that Descartes is concerned there with sense experience in the "restricted sense" needed for his case for dualism. In that sense Descartes is committed only to seeing sense experiences as "second-order" awarenesses of first-order sense experiences. However, with respect to the latter—Descartes's example is of first-order dreaming—his position appears to be that they do depend on the body (see chapter 1, section 1.5, for the case for this).

If we now take the perception of primary qualities at issue in *Principles* I, 71 to be first-order experiences, there is no warrant for denying that these perceptions might comprise a class of ideas directed toward the body and some warrant for affirming that they do comprise such a class.

39. *Principles* I, 45.

40. K. Clatterbaugh, "Descartes' Causal Likeness Principle," *Philosophical Review* 89, (1980): 379–402. Hereafter, Clatterbaugh, "Causal Likeness."

41. E. O'Neill, "Mind-Body Interaction and Metaphysical Consistency: A Defense of Descartes," *Journal of the History of Philosophy* 25 (1987): 227–245. Hereafter, O'Neill, "Mind-Body."

42. Clatterbaugh, "Causal Likeness," 391.

43. Ibid., 390.

44. Ibid., 391–392.

45. O'Neill, "Mind-Body," 237.

46. *Ibid.*, 235.

47. Quoted ibid., on 239. The selection is from *Disputationes Metaphysicae* 4 (XXX, I, 10) (Hildesheim: G. Olms, 1965). The translation is by A. Freddoso.

48. The distinction between misperception and inadequate perception is important for us later in the book when I deal with the doctrine of the material falsity of ideas. I reserve a fuller discussion of this distinction until then. See chapter 7, section 1.

Chapter 4

1. I will sometimes use an abbreviated title, the *Rules*, to refer to this work.

2. *De Anima* III, 7: 431a1.

3. Here and in what follows I am much indebted to Epstein and Hatfield (W. Epstein and G. Hatfield, "The Sensory Core and the Medieval Foundations of Early Modern Perceptual Theory," *Isis* 70 (1979): 363–384. (Hereafter Epstein and Hatfield, "Sensory Core.") See also the intro. to S. Gaukroger (trans. and ed.), *Antoine Arnauld's "On True and False Ideas"* (Manchester: Manchester University Press, 1990), for a helpful background to Cartesian theory of perception.

4. I am indebted here to Cohen's interpretation of the doctrine: J. Cohen, "St. Thomas Aquinas on the Immaterial Reception of Sensible Forms," *Philosophical Review* 41 (1982): 193–209.

5. Aristotle presents his account of human perception mainly in *De Anima* II, 5–III, 8. On the specific points made here see *De Anima* II, 12, and *De Anima* III, 8: 431b 20–432a 8.

6. *De Anima* II, 6.

7. *De Anima* II, 12.

8. I say "more or less" because the hard and fast distinction between the mental and the material characteristic of post-Cartesian thinking is not present in this period. See Epstein and Hatfield, "Sensory Core," 371.

9. The *Dioptrics* was published in 1611.

10. See especially *Optics* VI (AT VI, 130; CSM I, 167) and the Sixth Replies, 9 (AT VII, 437–438; CSM II, 294–295).

11. See, e.g., *Summa Theologiae* 1a 78, A3.

12. Brian O'Neil is such an interpreter. See B. O'Neil, *Epistemological Direct Realism in Descartes' Philosophy* (Albuquerque: University of New Mexico Press, 1974), for a defense of this intepretation. Hereafter O'Neil, *Direct Realism*.

13. There is much uncertainty about the underlying metaphysics of the *Rules for the Direction of the Mind*. This is due in part to Descartes's abrupt abandonment of that work before it was completed, in part to its appearance of cobbling together different lines of thought developed over a decade or so, in part to the uncertainties of inferring from mature doctrines what their origins must have been in the *Rules*, and, finally, to the general uncertainty surrounding which intellectual currents most affected the development of Descartes's thinking.

For a very good overall discussion of these issues see J. A. Schuster, "Descartes' *mathesis universalis*, 1619–1628," in S. Gaukroger (ed.), *Descartes: Philosophy, Mathematics and Physics* (Towata, N.J.: Harvester Press, 1980). For an interpretation that sees Descartes's mature mechanistic metaphysics already in place in the *Rules* see Caton, *Subjectivity*, 164ff.; for an interpretation that locates the overall doctrine of the *Rules* more within the Scholastic tradition see O'Neil, *Direct Realism*.

14. See the passage quoted at the beginning of section 2, below: passage A.

15. I owe this suggestion to John Barresi. See his "Descartes: Life, History and Intellectual Development," chap. 5 of an unpublished manuscript.

16. For a recent discussion of Descartes's case see D. Garber, *Metaphysical Physics* (Chicago: University of Chicago Press, 1992), chap. 4.

17. When I use the terminology of "primary qualities" and "secondary qualities," I intend these words to be taken as names for the list of properties customarily described by them, geometrical properties in case of "primary qualities," and colors, sounds, heat, cold, in the case of "secondary qualities." I will also sometimes use the terminology "geometrical properties" and "sensory qualities" to designate the same lists respectively. There are, course, many controversies that center on these concepts, e.g. what theoretical significance the distinction possesses, precisely which properties get on which list, etc. I do not intend any prejudgment of these controversies by my use of this terminology.

18. Direct realism should be distinguished from what I have been calling "commonsense realism," a prototheoretical commitment of common sense to a hylomorphic metaphysics in which colors and other secondary qualities are regarded as qualities (forms) present in extended matter. I regard Descartes as maintaining direct realism (in my sense) throughout his philosophical life, though with changing conceptions of what content we are *really* aware of and, correspondingly, with changing conceptions of which direct objects we need to postulate to account for that awareness. On the other hand, while Descartes may give some evidence here of also being a commonsense realist, he certainly abandoned that doctrine by the time he wrote *The Treatise on Light*.

19. See, e.g., W. Sellars, "Berkeley and Descartes: Reflections on the Theory of Ideas," in P. K. Machamer and R. G. Turnbull (eds.), *Studies in Perception* (Columbus: Ohio State University Press, 1978), sect. 4; also MacKenzie, "Sensory Representation," 117–120.

20. See the Sixth Replies: AT VII, 437–439; CSM II, 294–295.

21. See Meditation III: AT VII, 43; CSM II, 29–30; see Meditation VI: AT VII, 79–80; CSM II, 55.

22. See Sixth Replies: AT VII, 437–439; CSM II, 294–295.

23. Chapter 1, section 1.5.

24. That all sense experience may have an intellectual *component* is another matter. See Meditation VI: AT VII, 78; CSM II, 54.

25. "Sensory Core," 376.

26. G. Hatfield, "The Senses and the Fleshless Eye: The Meditations as Cognitive Exercises," in A. Rorty (ed.), *Essays on Descartes' "Meditations"* (Berkeley: University of California Press, 1986) (hereafter, Rorty [ed.], *Essays*), 45–80. See esp. 64–65.

27. The quotation is from the Sixth Replies (AT VII, 437–438; HR II, 252), reproduced on p. 376 of their article, their emphasis.

28. Wilson also suggests that in those texts in which Descartes is most disparaging about the positive role of the senses he may not be using sensing terminology in "the broad common usage" but rather in a more narrow technical sense. (Her suggestion for the technical sense is that it is second-grade sensing. See Margaret D. Wilson, "Descartes on the Perception of Primary Qualities," in Stephen Voss (ed.), *Essays on the Philosophy and Science of René Descartes* (New York: Oxford University Press, 1993), 170.

29. The passage from the *Conversation with Burman* is intended to clarify the doctrine of imagination in Meditation VI (AT VII, 73; CSM II, 51).

30. H. Caton, *Subjectivity:* 165, n., argues that the corporeal imagination and the common sense were taken by Descartes as separate structures in the *Rules for the Direction of the Mind* but as a single structure in later works. However, the text that I am just about to quote from the *Treatise on Man* seems to indicate that the dual structure account doctrine of the *Rules* was in place even in the later works.

31. I owe this way of seeing the ordering principle to Hatfield. See G. Hatfield, "Descartes' Physiology and Its Relation to His Psychology," in John Cottingham (ed.), *The Cambridge Companion to Descartes* (Cambridge: Cambridge University Press, 1992), 335–370.

32. See for example his discussion of the wise man and the man afflicted with jaundice in Rule 12 (AT X, 423; CSM I, 47).

33. The Sixth Discourse, esp. AT VI, 138: CSM I, 170.

34. See, e.g., the *Discourse on Method* (AT VI, 55ff; CSM I 139ff.), the *Treatise on Man;* various letters, e.g., to More, February 5, 1649 (*Letters*, 243) ; to Plempius, October 3, 1637 (*Letters*, 36); to Newcastle, November 23, 1646 (*Letters*, 206). For recent helpful descriptions of this project see A. MacKenzie, "Descartes on Life and Sense," *Canadian Journal of Philosophy* 19 (June 1989): 163–192 (hereafter, "Life and Sense"), esp. 164–176.

35. See the Fourth Discourse, esp. AT VI, 109; CSM I 164.

36. See Caton, *Subjectivity*, 91ff. and MacKenzie "Life and Sense," 172ff. for helpful summary discussions of the neurophysiological mechanisms postulated in the *Treatise on Man*.

37. These points are extracted from passages running from AT XI 159–161; Hall 59–63.

38. Of course there is always available in the pineal gland a representation of *the size of the retinal image*, but I find no indications in the *Treatise on Man* or in the *Optics* that Descartes wished to treat this as representational *of the size of the object* producing the retinal image.

39. R. Cummins, *The Nature of Psychological Explanation* (Cambridge, Mass.: MIT Press, 1983), 42–43.

40. The distinction between computational and computational-simulation systems is, admittedly, hard to draw in a precise and nonarbitrary way for it depends on which states are considered "discrete" and how the line between "internal workings" and "behavior" is drawn.

41. R. L. Gregory, "Emmert's Law," *The Oxford Companion to the Mind* (Oxford: Oxford University Press, 1991), 218.

42. See also AT VI, 55; CSM I, 139.

43. Cf. T. Lennon, "Representationalism, Judgment and Perception of Distance. Further to Yolton and MacRae," *Dialogue* 19 (March 1980): 151–162, 153ff.

44. See AT VI, 57; CSM I, 140.

45. See, e.g, I. Rock, *The Logic of Perception* (Cambridge, Mass.: MIT University Press, 1983), 280.

46. These passages are taken from AT IX, 346; CSM I, 337.

47. Cf. S. Voss (trans. and ann.) *The Passions of the Soul* (Indianapolis: Hackett, 1989), 30, n.23. Cf. R. McRae, "Descartes' Definition", 65.

48. See note 18 for a descripion of this doctrine.

49. I owe this term to Mark Glouberman.

50. This discussion occurs in chapters 5 and 7.

51 We might thus see Descartes as a precursor to contemporary developmental psychologists who trace the origins of our commonsense view of the world to the evolution of theoretical concepts in childhood. See, e.g., L. Forguson, *Common Sense* (London: Routledge, 1989).

52. In trying to sort out Descartes's doctrine it is important to keep clear about the difference between the use of the notion of resemblance in the resemblance principle just discussed and its use as Descartes's preferred way of describing the content of commonsense realism. (See chapter 5, for a fuller discussion of these and other Cartesian notions of resemblance.) The former has a causal role to play in the production of referred sensations, which themselves serve as the basis for our inclinations to hold the latter. One of the great difficulties facing an interpreter who wishes to arrive at a clear statement of Descartes's account of these matters is Descartes's tendency not to mark distinctions within his theoretical concepts by distinctions within his theoretical terminology.

53. Section 3.5.

54. Rule 12: AT X, 420: CSM I, 54.

55. Meditation VI: AT VII, 51; CSM II, 73; Second Replies: AT VII, 160; CSM II, 113.

56. Meditation II: AT VII, 29ff.; CSM II, 20ff.

57. Meditation VI: AT VII, 73; CSM II, 51.

58. See chapter 3, section 3.6.

59. Chapter 6, section 6.5.

60. Readers familiar with Descartes's doctrine in the *Meditations* on what falls within the scope of the union of mind and body—sensations of "secondary qualities" alone—will find this interpretation inconsistent with that doctrine; and in this inconsistency some will see reason to discount the interpretation. (For a discussion of the doctrine of the *Meditations* see below, chapter 6.) The fact remains that Descartes does speak in *Principles* I, 71 of the *mind that is attached to the body* as the mind that is presented with perceptions of corporeal bodies (geometrical properties), whereas the presentation of geometrical properties in the *Meditations* seems to be exclusively an affair of the intellect. In that work, the role of the imagination is either discredited or ignored altogether.

61. This contention is controversial. I assume it throughout most of the book but argue for it only in chapter 7, section 7.1.

62. See chapter 2, section 2.5.
63. MacKenzie, "Sensory Representation," 117.
64. Ibid., 120.
65. Ibid., 115ff.

Chapter 5

1. In chapter 2, section 2.8.
2. For a discussion of the naturalistic elements in Descartes's theory of representation present in these passages see J. Yolton, *Perceptual Acquaintance* chap. 1; and MacKenzie, "Life and Sense" and "Sensory Representation." It is not entirely clear to me how to categorize these accounts within the set of theory types at issue here, but they both seem to be closer to the constitutive type than the minimal type.
3. Something noted by Curley. See E. M. Curley, *Descartes against the Skeptics* (Cambridge, Mass.: Harvard University Press, 1978), 208.
4. *Pace* Wilson. See M. D. Wilson, "Descartes on Sensation," in J. Cover and M. Kulstad (eds.), *Central Theories in Early Modern Philosophy* (Indianapolis: Hackett, 1990).
5. See chapter 7, section 7.9.
6. Chapter 4, section 4.4.
7. In my discussion of the resemblance principle I shall be concerned with it in the form it takes within the theory of ideas, specifically in connection with the role it plays in explaining various errors about sensory ideas, not in its form as what Clatterbaugh calls "the Causal-Likeness Principle." (K. Clatterbaugh, "Descartes' Causal Likeness Principle.")
8. See chapter 4, section 4.4.
9. Chapter 7, section 7.2.
10. "Some of my thoughts are as it were images of things, and it is only in these cases that the term 'idea' is strictly appropriate" (Meditation III: AT VII, 37; CSM II, 25).
11. See *Principles* IV, 198 (AT VIIIA, 32–323; CSM II, 284–285).
12. Chapter 7, section 7.9.
13. I am indebted to Grene for this reference. See M. Grene, *Descartes* (Minneapolis: University of Minnesota Press, 1985), 22, n.5.
14. Let me say that I do not find the justification for this taxonomy to be very convincing. The grounds on which Descartes declines to treat ideas of secondary qualities as adventitious is that resemblances (generic or specific) of these qualities are not transmitted to our mind and brain from external objects. In the case of primary qualities, specific spatial patterns *are* transmitted to our mind and brain where they are processed by inferential reasoning into ideas of the objective qualities. However, for reasons we have discussed previously, these qualities will generally not be of the same specific sort as the patterns in the medium of transmission and for this reason Descartes declines to allow that these ideas are adventitious. But if this is the case, then it is equally true that the idea of the town of Leiden is not a resemblance of the physical cause occasioning it, namely Leiden itself. So consistency of rationale would suggest that the idea of Leiden is no more adventitious than the basic elements of which the idea is composed. On the other hand, if Descartes means to treat the idea of Leiden as adventitious on the grounds that the remote causes of this idea lie in stimuli outside our brains, then consistency of rationale would suggest that ideas of primary and secondary qualities, which also have remote causes lying in the environment outside our brains, should also be treated as adventitious.
15. See the passage from *Optics* IV (AT VI, 112; CSM I, 165), quoted in my discussion of the "Scholastic use" of Descartes notion of resemblance.

16. For a more extensive discussion of this account and of its relation to Descartes's mature account of psychological causation, see the next chapter.

17. This is how Loeb takes it. L. Loeb, "The Priority of Reason in Descartes," *Philosophical Review* 41 (1990): 3–43. See esp. 13–14.

18. See M. D. Wilson, *Descartes*, 102ff.

19. The suggestion derives from her account of the "representational character" of ideas. She describes ideas as having this property when they "are received by the mind as if exhibiting to it various things—or as if making things cognitively accessible" (102). She maintains that when Descartes wishes to ascribe this property to an idea he does so by saying that the idea is "like an image of a thing" (*tanquam rerum imaginies*) (*Descartes*, 109) noting that Descartes describes sensory ideas in this characteristic way.

20. See M. Bolton, "Confused and Obscure Ideas of Sense," in A. Rorty (ed.), *Essays:* 389–404, esp. 401, n. 2. Bolton maintains that material falsity is unconnected with any intrinsic property of the ideas themselves or their objects, arguing that the source of the error embodied in the material falsity of ideas of sensory qualities lies in an assumption extraneous to the ideas themselves concerning the way in which ideas in general can come to represent real qualities (396). The assumption is the resemblance principle. I have just argued, however, that this principle does not serve as the basis for the error of referred judgments.

21. Even Descartes himself seems to have accepted the commonsense view in his early work, the *Rules for the Direction of the Mind*: "Take colour for example: whatever you may suppose colour to be, you will not deny that it is extended and consequently has shape" (Rule 12: AT X, 413; CSM I, 40–41).

22. See chapter 6, section 6.2.

23. See also *Principles* I, 46.

Chapter 6

1. All these propositions appear on AT VII 80–81; CSM II, 56.

2. R. Mattern, "Descartes: 'All Things Which I Conceive Clearly and Distinctly in Corporeal Objects Are in Them'" in A. Rorty, (ed.), *Essays:* 473–490.

3. See Chapter 3, section 3.7.

4. See Chapter 3, section 3.5.

5. For an especially clear statement of this see *Comments on a Certain Broadsheet* (AT VIIIB, 363: CSM I, 307).

6. Meditation IV: AT VII, 57; CSM II, 40; the next few references are from this text and those immediately following.

7. "I could not but judge that something [that I exist] which I understood so clearly was true; but this was not because I was compelled so to judge by any external force, but because a great light in the intellect was followed by a great inclination in the will" AT VII, 58–59; CSM II, 41. See also Meditation V AT VII, 69; CSM II, 48.

8. See chapter 5, section 5.3.

9. See chapter I, section 1.2.

10. *Principles* I, 71.

11. Meditation III: AT VII, 46; CSM II, 31.

12. See chapter 5, section 5.1, for a discussion of this notion.

13. See the Second Replies (AT VII, 141; CSM II, 101) for an analogous point made in respect of an atheist mathematician.

14. I use this term with roughly the sense given to it by Sellars in W. Sellars, "Empiricism and the Philosophy of Mind" in *Science, Perception and Reality*, (London: Routledge, 1963) 127–197, especially 164–170. Hereafter: "Empiricism."

15. See also the appendix to this chapter (appendix A).

16. Section 5.1.

17. Following Pollock (J. Pollock, *Knowledge and Justification* [Princeton: Princeton University Press, 1974], 42–43) we can distinguish two classes of defeaters for prima facie justified propositions. *Class 1 defeaters* are reasons for thinking that a prima facie proposition *p* is itself false; *class 2 defeaters* are reasons for thinking that in the circumstances at hand, accepting a proposition in accord with the applicable warrant principle is unlikely to lead to the truth. In their extension to particular perceptual judgments, Cartesian teachings of nature face potential defeaters of both kinds. (For further discussion of this last point see section 6.3.)

18. See section 6.1.

19. See note 17.

20. See chapter 4, section 4.4.

21. Chapter 3, section 3.5.

22. I have discussed Descartes's error theory in chapter 5.3.

23. See the Sixth Replies (AT VII 438; CSM II, 295).

24. I.e. in the mechanism of immature referral. See chapter 4, section 4.3.

25. G. Dicker, *Descartes: An Analytical and Historical Introduction* (New York: Oxford University Press, 1993), 199–205.

26. Ibid., 204.

27. I note that the only deception device in Meditation I whose deceptive powers remain intact at the end of that meditation is the "deceiving God" introduced just after the sequal to the dream argument (AT VII, 21; CSM II, 14). The "evil demon" introduced toward the end of the chapter seems to have a mainly heuristic function.

28. Meditation V: AT VII, 69–71; CSM II, 48–49.

29. Chapter 4, section 4.3.

30. See the *Comments on a Certain Broadsheet*, AT VIIIB, 359; CSM I, 304.

31. Chapter 3, section 2.

32. The main discussion of Descartes's general theory of existential reasoning is given in chapter 2, section 2.3.

33. The term comes from W. Epstein and G. Hatfield, "The Sensory Core": 363–364. For the role of the sensory core in Cartesian theory of perception see 373.

34. Ibid., 377.

35. See chapter 4, section 4.3.

36. See *Optics* VI: AT VII, 144; CSM I, 173.

37. See *Optics* VI: (AT VI, 144; CSM I, 173).

38. I explored the first way in Chapter I, appendix A.

39. See Sellars, "Empiricism" and "Givenness and Explanatory Coherence," *Journal of Philosophy* 70 (1973): 612–624.

Chapter 7

1. Section 5.3.

2. I use the term "(re)presents" to indicate that I take the Cartesian term usually translated as "represents" to mean something closer to "presents." This convention is explained at the end of chapter 2, section 2.8.

3. Note especially that sentence 3 begins, "For example. . . ."

4. N. J. Wells, "Material Falsity in Descartes, Arnauld and Suarez," *Journal of the History of Philosophy* 22 (1984): 25–50.

5. See chapter 2, section 2.7.

6. See chapter 5, section 5.3.

7. Quoted above, chapter 4, section 4.4.

8. It is also in this text that Descartes draws a sharp contrast between the clarity and distinctness of our ideas of geometrical qualities and the obscurity of ideas of sensory qualities like heat and cold. I surmise that these two contrasts may be the same.

9. This bit of reasoning is somewhat analogous to the following. Suppose that we are looking through a microscope and see a pattern of light and colors. If we wonder whether this visual content is of real things or is merely an artifact of the lens, we might try turning up the power to see if more structure appears in the visual content. If it does, we are likely to infer that what we are seeing is a structure of real things; if it does not we are likely to infer that what we are seeing is an artifact, a content not revelatory of how things are in themselves.

10. See *Principles* I, 46. See section 7.2 for a full discussion of clear ideas of sense.

11. *Principles* II, 1: AT VIIIA, 41–42; CSM I, 224.

12. This puzzle was suggested to me by Steven Nadler in correspondence.

13. See also M. D. Wilson, *Descartes* (London: Routledge and Kegan Paul, 1978), 104ff. (hereafter, Wilson, *Descartes*).

14. I am indebted to Stephen Menn in conversation for this point.

15. For a discussion of aspects of this account see Garber, *Metaphysical Physics* (Chicago: Chicago University Press, 1992), 96–97. (hereafter, Garber, *Metaphysical Physics*). Garber takes this account to be the chief obstacle that Descartes needs to overcome to complete his program of mechanism. I believe, however, that there is another view, closer to commonsense epistemology than to Scholastic physics, which is the chief obstacle. This is the view I am about to discuss.

16. For Descartes's definition of this notion see *Principles* I, 60.

17. See chapter 4, section 4.4 for a detailed discussion of this claim.

18. To get the result that the objects in question are Aristotelian objects in our sense we interpret "resemblance" here in the *de re* sense. (See chapter 5, section 5.2.)

19. Chapter 5, section 5.3.

20. See chapter 2, sections 2.2, 2.6.

21. See chapter 3, section 3.6.

22. This is so even for someone engaged in what Williams has called "the project of pure inquiry." See B. Williams, *Descartes: The Project of Pure Inquiry* (London: Penguin, 1990). Also see the introduction for a further discussion of this issue.

23. See H. Frankfurt, *Demons, Dreamers, and Madmen* (Indianapolis: Bobbs-Merrill, 1970), chap. 4, for the whole story.

24. Wilson, *Descartes*, 110.

25. In chapter 5, section 5.3.

26. Garber, *Metaphysical Physics*, 96ff.

27. M. Gueroult (*Descartes' Philosophy Interpreted According to the Order of Reasons*, vol. 2, ed. and trans. R. Ariew (Minneapolis: University of Minnesota Press, 1985), 24ff.) (hereafter, Gueroult, *Descartes*) recognizes a distinction between absolute impossibility and "impossibility for the understanding." The two kinds of impossibilities under discussion here are both impossibilities for the understanding.

28. Since writing this portion of the chapter I have seen an article by Mark Bedeau, "Cartesian Interaction", *Midwest Studies in Philosophy* 10 (*Studies in the Philosophy of Mind*) (1986): 483–502, in which he shows that Descartes accepts the nonentailment thesis (487–88). However, in applying this theoretical apparatus in a discussion of Descartes's theory of mind-body interaction, Bedeau's purposes are somewhat different than mine here. (I consider this application in the next section.)

29. The notion plays a role in Descartes's proof that the idea of God is an innate idea, hence an idea with a real object that can be known. See J. Marion, "The Essential Incoherence of Descartes' Definition of Infinity," in Rorty (ed.), *Essays*, 297–338. See esp. 309–310.

30. Garber has also recently claimed that Descartes's case against his opponents fails, but for reasons different from those I have advanced here. His case depends on showing that the opposing theory, which he takes to be the Scholastic doctrine of substantial forms, is not logically inconsistent with the fundamental tenets of Cartesian metaphysics. See Garber, *Metaphysical Physics*, 111.

31. Gueroult has also insisted on the importance of seeing in the Cartesian doctrine of mind-body union a deliberate commitment to the irreducible "incomprehensibility" of that relation. See Gueroult, *Descartes* II: 107ff.

32. See the letters to Regius of December 1641 (AT III, 459; *Letters*, 121ff.) and January 1642 (AT III, 49; *Letters*, 126ff.).

33. Bedeau, "Cartesian Interaction."

34. *Descartes*, 114–119.

35. Wilson has since revised her account of the doctrine of material falsity and of the crucial text from the Reply to Arnauld quoted above. See M. D. Wilson, "Descartes on Sensation," in J. Cover and M. Kulstad (eds.), *Central Theories in Early Modern Philosophy* (Indianapolis: Hackett, 1990). This revision is due to a newfound conviction on her part that although sensory ideas do not "present" their objects, there is a minimal but genuine sense in which they "referentially represent" them. My own treatment of the notion of referred sensations does not count referral as a legitimate form of representation. For this reason I find Wilson's original treatment preferable.

36. E. J. Ashworth, "Descartes' Theory of Clear and Distinct Ideas," in R. J. Butler (ed.), *Cartesian Studies* (London: Oxford University Press, 1972), 97.

37. P. Markie, *Descartes*, 182.

38. See the next subsection.

39. AT V, 289; *Letters*, 246. This letter is quoted extensively in the next subsection.

40. E.g., in the *Treatise on Light*: AT XI, 3; CSM I, 81 and AT XI, 9; CSM I, 84, and *Principles* IV, 198: AT VIIIA, 322; CSM I, 285.

41. For pointing out the existence of this general distinction within Descartes's writings, I am again indebted to Murray Miles.

42. This is the case with the Latin text. Unfortunately the French text speaks of clearly *and distinctly* perceived sensations. I take this to be inadvertently introduced into the French translation since the last text in which clear ideas of sensations are mentioned, article 46, is the one in which Descartes first specifically introduces the notion of ideas of sensations that are clear but not distinct, and when Descartes explictly deals with the property of clarity *and* distinctness in our perceptions of sensations he does so two articles later, in article 68.

43. Why Descartes maintains this is a point I have taken up in section 7.3.

44. This entity will be one dependent on a substance, so we can infer from the antecedent of the principle that there is an existing substance having at least this property: it is the substance upon which entity *x* depends.

45. See section 7.3.

46. See section 7.6.

47. See the epilogue for a discussion of this method.

48. F. Dretske, "Epistemic Operators," *Journal of Philosophy* 67 (1971): 1007–1023.

49. N. Maull, "Cartesian Optics and the Geometrization of Nature," *Review of Metaphysics* 32 (1978): 254–272. See esp. 267.

50. Ibid., 266.

Epilogue

1. See the introduction.

2. See chapter 1.

3. L. BonJour, *The Structure of Empirical Knowledge* (Cambridge, Mass.: Harvard University Press, 1986).

4. This account is a crude version of an elegant and subtle line of argument BonJour carries out in the book.

5. I am indebted here to Schouls, *The Imposition of Method* (Oxford: Clarendon Press, 1981), 9–16. (hereafter, Schouls, *Method*)

6. This point is argued by Schouls in the first five chapters of *Method*.

7. See Schouls, ibid., 16–17.

8. See note 21 for a suggestion for a fourth reason.

9. The phrase comes from the *Conversation with Burman* (AT V, 147; CSM III, 333). See appendix A of chapter 3 for a fuller discussion of this doctrine.

10. L. BonJour, "Can Empirical Knowledge Have a Foundation?" *American Philosophical Quarterly* 15 (1978): 1–13.

11. Some, like Sellars (W. Sellars, *Science and Metaphysics* [New York: Routledge and Kegan Paul, 1968], chap. 2) have advocated identifying truth in general with warranted assertability, others like Richard Rorty (see, e.g., R. Rorty, *Philosophy and the Mirror of Nature* [Princeton: Princeton University Press, 1979], hereafter, Rorty, *Mirror*), have advocated an eliminative reduction of truth in favor of current justificatory practices.

12. In her book *Evidence and Inquiry* (Oxford: Blackwell, 1995) Susan Haack has had a great deal to say of immediate relevance to what I have to say here. Unfortunately her ideas have come to my attention too late for me to do justice to them here.

13. W. V. O. Quine, "Epistemology Naturalized," in *Ontological Relativity and Other Essays* (New York: Columbia University Press, 1969), 69–90.

14. See chapter 4, section 4.4; chapter 5, section 5.5; and chapter 7, sections 7.1–7.4.

15. See, e.g., D. M. Armstrong, *Belief, Truth and Knowledge* (London: Routledge and Kegan Paul, 1973), and R. Nozick, R., *Philosophical Explanations* (Cambridge, Mass.: Harvard University Press, 1981).

16. Some philosophers such as W. P. Alston have argued that first-level foundationalism can sit comfortably with second-level coherentism. See W. P. Alston, "Two Types of Foundationalism," in *Epistemic Justification* (Ithaca: Cornell, 1989). However, I have argued elsewhere that mixing styles of epistemology in this way is unstable. See my "Why Is There Analytic Epistemology?" *Dialogue* 23 (1994): 517–532. See esp. 525ff.

17. See chapter 1, section 1.8.

18. Cf. Schouls, *Method* 110ff. Schouls correctly observes that doubts are involved in the tasks of identifying basic intuitions and distinguishing them from hypotheses. He does not, however, distinguish between this use of doubts (the classification use) and the method of doubt proper, arguing that the latter is identical with the method of resolution. This, as I see it, is a mistake.

19. See chapter 1, section 1.5.

20. A reconstruction of this taxonomy is provided in chapter 5.

21. It may be consistent with characterizing the difference between the analytic and the synthetic method as the difference between semantic and syntactic approaches to proof theory ([5] above in the text following note 7), that a formal theory set out in the traditional geometrical manner occurs within the analytic method as long as the inferences are drawn on a semantic rather than a purely syntactic basis. (The reverse is not true: to represent an immediate inference—the kind occurring within the analytic method—as valid syntacti-

cally requires adding other premises, thus transforming the proof as it stands. This is another reason that Descartes might see analysis as more fundamental than synthesis.) However, for my purposes any argument set out in the traditional geometrical manner will count as synthetic reasoning.

22. Gaukroger criticizes Descartes for failing to see that the unique ability of a synthetic exposition to reveal the systematic properties of a subject is an important epistemic virtue: S. Gaukroger, *Cartesian Logic* (Oxford: Clarendon Press, 1989), 87–88. However, the existence of a general statement of the rule of truth taken together with the taxonomic exercise a few paragraphs later in Meditation III suggests that in practice if not in pronouncement Descartes does recognize these virtues even in the *Meditations*. In the *Principles* Descartes recognizes these virtues both in practice and pronouncement. See the preface to the French edition, AT IXB, 16–17, also *Principles* II, 64. For a discussion of the degree to which these pronouncements and practices can be reconciled with Descartes's negative views on the virtues of the synthetic method see Gaukroger, *Cartesian Logic*, 104ff.

23. I have discussed this method in ch. 7 under the rubric of Descartes's error theory.

24. In what I take to be a reference at the end of Meditation VI (AT VII, 89; CSM II, 61) to the kind of doubts which these arguments are intended to generate, Descartes himself describes them as "ridiculous." I have discussed some of the issues arising from classical Cartesian skepticism in three articles, "Skepticism and Doxastic Conservatism," *Pacific Philosophical Quarterly* 64 (1983): 341–350; "A Critical Notice of Peter Klein *Certainty: A Refutation of Skepticism*," *Canadian Journal of Philosophy* 14 (1984): 125–145; and "A Critical Notice of Barry Stroud *The Significance of Philosophical Skepticism*," *Canadian Journal of Philosophy* 16 (1986): 559–574.

25. See chapter 7, section 7.4.

26. See chapter 7, section 7.5.

27. See chapter 4, section 4.4; chapter 5, section 5.5; and chapter 7, sections 7.1–7.4.

28. D. Dennett, *Consciousness Explained* (Boston: Little Brown, 1991), chap. 4, 66ff.

29. This point should be distinguished from the claim that skeptical scenarios show that our conviction that there are external objects is epistemically unwarranted. Perhaps they do show this.

30. There are several forms that such an explanation might take. It might, for example, specify a set of causal processes from those generally available within the alternative theory, a set which does not of course include the state of affairs that is the object of the original conviction but which also does not include states of affairs that are incompatible with it. Alternatively, the explanation might specify causal processes that either include or presuppose states of affairs that are incompatible with the object of the original conviction. My thanks to Steve Maitzen for helpful discussion of this point.

31. My thanks again to Steve Maitzen.

32. Let me address a potential objection to clause 2. (My thanks again to Steve Maitzen.) If I am to be convinced that there is an error explanation for my conviction that *p* is obvious, I need to be convinced that an explanation can be drawn within terms consistent with the premises of the alternative proof. This is a hypothetical matter—we assume for the sake of argument that these premises are true and then see if we can construct a convincing explanation. If we had to be antecedently convinced that the premises are true in order to do this, then clause 2 would make clause 1 redundant—but we do not have to be antecedently convinced of this. Of course the fact that a set of premises allows a good error theory to be constructed for a given explanandum—in this case the explanandum is my conviction that *p* is obviously true—provides some degree of confirmation of the truth of the premises, and hence of the falsity of the original belief, but it is not a very powerful confirmation taken by itself. Certainly, it is no substitute for the powerful proof mentioned in clause 1.

33. The reliance of the error theory method on cognitive science is one affinity that Cartesian epistemology has with Quinean naturalized epistemology.

34. R. Foley, *Working Without a Net* (New York: Oxford University Press, 1993). See page 44.

35. Ibid., 122.

36. Ibid., 121.

37. Ibid., 122.

38. Ibid., 122.

39. The distinction that I have in mind here can be illustrated by different attitudes which we might take to winning a game. If winning a game is scoring more legal points than one's opponent and playing the game well is making the best legal moves in the circumstances, then we can arbitrarily choose which of these to make our ultimate objective. There is, to be sure, an internal relationship between making a good move and attempting to facilitate the scoring of points, but there is still a difference between the two objectives: whichever we choose will become the standard by means of which to assess success in our games and there are cases of winning games that are not cases of having played well and there are cases of having played well that are not cases of winning games. However, even someone who chooses playing well as the standard of ultimate success can still find winning a desirable outcome. It is just that not winning is not failing from this person's point of view, a point of view that is more in accord with an egocentric standard of rationality than the alternative.

40. The clearest text for this is in the Second Set of Replies:

> as soon as we think that we correctly perceive something, we are spontaneously convinced that it is true. Now if this conviction is so firm that it is impossible for us ever to have any reason for doubting what we are convinced of, then there are no further questions for us to ask: we have everything that we could reasonably want. What is it to us that someone may make out that the perception whose truth we are so firmly convinced of may appear false to God or an angel, so that it is, absolutely speaking, false? Why should this alleged "absolute falsity" bother us, since we neither believe in it nor have the slightest suspicion of it? For the supposition which we are making here is of a conviction so firm that it is quite incapable of being destroyed; and such a conviction is clearly the same as the most perfect certainty. (AT VII, 144–145; CSM II, 103)

41. Ibid., 134.

42. For a defense of this assertion, see my "What is the Ground for the Identity of Indiscernibles in Leibnitz's Correspondence with Clarke?" *Journal of the History of Philosophy* 12 (Jan. 1974); 95–101.

43. R. Rorty, *Mirror*, 389–390.

44. See Gaukroger, *Cartesian Logic*, chap. 1.

Bibliography

Alston, William P. "The Deontological Conception of Epistemic Justification." In Alston, *Epistemic Justification*, 115–152.
——. *Epistemic Justification* (Ithaca: Cornell, 1989).
——. "Two Types of Foundationalism." In Alston, *Epistemic Justification*, 19–38. Originally printed in *Journal of Philosophy* 73 (1976): 165–85.
Aquila, Richard E. "Brentano, Descartes, and Hume on Awareness." *Philosophy and Phenomenological Research* 35 (1974–75): 228–231.
Arbini, Ronald. "Did Descartes Have a Philosophical Theory of Sense Experience?" *Journal of the History of Philosophy* 21 (1983): 317–337.
Aristotle. *The Basic Works of Aristotle*. Edited by Richard McKeon. (New York: Random House, 1966).
Armstrong, David M. *Belief, Truth and Knowledge* (London: Routledge and Kegan Paul, 1973).
Ashworth, E. Jennifer. "Descartes' Theory of Clear and Distinct Ideas." In Ronald. J. Butler (ed.), *Cartesian Studies* (London: Oxford University Press, 1972): 89–105.
Audi, Robert. *The Structure of Justification* (Cambridge: Cambridge University Press, 1993).
Barresi, John. "Descartes: His Life, History and Intellectual Development," chap. 5 of an unpublished manuscript.
Bedeau, Mark. "Cartesian Interaction." *Midwest Studies in Philosophy* 10 (*Studies in the Philosophy of Mind*) (1986): 483–502.
Bennett, Jonathan. "Descartes' Theory of Modality." *Philosophical Review* 103 (1994): 639–667.
Berkeley, G. A. *Treatise Concerning the Principles of Human Knowledge*. Section 49 in A. A. Luce and T. E. Jessop (eds.), *The Works of George Berkeley, Bishop of Cloyne*, vol. 2 (London: Nelson, 1948–1957).
Bolton, Martha B. "Confused and Obscure Ideas of Sense." In Rorty (ed.), *Essays*, 389–404.

BonJour, Laurence. "Can Empirical Knowledge have a Foundation?" *American Philosophical Quarterly* 15 (1978): 1–13.

———. *The Structure of Empirical Knowledge* (Cambridge, Mass.: Harvard University Press, 1986).

Broughton, Janet, and Mattern, Ruth. "Reinterpreting Descartes on the Notion of the Union of Mind and Body." *Journal of the History of Philosophy* 16 (1978): 23–32.

Carriero, John. "The Second Meditation and the Essence of the Mind." In Rorty (ed.), *Essays*, 199–223.

Caton, Hiram. *The Origin of Subjectivity* (New Haven: Yale University Press, 1973).

Chappell, Vere. "The Theory of Ideas." In Rorty (ed.), *Essays*, 177–198.

Clarke, Desmond. *Descartes' Philosophy of Science* (Manchester: Manchester University Press, 1982).

Clatterbaugh, Kenneth. "Descartes' Causal Likeness Principle." *Philosophical Review* 89 (1980): 379–402.

Cohen, Joshua. "Thomas Aquinas on the Immaterial Reception of Sensible Forms." *Philosophical Review* 91 (1982): 193–209.

Costa, Michael. "What Cartesian Ideas Are Not." *Journal of the History of Philosophy* 21 (1983): 237–238.

Cottingham, John, (trans.). *Descartes' Conversation with Burman.* (Oxford: Clarendon Press, 1976).

———. *Descartes* (Oxford: Blackwell, 1986).

———. (ed.). *Reason, Will and Sensation* (Oxford: Clarendon Press, 1994).

———. (ed.). *The Cambridge Companion to Descartes* (Cambridge: Cambridge University Press, 1992).

Cover, Jan, and Mark Kulstad (eds.). *Central Theories in Early Modern Philosophy* (Indianapolis: Hackett, 1990).

Cummins, Robert. *The Nature of Psychological Explanation* (Cambridge, Mass.: MIT Press, 1983).

Curley, Edwin M. *Descartes against the Skeptics* (Cambridge, Mass.: Harvard University Press, 1978).

Dennett, Daniel. *Consciousness Explained* (Boston: Little Brown, 1991).

Dicker, Georges. *Descartes: An Analytical and Historical Introduction* (Oxford: Oxford University Press, 1993).

Doney, Willis. "The Cartesian Circle." *Journal of the History of Ideas* 16 (1955): 324–338.

Epstein, William, and Hatfield, Gary. "The Sensory Core and the Medieval Foundations of Early Modern Perceptual Theory." *Isis* 70 (1979): 363–384.

Field, Richard. "Descartes' Proof of the Existence of Matter." *Mind* 44 (1985): 244–249.

Foley, Richard. *Working without a Net: A Study of Egocentric Epistemology* (New York: Oxford University Press, 1993).

Forguson, Lynd. *Common Sense* (London: Routledge, 1989).

Frankfurt, Harry. *Demons, Dreamers, and Madmen* (Indianapolis: Bobbs-Merrill, 1970).

Garber, Daniel, "Science and Certainty." In Michael Hooker (ed.), *Descartes: Critical and Interpretative Essays*, 114–151 (Baltimore: Johns Hopkins University Press, 1978).

———. "Descartes and Experiment in the *Discourse* and *Essays*." in Voss (ed.), *Essays on the Philosophy and Science of René Descartes*, 288–312.

———. *Metaphysical Physics* (Chicago: University of Chicago Press, 1992).

———. "*Semel in vita:* The Scientific Background to Descartes' *Meditations.*" In Rorty (ed.), *Essays*, 81–117.

Gaukroger, Stephen. *Cartesian Logic* (Oxford: Clarendon Press, 1989).

——. *Descartes: An Intellectual Biography* (Oxford: Clarendon, 1995).
—— (ed.). *Descartes: Philosophy, Mathematics and Physics* (Towata, N.J.: Harvester Press, 1980).
—— (ed. and trans.). *Antoine Arnauld's "On True and False Ideas"* (Manchester: Manchester University Press, 1990).
Glouberman, Mark. *The Probable and the Certain* (Amsterdam: Rodopoi, B.V., 1986).
Gregory, Richard, L. *The Oxford Companion to the Mind* (Oxford: Oxford University Press, 1991).
Grene, Marjorie. *Descartes* (Minneapolis: University of Minnesota Press, 1985).
Gueroult, M. *Descartes' Philosophy Interpreted According to the Order of Reasons*, vol. I: *The Soul and God*, and vol. II: *The Soul and the Body*. Edited and translated by Roger Ariew (Minneapolis: University of Minnesota Press, 1985).
Haack, Susan. *Evidence and Inquiry* (Oxford: Blackwell, 1995).
Hatfield, Gary. "Descartes' Physiology and Its Relation to His Psychology." In Cottingham (ed.), *The Cambridge Companion to Descartes*.
——. "The Senses and the Fleshless Eye: The *Meditations* as Cognitive Exercises." In Rorty (ed.), *Essays*,: 45–79.
Hempel, Carl G. *Aspects of Scientific Explanation* (New York: Macmillan, 1965).
Hintikka, Jaako. "*Cogito Ergo Sum*: Inference or Performance." *Philosophical Review* 71 (1962): 3–32.
Jeffrey, Richard C. "Statistical Explanation vs. Statistical Inference." in Salmon (ed.), *Statistical Explanation and Statistical Relevance*, 19–28.
Jolly, Nicholas J. *The Light of the Soul* (New York: Oxford University Press, 1990).
Kant, Immanuel. *The Critique of Pure of Reason*, translated by Norman K. Smith (New York: St. Martin's, 1965).
Kenny, Anthony. *Descartes* (Random House: New York, 1968).
Lehrer, Keith. *Knowledge* (London: Oxford University Press, 1974).
Klein, Peter. *Certainty: A Refutation of Skepticism* (Minneapolis: University of Minnesota Press, 1981).
Lennon, Thomas. *The Battle of the Gods and the Giants* (Princeton: Princeton University Press, 1993).
——. "Representationalism, Judgment and Perception of Distance: Further to Yolton and McRae." *Dialogue* 19 (March 1980): 151–162.
Lewis, David K. "Attitudes *De Dicto* and *De Se*." *Philosophical Review* 88 (1979): 523–514.
Loeb, Louis. "Is There a Problem of Cartesian Interactionism." *Journal of the History of Philosophy* 23 (1985): 227–231.
——. "Is There Radical Dissimulation in Descartes' *Meditations*?" in Rorty (ed.), *Essays*, 243–270.
——. "The Priority of Reason in Descartes." *Philosophical Review* 91 (1990): 3–43.
MacKenzie, Anne. "Descartes on Life and Sense." *Canadian Journal of Philosophy* 19 (1989): 163–192.
——. "Descartes on Sensory Representation: A Study of the Dioptrics." *Canadian Journal of Philosophy* suppl. vol. 16 (1990): 109–147.
McRae, Robert. "Descartes' Definition of Thought." In Ronald J. Butler (ed.) *Cartesian Studies* (Oxford: Blackwell, 1972).
Marion, Jean-Luc. "The Essential Incoherence of Descartes' Definition of Infinity." In Rorty (ed.), *Essays*, 297–338.
Markie, Peter. *Descartes' Gambit* (Ithaca: Cornell University Press, 1986).
——. "Descartes' Concept of Substance." In Cottingham (ed.), *Reason, Will and Sensation*, 63–88.

Maull, Nancy. "Cartesian Optics and the Geometrization of Nature." *Review of Metaphysics* 32 (1978): 254–272.

Miles, Murray. *Insight, and Inference* (Unpublished manuscript)

Nadler, Steven. *Arnauld and the Cartesian Philosophy of Ideas* (Princeton: Princeton University Press, 1989).

Nelson, A. "Cartesian Actualism in the Leibnitz-Arnauld Correspondence," *Canadian Journal of Philosophy* 23:675–694.

Normore, Calvin. "Meaning and Objective Being: Descartes and His Sources." In Rorty (ed.), *Essays*, 223–241.

Nozick, Robert. *Philosophical Explanations* (Cambridge, Mass.: Harvard University Press, 1981).

O'Neil, Brian. *Epistemological Direct Realism in Descartes' Philosophy* (Albuquerque: University of New Mexico Press, 1974).

O'Neill, Eileen. "Mind-Body Interaction and Metaphysical Consistency: A Defense of Descartes." *Journal of the History of Philosophy* 25 (1987): 227–245.

Pollock, John. *Knowledge and Justification* (Princeton: Princeton University Press, 1974).

Quine, Willard. "Epistemology Naturalized." In *Ontological Relativity and Other Essays*, 69–90 (New York: Columbia University Press, 1969).

Quinton, Anthony. "The Problem of Perception." In Robert Schwartz (ed.), *Perceiving, Sensing and Knowing*, 497–526 (New York: Anchor, 1965).

Radner, Daisie. "Descartes' Notion of the Union of Mind and Body." *Journal of the History of Philosophy* 9 (1971): 159–170.

———. "Is There a Problem of Cartesian Interaction?" *Journal of the History of Philosophy* 23 (1985), 35–49.

———. "Thought and Consciousness in Descartes." *Journal of the History of Philosophy* 26 (1988): 439–470.

Richardson, Robert. "Union and Interaction of Body and Soul." *Journal of the History of Philosophy* 23 (1985): 221–226.

Rock, Irwin. *The Logic of Perception* (Cambridge, Mass.: MIT University Press, 1983).

Rorty, Amélie (ed.). *Essays on Descartes' "Meditations"* (Berkeley: University of California Press, 1986).

Rorty, Richard. *Philosophy and the Mirror of Nature* (Princeton: Princeton University Press, 1979).

Russell, Bertrand. "On Denoting." In Robert. C. Marsh (ed.), *Logic and Knowledge*, 39–56 (London: Allen and Unwin, 1956).

Salmon, Wesley. "Statistical Explanation." In Salmon, *Statistical Explanation and Statistical Relevance*, 29–88.

——— (ed.). *Statistical Explanation and Statistical Relevance* (Pittsburgh: University of Pittsburgh Press, 1971).

Schmitt, Frederick F. "Why Was Descartes a Foundationalist?" In Rorty (ed.), *Essays*, 419–512.

Schouls, Peter. *The Imposition of Method* (Oxford: Clarendon Press, 1981).

Schuster, John A. "Descartes' *mathesis universalis*, 1619–1628." In Gaukroger (ed.), *Descartes: Philosophy, Mathematics and Physics*, 41–95.

Sellars, Wilfrid. "The Adverbial Theory of the Objects of Sensation." *Metaphilosophy* 6 (1975): 144–160.

———. "Berkeley and Descartes: Reflections on the Theory of Ideas." In Peter Machamer and Robert Turnbull (eds.), *Studies in Perception* (Columbus: Ohio State University Press, 1978).

———. "Empiricism and the Philosophy of Mind." In *Science, Perception and* Reality, 127–196.

———. "Givenness and Explanatory Coherence." *Journal of Philosophy* 70 (1973): 612–624.

———. "Philosophy and the Scientific Image of Man." In *Science, Perception and Reality*, 1–40.

———. *Science and Metaphysics* (New York: Routledge and Kegan Paul, 1968).

———. *Science, Perception and Reality* (London: Routledge, 1963).

Sosa, Ernest. "The Raft and the Pyramid." *Midwest Studies in Philosophy* 5 (1980): 3–25.

Stich, Stephen. *The Fragmentation of Reason* (Cambridge, Mass.: MIT Press, 1990).

Stroud, Barry. *The Significance of Philosophical Skepticism* (Oxford: Clarendon Press, 1984).

Van Cleve, James. "Foundationalism, Epistemic Principles and the Cartesian Circle." *Philosophical Review* 88 (1979): 55–91.

Van De Pitt, Frederick. "Intuition and Judgment in Descartes' Theory of Truth." *Journal of the History of Philosophy* 26 (1988): 446–466.

Vinci, Thomas. "Critical Notice of Barry Stroud, *The Significance of Philosophical Skepticism.*" *Canadian Journal of Philosophy* 16 (1986): 559–574.

———. "Critical Notice of Peter Klein, *Certainty: A Refutation of Skepticism.*" *Canadian Journal of Philosophy* 14 (1984): 125–145.

———. "Skepticism and Doxastic Conservatism." *Pacific Philosophical Quarterly* 64 (1983): 341–350.

———. "Why Is There Analytic Epistemology?" Critical notice of William Alston, *Epistemic Justification. Dialogue* 33 (1994): 517–532.

Voss, Stephen. (ed.) *Essays on the Philosophy and Science of René Descartes* (Oxford: Oxford University Press, 1993).

———. (trans. and ann.) *The Passions of the Soul* (Indianapolis: Hackett, 1989).

Wells, Norman J. "Material Falsity in Descartes, Arnauld and Suarez." *Journal of the History of Philosophy* 22 (1984): 25–50.

Williams, Bernard. *Descartes: The Project of Pure Inquiry* (Hammondsworth: Penguin, 1990).

Wilson, Margaret D. *Descartes* (London: Routledge and Kegan Paul, 1978).

———. "Descartes on Sensation." In Cover and Kulstad (eds.), *Central Theories*, 1–22.

———. "Descartes on the Perception of Primary Qualities." In Voss, *Essays on the Philosophy and Science of René Descartes*, 162–176.

———. "Skepticism without Indubitability." *Journal of Philosophy* 81 (1984): 537–544.

Yolton, John. *Perceptual Acquaintance from Descartes to Reed* (Minneapolis: University of Minnesota Press, 1984).

Index